ASCENT®

CENTER FOR TECHNICAL KNOWLEDGE

AutoCAD® 2023
3D Drawing and Modeling

Learning Guide

Mixed Units - 1st Edition

AUTODESK

Authorized Publisher

ASCENT - Center for Technical Knowledge®
AutoCAD® 2023
3D Drawing and Modeling

Mixed Units - 1st Edition

Prepared and produced by:

ASCENT Center for Technical Knowledge
630 Peter Jefferson Parkway, Suite 175
Charlottesville, VA 22911

866-527-2368
www.ASCENTed.com

Lead Contributor: Renu Muthoo

ASCENT - Center for Technical Knowledge (a division of Rand Worldwide Inc.) is a leading developer of professional learning materials and knowledge products for engineering software applications. ASCENT specializes in designing targeted content that facilitates application-based learning with hands-on software experience. For over 25 years, ASCENT has helped users become more productive through tailored custom learning solutions.

We welcome any comments you may have regarding this guide, or any of our products. To contact us please email: feedback@ASCENTed.com.

AS-ACD2301-3DM1MU-SG // IS-ACD2301-3DM1MU-SG

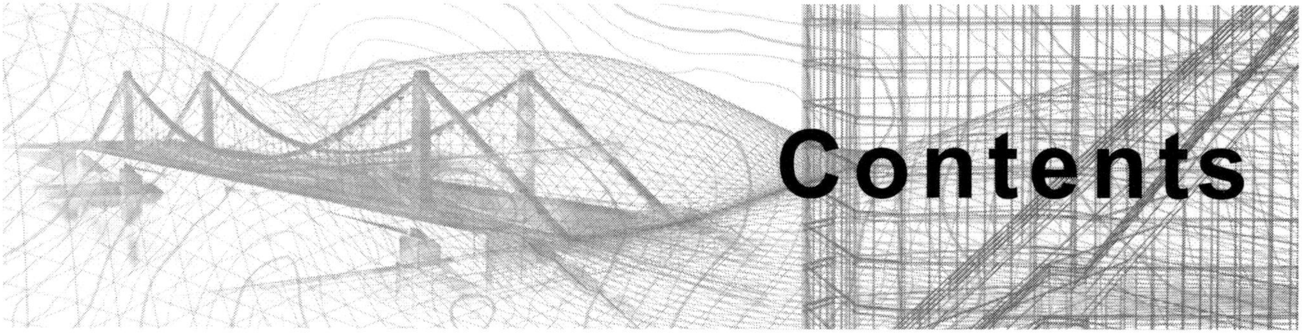

Contents

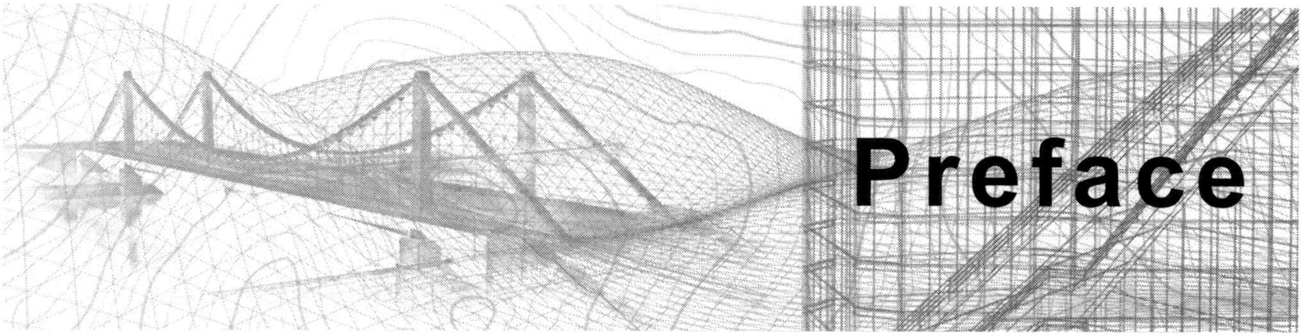

Preface

The *AutoCAD® 2023: 3D Drawing and Modeling* guide is designed for those using AutoCAD® 2023 with a Windows operating system. This guide is not designed for the AutoCAD for Mac software.

The *AutoCAD 2023: 3D Drawing and Modeling* guide introduces users, who are proficient with the 2D commands in the AutoCAD software, to the concepts and methods of 3D modeling. The guide provides a thorough grounding in the fundamentals of 3D and explores the main features of the advanced 3D Modeling workspace in the AutoCAD software.

Topics Covered

- 3D viewing techniques
- Working with simple and composite solids
- Creating complex solids and surfaces
- Modifying objects in 3D space
- Editing solids
- Creating sections, camera perspectives, and animations
- Working with point clouds
- Converting 3D objects
- Setting up a rendering with materials and lights
- Creating 2D drawings from 3D models
- Working with the User Coordinate System
- Set up a drawing for 3D Prints

Prerequisites

- Access to the 2023.0 version of the software, to ensure compatibility with this guide. Future software updates that are released by Autodesk may include changes that are not reflected in this guide. The practices and files included with this guide might not be compatible with prior versions (e.g., 2022).
- A good working skill level in the AutoCAD software, i.e., a minimum of 80 hours of work experience with the AutoCAD software, is recommended.

Note on Software Setup

This guide assumes a standard installation of the software using the default preferences during installation. Lectures and practices use the standard software templates and default options for the Content Libraries.

Lead Contributor: Renu Muthoo

Renu uses her instructional design training to develop courseware for AutoCAD and AutoCAD vertical products, Autodesk 3ds Max, Autodesk Showcase and various other Autodesk software products. She has worked with Autodesk products for the past 20 years with a main focus on design visualization software.

Renu holds a bachelor's degree in Computer Engineering and started her career as a Instructional Designer/Author where she co-authored a number of Autodesk 3ds Max and AutoCAD books, some of which were translated into other languages for a wide audience reach. In her next role as a Technical Specialist at a 3D visualization company, Renu used 3ds Max in real-world scenarios on a daily basis. There, she developed customized 3D web planner solutions to create specialized 3D models with photorealistic texturing and lighting to produce high quality renderings.

Renu Muthoo has been the Lead Contributor for *AutoCAD: 3D Drawing and Modeling* since 2019.

In This Guide

The following highlights the key features of this guide.

Feature	Description
Practice Files	The Practice Files page includes a link to the practice files and instructions on how to download and install them. The practice files are required to complete the practices in this guide.
Chapters	A chapter consists of the following - Learning Objectives, Instructional Content, Practices, Chapter Review Questions, and Command Summary. • **Learning Objectives** define the skills you can acquire by learning the content provided in the chapter. • **Instructional Content**, which begins right after Learning Objectives, refers to the descriptive and procedural information related to various topics. Each main topic introduces a product feature, discusses various aspects of that feature, and provides step-by-step procedures on how to use that feature. Where relevant, examples, figures, helpful hints, and notes are provided. • **Practice** for a topic follows the instructional content. Practices enable you to use the software to perform a hands-on review of a topic. It is required that you download the practice files (using the link found on the Practice Files page) prior to starting the first practice. • **Chapter Review Questions**, located close to the end of a chapter, enable you to test your knowledge of the key concepts discussed in the chapter. • **Command Summary** concludes a chapter. It contains a list of the software commands that are used throughout the chapter and provides information on where the command can be found in the software.
Appendices	Appendices provide additional information to the main course content. It could be in the form of instructional content, practices, tables, projects, or skills assessment.

Practice Files

To download the practice files for this guide, use the following steps:

1. Type the URL ***exactly as shown below*** into the address bar of your Internet browser, to access the Course File Download page.

   Note: If you are using the ebook, you do not have to type the URL. Instead, you can access the page simply by clicking the URL below.

   https://www.ascented.com/getfile/id/dipterostelePF

2. On the Course File Download page, click the **DOWNLOAD NOW** button, as shown below, to download the .ZIP file that contains the practice files.

3. Once the download is complete, unzip the file and extract its contents.

   The recommended practice files folder location is:
   C:\AutoCAD 2023 3D Drawing and Modeling Practice Files

   Note: It is recommended that you do not change the location of the practice files folder. Doing so may cause errors when completing the practices.

Stay Informed!

To receive information about upcoming events, promotional offers, and complimentary webcasts, visit:

www.ASCENTed.com/updates

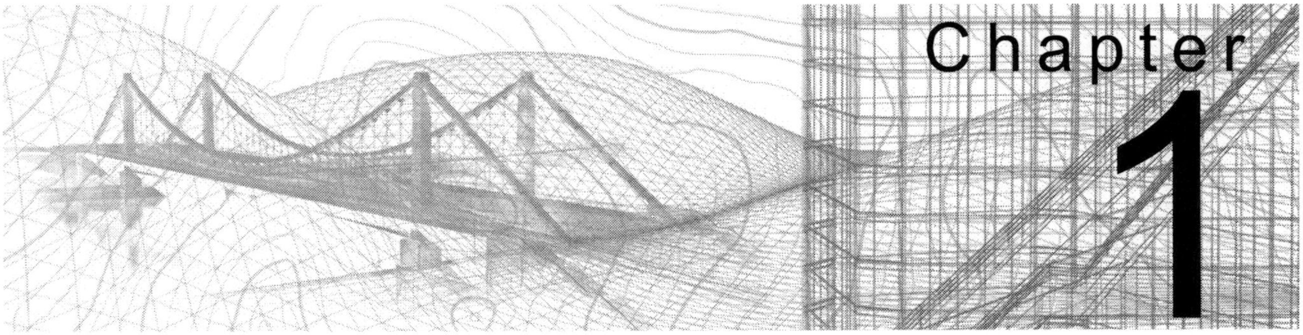

3D Foundations

In this chapter, you learn how to identify 3D models, use the 3D workspace, view a 3D model from different angles, shade the model using visual styles, and understand the user coordinate system (UCS).

Learning Objectives in This Chapter

- Describe the differences between 2D drawings and 3D models.
- Access the 3D drawing and viewing tools using the ribbon through 3D-specific workspaces.
- View objects from all directions using preset 3D views and 3D orbiting tools.
- Control how elements display in a view using the visual styles.
- Navigate 3D drawings with additional tools, including the ViewCube and the SteeringWheel.
- Move the UCS to a face on a 3D object using the Dynamic UCS.

1.1 Why Use 3D?

2D plans and schematics are diagrams that represent an object by reducing it to a simpler form. For example, two parallel lines are easily recognized as the symbol for a wall, although they are not actually a wall. However, a 3D model is a complete object in all its dimensions. A complete 3D model of a wall can include all interior framing, the drywall, the baseboards, etc. At the very least, it would display the height, length, and width of the wall.

Likewise, a three-view 2D mechanical drawing is a symbolic representation of an object from various directions. If you want to view the object from another angle, you must draw another 2D view. However, a 3D mechanical model is a single object that can be viewed from many directions, as shown in Figure 1–1.

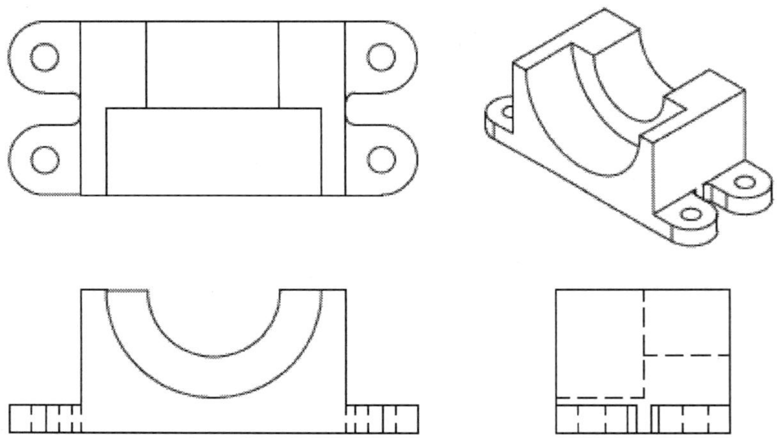

Figure 1–1

A 3D model:

- Can be viewed from any direction.
- Can be used to generate 2D views as required.
- Can be rendered to create photo-realistic images of the finished model.

Types of 3D Models

You can create four types of 3D models with the AutoCAD® software: wireframe, surface, mesh, and solid, as shown in Figure 1–2.

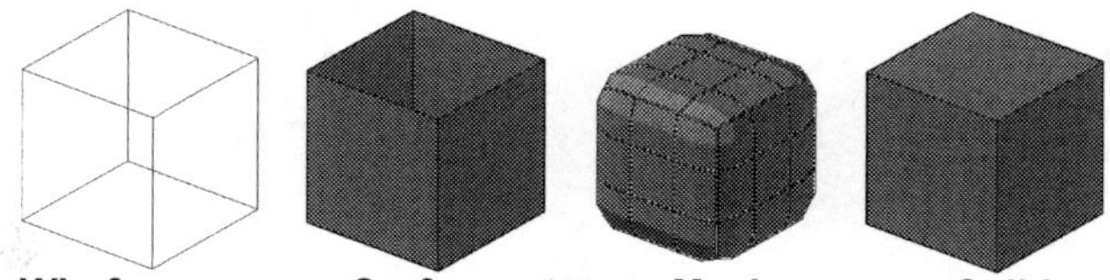

Figure 1–2

Wireframe models: Represent the 3D object by indicating its edges. There are no surfaces between the edges. Therefore, you can see through the object. For example, you can use a wireframe drawing to display a plumbing riser diagram. You can also use wireframe objects as paths or frameworks for other 3D objects.

Surface models: Consist of infinitely thin surfaces that represent the *shell* of an object. Since the surfaces are opaque, the edges behind them can be hidden. However, the model cannot be used for mechanical or thermal analysis because the thin surfaces do not have a mass. You can use surfaces to create contour maps or other complex geometry, such as a car body or cell phone design. You can also use surfaces to cut solids and apply complex geometry to them.

Mesh models: Consist of polygons that form edges, faces, and vertices. They do not have mass and can be used to create complex shapes that can be creased, split, and deformed as required. They can be shaded and rendered without having a mass and can be a useful alternative to solids.

Solid models: Can look like surface models, but are solid blocks of material, rather than hollow. A solid model has mass and can be used for mechanical and thermal analysis, and renderings. Solids can be used to create anything from a doorknob, to a large machine, or to a massing study for a new high-rise.

Hint: Advanced 3D Modeling

The 3D tools in the AutoCAD software are primarily for conceptual design, but can be used to create objects and then to create working drawings from them. Autodesk supplies *vertical* software, such as Autodesk® Inventor® for mechanical design, Autodesk® Revit® Architecture for architectural design, and Autodesk® Civil 3D® and Autodesk® InfraWorks® for civil design, each of which are more powerful in their specific disciplines. For advanced rendering and animations, you would use the Autodesk® 3ds Max® software.

1.2 Introduction to the 3D Modeling Workspace

When you are ready to begin working in 3D, you need special tools and visual clues to help you move from the flat 2D world into the full-featured world of the third dimension. The AutoCAD software includes a 3D modeling workspace with easy access to 3D drawing and viewing tools, as shown in Figure 1–3.

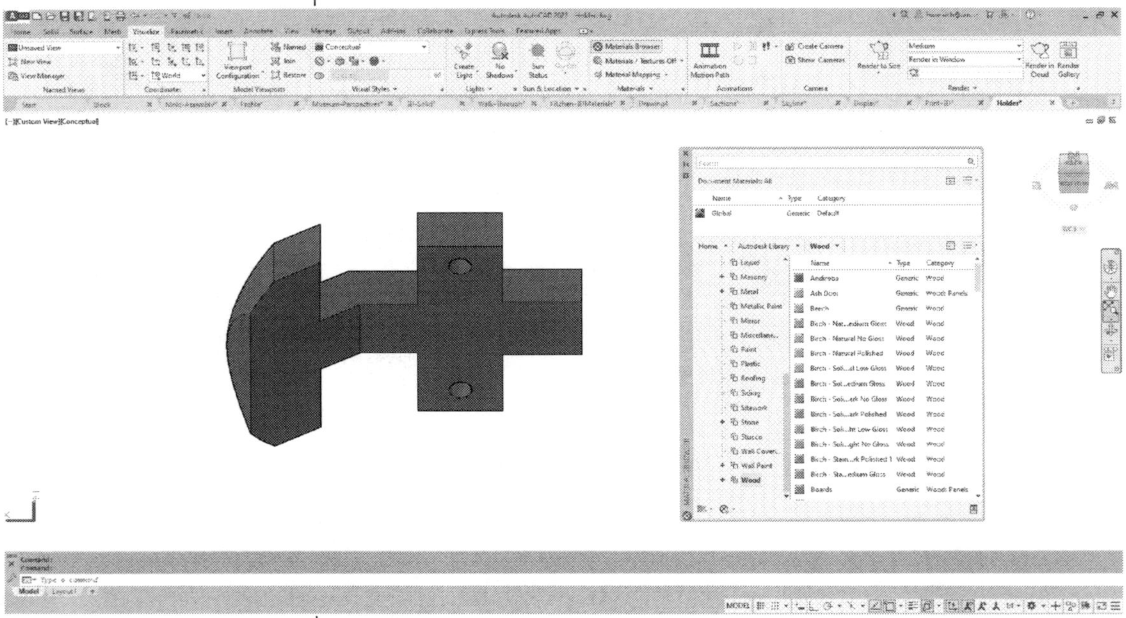

Figure 1–3

- The 3D Modeling workspace might not be available and is required to be turned on. You can open the 3D Modeling workspace by selecting **3D Modeling** in the Status Bar, as shown in Figure 1–4.

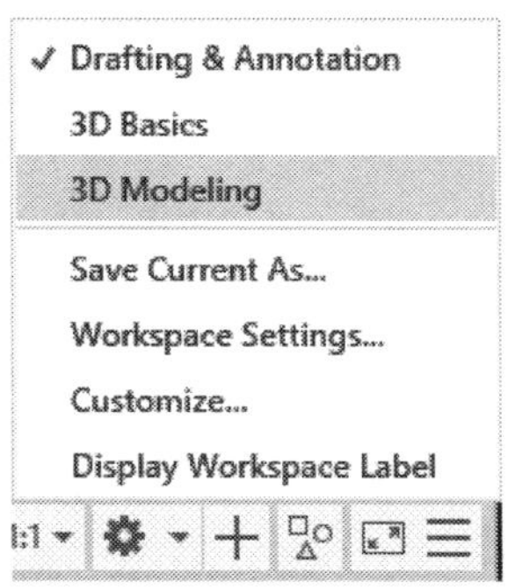

Figure 1–4

*To display the Workspace list in the Quick Access Toolbar, toggle on **Workspace** in the (Customize Toolbar).*

- You can also open the 3D Modeling workspace in the Quick Access Toolbar by selecting **3D Modeling** in the Workspace drop-down list.
- You can also use the 3D Basics workspace, which contains many commonly used commands.
- Use the ribbon tabs and panels to access the 3D tools.
- Toggle the Tool Palettes off or set them to **Auto-Hide** to save space in the drawing window. They are primarily used for lights and other visualization commands.

3D Ribbon Panels

The 3D Modeling workspace includes ribbon tabs and panels that contain commonly used 3D tools. The tabs are: *Home*, *Solid*, *Surface*, *Mesh*, *Visualize*, *Parametric*, *Insert*, *Annotate*, *View, Manage, Output, Add-ins, Collaborate, Express Tools, and Featured Apps tabs.*

- The 3D Basics workspace contains the *Home*, *Visualize*, *Insert*, *View*, *Manage*, *Output, Add-ins, Collaborate, Express Tools, and Featured Apps* tabs.

The *Home* tab of the 3D Modeling workspace includes the following panels: Modeling, Mesh, Solid Editing, Draw, Modify, Section, Coordinates, View, Selection, Layers, Groups, and View, as shown in Figure 1–5.

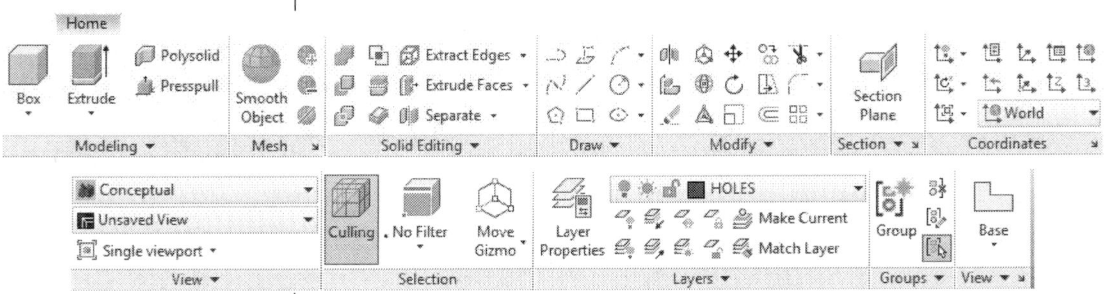

Figure 1–5

The *Solid* tab includes the following panels: Primitives, Solid, Boolean, Solid Editing, Section, and Selection, as shown in Figure 1–6.

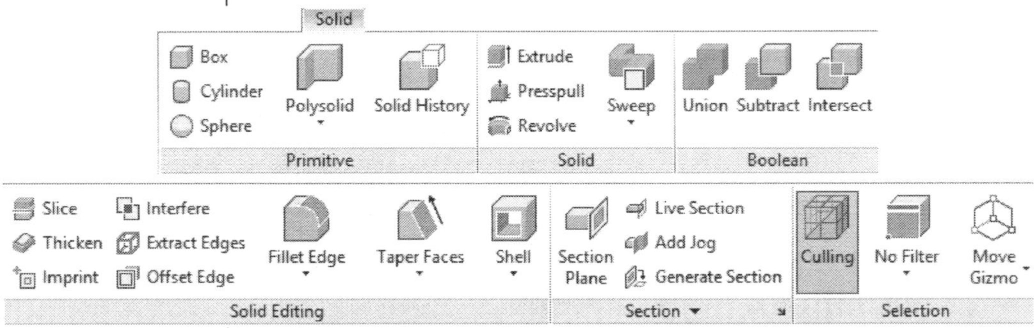

Figure 1–6

The *Surface* tab includes the following panels: Create, Edit, Control Vertices, Curves, Project Geometry, and Analysis, as shown in Figure 1–7.

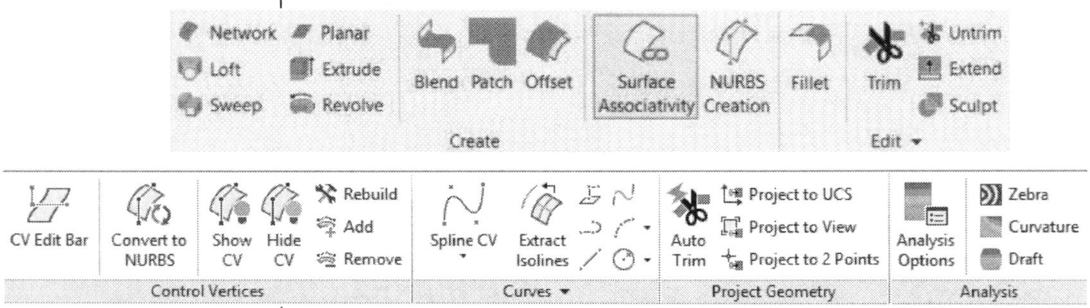

Figure 1–7

The *Mesh* tab includes the following panels: Primitives, Mesh, Mesh Edit, Convert Mesh, Section, and Selection, as shown in Figure 1–8.

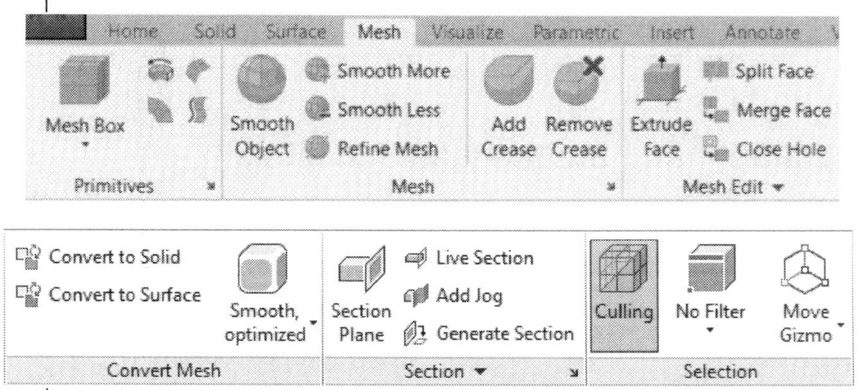

Figure 1–8

The *Visualize* tab includes the following panels: Named Views, Coordinates, Model Viewports, Visual Styles, Lights, Sun & Location, Materials, Camera, and Render, as shown in Figure 1–9.

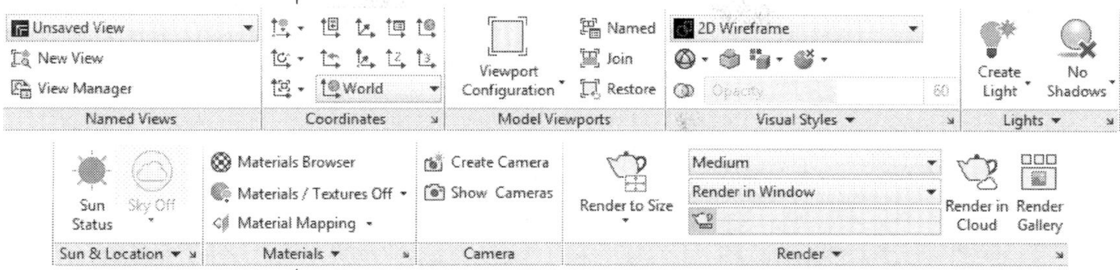

Figure 1–9

The *View* tab includes the following panels: Viewport Tools, Named Views, Palettes, and Interface, as shown in Figure 1–10.

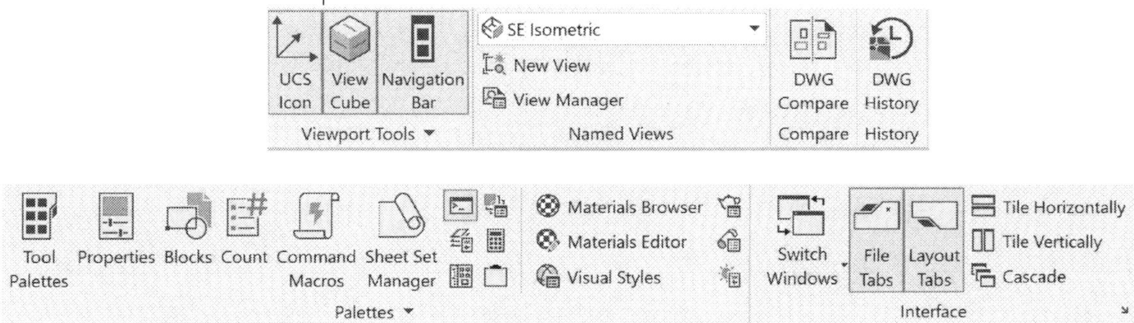

Figure 1–10

1.3 Basic 3D Viewing Tools

As you are working in 3D, you need to be able to view objects from all directions. There are several basic tools that enable you to do so: preset 3D views, orbiting, and Visual Styles.

Preset 3D Views

The AutoCAD software provides a number of standard preset 3D views (orthographic and isometric) that enable you to quickly change the viewing angle. They are located in the *Home* tab> View panel or in the **View Controls** label of the drawing window, as shown in Figure 1–11.

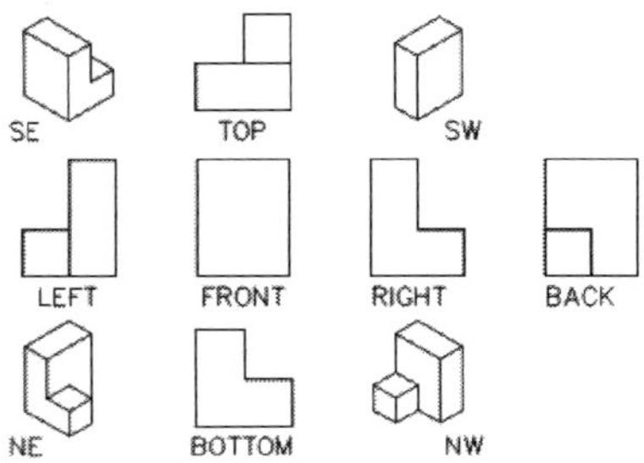

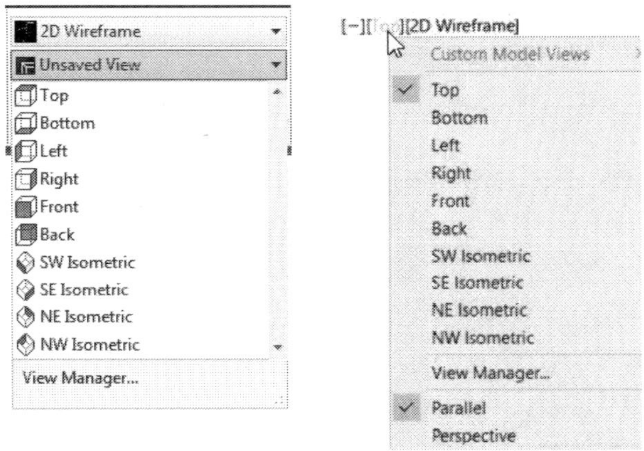

Home tab>View panel ***Drawing window>View Controls label***

Figure 1–11

Orthographic views display as if you are facing directly onto one side of a part. Isometric views typically display three sides, as if you are facing a corner. For example, an orthographic view of the cube would display one face: a square. An isometric view might display the top, left, and front sides of the cube.

- Orthographic views change the active drawing plane (UCS) of the view. This means that you can draw on that plane without having to manually change the UCS.
- Isometric views do not change the active drawing plane (UCS). To return to the flat drawing plane, select the **Top** view before continuing with a non-orthographic 3D view.

Drawing Window Setup

When you are new to working in 3D, you might find it helpful to setup your drawing window so that you can see the model you are working on from multiple viewing angles at the same time. For instance, you might want to view the model from the top view, a side view, and the front view all at once, while also viewing it in 3D, as shown in Figure 1–12.

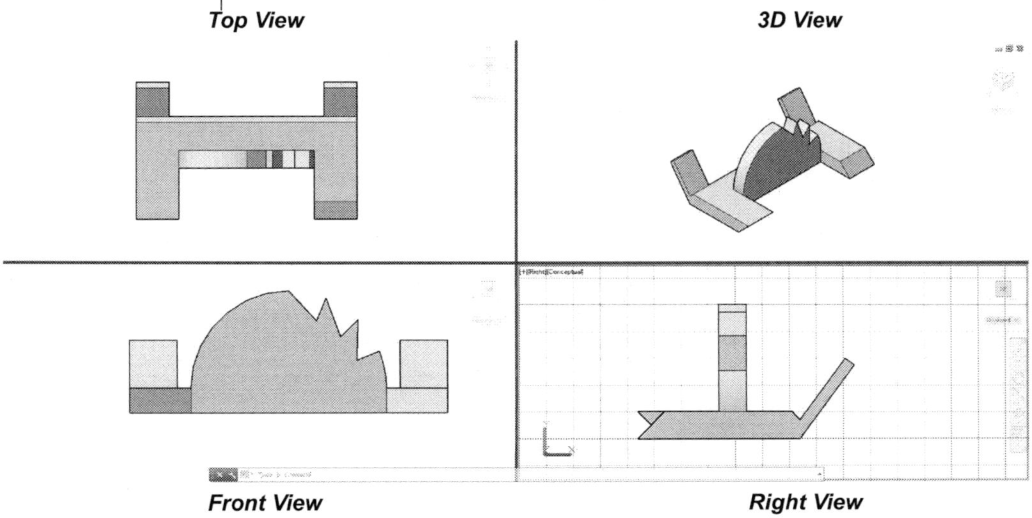

Figure 1–12

How To: Set Up the Drawing Window for Multiple Viewing Angles

1. In the *Visualize* tab>Model Viewports panel, expand  (Viewport Configuration) and select the desired configuration, as shown in Figure 1–13.

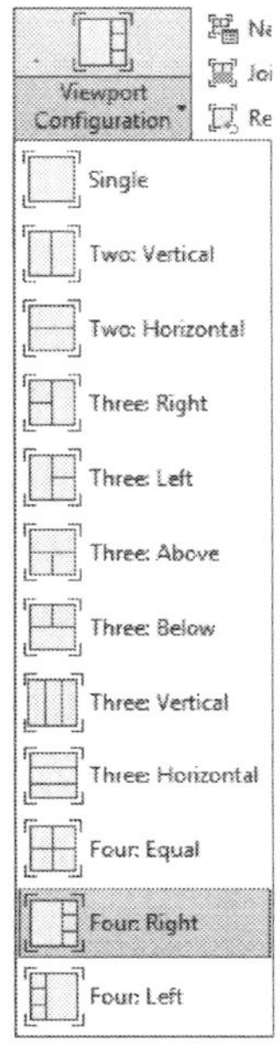

Figure 1–13

2. Click inside a viewport and change the viewing angle as required.
3. Click inside each of the other viewports and change their viewing angle so that each one is different.

Orbiting in 3D

The best tools for viewing in 3D are the mouse and keyboard. You can zoom in and out using the mouse's scroll wheel and can pan by holding the scroll wheel and dragging the mouse. Both methods are useful in 2D and 3D. However, in 3D you also need to view the model from all sides. Hold <Shift> and the scroll wheel of the mouse to temporarily orbit the objects in your drawing, as shown in Figure 1–14.

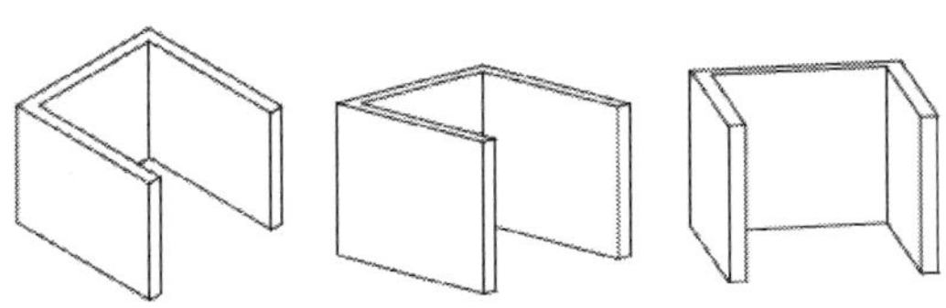

Figure 1–14

- When you orbit, the target (what you are viewing) stays stationary while the camera (your viewpoint) moves.
- You can also hold <Ctrl> and the scroll wheel to temporarily swivel. This is similar to panning the camera as you drag the mouse. The target of the view changes.
- If you select objects before you start orbiting, only those objects display as you move around the drawing. This is useful in complex drawings, because limiting the number of objects results in a smoother rotation of the view.

Additional Orbiting Commands

If the Navigate panel is not visible, right-click in the ribbon area and select Show Panels>Navigate.

Additional orbiting commands are available in the *View* tab> Navigate panel and in the Navigation Bar, as shown in Figure 1–15.

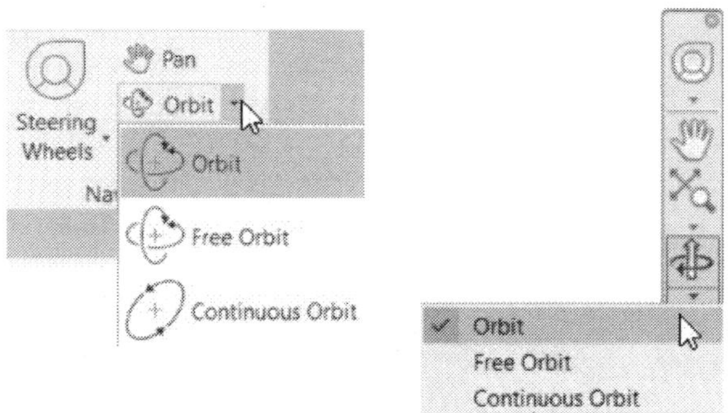

Figure 1–15

	**Orbit:** Orbits along the XY plane or Z-axis.
	**Free Orbit:** Orbits without any constraint to a plane or axis. A green circle called an arc ball displays. When you move the cursor over different parts of the arc ball, the view moves in different directions.
	**Continuous Orbit:** Rotates the viewpoint at a constant speed until you stop the rotation. Gives the impression of spinning the object in 3D space. To start the rotation, hold the mouse button, move the cursor, and release the button. The speed at which you move the cursor determines the speed of rotation, and the direction in which you move the cursor determines the direction of rotation.

- Use the mouse button rather than the scroll wheel to move around the drawing.
- When you are in a command, right-click to change between the various 3D viewing commands.

Using Visual Styles

While viewing a model, setting a visual style can help you gain a clearer understanding of the model. Visual styles control how elements display in a view. They might display all edges of the objects at the same time or just the ones closest to the viewer. Materials associated with the objects might be displayed or only shaded surfaces. You can add and modify objects and orbit in any of the visual styles.

Many preset visual styles come with the AutoCAD software, such as: 2D Wireframe, Conceptual, Realistic, Shaded, Shades of Gray, etc. Select a Visual Style by expanding Realistic in the *Home* tab>View panel and then selecting an option, as shown on the left in Figure 1–16. Some of the visual styles are also available in the Visual Style Controls label in the drawing window, as shown on the right in Figure 1–16.

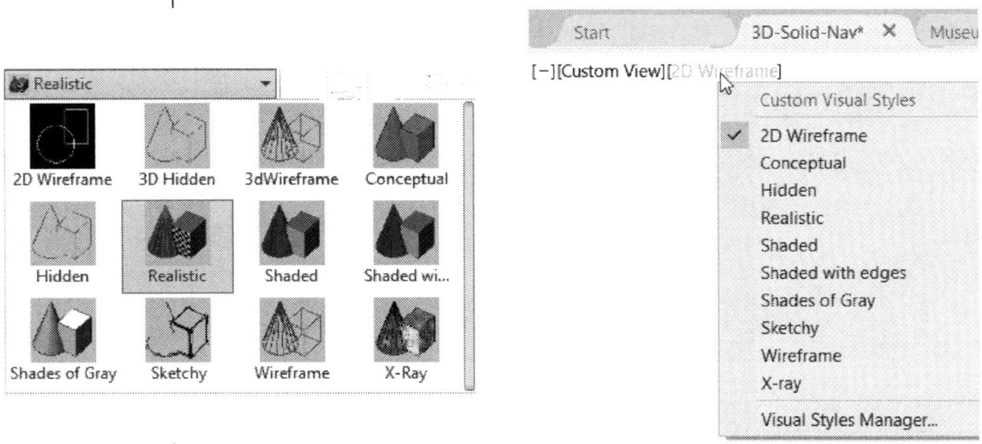

Figure 1–16

- If you are working in an orthographic view, set the *visual style* to **2D Wireframe** for the best results.
- In Paper Space, you must be in an active Model Space viewport before applying a visual style.

1.4 3D Navigation Tools

The AutoCAD software includes two additional tools to help you navigate 3D drawings: the ViewCube and the SteeringWheel (located in the Navigation Bar), as shown in Figure 1–17.

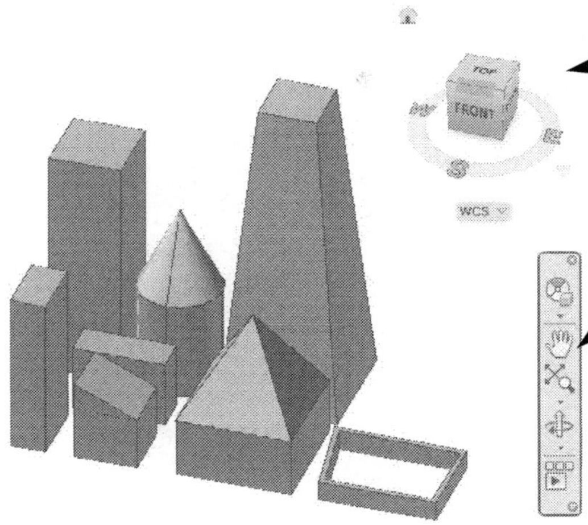

Figure 1–17

ViewCube

The ViewCube provides visual clues as to where you are in a 3D drawing and makes it easier to navigate to standard views, such as top, front, right, corner and directional views. Move the cursor over one of the highlighted options and select it. You can also click and drag on the ViewCube to rotate the box, which rotates the model. The ViewCube is shown in Figure 1–18.

*To change the Home view, set the view you want, right-click on the ViewCube, and select **Set Current View as Home**.*

Figure 1–18

-  (Home) displays when you move the cursor over the ViewCube. Click it to return to the view defined as **Home**.
- To toggle the ViewCube on and off, in the *View* tab>ViewPort Tools panel, select **ViewCube**.

Hint: Parallel and Perspective Views

Traditional 2D drawings display objects in orthographic (parallel) views, where parallel edges on the object seem to be parallel in the drawing. Perspective views display as the eye sees and parallel edges seem to converge at a vanishing point on the horizon. You can view the model in either Parallel or Perspective projection, as shown in Figure 1–19.

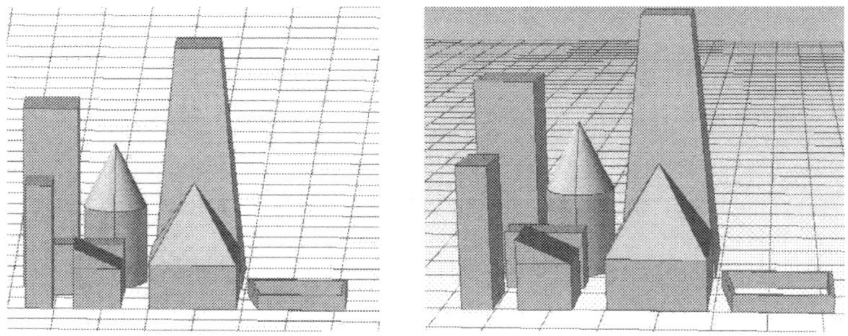

Figure 1–19

A parallel view helps you to evaluate the object's shape and size proportions without any distortion, while a perspective view gives you a better sense of space and depth, especially with large objects (such as buildings).

- You can draw, select, and modify objects while you are in a perspective view.
- You can switch between **Parallel**, **Perspective**, and **Perspective with Ortho Faces** when you right-click on the ViewCube or while you are in a **3D Orbit** command.
- You can also switch between **Parallel** and **Perspective** in the **View Controls** label list of the drawing window.
- Perspective mode is not available in the 2D wireframe visual style.
- If you save a drawing as a version earlier than the AutoCAD 2007 software, the Perspective view is automatically toggled off.

ViewCube Settings

ViewCube settings control the display of the ViewCube, how it works when you are dragging or clicking, and several other settings. Right-click on the ViewCube and select **ViewCube Settings...** to open the ViewCube Settings dialog box, as shown in Figure 1–20.

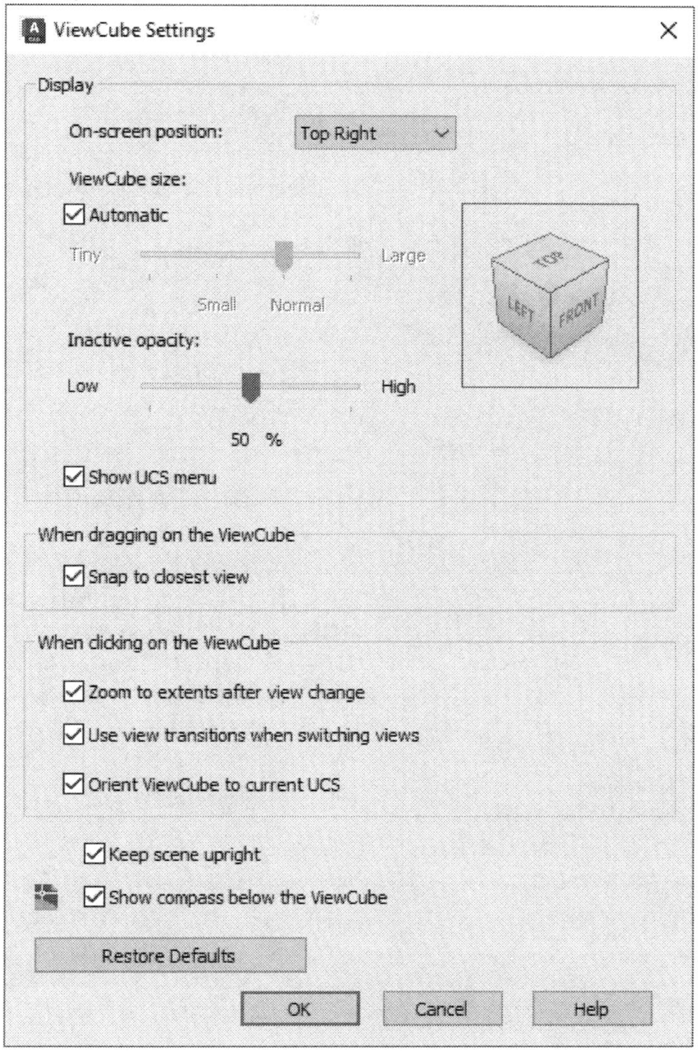

Figure 1–20

SteeringWheel

The SteeringWheel provides access to navigation commands such as **Zoom**, **Pan**, **Orbit**, and **Rewind**. The **Rewind** command navigates through all previous views of the model.

How To: Use the SteeringWheel

1. In the Navigation Bar, expand  (Full Navigation Wheel) and select a SteeringWheel.
    - Alternatively, you can expand  (Steering Wheel) in the Navigation Bar or type **navswheel** in the command line.
2. In the SteeringWheel, hover the cursor over the navigation command that you want to use.
3. Click and hold the mouse button to start the navigation command.
4. Move the cursor to change the view as required.
5. Release the mouse button to end the navigation command.
6. Close the SteeringWheel.

- The SteeringWheel follows the cursor in the drawing window. Verify that the cursor is positioned correctly before launching a navigation command.

Full SteeringWheels

You can select from three different full wheels: Full Navigation, View Object, and Tour Building. The Full Navigation wheel includes all of the navigation tools, the Basic View Object wheel contains **Center**, **Zoom**, **Rewind**, and **Orbit**, and the Basic Tour Building wheel contains **Forward**, **Look**, **Rewind**, and **Up/Down**. The full wheels are shown in Figure 1–21.

*To close the SteeringWheel, press <Esc> or <Enter> or click the **X** in the SteeringWheel.*

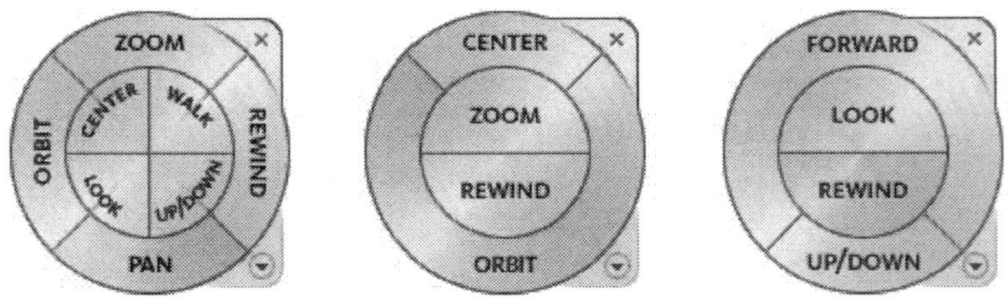

Full Navigation ***Basic View Object*** ***Basic Tour Building***

Figure 1–21

Mini Wheels

The mini wheels provide access to similar commands as the full wheels, but use a smaller icon with pie-shaped wedges. As the icon moves with the cursor (while you are in the **SteeringWheel** command), the mini wheels provide more screen space by eliminating the text descriptions on the wheel. The mini wheels and their commands are shown in Figure 1–22.

Right-click on the SteeringWheel to change between the different types of wheels.

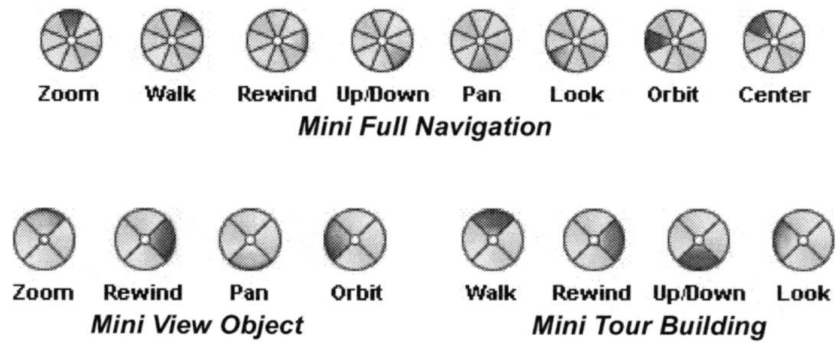

Figure 1–22

Rewind Command

Use the **Rewind** command to navigate to previously displayed views of the model, as shown in Figure 1–23.

Figure 1–23

How To: Use the Rewind Command

1. Start the **SteeringWheel** command.
2. Hover the cursor over the **Rewind** option.
3. Click and hold the mouse button to start the **Rewind** command. A series of thumbnails display.
4. Move the cursor over the thumbnails to navigate to the highlighted view. The model updates as you move over the thumbnails.
5. Release the mouse button to make the highlighted view active.

SteeringWheel Settings

The SteeringWheels Settings dialog box controls the appearance of the SteeringWheels. With a SteeringWheel active, right-click and select **SteeringWheels Settings...** to open the dialog box, as shown in Figure 1–24.

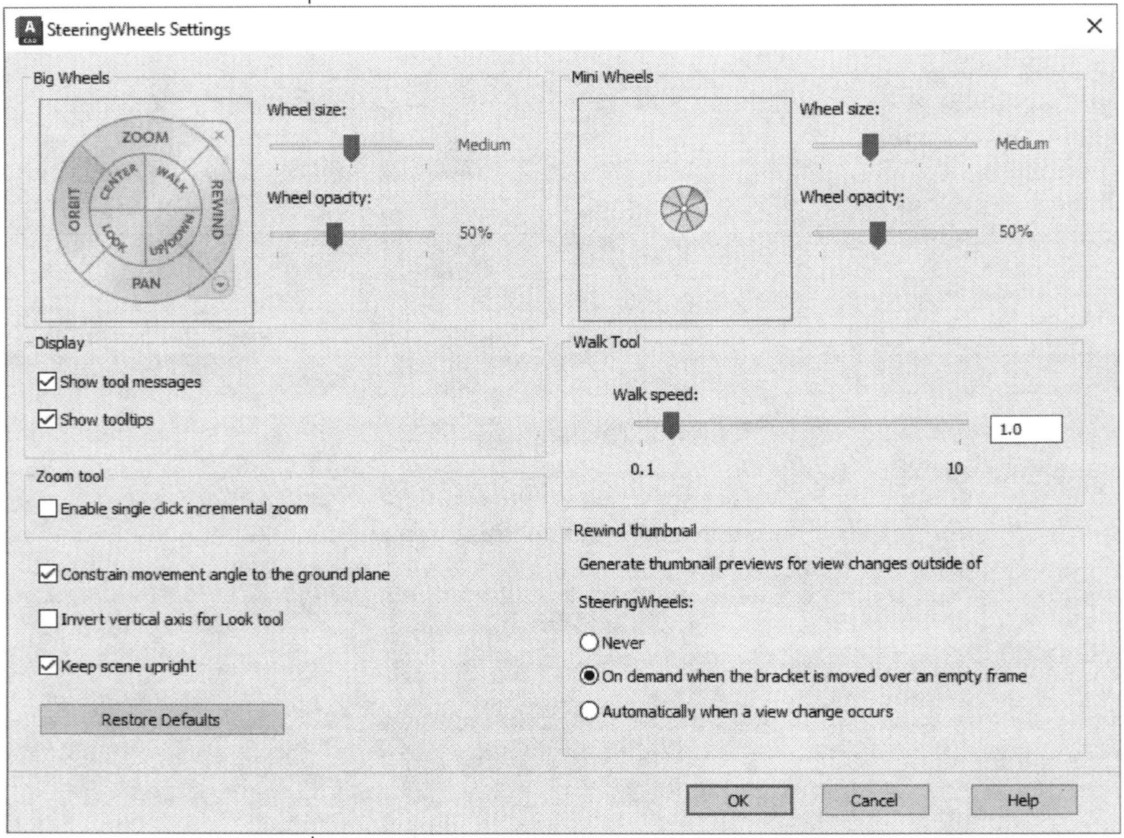

Figure 1–24

Practice 1a 3D Navigation Tools

Practice Objectives

- Navigate around a 3D model using preset views, manual orbiting tools, ViewCube, and the SteeringWheel.
- Modify the display and appearance of a 3D model by changing the visual style.

In this practice, you will access preset views, orbit the drawing, and test visual styles. You will also use the ViewCube and SteeringWheel to view the drawing. You can use an architectural drawing (as shown in Figure 1–25) or a mechanical drawing (as shown in Figure 1–26).

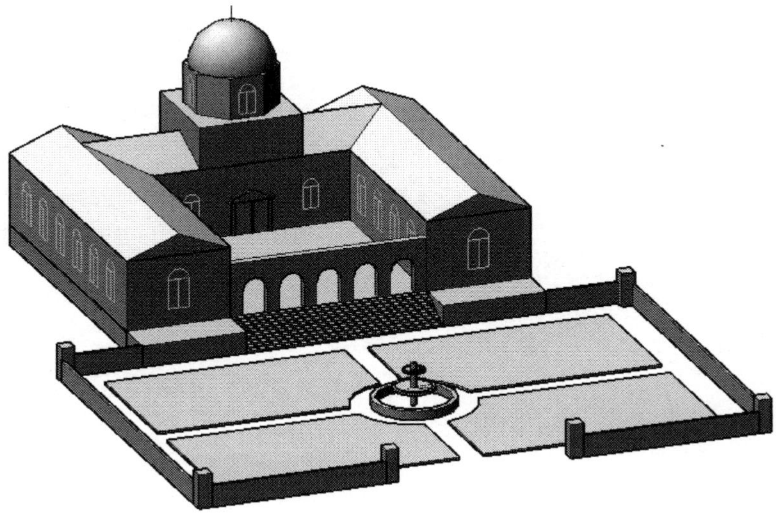

Figure 1–25

Task 1 - Navigate the model.

1. Open **3D-Solid-Nav.dwg** (mechanical) or **Museum-Concept.dwg** (architectural).
2. In the Status Bar>Workspace Switching list or in the Quick Access Toolbar>Workspace drop-down list, select **3D Modeling**.
3. In the *Home* tab>View panel, use the view presets to display several views of the part or building (Left, Right, SE Isometric, etc.). Finish by selecting the **Top** view to reset the UCS and then select an isometric view.

You can also select the various views in the ***View Controls*** *drop-down list in the drawing window.*

4. Hold <Shift> + the middle mouse wheel to use **3DOrbit** and move around the part or building, displaying the different sides.

*You can also select the various visual styles in the **Visual Style Controls** list in the drawing window.*

5. In the *Home* tab>View panel, change the different visual styles to display different appearances for the part or building (Realistic, Conceptual, etc.).

Task 2 - Work with the ViewCube

1. Use the ViewCube and navigate to different views using the various sides and corners of the cube.
2. Click (Home) to return to the **Home** view.
3. Hold <Shift> + the middle mouse button and orbit to a different view. The ViewCube follows the direction of the cursor.
4. Right-click on the ViewCube and select **Set Current View as Home**.
5. Use the ViewCube to change the view and click (Home) again. It returns to the view you specified as Home.
6. In the drawing window, select the *Visual Style Controls* label and select **Top**.

Task 3 - Use the SteeringWheel.

1. In the Navigation Bar, expand (Full Navigation Wheel) and select **Mini Full Navigation Wheel**.
2. Zoom, orbit, and pan using the SteeringWheel tools, as shown with the mechanical part in Figure 1–26.

Figure 1–26

3. Rewind back to your first view.

4. Right-click on the SteeringWheel, expand Basic Wheels, and select **View Object Wheel**.

5. Try the viewing tools in this SteeringWheel.

6. Right-click again and select **Mini View Object Wheel**. Change the view using this SteeringWheel.

7. Change to one of the other mini wheels and try any tools you have not yet used, such as **Walk** or **Look**.

8. When you have finished trying the new tools, right-click and select **Go Home**. The view returns to the last specified home.

9. Right-click and select **Close Wheel**.

10. Save the drawing.

Task 4 - Set up the model space with multiple viewing angles.

1. Open **Museum-Concept.dwg**, if not already open.

2. In the *Visualize* tab>Model Viewports panel, expand  (Viewport Configuration) and select the **Four: Equal** configuration, as shown in Figure 1–27.

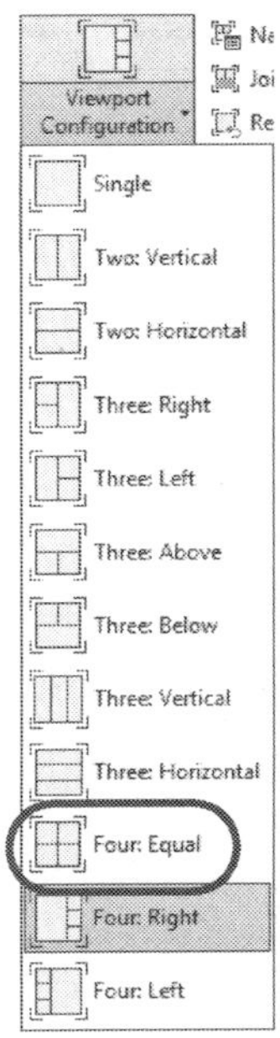

Figure 1–27

3. Click inside each viewport and change the viewing angles to the preset views shown in Figure 1–28. (The visual style is set to **2D Wireframe**.)

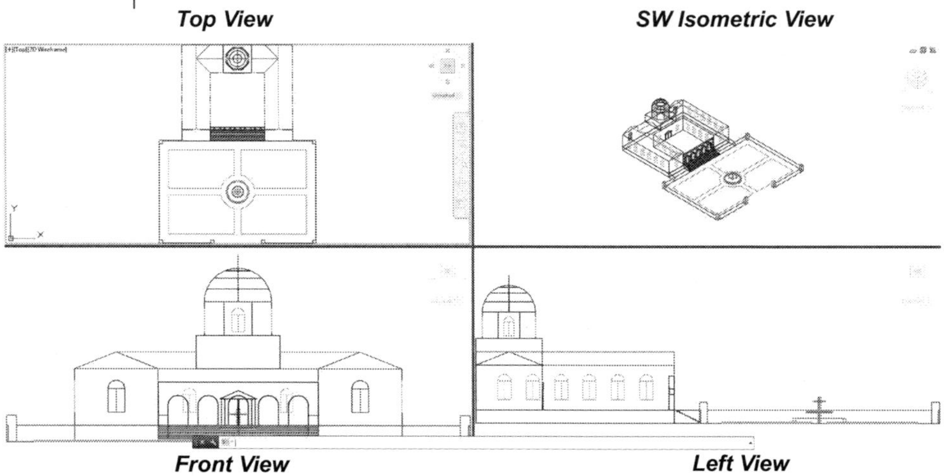

Figure 1–28

4. Close the drawing without saving.

1.5 Introduction to the User Coordinate System (UCS)

In the AutoCAD software, 2D objects are created on a single flat plane, which is usually the XY plane. In 3D, you can work on the XY plane or change to another plane, as shown in Figure 1–29.

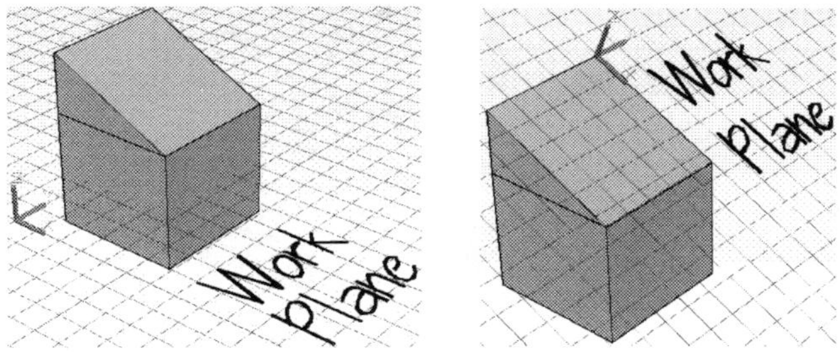

Figure 1–29

There are three axes: the X-axis, Y-axis, and Z-axis. Three planes are also automatically created by the intersections of these axes. They are the XY plane, the YZ plane, and the XZ plane. Together these three axes and their planes make up a user coordinate system, or UCS. The UCS is a user-defined working plane with X,Y coordinates that can be positioned at any location or orientation in space.

When you draw on the UCS, you can use the same commands and methods regardless of the angle or location to which the XY plane has changed. Drawing in 3D is very similar to drawing in 2D. The only difference is that you add information for the Z-direction as well for the thickness, elevation, or height. Many 2D commands can be used to start or add to 3D drawings.

- Do not confuse the UCS position with the viewing direction. The position from which you view your drawing, known as the viewpoint, determines how you see your drawing. The UCS determines where you are drawing. It sets the position of the working plane.
- Each viewport can have its own UCS.

Modeling with Dynamic Feedback

Most of the 3D commands display dynamic feedback as you draw. Not only can you select points to define the dimensions of the object, including its height, but this information also displays in the drawing window as you work. You can type specific numbers or select points with the cursor, as shown in Figure 1–30.

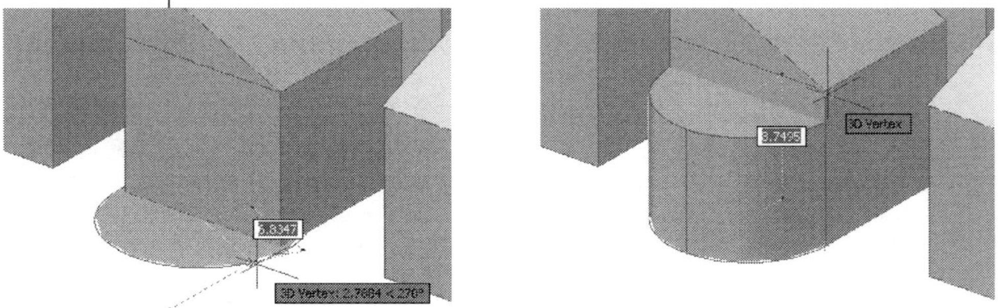

Figure 1–30

- POLAR, OTRACK, and ORTHO work with dynamic input in the Z-axis direction.

Dynamic UCS

Rather than frequently changing the UCS, you can use the **Dynamic UCS (DUCS)** command to temporarily move the UCS to a face on a 3D object while you are drawing, as shown in Figure 1–31. While you are in a command, move the cursor over the edge of a face until it is highlighted, and then proceed with the command. The UCS icon moves to that face and the next objects created align with the coordinate system of the face. When the command is finished, the UCS returns to its previous location.

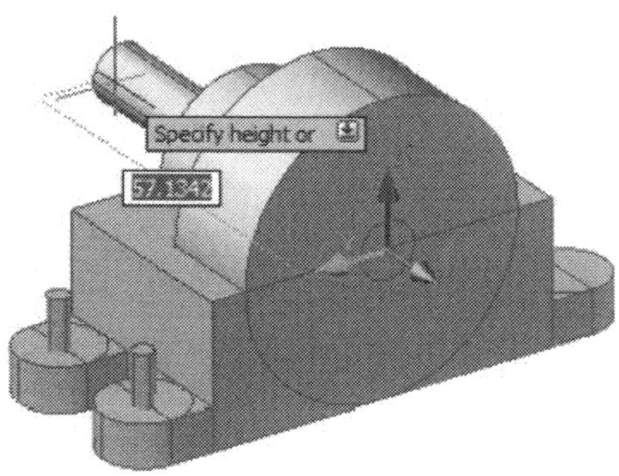

Figure 1–31

- The Dynamic UCS can be toggled on and off by clicking (Dynamics UCS) in the Status Bar, as shown in Figure 1–32.

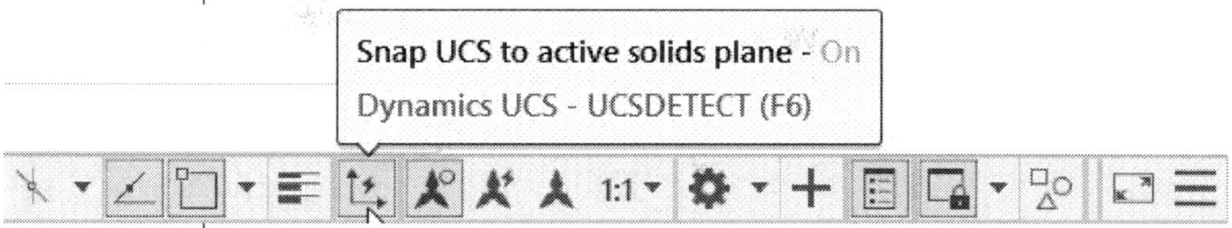

Figure 1–32

- When the cursor is moved over to a face, the crosshair takes the orientation of the edge (side) over which the cursor was being passed.

- Object Snaps can be used with **Dynamic UCS**. Sometimes, object snaps can interfere with the selection when you are identifying the face you want to use. Toggle off (Object Snap) in the Status Bar or press <F3> until you have selected the face you want to use. You can also use the **None** Object Snap Override to temporarily toggle off Object Snap.

- You can use 3D object snaps by toggling on (3D Object Snap) in the Status Bar. They include: **Vertex**, **Midpoint on edge**, **Center of face**, **Knot**, **Perpendicular**, and **Nearest to face** and are useful when snapping to points on 3D objects.

- To change the current UCS to a different face in the drawing, start the **UCS** command, select the face, and press <Enter>. The UCS moves to the selected face. If the grid is on, it aligns with the new UCS as well.

- The World Coordinate System is the drawing's original and master coordinate setup. Type **UCS** and select **World** to restore the drawing coordinates to the master coordinate system.

Practice 1b Introduction to the User Coordinate System

Practice Objective

- Add 2D objects to various faces on a 3D model using Dynamic UCS.

In this practice, you will add 2D objects to a simple solid model using Dynamic UCS, and view the model with 3D Navigation commands.

1. Open **DUCS.dwg**.

2. In the Status Bar, toggle on (Grid Display), (Dynamic UCS), (Dynamic Input), and (Lineweight), if they are not already on.

3. In the Status Bar, toggle off (Object Snap) and (3D Object Snap).

4. Orbit the model to display the faces labeled A, B, C, D, and E. Finish with a view in which Face A displays.

5. In the *Home* tab>Draw panel, click (Line). Hover over Face A until it highlights and add several lines to the surface, similar to those shown in Figure 1–33.

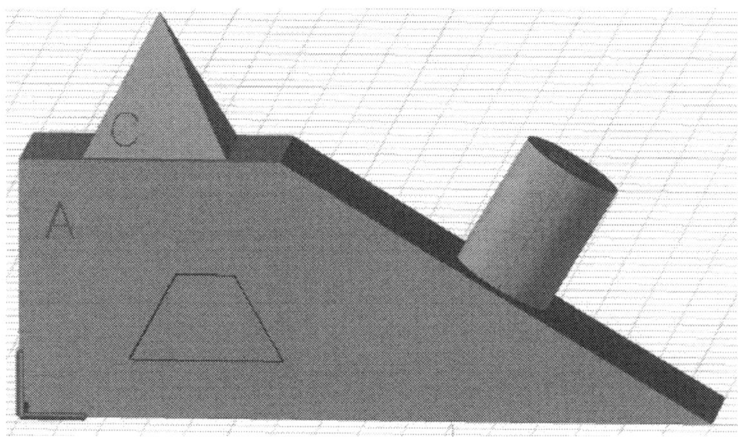

Figure 1–33

6. Click  (Circle). Hover over Face B until it highlights. Draw a small circle anywhere on Face B, similar to that shown in Figure 1–34.

7. Draw another circle on Face C, similar to that shown in Figure 1–34.

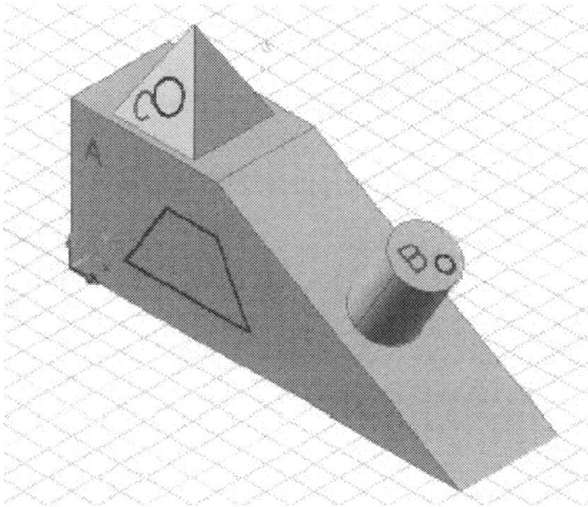

Figure 1–34

8. Orbit the model to display Faces D and E. Draw objects on those faces.

9. Finish with the **SE Isometric** view and save the drawing.

Chapter Review Questions

1. Which of the following is a type of 3D model?
    a. Cone
    b. Mesh
    c. Box
    d. Cylinder
2. The *Visualize* tab contains tools that enable you to add lights and materials to the model.
    a. True
    b. False
3. Which of the following is a preset 3D view?
    a. SW Isometric
    b. Top
    c. Front
    d. All of the above
4. When using the ViewCube to view a model in 3D, which of the following icons near the ViewCube can you click to return to the original view?
    a. **Top**
    b. **WCS**
    c. **W**
    d. **Home**
5. Which of the following is true of the Dynamic UCS?
    a. When you move the UCS to a selected face on a 3D object, it remains there permanently.
    b. It cannot be used with object snaps.
    c. It cannot be toggled on or off.
    d. Temporarily moves the UCS to a selected face on a 3D object.

6. A perspective view helps you to evaluate the object's shape and size proportions without any distortion, while a parallel view gives you a better sense of space and depth.
    a. True
    b. False

Command Summary

All ribbon names reference the 3D Modeling workspace.

Button	Command	Location
	Allow/Disallow Dynamic UCS	• **Status Bar**
	Continuous Orbit	• **Ribbon:** *View* tab>Navigate panel • **Navigation Bar**
	Free Orbit	• **Ribbon:** *View* tab>Navigate panel • **Navigation Bar**
	Home	• **ViewCube**
	Orbit	• **Ribbon:** *View* tab>Navigate panel • **Navigation Bar**
	Preset Views	• **Ribbon:** *Home* tab>View panel
	SteeringWheel	• **Ribbon:** *View* tab>Navigate panel • **Navigation Bar**
	User Interface	• **Ribbon:** *View* tab>User Interface panel
N/A	**ViewCube Display**	• **Ribbon:** *View* tab>User Interface panel>User Interface drop-down list
	Visual Styles	• **Ribbon:** *Home* tab>View panel or *View* tab>Visual Styles panel
	Workspace Switching	• **Quick Access Toolbar** • **Status Bar**

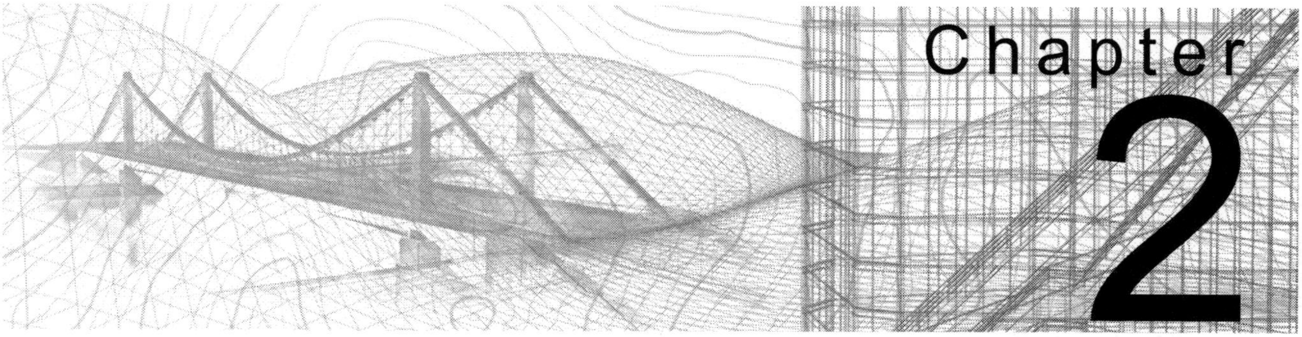

Simple Solids

In this chapter, you learn how to create and modify solid primitives, including boxes, wedges, pyramids, cylinders, cones, spheres, and tori. You learn to use Boolean commands to join, subtract, and find the common volume between solids, and modifying composite solids. You also learn how to create, modify, and convert to and from mesh models.

Learning Objectives in This Chapter

- Modify existing solid primitives.
- Create solid primitives and polysolids.
- Combine two or more solids to form a single, more complicated solid.
- Create mesh models.

2.1 Working with Solid Primitives

Solid primitives are the simplest form of solids, much like building blocks, as shown in Figure 2–1. They help you to create the basic mass of the model and are useful as temporary objects. They are easy to use with dynamic feedback, since their prompts are similar to 2D commands. For example, **Box** and **Wedge** start with a rectangle, **Pyramid** starts with a polygon, **Cylinder** and **Cone** start with a circle, and a **Polysolid** is similar to a polyline with a width and height.

You can use a solid primitive with Dynamic UCS to set a UCS or specify an object snap point in 3D space. When you no longer need the solid primitive, you can erase it.

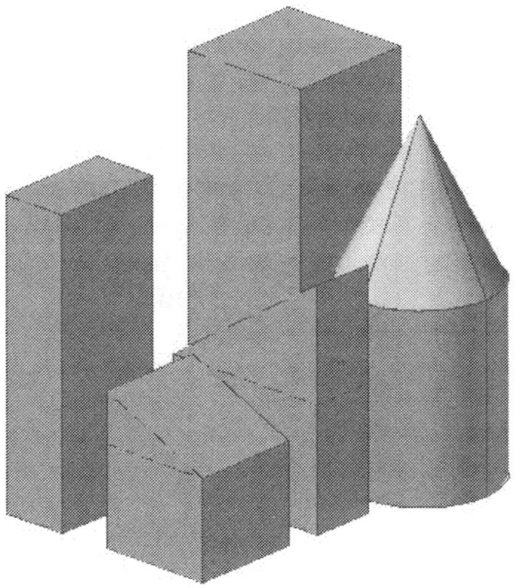

Figure 2–1

Drawing Solid Primitives

The basic method of drawing a solid primitive is simple. In most cases, you draw the 2D object first and then add the height, as shown in Figure 2–2. All of this can be done by selecting points on the screen without any typing. You can also type a distance value to specify each dimension.

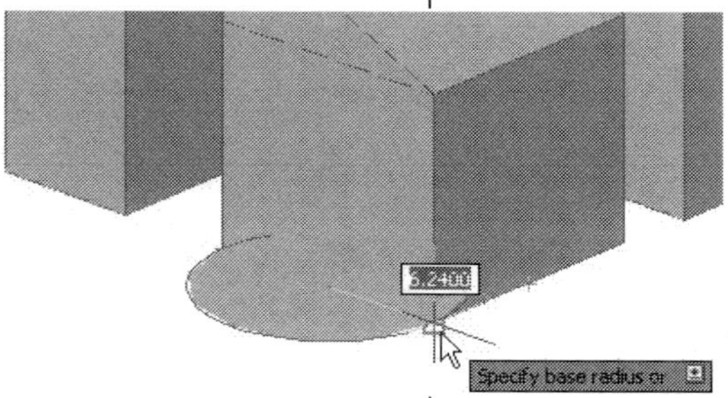

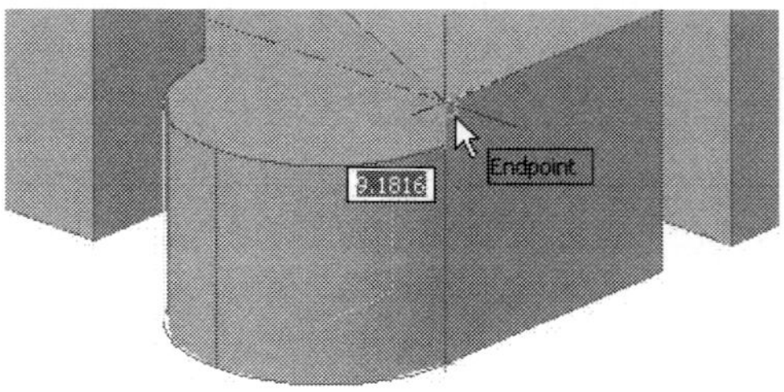

Figure 2–2

Editing Solid Primitives

You can modify solid primitives with grips and in Properties after you have created the solid primitive, as shown in Figure 2–3. When you edit solid primitives with grips, both square and arrow grip styles display on most solid primitives. Each one has a specific purpose, depending on the type of solid primitive you have selected.

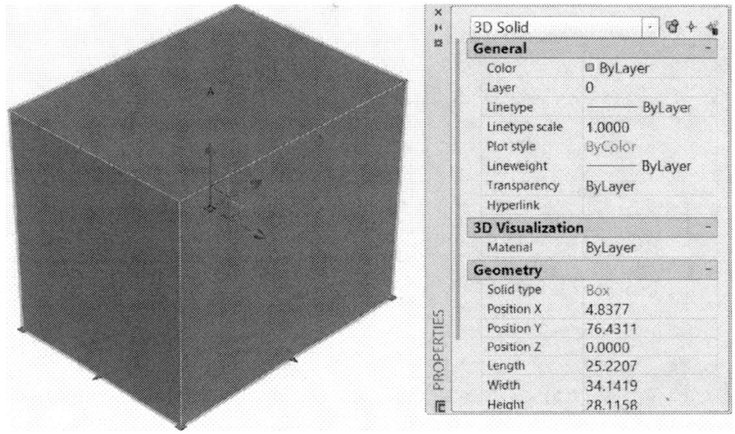

Figure 2–3

Grip Types

	The square grip in the center of any solid primitive is the location grip. You can use it to move or rotate the entire solid primitive.
	A square grip at each vertex of polygonal solid primitives (boxes, wedges, and pyramids) resizes the base polygonal shape. The base always stays polygonal.
	Arrows on each edge of a polygonal base modify one side of the base. Any arrow grip on a pyramid changes the length on all sides.
	Cylinders, cones, spheres, and tori have arrow grips that modify their radius.
	Arrows that point up or down modify the height of the object.

- If you modify a solid primitive with grips, the object remains the same but is a different size or height, etc. For example, a cone remains a cone even if you change its point to be a flat circular surface.

Dynamic Dimensions and Grips

You can hover over a grip to display the related dimensions of the solid primitive, as shown in Figure 2–4. For example, if you hover over the vertex of the box, its length displays in each direction from the grip. If you hover over the height grip, the height of the solid primitive displays.

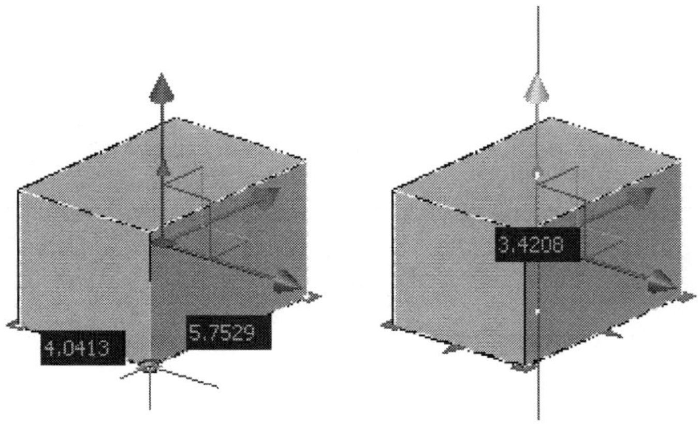

Figure 2–4

Select the grip to change the size (such as height or length) of solid primitives. You can type the distance values if you want more control. When you select the grip, the associated dynamic dimensions are available for typed input.

- To toggle through the dynamic dimensions, press <Tab>.
- To modify a grip that only adjusts the object in a single direction (such as height or edge), click on the grip, move the cursor in the required direction, and type a value for the change in that direction. If you want to change the overall value in that direction, press <Tab> before typing the number.

2.2 Solid Primitive Types

Solid primitives are the building blocks when using 3D in the AutoCAD® software. They are located in the *Home* tab>Modeling panel and in the *Solid* tab>Primitive panel, as shown in Figure 2–5. They include Box, Cylinder, Cone, Sphere, Pyramid, Wedge, and Torus.

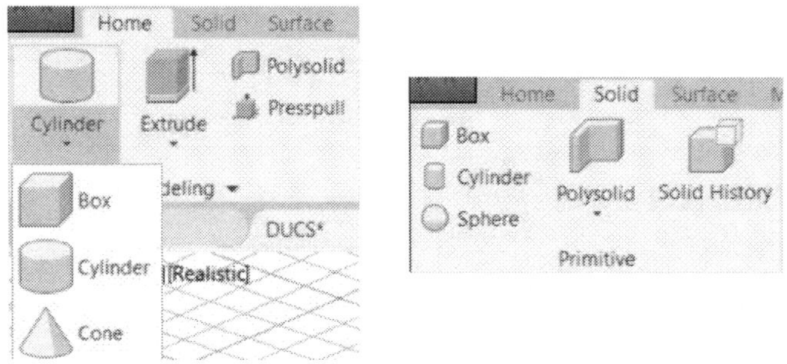

Figure 2–5

Creating Boxes and Wedges

The box, as with the line and rectangle in 2D drawings, is a standard building block for many different 3D objects. Boxes are used to draw buildings (as shown in Figure 2–6), furniture, electrical, mechanical, and structural parts. Wedges are boxes that have been cut diagonally. They are used to draw roof lines and other tapered parts.

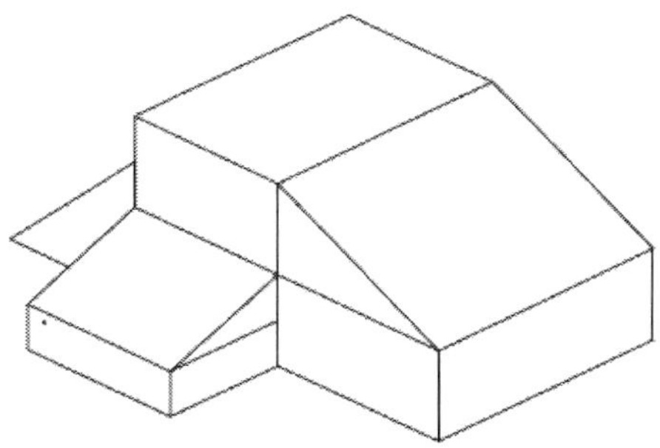

Figure 2–6

How To: Create Boxes and Wedges

1. In the *Home* tab>Modeling panel, click  (Box) or click  Wedge.
   - Alternatively, you can access the commands in the *Solid* tab>Primitive panel or type **box** or **wedge** in the command line.

2. Select two corners of the box or wedge as if you were creating a rectangle.
3. Type a value or pick in the drawing window to set the height.

- A wedge slopes down from the first selected point. When you move the cursor to set the height, the slope is created dynamically.
- There are several options for using the **Box** and **Wedge** commands. In most cases, it is easier to draw the solid and then manipulate its size or location once it is in the drawing.

Box and Wedge Options

Center	Starts the box or wedge at the geometric center.
Cube	Creates a box or wedge with equal length, width, and height.
Length	Prompts for the length, width, and height. Length refers to the distance in the X-direction, width refers to the distance in the Y-direction, and height refers to the Z-direction.
2Point	Enables you to select two points on the screen to establish the height of the box.

Editing Boxes and Wedges

You can modify boxes and wedges with edge, vertex, and height grips. Moving a vertex grip expands the overall shape of the box or wedge from the corner. Moving an edge grip modifies the length of that edge. You can also modify the geometry in Properties, as shown in Figure 2–7.

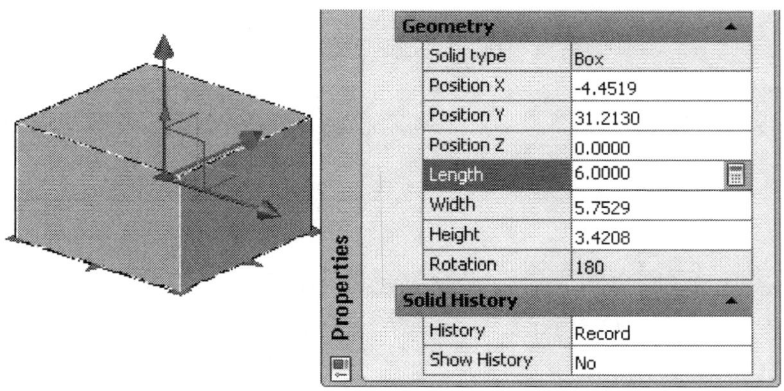

Figure 2–7

Creating Pyramids

A pyramid is a solid with three or more equal sides. The base options are similar to the **Polygon** command, in which you can specify the number of sides for the base, and the method (**Edge**, **Circumscribed**, or **Inscribed**) of creating the base. You can have a point at the top, create a frustum pyramid that has its top cut off, or set the top and bottom radius to be equal to create a cylindrical polygon, as shown in Figure 2–8.

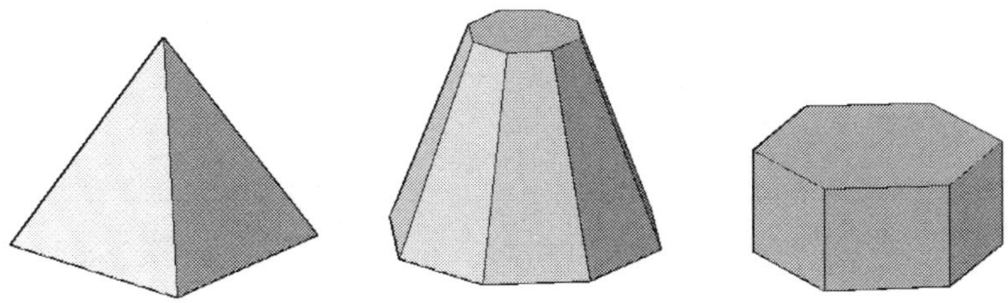

Figure 2–8

How To: Create a Pyramid

1. In the *Home* tab>Modeling panel, click  (Pyramid).
   - Alternatively, you can click  (Pyramid) in the *Solid* tab>Primitive panel or type **pyramid** in the command line.
2. The Command Line displays the default number of sides and the default method. Select **Sides** to specify the number of sides.
3. Select a center point or change to the **Edge** method.
4. If you are starting with a center point, select the **Circumscribed** or **Inscribed** method, as shown in Figure 2–9, and set the base radius. If you have selected the **Edge** method, specify the first and second end points of the edge.

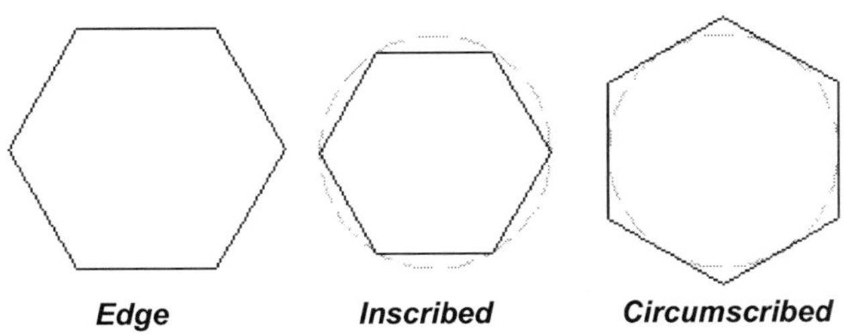

Figure 2–9

5. Specify the height of the pyramid or use one of the pyramid options.

Pyramid Options

2Point	Enables you to select two points on the screen to establish the height of the pyramid.
Axis Endpoint	Enables you specify the end point of the pyramid. This point can be anywhere in 3D space and sets the height and orientation of the pyramid.
Top Radius	Enables you to specify the dimension of the top radius if you want to have a flat surface rather than a point.

Editing Pyramids

You can modify pyramids with edge, vertex, and height grips. You can also modify the geometry in Properties, as shown in Figure 2–10. Moving a vertex or edge grip expands the overall base of the pyramid. In Properties, you can also set the *Type* to **Circumscribed** or **Inscribed** and change the number of sides.

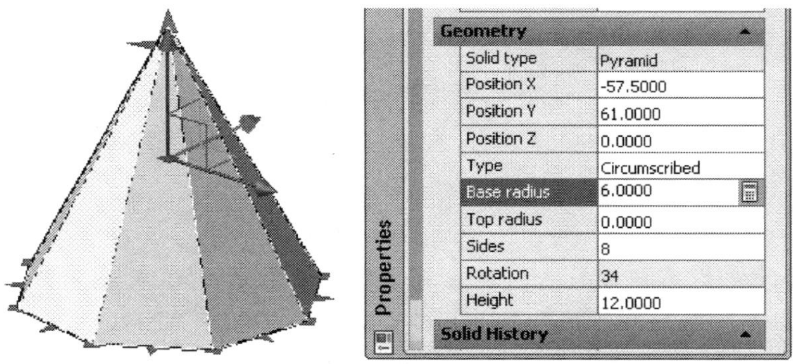

Figure 2–10

- Pyramids have an arrow grip near the top that changes the point to a flat surface, which you can independently resize, thus creating a frustum pyramid. You can also modify the *Top radius* in Properties to make this change.

Creating Cylinders and Cones

The **Cylinder** command creates a solid column with an elliptical or circular base. Cylinders can be used for columns, pipes, holes, and wires. The **Cone** command creates a cone with an elliptical or circular base. Cones can be used to create nozzles, pedestals, and some roofs. Examples of cylinders and cones are shown in Figure 2–11.

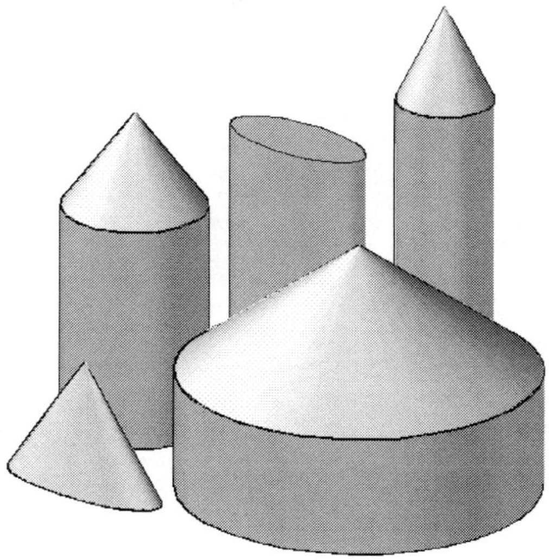

Figure 2–11

How To: Draw a Cylinder or Cone

1. In the *Home* tab>Modeling panel, click  (Cylinder) or  (Cone).
   - Alternatively, you can access the commands in the *Solid* tab>Primitive panel or type **cylinder** or **cone** in the command line.
2. Select the center point of the base
3. Specify the radius.
4. Specify the height.

- As with the **Circle** command, you can use the **3P**, **2P**, and **Ttr** options to create the base and can specify a diameter rather than the radius.
- To create an elliptical cylinder or cone, select the **Elliptical** option before specifying any other points. You are then prompted to specify the first and second axes for the ellipse before you specify the height.

- At the *Specify Height:* prompt, the options are **2Point**, **Axis endpoint**, and **Top radius**.
- You can use the **Center**, **Quadrant**, and **Tangent** object snaps with cylinders and cones.

Editing Cylinders and Cones

You can modify cylinders and cones with radius and height grips in Properties, as shown in Figure 2–12. Moving a radius grip expands the overall base of the cylinder or cone. In Properties, if the *Elliptical* property is set to **Yes**, modifying the radius grips changes one axis at a time.

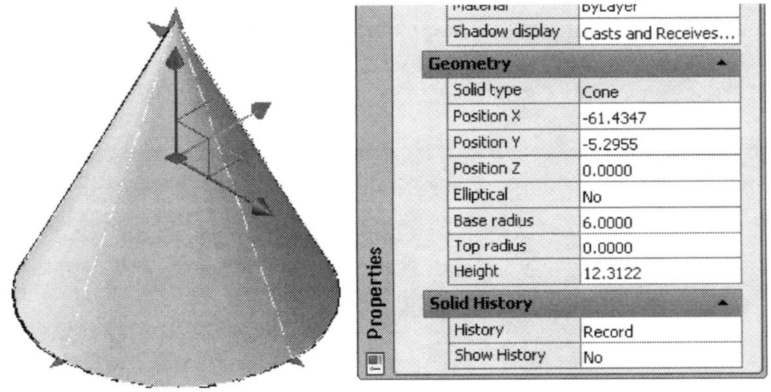

Figure 2–12

- Cones have a grip arrow near the top that changes the point to a flat surface, which you can independently resize. You can also modify the geometry in Properties.
- Cylinders cannot be changed to cones, but a cone can have its top radius set to the same dimensions as the base radius to look like a cylinder.

Creating Spheres and Tori

Spheres are used for drawing many mechanical parts, balls and globes. A Torus is a donut or inner-tube shape. Tori are used to put grooves in cylinders, cones, and spheres. They can also be used to draw pipes and wires. Examples of spheres and tori are shown in Figure 2–13.

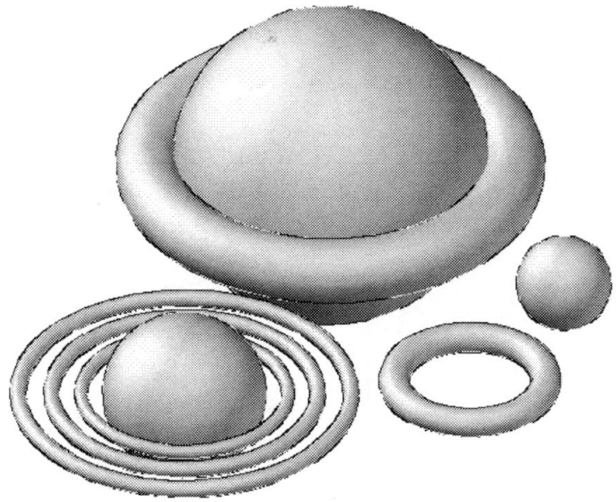

Figure 2–13

How To: Create Spheres

1. In the *Home* tab>Modeling panel, click  (Sphere).
   - Alternatively, you can access the command in the *Solid* tab>Primitive panel or type **sphere** in the command line.
2. Specify the center of the sphere.
3. Specify the radius (or diameter) of the sphere.

How To: Create Tori

1. In the *Home* tab>Modeling panel, click  (Torus).
   - Alternatively, you can access the command in the *Solid* tab>Primitive panel or type **torus** in the command line.
2. Specify the center of the torus.
3. Specify the radius (or diameter) of the entire torus.
4. Specify the radius (or diameter) of the tube.

- The **Center** object snap and **Nearest to face** 3D object snap are the only ones that work on spheres and tori.

- A torus that has a tube radius so large that there is no hole in the center of the ring is called a self-intersecting torus. You can create this type of torus in the AutoCAD software.

- A football shape can be created by setting the diameter or radius of the torus to a negative value, and setting the radius of the tube to a larger absolute value than that of the torus.

Modifying Spheres and Tori

You can modify spheres and tori with radius grips and in Properties, as shown in Figure 2–14. Moving a radius grip expands the overall size of the sphere. Tori have four arrow grips around the edge of the tube profile that change its tube radius. They also have an arrow in the center of the tube profile that changes the radius of the torus (or full tire).

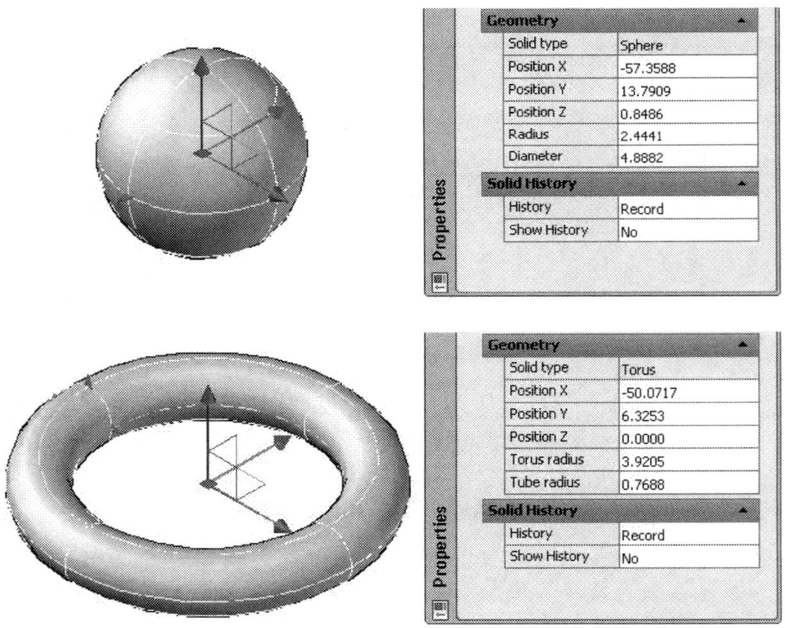

Figure 2–14

Creating Wall-like Solids with Polysolid

A polysolid is a 3D polyline that can help you draw walls or any type of linear 3D object, as shown in Figure 2–15. The process is similar to working with the **Polyline** command in drawings. It can have arcs or lines and can be closed from end point to end point after a minimum of two segments have been drawn.

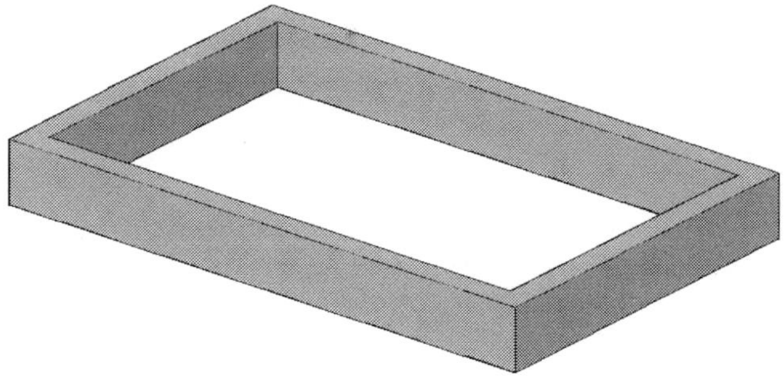

Figure 2–15

How To: Create a Polysolid

1. In the *Home* tab>Modeling panel, click  (Polysolid).
    - Alternatively, you can access the command in the *Solid* tab>Primitive panel or type **polysolid** in the command line.
2. Set the **Height**, **Width**, and **Justify** options as required before you start drawing.
3. Specify the first point and other points as required. The options are similar to polylines. You can add arc segments as you draw.
4. Press <Enter> to end the command. You can also select **Close** to create a closed profile object and end the command.

- You can also convert a line, polyline, spline, circle, or arc into a polysolid. Start the **Polysolid** command and press <Enter> to launch Object mode. The height and width are controlled by the **Polysolid** command options.

- While you can modify polysolids with grips, you are actually modifying a profile rather than a primitive. Changing the height or width is more complicated than on a typical primitive.

Hint: Controlling the Appearance of Solids

Isolines are lines drawn on a curved surface to indicate that the surface exists. The **Isolines** variable controls how many isolines display on curved solids. The default value is 4. A larger number creates a more tightly curved object, as shown in Figure 2–16.

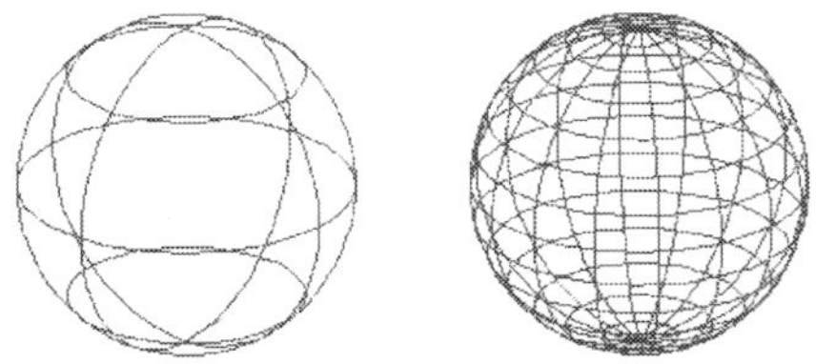

Isolines = 4 *Isolines = 16*

Figure 2–16

Silhouette edges (**Dispsilh**) are lines that indicate where a curved surface disappears from sight, as shown in Figure 2–17.

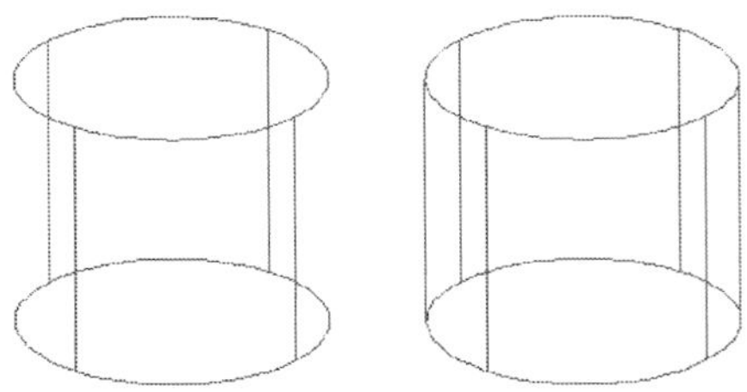

Dispsilh = 0 *Dispsilh = 1*

Figure 2–17

- The **Isolines** and **Dispsilh** variables affect the plotting of shapes when the lines are hidden.

Facet resolution (**Facetres**) sets the smoothness of shaded and rendered objects, and objects with hidden lines removed, as shown in Figure 2–18.

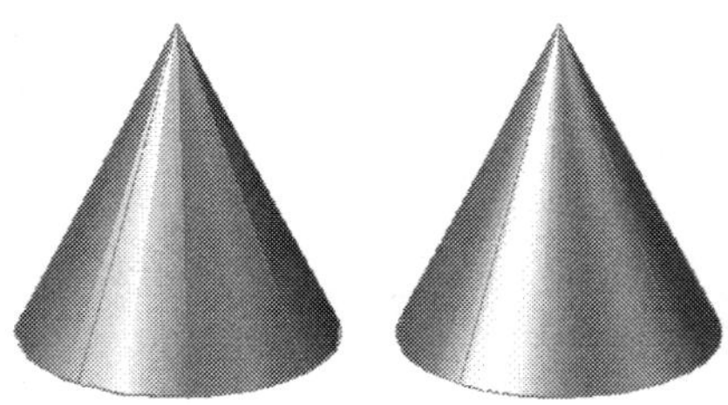

Facetres = 0.2 *Facetres = 10*

Figure 2–18

- Type **Regen** to display the change, as required.

Practice 2a Working with Solid Primitives - Architectural

Practice Objective

- Create a conceptual skyline by drawing solid primitives using dynamic inputs and dynamic UCS.

In this practice, you will draw solid primitives using dynamic input and dynamic UCS to create a conceptual skyline, as shown in Figure 2–19. You will also add a polysolid wall.

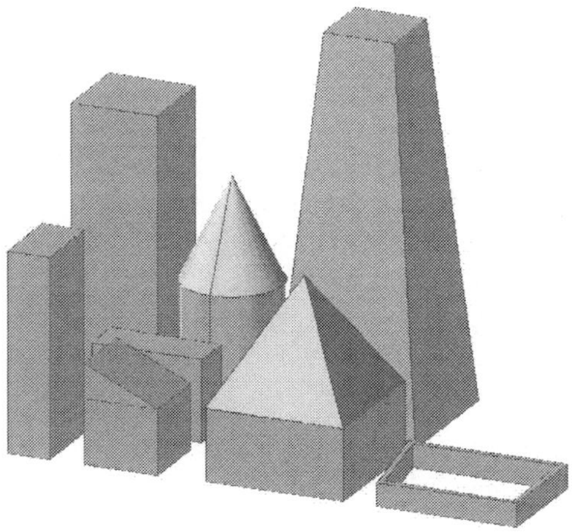

Figure 2–19

Use (New) to open the Select template dialog box in the AutoCAD Template folder.

1. Start a new drawing based on **acad3D.dwt** (located in the **Template** folder provided with the AutoCAD software) and save it in your practice files folder as **New-Skyline.dwg**.
2. Using the grid as if it were a city map, draw boxes, cylinders, pyramids, and other solid primitives, as shown in Figure 2–19 (*Home* tab>Modeling panel). Use Dynamic UCS and 3D Object Snaps to help when you draw on top of other primitives and to create areas of roof lines. You can also draw on other faces. Use the various grips and Properties to modify the objects.
3. On the *Solid* tab>Primitive panel, click (Polysolid) and create a garden wall in one area. Use the **Close** option to create a closed area.
4. Save and close the drawing.

Practice 2b Working with Solid Primitives - Mechanical

Practice Objective

- Add solid primitives to a simple solid model using Dynamic UCS.

In this practice, you will add primitives to a simple solid model using Dynamic UCS, as shown in Figure 2–20.

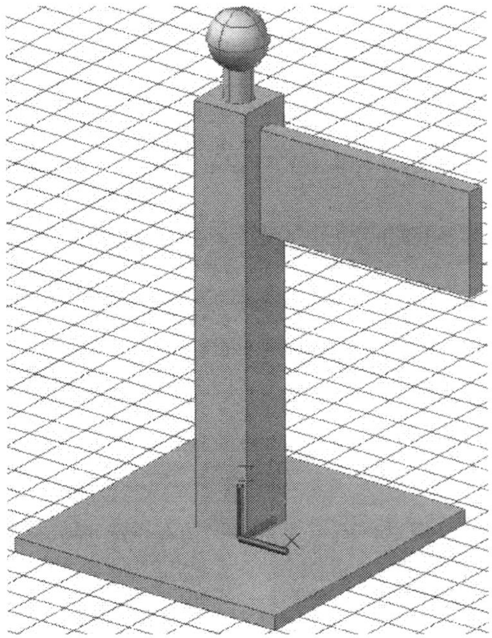

Figure 2–20

1. Open **Sign-Post.dwg**.
2. In the Status Bar, toggle on (Grid Display), (Object Snap), (3D Object Snap), (Dynamic UCS), and (Dynamic Input).
3. Zoom in on the top square surface of the upright post.
4. On the *Solid* tab>Primitive panel, click (Cylinder).

5. Hover over the top square surface to highlight the face, such that the cursor crosshairs are on the face and you can create objects on it.

6. At the *Specify center point of base:* prompt, snap to the center of the square face, then specify a radius of **1** and a height of **4** for the cylinder.

7. On the *Solid* tab>Primitive panel, click (Sphere).

8. Hover over the top circular face of the cylinder you just drew to highlight it.

9. At the *Specify center point:* prompt, snap to the center of the face. Specify a *Radius* of **2**.

10. On the *Solid* tab>Primitive panel, click (Box).

11. Hover over one of the vertical faces of the post to highlight it. Create a box to represent a sign projecting from that surface. The exact size and placement are not critical. You might need to toggle off Object Snap and 3D Object Snap to make it easier to pick points on the vertical face.

12. Save and close the drawing.

2.3 Working with Composite Solids

Some projects require you to put a hole through a solid or join two solids to create one object. Two or more solids can be combined through Boolean operations to form a single, more complicated solid, as shown in Figure 2–21.

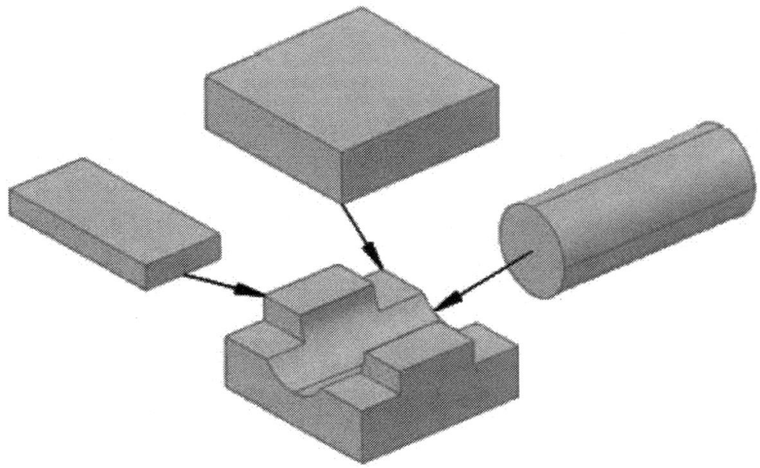

Figure 2–21

Creating Composite Solids

Boolean operations include  (Union) (the sum of two or more solids),  (Subtract) (the volume of a single solid minus the volume it shares in common with another solid(s)), and  (Intersect) (the common volume of two or more solids).

- These tools are located in the *Home* tab>Solid Editing panel and the *Solid* tab>Boolean panel, as shown in Figure 2–22.

If the solids selected for a Boolean operation are on different layers, the composite solid is created on the layer of the first object selected.

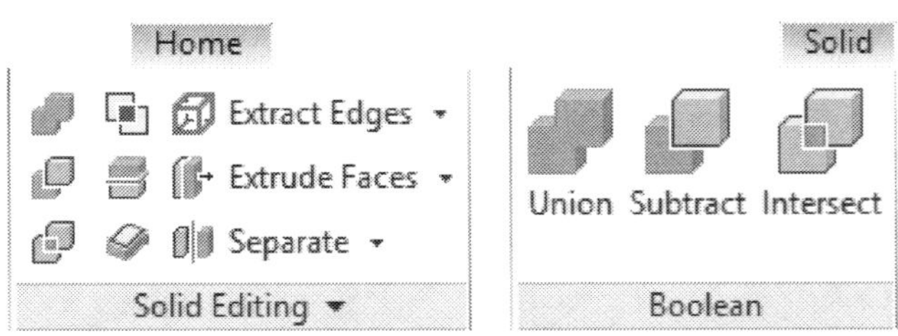

Figure 2–22

Union: Joining Solids

The **Union** command joins two or more selected solids, as shown in Figure 2–23. When the solids have been joined, the resulting solid can be manipulated as one object.

Parts that are unioned but do not touch behave as if they are grouped (acting as a single object).

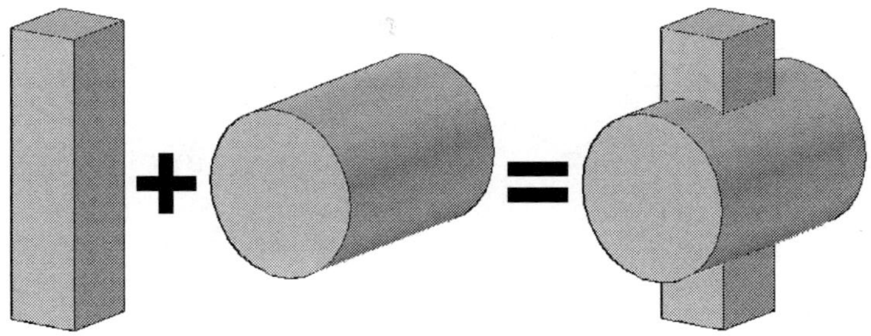

Figure 2–23

How To: Union Solids

1. In the *Home* tab>Solid Editing panel, click  (Union).
   - Alternatively, you can access the command in the *Solid* tab>Boolean panel or type **union** in the command line.
2. Select the objects that you want to join.
3. Press <Enter> to join the objects.

Subtract: Removing Solids from Other Solids

Another way to turn solids into shapes that are more complex is to remove one solid from another, as shown in Figure 2–24. For example, you might want to place a hole or cutout in an object.

Subtract automatically performs a union of all source objects.

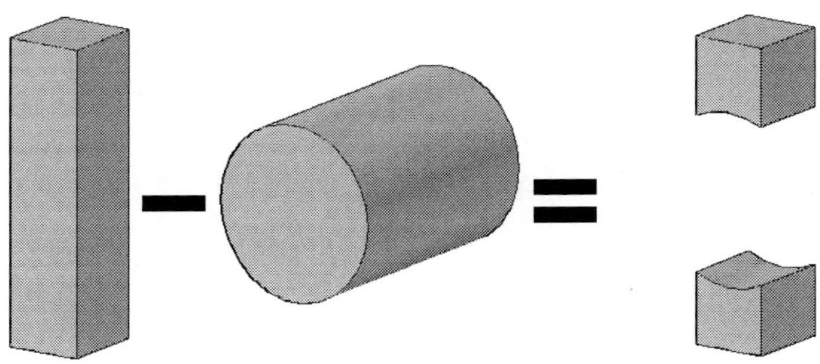

Figure 2–24

How To: Subtract Solids

1. In the *Home* tab>Solid Editing panel, click (Subtract).
   - Alternatively, you can access the command in the *Solid* tab>Boolean panel or type **subtract** in the command line.
2. Select the objects from which you want to subtract.
3. Press <Enter> and then select the objects that you want to subtract.

Intersect: Finding the Common Volume

You can also create complex solids from parts where other solids overlap. For example, you might want to create a solid from the volume of two or more intersecting solids. The **Intersect** command creates a solid of the intersection (common volume) from the selected solids, as shown in Figure 2–25.

If selected solids do not overlap, they are deleted.

Figure 2–25

How To: Intersect Solids

1. In the *Home* tab>Solid Editing panel, click (Intersect).
   - Alternatively, you can access the command in the *Solid* tab>Boolean panel or type **intersect** in the command line.
2. Select the objects that you want to intersect.
3. Press <Enter> to display the common volume.

Modifying Composite Solids

*To remove a subobject from a composite solid, select it and then start the **Erase** command or press <Delete>.*

When you first select a composite solid object, only the location grip displays. It can be used to move the object around. However, if you want to modify the radius of a cylinder that you have cut out of other solids, you need to select it separately. To do this, hold <Ctrl> before selecting the composite solid and move the cursor over the solids. Highlight the one you want to select and click to select it. You can then use grips or Properties to modify it, as shown in Figure 2–26.

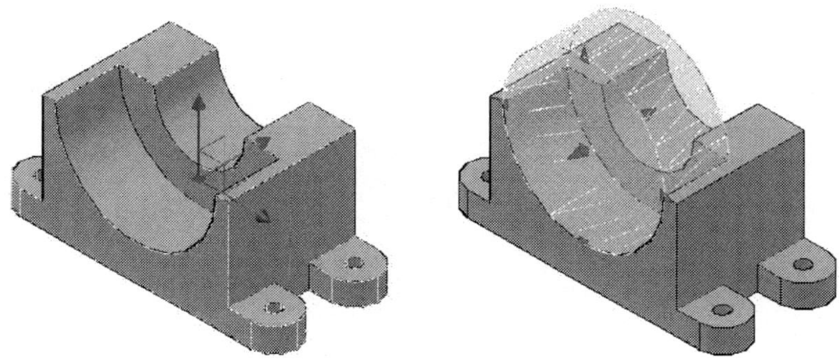

Figure 2–26

- If two or more solids are unioned but not touching, you can click (Separate) in the *Home* tab>Solid Editing panel to divide them into individual solids. The command is also located in the *Solid* tab>Solid Editing panel, expanded **solidedit** flyout.
- Solid History must be set to Record before the composite object is created so that you can select a subobject from a composite solid.

Hint: Setting the Solid History

By default, the Solid History is set to **None** (Solidhist=0). You need to change it to **Record** (Solidhist=1) for it to remember the various component solids that make up the composite solid. Having the Solid History set to **Record**, enables you to use <Ctrl> to select sub-objects individually and manipulate them. Hold <Ctrl>, hover the cursor over the composite solid, and select the simple solid when highlighted. You can then modify the individual solid. If the Solid History is set to **None**, you cannot select sub-objects. However, you can edit the faces, edges, and vertices of the composite solid.

- When solids have been created, you can change their Solid History using Properties, as shown in Figure 2–27. If you set the *History* to **None**, you cannot restore the record of the existing solid. However, if you set the *History* to **Record** and add other composite objects, those sub-objects are accessible.

Solid History	
History	Record
Show History	No

Figure 2–27

- *Show History* displays each solid in a composite solid as if it were still separate. Any objects that have been subtracted display in wireframe, as shown in Figure 2–28.

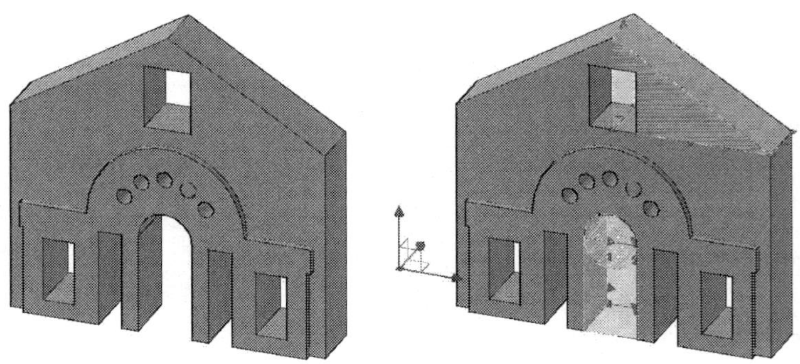

Show History: No ***Show History: Yes***

Figure 2–28

- If you modify **SolidHist**, it changes how new composite solids are created from that point forward. It does not change the history of existing solids.

Practice 2c Working with Composite Solids

Practice Objective

- Combine 3D objects to create a single 3D object using the **Intersect** and **Subtract** commands.

In this practice, you will use **Intersect** to find the common volume between two solids. You will also use **Subtract** to create holes, as shown in Figure 2–29.

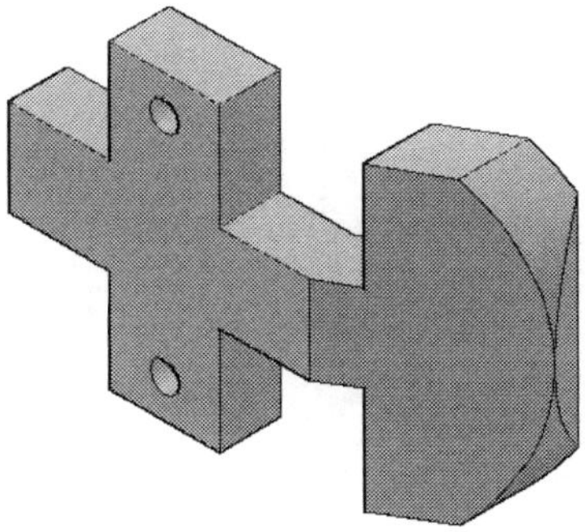

Figure 2–29

1. Open **Holder.dwg**. The drawing contains four overlapping solids.

*To better comprehend the shape of each object, you might want to switch to the **Conceptual** visual style and toggle off the various layers individually. Remember to toggle all layers back on and return to the **3dWireframe** visual style.*

2. Change to the **Conceptual** visual style. Orbit the drawing to view the parts from several angles. Change back to the **3DWireframe** visual style.
3. On the *Solid* tab>Boolean panel, click (Intersect).
4. At the *Select objects:* prompt, select the cyan object first and then the gray object (if the background is set to black, the object displays in white). Press <Enter>.
5. Orbit the drawing to examine the resulting part.
6. On the *Solid* tab>Boolean panel, click (Subtract).
7. At the *Select objects:* prompt, select the main body (cyan) of the part and press <Enter>.
8. At the *Select objects:* prompt, select both the red cylinders and press <Enter>.
9. Change the visual style and orbit to view the drawing.
10. Save and close the drawing.

Practice 2d Mechanical Project - Machine Part

Practice Objective

- Create a composite solid using solid primitives and Boolean commands.

In this practice, you will use solid primitives and Boolean commands to create a composite solid: the machine part shown in Figure 2–30. Use the top and front views for dimensions.

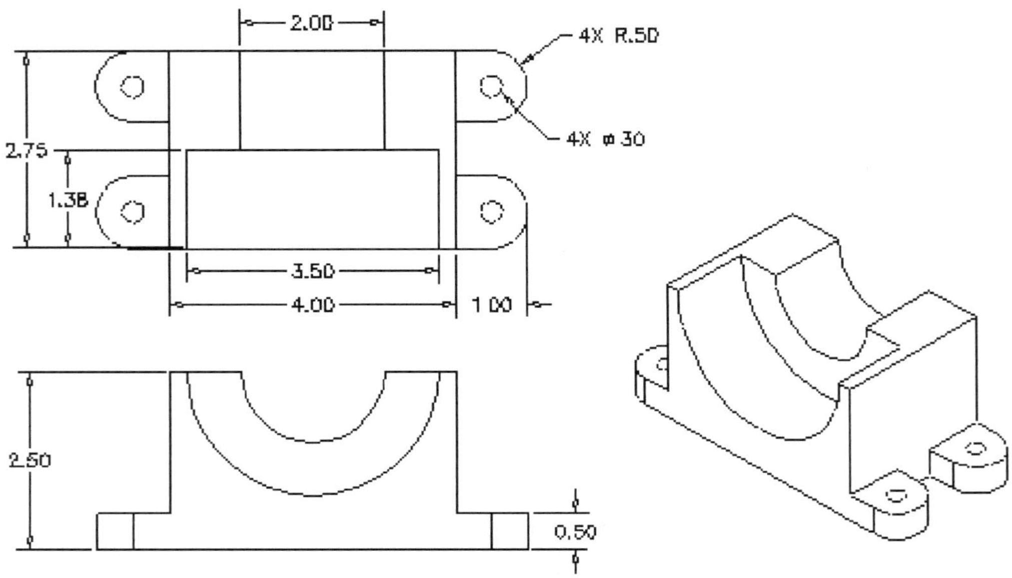

Figure 2–30

1. Start a new drawing based on **acad3D.dwt** and save it in your practice files folder as **Rollerbase.dwg**.
2. In the *Home* tab>View panel or from the *View Control* list in the drawing window, select the **Top** view and Parallel orientation. This sets the view and the UCS (workplane) to the top.
3. On the *Home* tab>Modeling panel, click (Box) and draw the main section of the part (a box **4.00 x 2.75 x 2.50**).

*Use **Orthomode** to restrict the cube to be drawn orthogonally.*

4. In the *Home* tab>View panel, select the **Front** view.

*Use the appropriate **3D Object Snaps.***

5. On the *Solid* tab>Primitive panel, click (Cylinder) and add two cylinders (one with diameter **2.00** and height **2.75**, and the other with diameter **3.50** and height **1.38**) to the box.
6. Use the **SW Isometric** view and **XRay** visual style to display the solids, as shown in Figure 2–31. (Use (Move) to place the cylinders at the required location with the bottom face of both the cylinders flush with front face of the cube).

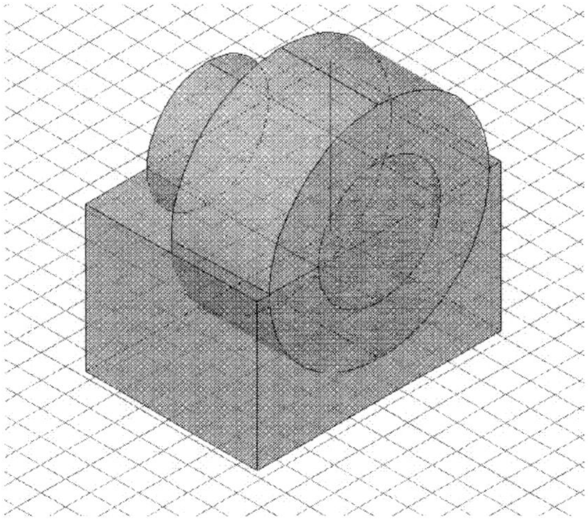

Figure 2–31

7. On the *Solid* tab>Boolean panel, click (Subtract) and remove the cylinders from the box, to get the solid shown in Figure 2–32.

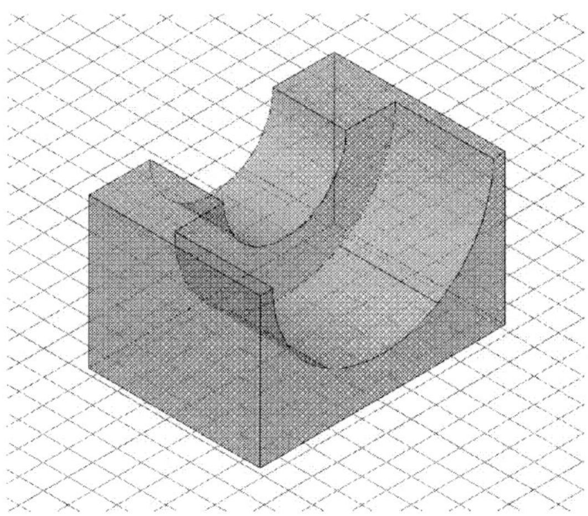

Figure 2–32

Refer to Figure 2–30 to check the dimensions and position of elements.(Use

(Move) to place the elements at the required location).

8. Switch to the **Top** view and add the elements of one of the feet to the front right corner of the object - a box(0.50 X 1.00 X 0.5), a cylinder (R 0.50 and H 0.50), and a smaller cylinder (R 0.15 and H 0.50).

9. Use the **SE Isometric** view and **XRay** visual style to display the solids, as shown in Figure 2–33.

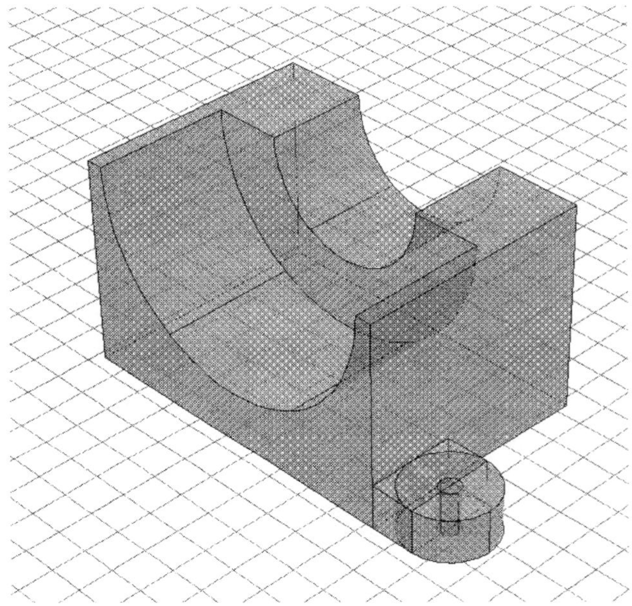

Figure 2–33

10. On the *Solid* tab>Boolean panel, click (Union) to join the foot cube and the R0.50 cylinder.

11. On the *Solid* tab>Boolean panel, click (Subtract) and remove the R0.15 cylinder to create a hole in the foot element.

12. Copy the feet to the back corner of the bigger solid.

13. Mirror the two feet to the left side of the bigger solid.

14. On the *Solid* tab>Boolean panel, click (Union) to convert all the pieces into a single solid.

15. Save and close the drawing.

Practice 2e

Architectural Project - Facade Puzzle

Practice Objective

- Create a composite solid using solid primitives and Boolean commands.

In this practice, you will create a puzzle of a building facade using solid primitives and Boolean commands, as shown in Figure 2–34.

Figure 2–34

1. Start a new drawing based on **acad3D.dwt** and save it in your practice files folder as **Facade.dwg**.
2. Create the solid primitives shown in Figure 2–35 with a depth of **1.75**. Union the large rectangle and the two wedges. Subtract the small rectangle.

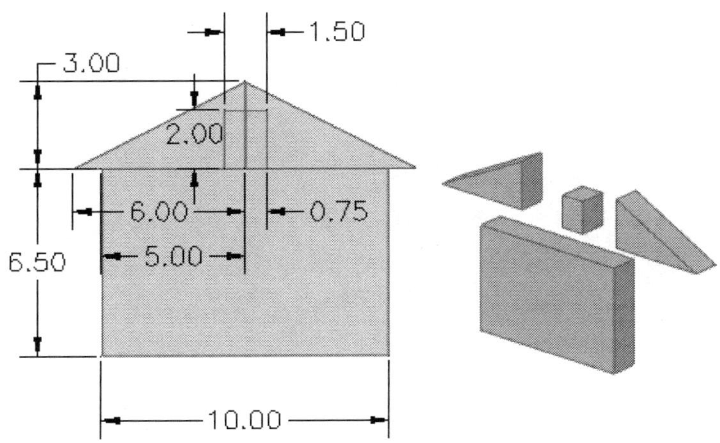

Figure 2–35

3. Create the solid primitives shown in Figure 2–36 with a depth of **2**.

Place UCS on the cylinder face, if the array of the cylinders doesn't array in the required direction.

4. Create an array of cylinders with the diameter shown in Figure 2–37. Draw the first one on the left and array them **180** degrees around the center of the large cylinder. Union all of the pieces, except for the small cylinders. Do not subtract the small cylinders.

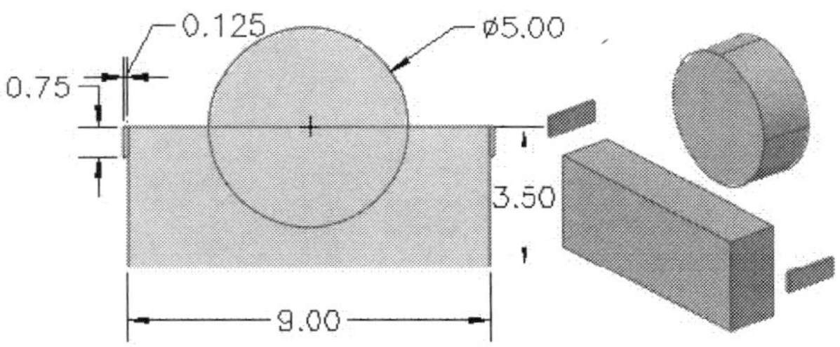

Figure 2–36

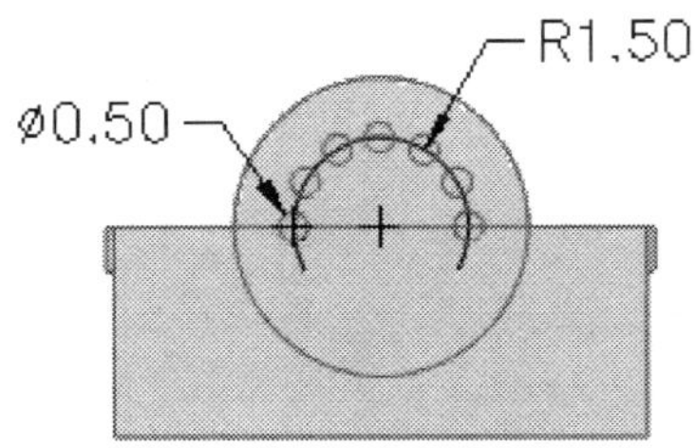

Figure 2–37

5. Explode the array of small cylinders so that they each become their own object rather than part of an array. Erase the two that intersect the box.

6. Create the solid primitives shown Figure 2–38 with a depth of **2**.

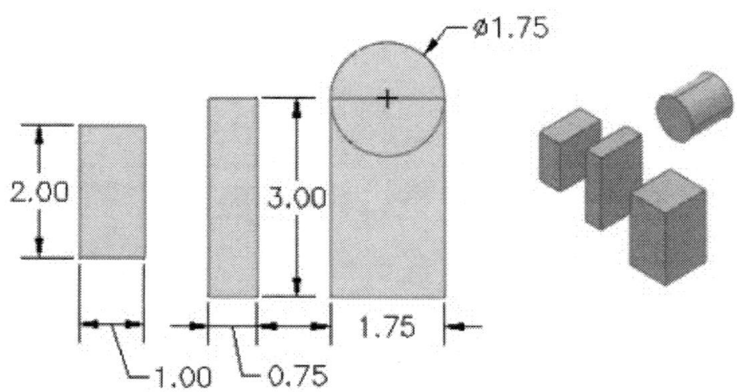

Figure 2–38

You can create reference lines for placing the objects at the required points.

7. Move and copy the building blocks as required so that they are arranged on the rest of the solids, as shown in Figure 2–39.

8. Move the objects together so that the front piece and the main building match at the back. The front piece sits away from the main building by **0.25**.

9. Union the two larger groups of solids together and then subtract the openings, as shown in Figure 2–40.

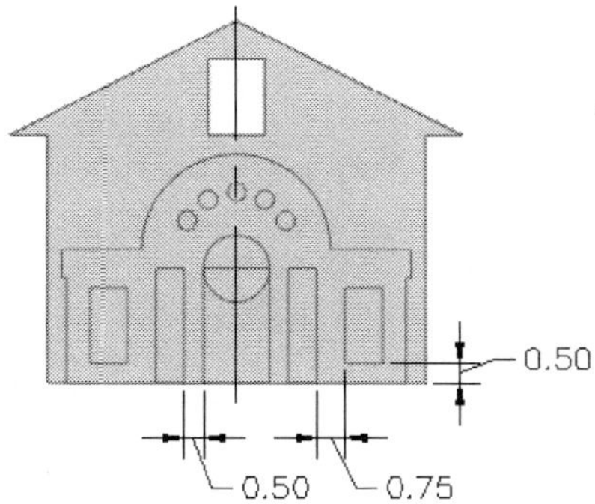

Figure 2–39

Figure 2–40

10. Save and close the drawing.

2.4 Working with Mesh Models

Free-form design in the AutoCAD software helps create and modify mesh models in a free-form and flowing method. Mesh models can be incrementally smoothed to create curved shapes. The *Mesh* tab provides tools to help you easily create and modify mesh models. The creation of mesh primitives uses tools similar to creating solid primitives. The smoothness level of mesh models can be adjusted from straight to rounded edges. You can create mesh primitives from standard shapes, or mesh models from other objects or object types (such as solids and surfaces). The mesh tools help you to create free-form shapes, as shown in Figure 2–41.

Mesh model before conversion to solid

Mesh model after conversion to solid

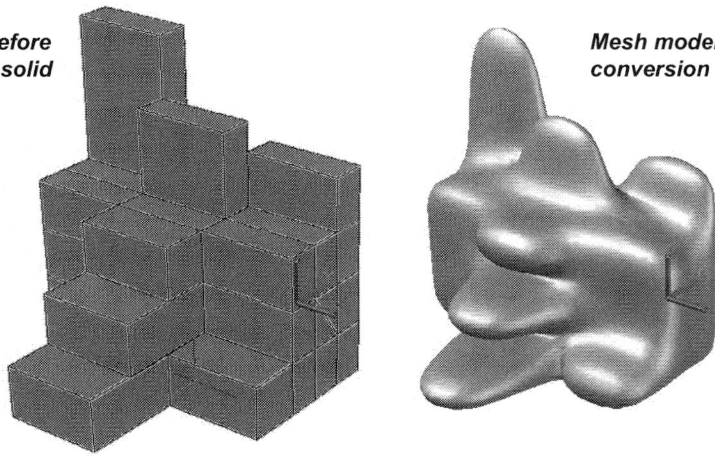

Figure 2–41

Creating Mesh Primitives

The basic method of creating a mesh primitive is similar to drawing a solid primitive. You draw the 2D object first and then add the height, as shown in Figure 2–42. This can be done by selecting points in the drawing window or by typing the dimension values.

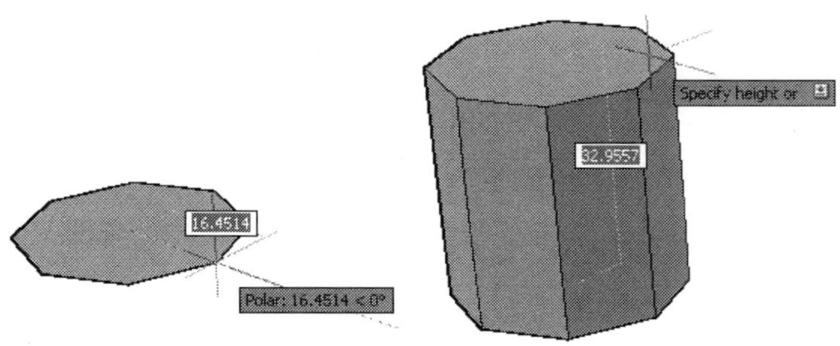

Figure 2–42

The tools to create a mesh primitive are located in the *Mesh* tab> Primitives panel>Mesh drop-down list, as shown in Figure 2–43.

You can create various mesh shapes: (Mesh Box), Mesh Cone), (Mesh Cylinder), (Mesh Pyramid), (Mesh Sphere), (Mesh Wedge), and (Mesh Torus). The steps to create mesh shapes are identical to those for creating solid primitives.

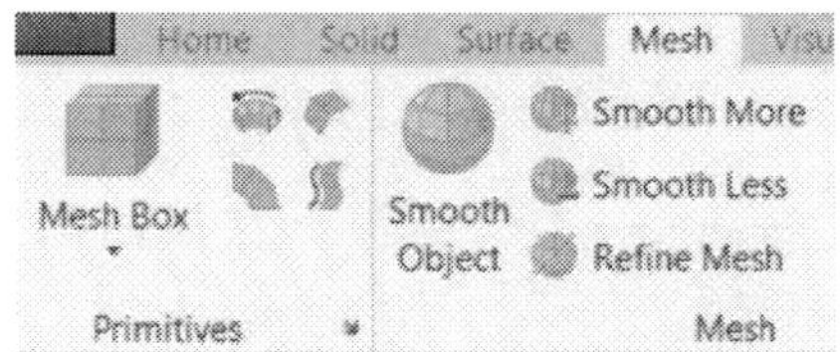

Figure 2–43

You can control the default tessellation divisions for each type of mesh primitive using the Mesh Primitive Options dialog box, as shown in Figure 2–44. To access these options, click in the *Mesh* tab>Primitives panel. In the Mesh Tessellation Options dialog box that opens, click **Mesh Primitives**. You can set the Tessellation Divisions for **Length**, **Width**, and **Height** for each type of mesh primitive. The preview displays the results and you can pan, zoom, and orbit to view it from all angles. You can also set the **Smoothness Level**.

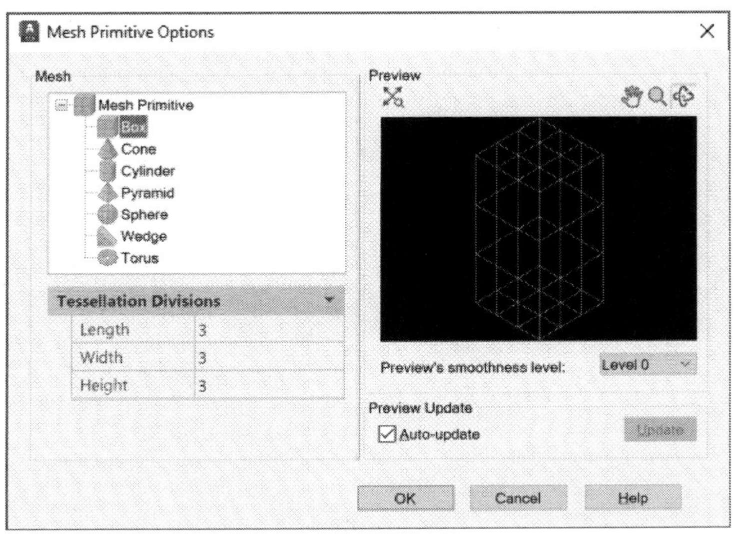

Figure 2–44

Creating Mesh Models from Objects

You can convert solids into mesh models. The tools for converting a solid into a mesh are located in the *Mesh* tab>Mesh panel, as shown in Figure 2–45. Some of these tools can also be used to modify existing mesh models.

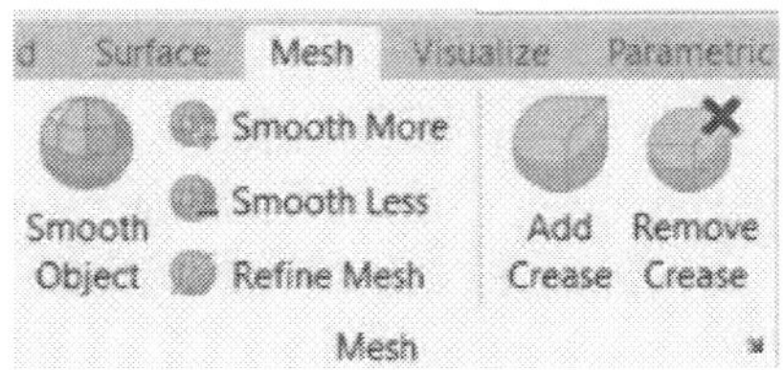

Figure 2–45

To convert a solid (or surface) to a mesh, you can click (Smooth Object) and then select the objects to be converted. This command uses the options set in the Mesh Tessellation Options dialog box (shown in Figure 2–46) to control how the object is going to be converted. Set the object's **Smoothness level** in the *Smooth Mesh After Tessellation* area.

To open the Mesh Tessellation Options dialog box, click in the bottom right corner of the Mesh panel in the *Mesh* tab or *Home* tab>Mesh panel.

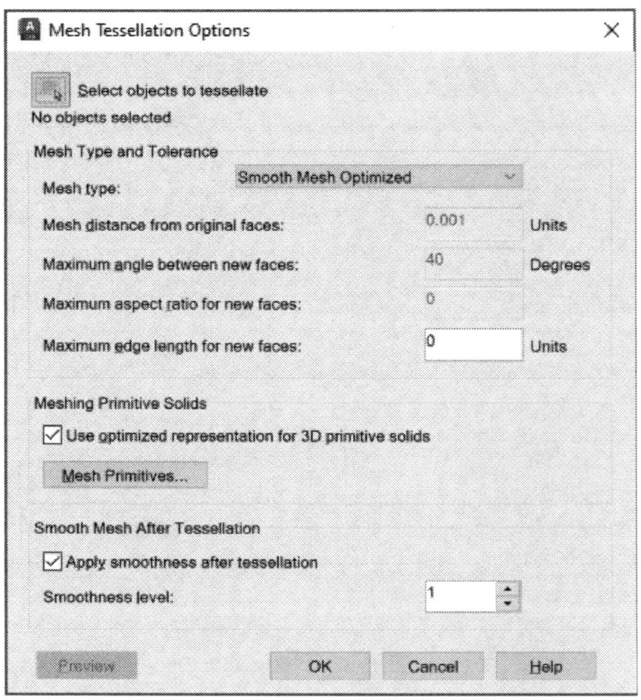

Figure 2–46

Editing Mesh Models

After a mesh model has been created, you can modify it in many ways. You can increase or decrease its smoothness, refine its mesh, split a mesh face, or extrude a mesh face. The mesh editing tools are located in the *Mesh* tab>Mesh and Mesh Edit panels, as shown in Figure 2–47.

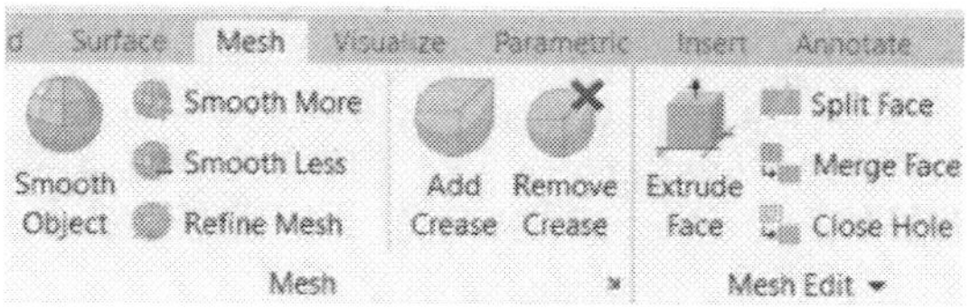

Figure 2–47

Smoothness

The Smoothness Level determines how smooth (straight or round) an object's edges are, as shown in Figure 2–48.

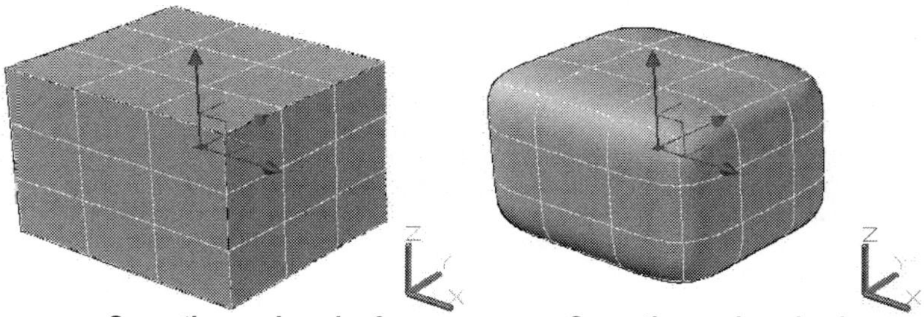

Smoothness Level = 0 ***Smoothness Level = 4***

Figure 2–48

Alternatively, you can increase or decrease an existing object's ***Smoothness Level*** *using (Smooth More) or (Smooth Less) in the Mesh tab> Mesh panel.*

The **Smoothness Level** ranges from **0** (straight edges) to a maximum of **4** (rounded edges). It can be set in the Mesh Primitive Options dialog box or in the Mesh Tessellation Options dialog box. You can also edit an object's **Smoothness Level** in Properties, as shown in Figure 2–49.

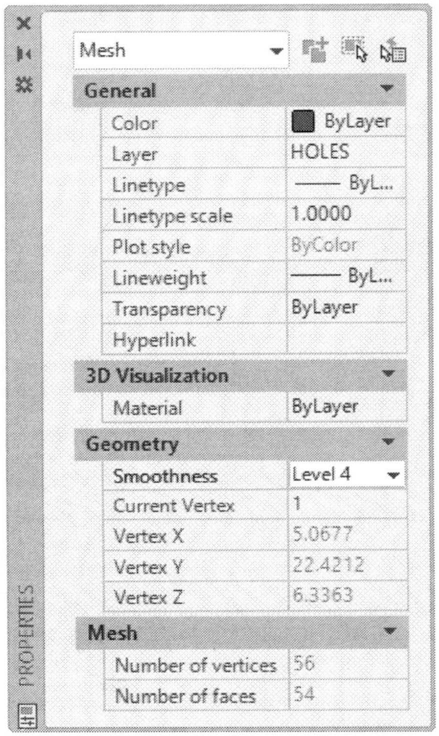

Figure 2–49

Refine a Mesh

After increasing an object's **Smoothness Level** (to anything greater than **0**), you might need to display a finer mesh grid on the object. After a mesh has been refined, the **Smoothness Level** of the object resets back to **0**, enabling you to continue to smoothing the object. (Refine Mesh) in the *Mesh* tab>Mesh panel converts the underlying facet (mesh) grid into more detailed or finer editable faces, as shown in Figure 2–50. The object on the left has a *Smoothness Level* of **1**. The object on the right has been refined. It contains a greater number of smaller grids and its *Smoothness Level* has been set to **0**.

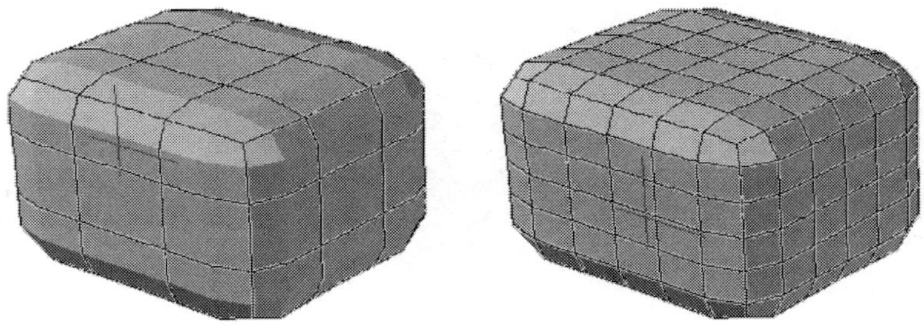

Figure 2–50

How To: Refine the Mesh

In the *Mesh* tab>Mesh panel, click (Refine Mesh).

- Increasing both the smoothness and refinement adds complexity to the object, which can cause performance issues.
- Develop your model at lower smoothness levels, increasing the levels as it nears completion.
- To confine complexity to specific areas of an object, you can refine individual (mesh grid) faces. Hold <Ctrl> while making selections. Doing so does not reset the object's baseline level of smoothness.

Split a Mesh Face

There are times when you need to manually refine a mesh. This can be done by splitting an existing face, enabling you to select and edit each new face independently. To split a mesh face, use (Split Face), which is located in the *Mesh* tab>Mesh Edit panel. Figure 2–51 shows the object before and after the **Split Face** command has been used.

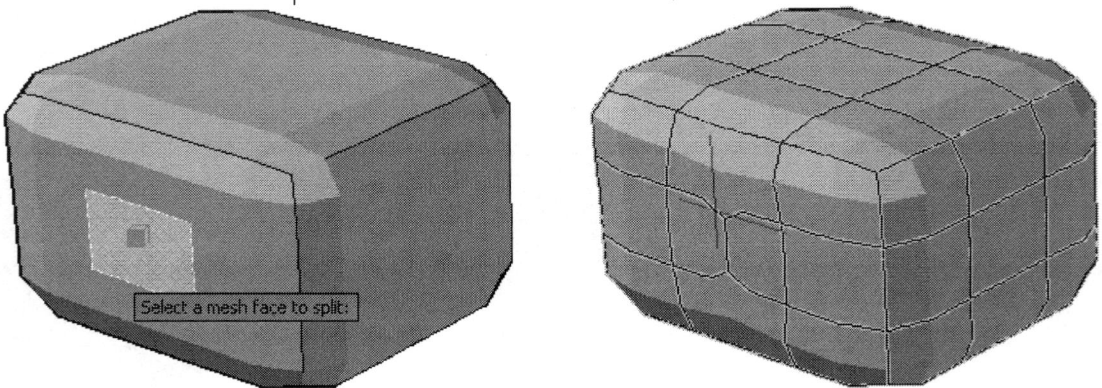

Figure 2–51

How To: Split a Face

In the *Mesh* tab>Mesh Edit panel, click (Split Face).

- After selecting the mesh face to split, you need to specify the first and second split points.
- Each new face created using the **Split Face** command can be edited independently.
- You can apply different materials to individual mesh faces.

Extrude a Mesh Face

You can extrude any mesh face individually or in multiples using  (Extrude Face) in the *Mesh* tab>Mesh Edit panel. The extrusions extend and deform the mesh object without creating new solid objects. You can type the extrusion height or select a point in the drawing window, as shown in Figure 2–52.

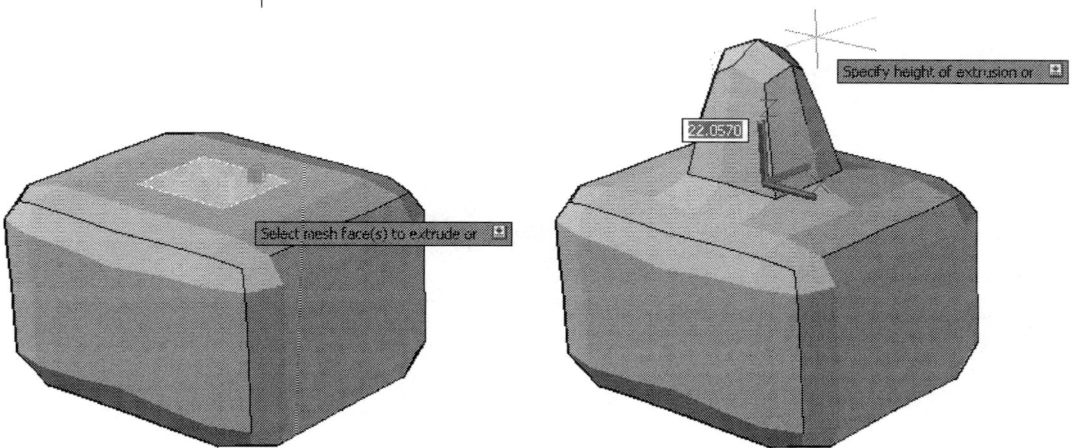

Figure 2–52

How To: Extrude a Face

In the *Mesh* tab>Mesh Edit panel, click  (Extrude Face).

- Hold <Ctrl> while selecting faces to extrude.
- Multiple faces can be extruded. Each face extrudes independently, but all extrude to the same specified height.
- Select an option (**Direction**, **Path**, or **Taper angle**) at the *Specify height of extrusion* prompt for additional modification methods.

Convert From Mesh Models

You can convert your final mesh objects to smooth or faceted solids or surfaces to union them with other solids or surfaces. The **Convert to** commands are located in the *Mesh* tab>Convert Mesh panel. Four options are available, as shown in Figure 2–53. They enable you to control how smooth or faceted the converted model is going to be when displayed.

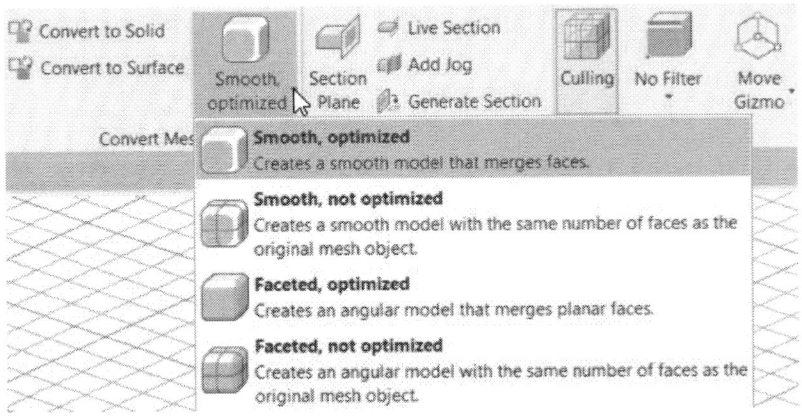

Figure 2–53

- **Optimized** options create less complex solids (or surfaces) than **not optimized** options.
- Mesh models with a large number of faces can take a long time to convert to solids (or surfaces) when the **not optimized** options are used during conversion.
- Use (Convert to Solid) to convert the mesh object into a solid and (Convert to Surface) to convert it into a surface.

Practice 2f Mesh Model

Practice Objective

- Create and modify a mesh model, by adjusting its smoothness, refining it, splitting and extruding a mesh face, and converting it into a solid.

In this practice, you will create a mesh object, modify its smoothness, apply refinement to its mesh, split a mesh face, extrude a mesh face, and convert the mesh model to a solid. The final model is shown in Figure 2–54.

Figure 2–54

1. Start a new drawing based on **acad3D.dwt** and save it in your practice files folder as **Mesh Edit.dwg**.

2. In the *Mesh* tab>Primitives panel, click  (Mesh Box) and create a mesh box with the *height*, *width*, and *length* all set to **50**, as shown in Figure 2–55.

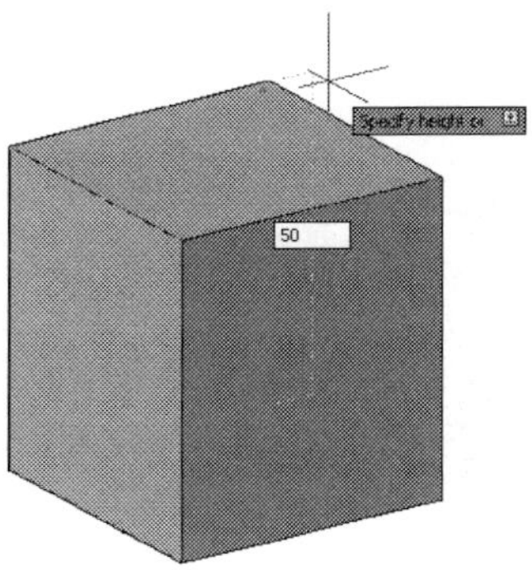

Figure 2–55

*Use the **Shaded with edges** visual style to display the individual faces. Verify that (Object Snap) and (3D Object Snap) are toggled on.*

3. Select the newly created mesh model. In its Properties palette, change the *Smoothness* to **Level 1**. The mesh model updates, as shown in Figure 2–56.

4. In the *Mesh* tab>Mesh Edit panel, click (Split Face) and select the top center face on the top side of the mesh model. For the two split points, select the left and right corners of the selected face, as shown in Figure 2–57.

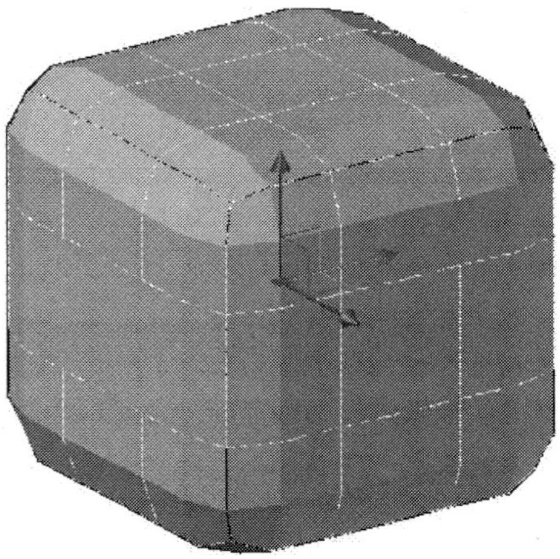

Figure 2–56

Figure 2–57

5. In the *Mesh* tab>Mesh Edit panel, click (Extrude Face). While holding <Ctrl>, select the face next to the split face. Press <Enter> and extrude the face upward with a value of **50**, as shown in Figure 2–58.

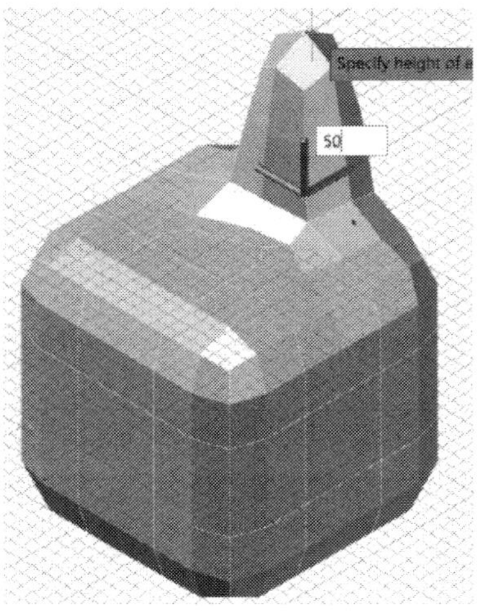

Figure 2–58

6. Select the mesh model. In Properties, the *Smoothness* is still set to **Level 1**. Change it to **None** and note how the mesh model updates. Set it back to **Level 1**.

7. In the *Mesh* tab>Mesh panel, click (Refine Mesh), select the mesh model and press <Enter>. Note the additional mesh faces that have been created.

8. Select the mesh model. In Properties, the *Smoothness* has automatically been set to **None**.

9. In the *Mesh* tab>Convert Mesh panel, expand (Smooth, optimized) and click (Smooth, optimized).

10. In the *Mesh* tab>Convert Mesh panel, click (Convert to Solid). Select the mesh model and press <Enter>. The model updates and displays a smooth appearance. Select the model to display its grips, as shown in Figure 2–59. In Properties, the model is no longer a Mesh. It is now a 3D Solid.

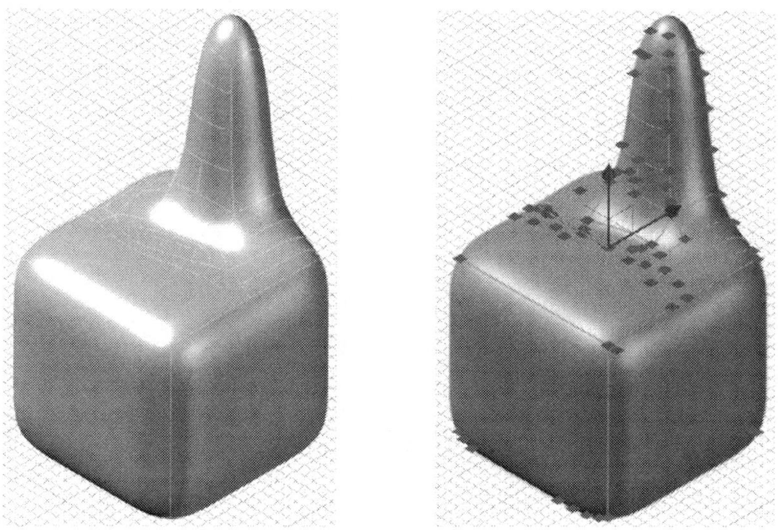

Figure 2–59

11. Undo the **Convert to Solid** command.

12. In the *Mesh* tab>Convert Mesh panel, expand (Smooth, optimized) and click (Faceted, not optimized).

13. In the *Mesh* tab>Convert Mesh panel, click  (Convert to Solid). Select the mesh model and press <Enter>. The new solid model contains many faces. Select the model to display the grips, which have also increased in number, as shown in Figure 2–60.

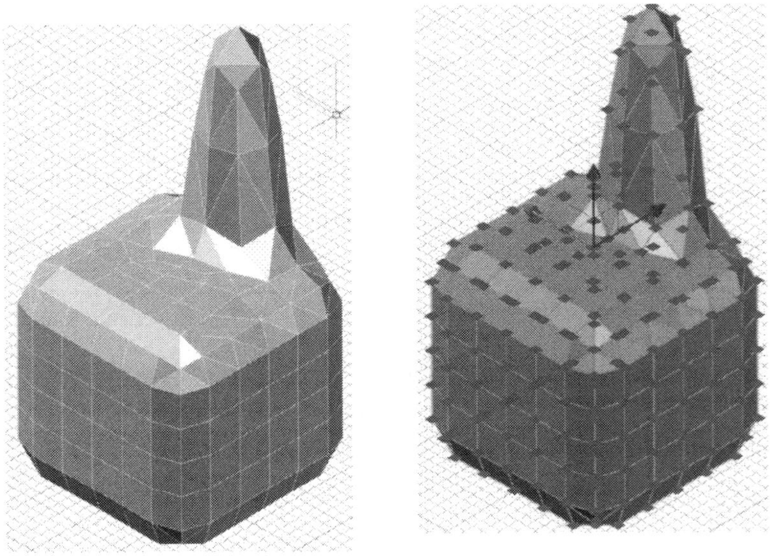

Figure 2–60

14. Save and close the drawing.

Chapter Review Questions

1. Which of the following is a type of simple solid primitive that enables you to build the basic mass of a model?
    a. Polyline
    b. Box
    c. Circle
    d. Triangle
2. What does the **Cube** option in the **Box** command do?
    a. Creates a triangular shape.
    b. Creates a box of varying dimensions based on two points selected in the drawing window.
    c. Creates a box with equal length, width, and height.
    d. Creates a box with unequal length, width, and height.
3. A torus is an inner-tube shape that can be used to put grooves in cylinders.
    a. True
    b. False
4. How many solids can you union at one time?
    a. One
    b. Two
    c. Sixteen
    d. Unlimited
5. The **Intersect** command creates a solid of the intersection (common volume) from the selected solids.
    a. True
    b. False

6. When simple solids are joined into composite solids, the individual solids can still be modified. Which of the following methods enables you to do this?
    a. Click on the face of the composite solid that was previously a simple solid.
    b. Hold <Ctrl>, hover the cursor over the composite solid, and select the simple solid when it highlights.
    c. Hover the cursor over the composite solid and select the highlighted simple solid.
    d. Hold <Shift>, hover the cursor over the composite solid, and select the simple solid when it highlights.

Command Summary

All ribbon names reference the 3D Modeling workspace.

Button	Command	Location
	Box	• **Ribbon:** *Home* tab>Modeling panel or *Solid* tab>Primitive panel
	Cone	• **Ribbon:** *Home* tab>Modeling panel or *Solid* tab>Primitive panel
	Convert to Solid	• **Ribbon:** *Mesh* tab>Convert Mesh panel
	Cylinder	• **Ribbon:** *Home* tab>Modeling panel or *Solid* tab>Primitive panel
	Extrude Face	• **Ribbon:** *Mesh* tab>Mesh Edit panel
	Intersect	• **Ribbon:** *Home* tab>Solid Editing panel or *Solid* tab>Boolean panel
	Mesh Box	• **Ribbon:** *Mesh* tab>Primitives panel
	Mesh Cone	• **Ribbon:** *Mesh* tab>Primitives panel
	Mesh Cylinder	• **Ribbon:** *Mesh* tab>Primitives panel
	Mesh Pyramid	• **Ribbon:** *Mesh* tab>Primitives panel
	Mesh Sphere	• **Ribbon:** *Mesh* tab>Primitives panel
	Mesh Wedge	• **Ribbon:** *Mesh* tab>Primitives panel
	Mesh Torus	• **Ribbon:** *Mesh* tab>Primitives panel
	Polysolid	• **Ribbon:** *Home* tab>Modeling panel or *Solid* tab>Primitive panel
	Pyramid	• **Ribbon:** *Home* tab>Modeling panel or *Solid* tab>Primitive panel
	Refine Mesh	• **Ribbon:** *Mesh* tab>Mesh panel
	Separate	• **Ribbon:** *Home* tab>Solid Editing panel or *Solid* tab>Solid Editing panel
	Smooth Less	• **Ribbon:** *Mesh* tab>Mesh panel
	Smooth More	• **Ribbon:** *Mesh* tab>Mesh panel
	Smooth Object	• **Ribbon:** *Mesh* tab>Mesh panel

	**Sphere**	• **Ribbon:** *Home* tab>Modeling panel or *Solid* tab>Primitive panel
	**Split Face**	• **Ribbon:** *Mesh* tab>Mesh Edit panel
	**Subtract**	• **Ribbon:** *Home* tab>Solid Editing panel or *Solid* tab>Boolean panel
	**Torus**	• **Ribbon:** *Home* tab>Modeling panel or *Solid* tab>Primitive panel
	**Union**	• **Ribbon:** *Home* tab>Solid Editing panel or *Solid* tab>Boolean panel
	**Wedge**	• **Ribbon:** *Home* tab>Modeling panel or *Solid* tab>Primitive panel

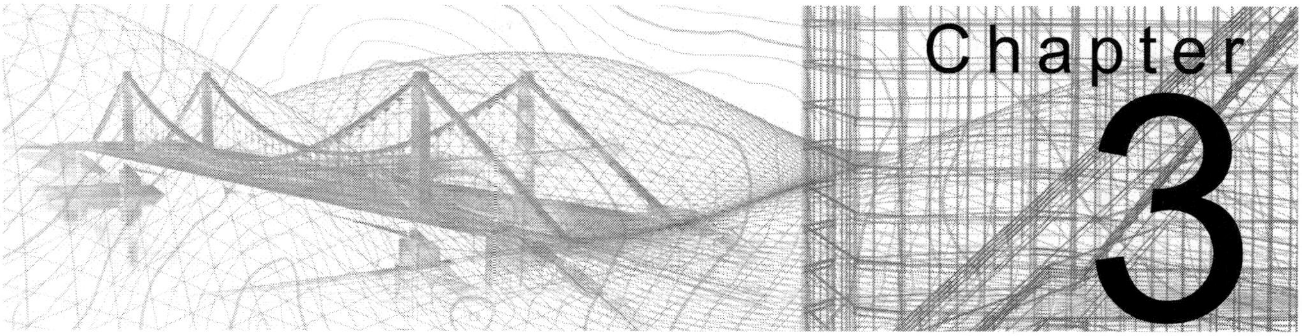

Working with the User Coordinate System

In this chapter, you learn how to use the user coordinate system (UCS), including setting up the UCS icon, moving the UCS Origin, picking three points to establish a UCS, using the UCS X-, Y-, and Z-options, using the UCS multi-functional grips, and saving a UCS by name.

Learning Objectives in This Chapter

- Move the UCS origin to a new location so that you can work at different elevations and locations in a 3D model.
- Change the display settings of the UCS.
- Rotate the UCS about its axis to move it from one plane to another.
- Change the origin and alignment of the UCS using multi-functional grips.
- Reuse a UCS in a drawing by defining and saving it in the UCS dialog box.

3.1 UCS Basics

(Dynamic UCS) (located in the Status Bar) is a powerful tool that can help you to draw using objects that are already in your drawing when drawing objects on temporary planes. You might also have selected a view (such as **Top**, **Front**, or **Right**) that changed the UCS so that you could draw on the associated plane. However, sometimes it might be required to set a specific coordinate plane and origin, as shown in Figure 3–1. The **UCS** command includes many options that can help you create User Coordinate Systems.

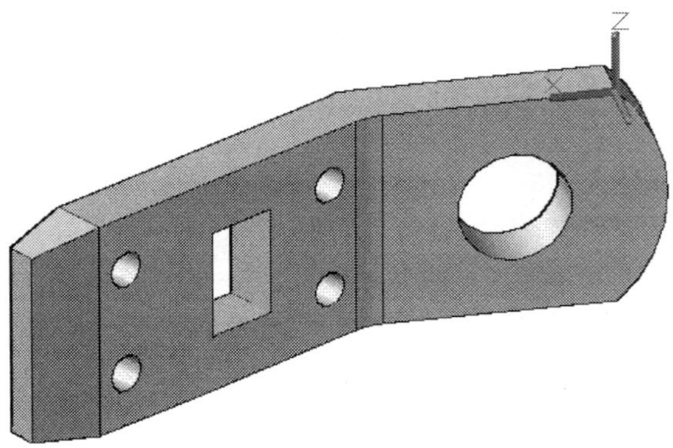

Figure 3–1

How To: Start the UCS Command

1. In the *Home* tab>Coordinates panel, click (UCS).
    - Alternatively, you can access the command in the *View* tab>Viewport Tools panel or type **UCS** at the command line.

- You should always be able to return to the UCS home position. The fastest way to do so is to restore the (World UCS). You can also type the command name: type **UCS**, press <Enter>, type **W**, and press <Enter>.
- To return to the last UCS used, click (UCS, Previous). The AutoCAD® software retains up to 10 previous UCSs.
- If you have multiple viewports in Model Space, each viewport can have a different UCS.

UCS Icon

In 2D drawings, you rarely need to use any other coordinate system than the World UCS. The UCS icon can be toggled off. However, in 3D models the UCS icon can be very helpful for indicating where the UCS is located and how it is oriented. You can toggle the UCS icon on and off, and have it display at the actual UCS origin point or always at the lower left corner of the screen.

- The UCS Icon is on by default in the **acad3D.dwt** template. It also is set to move to any new UCS origin.
- If you want to change the status of the UCS icon, on the *Home* tab>Coordinates panel, expand  (Show UCS Icon at Origin) and select an option, as shown in Figure 3–2.

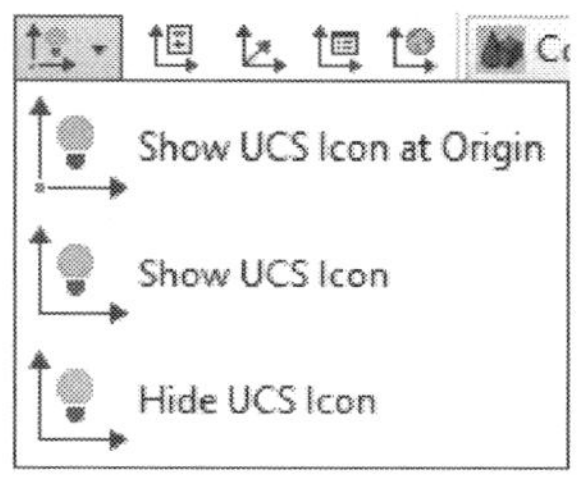

Figure 3–2

- The visual properties of the UCS icon can be modified in the UCS Icon dialog box. In the *Home* tab>Coordinates panel, click  (UCS Icon, Properties) to open the dialog box. You can modify the icon's style, size, and color, as shown in Figure 3–3.

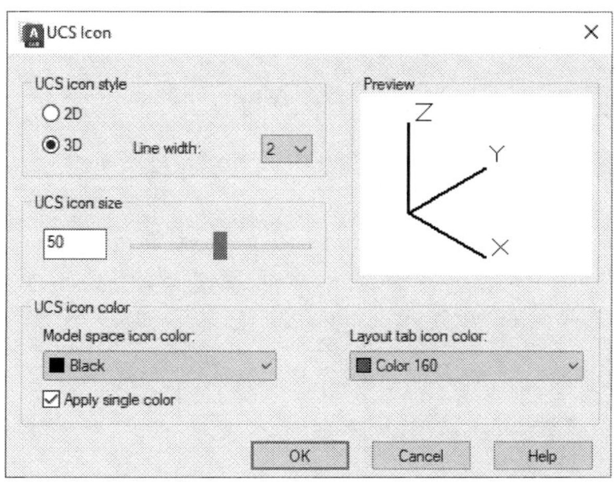

Figure 3–3

UCS and UCS Icon Settings

To modify the settings for the UCS and the UCS icon, click (UCS, UCS Settings) in the *Home* tab>Coordinates panel. The UCS dialog box opens to the *Settings* tab, as shown in Figure 3–4.

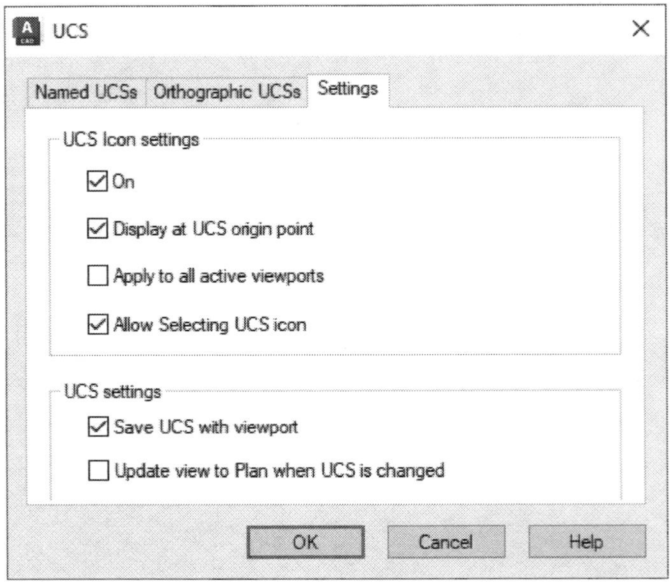

Figure 3–4

The UCS icon display and behavior settings for the current viewport enable you to:

- Toggle the display of the UCS icon.
- Display the UCS icon at its origin or (if the origin is hidden) in the lower left corner.
- Apply the settings to all active viewports.
- Enable the selection of the UCS icon.
- Save the UCS settings with the current viewport.
- Restore the view to Plan view when the UCS is changed.

If the UCS icon is set to be selectable, relevant options display in the Properties palette when the UCS icon is selected, as shown in Figure 3–5.

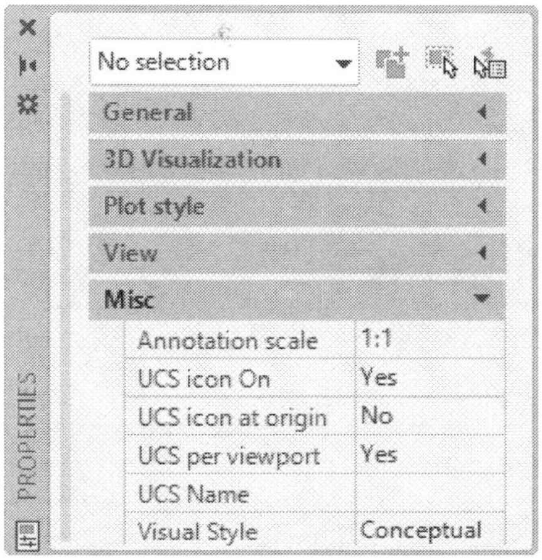

Figure 3–5

- Many UCS controls are also available in the shortcut menu by right-clicking on the UCS icon.

Moving the UCS Origin

The first UCS technique to learn is how to change the UCS origin, or 0,0,0 point. Moving the origin to a new location enables you to work at different elevations (by moving the UCS in the Z-direction) and different locations in your 3D model, as shown in Figure 3–6.

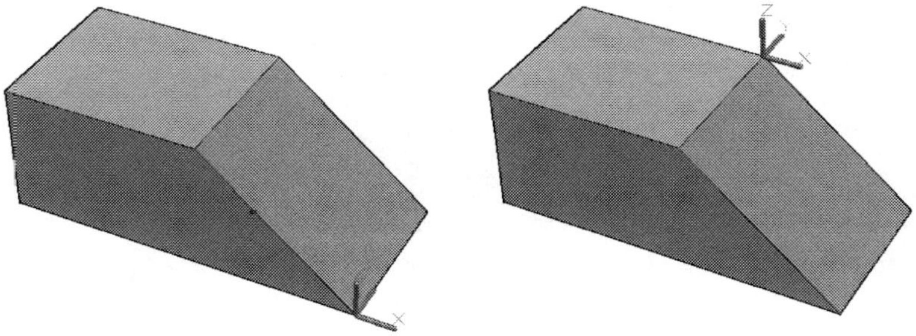

Figure 3–6

- If 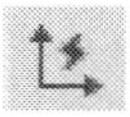 (Dynamic UCS) is toggled on in the Status Bar, you can hover the cursor over a face or point cloud to highlight it before selecting the new origin point. Doing so moves the UCS origin and changes the orientation to the face.

How To: Move the UCS Origin

1. In the *Home* tab>Coordinates panel, click (UCS, Origin).
2. Using object snaps, select a point on the object at which you want to locate the new origin or type the new coordinates.

- If (Grid Display) is toggled on in the Status Bar, the grid moves to the new origin/workplane.

Moving the UCS to a Face

When you are working with solids, you can place the UCS on a specific face. This option is useful when working with faces whose points are not easy to select.

How To: Move the UCS to a Solid Face

1. In the *Home* tab>Coordinates panel, expand the UCS, View flyout and click (UCS, Face).
2. Select a face to use as the UCS. Hold <Ctrl> to highlight specific faces.
3. In the menu:
    - Select **Next** to switch to a face nearby.
    - If you need to adjust the direction of the X- or Y-axis, you can use the **Xflip** and **Yflip** options to rotate the UCS.
4. When the UCS is located correctly, select **Accept** or press <Enter>.

Moving the UCS Using 3 Points

The **UCS, 3 Point** command enables you to specify a new working plane by selecting three points in 3D space, most typically on an object, as shown in Figure 3–7.

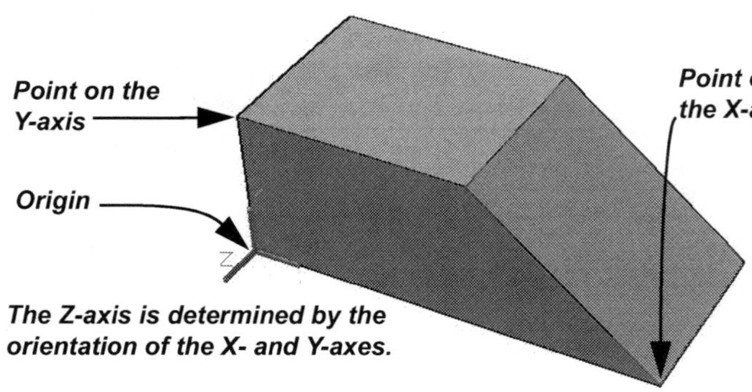

Figure 3–7

How To: Select 3 Points to Establish a UCS

1. In the *Home* tab>Coordinates panel, click (UCS, 3 Point).
2. Select a point for the new UCS origin.
3. Select a second point on the new X-axis.
4. Select a third point on the new Y-axis.

- Use object snaps when selecting points on objects.
- (UCS, World) sets the current UCS to align with the WCS (World Coordinate System), a fixed Cartesian coordinate system.

Hint: The UCS View Option

(UCS, View) uses the current screen orientation to create a new UCS. The location of the origin does not change, but the X-, Y-, and Z-directions do. This option is useful when adding text labels to the Isometric views of an object, as shown in Figure 3–8, and for creating the top, front, and side views of a drawing if you are not using a layout.

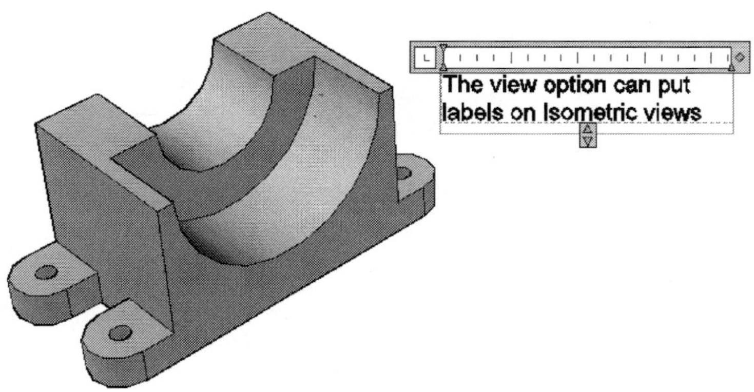

Figure 3–8

- (UCS, View) sets the UCS to be parallel to the screen.

Practice 3a

Using the UCS

Practice Objectives

- Change the current UCS to different locations and create similar objects at those locations.
- Align the current UCS with the WCS.

In this practice, you will change the current UCS to various locations using the **UCS, Origin**, and **UCS, Face** commands, as shown in Figure 3–9. You will create objects at the different UCS locations and align the current UCS with the WCS.

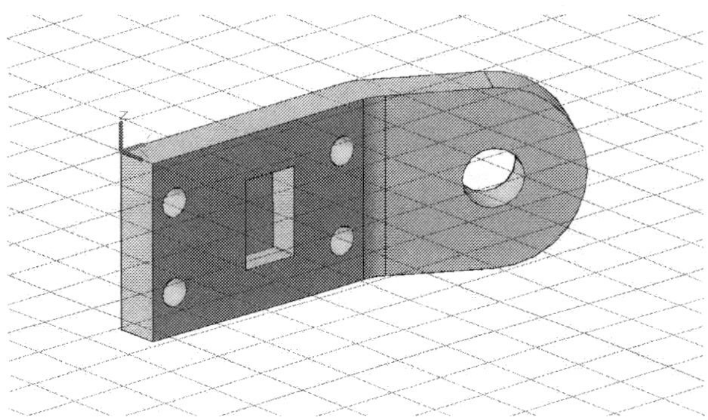

Figure 3–9

1. Open **Bracket-UCS.dwg**.
2. Open the Properties palette.
3. Select the **UCS icon**, which should be in the lower left corner of the drawing window.
4. In the Properties palette, set *UCS icon at origin* to **Yes**. The UCS icon should move to the corner of the bracket model, as shown in Figure 3–10.

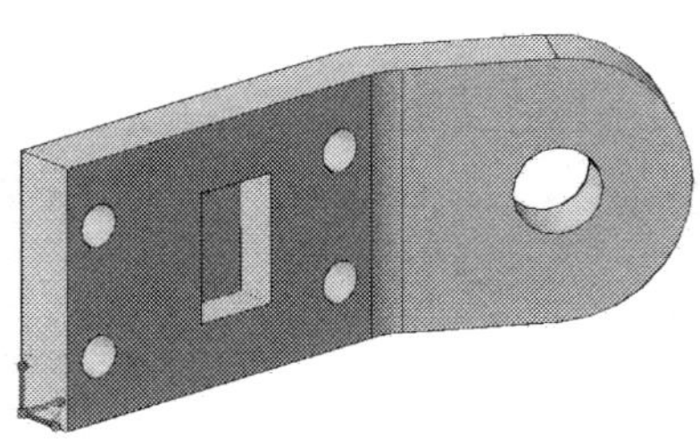

Figure 3–10

5. In the Status Bar, toggle on (Grid) to display the grid under the bracket model, as shown in Figure 3–11.

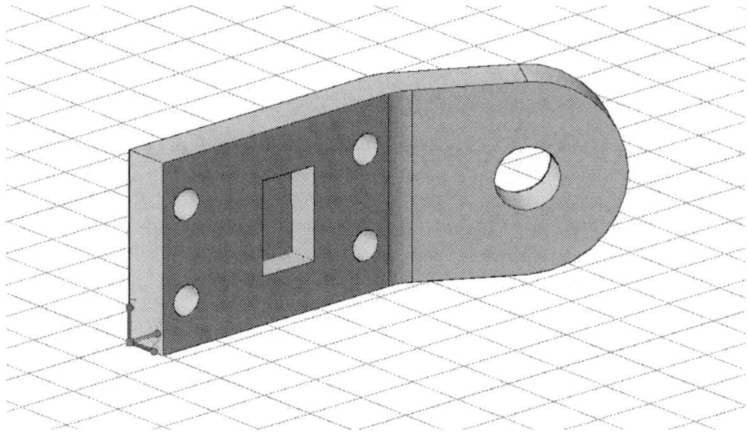

Figure 3–11

6. On the *Home* tab>Modeling panel, click (Box) to create a box. Specify the first corner at **0,0,0** and the other corner at **2,2,0**. Move your cursor above the base and then set the height to **2**. Note that it is placed at the origin lying on the grid, but is overlapping the bracket model, as shown in Figure 3–12.

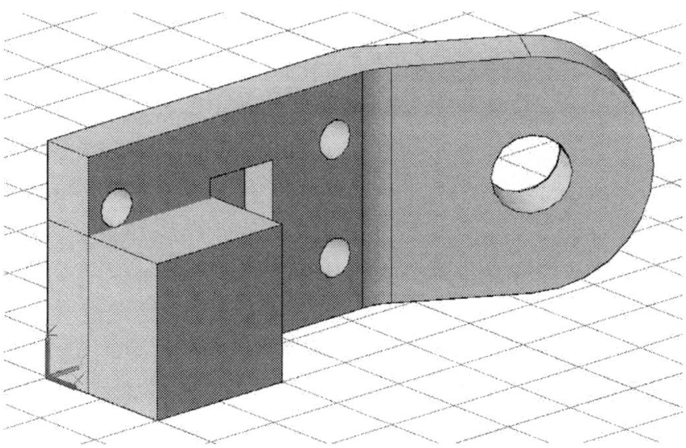

Figure 3–12

7. Delete the box that you just created.

8. On the *Home* tab>Coordinates panel, click (UCS, Origin).The UCS icon attaches itself to the cursor. At the *Specify new origin point* prompt, select the top left corner of the bracket model. Both the UCS icon and the grid move to the new location, as shown on the left in Figure 3–13.

9. Recreate the same box with its starting point at **0,0,0**, other point at **2,2,0**, and a height of **2**. Note that it still is created at the origin, but is no longer overlapping the bracket model. Instead, it is above the bracket model, as shown on the right in Figure 3–14.

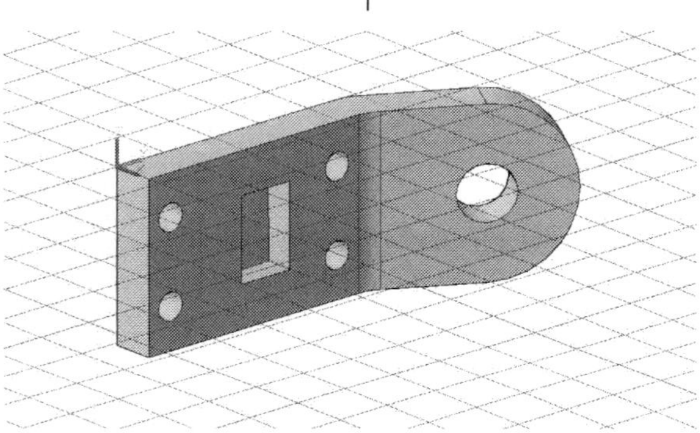

Figure 3–13

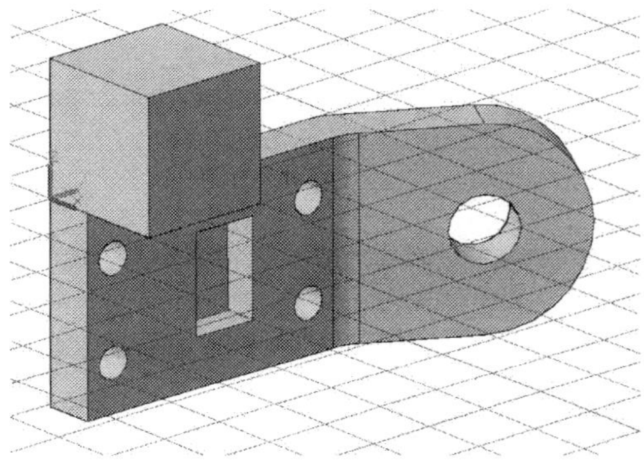

Figure 3–14

10. Delete the box that you just created.

11. On the *Home* tab>Coordinates panel (UCS, View flyout), click (UCS, Face). At the *Select face of solid, surface, or mesh* prompt, select any face of the bracket model and press <Enter> to accept the defaults. Note the change in location of the UCS icon and the grid display.

12. On the *Home* tab>Coordinates panel, click (UCS, World). The UCS icon and grid display move to align with WCS.

13. Save and close the file.

3.2 UCS X, Y, and Z Commands

Most 3D objects are made of several planes. If you know the relationship between the planes, you can move the UCS from one plane to another by rotating the UCS about an axis. The **UCS X**, **Y**, and **Z** commands enable the User Coordinate System to be rotated around the required axis by a specified number of degrees. You can use these tools to set the UCS before drawing objects such that you can draw on a different plane. For example, you might need to create a 3D model from a 3-view mechanical drawing and need to start on the front view, rather than the top view. To do this, you rotate the UCS 90 degrees around the X-axis, as shown in Figure 3–15.

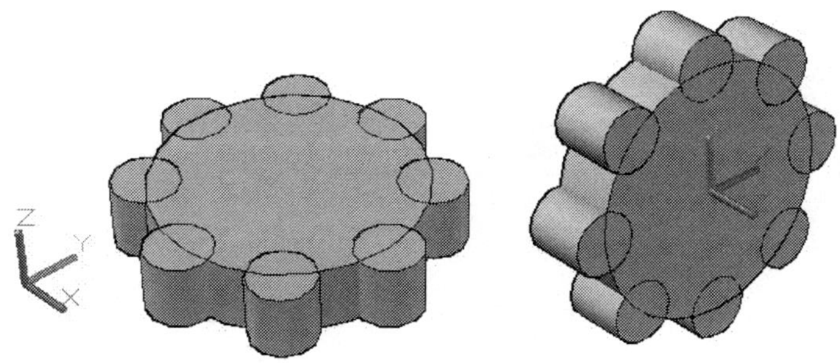

Model drawn at World UCS

UCS rotated before model is drawn

Figure 3–15

How To: Use the UCS X, Y, or Z Commands

1. In the *Home* tab>Coordinates panel>UCS, View flyout, click X, Y, or Z.
2. Specify the rotation around the axis. You can type a value for the angle or select two points on the screen to establish the angle.
3. The UCS rotates.

Right-hand Rule

Use the right-hand rule to help you to determine which way to rotate the UCS. By placing your right thumb in the direction of a particular axis, the curl of your fingers point in the direction of a positive angle, as shown in Figure 3–16. This is important when you define a UCS, or when you rotate or array objects.

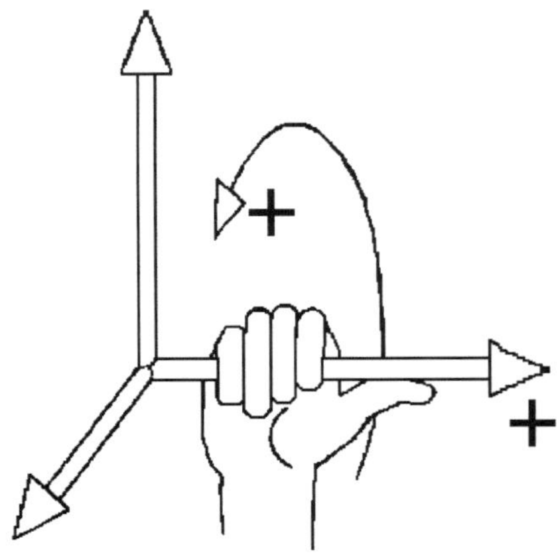

Figure 3–16

Hint: Z-axis Vector

 (Z-Axis Vector) uses two points to define a new Z-axis rather than rotating about the Z-axis. The first point you select is the new origin and the second point is the direction of the positive Z-axis. It rotates the XY plane and is very useful when defining the direction of an extrusion.

Moving the UCS to a 2D Object

With  (UCS, Object), the AutoCAD software enables the User Coordinate Systems to match the alignment of existing 2D objects in the drawing. The new working plane is perpendicular to the extrusion direction (positive Z-axis) of the object.

With this command, the point you select on the object generally determines the orientation of the new UCS. For example, if a circle is selected, the center of the circle is the new origin, and the positive X-axis passes through the point where the circle was selected. For a line or rectangle, the end point or corner closest to the selected point becomes the new origin.

Practice 3b X, Y, and Z Commands

Practice Objective

- Draw a mechanical part using the **UCS Origin**, **X**, **Y**, and **Z** commands to modify the location of the UCS.

In this practice, you will draw the part shown in Figure 3–17 using the **UCS X**, **Y**, and **Z** commands.

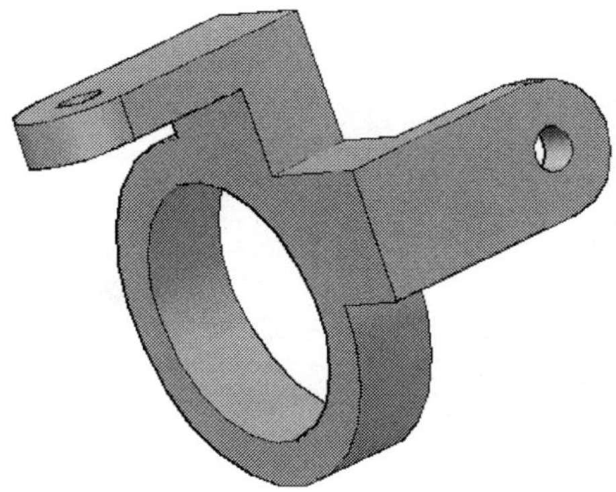

Figure 3–17

1. Start a new drawing based on **acad3D.dwt** and save it in your practice files folder as **Angle.dwg**.
2. In the Status Bar, toggle off 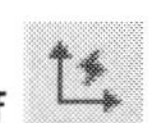 (Dynamic UCS). Right-click on the ViewCube and set the projection mode to **Parallel**.
3. In the **View Controls** list of the drawing window or in the *Home* tab>View panel, switch to the **Front** view (this also changes the UCS to the front).
4. Set the *Visual Style* to **2D Wireframe**.
5. Draw a cylinder with a *radius* of **3** and a *height* of **2**. Draw another cylinder on the same center with a *radius* of **4** and a *height* of **2**.

*Change the color of the layer **0** to a darker shade of gray if your drawing window background color is white.*

6. On the *Home* tab>Coordinates panel, click  (UCS, Origin) and place the origin at the center of the cylinders.
7. On the *Home* tab>Coordinates panel, click 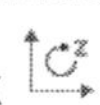 (UCS, Z) and rotate the UCS **30 degrees** around the Z-axis.
8. Verify that  (Polar Tracking) is toggled on.

9. On the *Home* tab>Draw panel, click (Polyline) and draw the pline object shown in Figure 3–18.

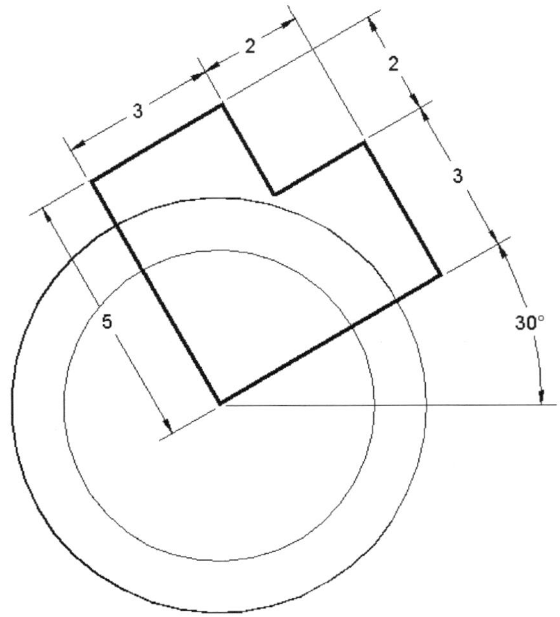

Figure 3–18

10. Set the *Visual Style* to **Shades of Gray**.
11. Use **Orbit** to orbit around such that the height of the cylinders is visible. If required, use (Move) to move the cylinders such that they overlap each other.
12. On the *Home* tab>Modeling panel, click (Extrude). Select the polyline and extrude it **2** units in the direction of the cylinders.
13. Switch to the **SE Isometric** view (**View Controls** list of the drawing window).

14. Union the outside cylinder and the extruded object. Subtract the inside cylinder, as shown in Figure 3–19.

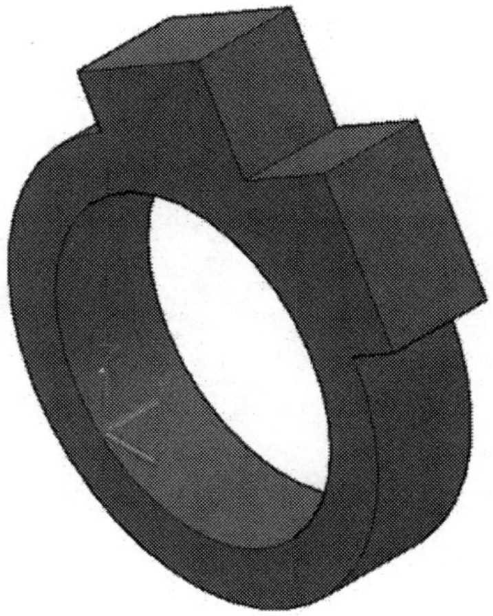

Figure 3–19

When you click to place the UCS, it might temporarily shift to some other location but will locate itself at the correct position once you press <Enter>.

15. On the *Home* tab>Coordinates panel, click (UCS, Face). At the *Select face of solid, surface, or mesh* prompt, move the cursor over the bottom edge of the face of the extruded polyline that is facing towards you. Verify that the X axis is parallel to the bottom edge of the face, as shown in Figure 3–20. Click to place the UCS on the face. Press <Enter>.

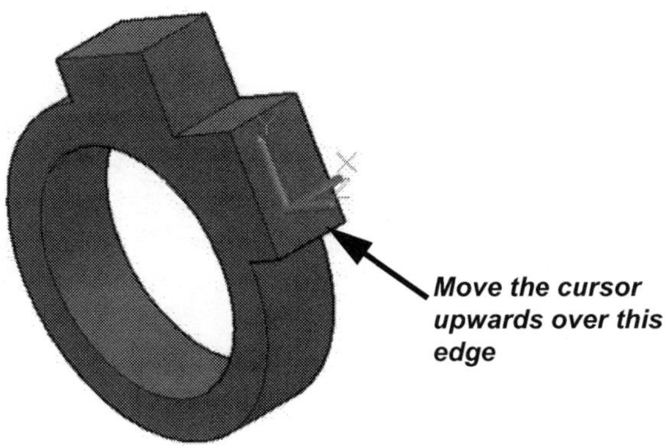

Figure 3–20

16. Draw the closed polyline and circle shown on the right in Figure 3–21, with the lower left corner of the polyline touching the lower left corner of the object's face. Hint: To draw the arc, use the **Arc** option of **Pline** command with a diameter of **3.0** (as shown on the left in Figure 3–21). Select the **Line** option of the **Pline** command to draw the rest of the lines.

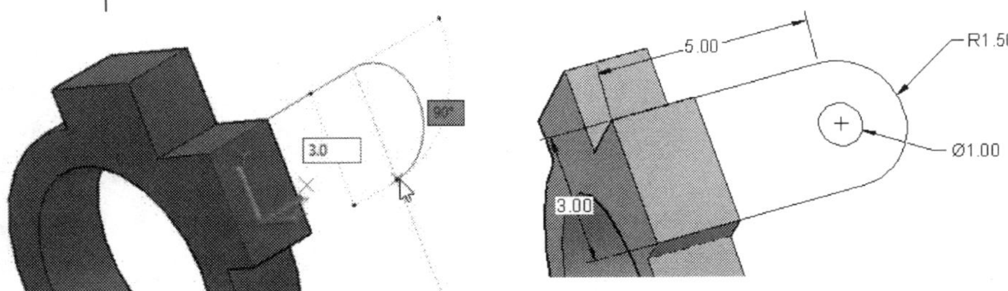

Figure 3–21

17. Extrude the polyline and circle **1** units away from the solid. Union the extruded polyline solid with the rest of the solid and subtract the cylindrical hole.

18. On the *Home* tab>Coordinates panel, click  (UCS, Face) and place the UCS as required to view the other angled face. Draw the same polyline and circle in the opposite direction to the one shown in Step 16.

19. Extrude and union the polyline and circle. The model displays as shown in Figure 3–22.

Figure 3–22

20. Save and close the drawing.

3.3 UCS Multi-functional Grips

When the UCS settings are set to permit selection of the UCS icon and the UCS icon is selected, it displays with multi-functional grips, as shown in Figure 3–23. These multi-functional grips permit direct manipulation of the UCS icon, enabling you to easily move the origin and align its axis to objects including curved surfaces and solids.

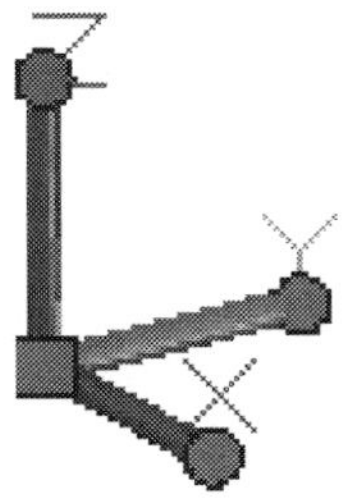

Figure 3–23

- To move the UCS icon and origin, select the square grip at the origin, move the cursor, and select a new location.
- To align the UCS icon and one of its axes, select the circle grip of the specific axis, move the cursor, and select a point to which to align it.

When you hover over one of the grips before selecting it, a dynamic multifunction grip list displays, as shown in Figure 3–24. Depending on which grip you hover over, the options might include move only, move and align, align only, rotate around, or move to the World UCS.

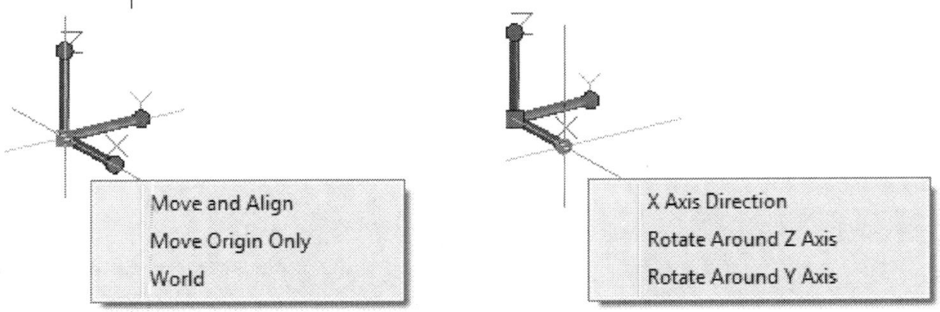

Figure 3–24

- After you select an option in the multifunction grip list, follow the Command Prompt for options to either select a point or enter a value.

3.4 Saving a UCS by Name

You often need to reuse a UCS in your drawing. The AutoCAD software enables any defined UCS to be saved and recalled by name, as shown in Figure 3–25. You can also access the Named and Orthographic UCSs in the UCS dialog box.

You can save an unlimited number of UCSs with each drawing.

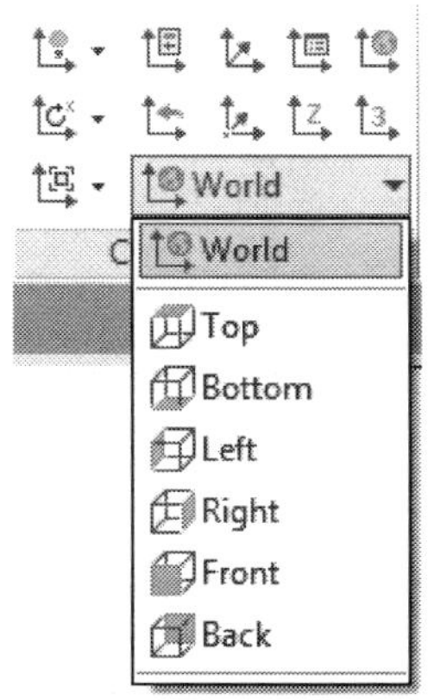

Figure 3–25

- The Named UCSs are located in the Named UCS Combo Control in the *Home* tab>Coordinates panel.

How To: Name and Save a UCS

1. Set up the UCS as required.
2. In the *Home* tab>Coordinates panel>, click  (Named UCS).
3. In the UCS dialog box, select the *Named UCSs* tab.
4. In the list, right-click on Unnamed and select **Rename**, as shown in Figure 3–26.

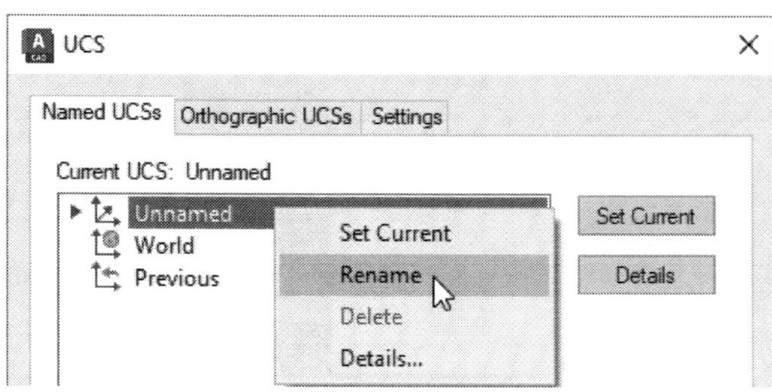

Figure 3–26

5. Type a new name for the UCS.

6. Click **OK**.

- To delete a named UCS, right-click on its name and select **Delete**.
- To make a UCS current, select its name and click **Set Current**, or double-click on the name. The current UCS displays an arrow to the left of its name.

How To: Set a UCS Relative to a Named UCS

Once you have named a UCS, you might want to define another UCS relative to it. For example, if you place the UCS on the top of a part, you might want to change the UCS quickly to the bottom or side of the part.

1. Start the **Named UCS** command.
2. In the UCS dialog box, select the *Orthographic UCSs* tab.
3. Select the Orthographic UCS that you want to use.
4. In the Relative to: drop-down list, select the named UCS you want to move relative to, as shown in Figure 3–27.

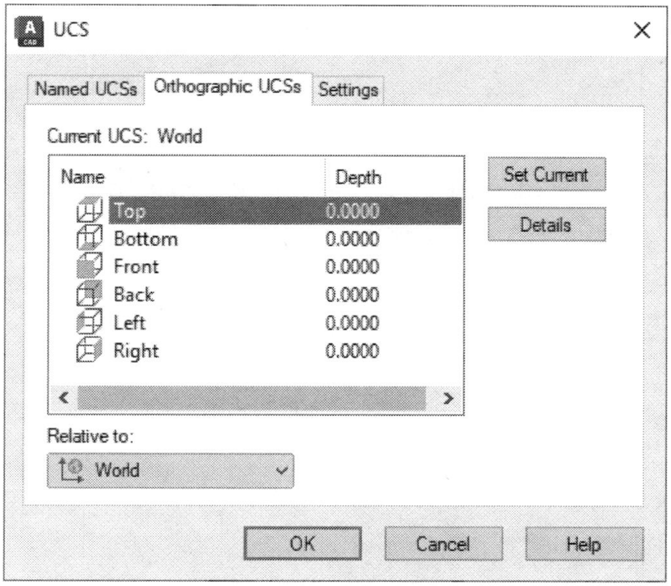

Figure 3–27

5. Click **OK**.

- The origin of these UCSs is the same as the origin of the *Relative to:* UCS.

Hint: Aligning the View to the UCS Manually

When you have defined a new UCS, you might want to view it head-on to make drawing easier. You can do this by changing the Plan View to the **Current UCS**, **World UCS**, or a **Named UCS**. Use the **Plan** command at the Command Prompt and select the appropriate options to change the Plan View.

Aligning the View to the UCS Automatically

To automatically update the view to the current UCS, open the UCS dialog box, switch to the *Settings* tab, and select **Update view to Plan when UCS is changed**, as shown in Figure 3–28. It is off by default.

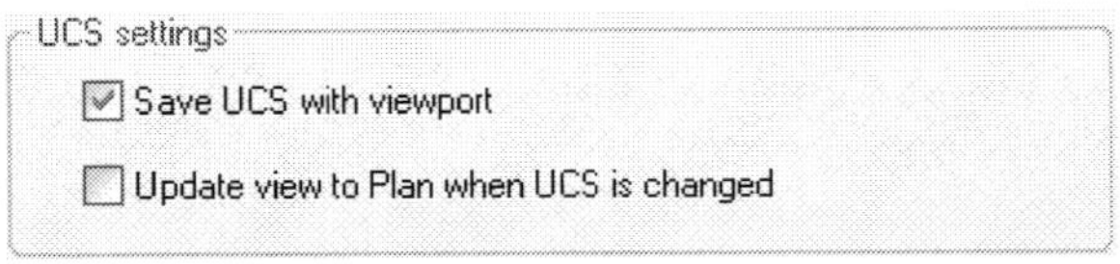

Figure 3–28

- This setting can be helpful when using multiple viewports. One viewport can be set to change with the UCS so that it always displays a head-on view of the current UCS. Other viewports would have views that would not be affected by UCS changes.
- The **Save UCS with viewport** option is on by default. It controls whether a viewport has its own UCS (option selected) or if it automatically matches the UCS of the active viewport (option not selected). If you are using the **Update view to plan when UCS is changed** option, you should toggle this setting off.

Practice 3c

Working with Named UCSs

Practice Objective

- Define, save, and restore UCSs in a model.

In this practice, you will save and restore the UCSs that you define on the ratchet drawing shown in Figure 3–29.

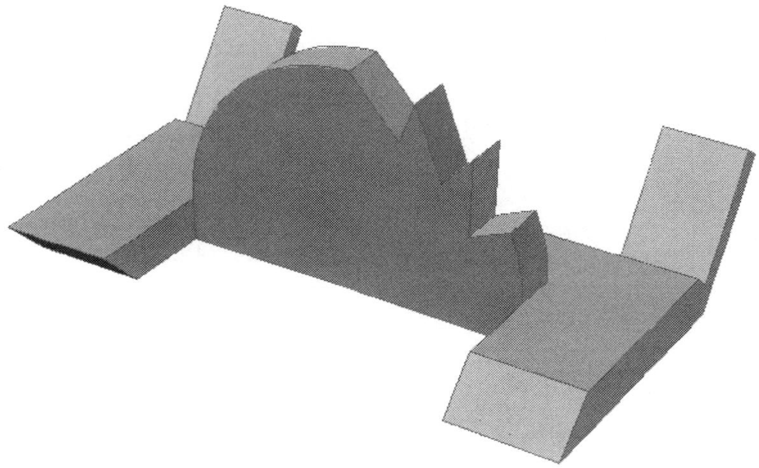

Figure 3–29

1. Open **Ratchet.dwg**.
2. On the *Home* tab>Coordinates panel, click (UCS, 3 Point) and set up a UCS on any face of the object.
3. On the *Home* tab>Coordinates panel, click (UCS, Named). In the UCS dialog box, right-click on the **Unnamed** UCS and select **Rename**. Type **RatchetUCS** and click **OK**. Click **OK** again to exit the dialog box.
4. Use different UCS commands and the UCS multi-functional grips to create 2 more UCSs on different faces of the object.

   Save them using (UCS, Named).
5. After you have saved the UCSs, restore and test each one by drawing circles on the object.
6. Save and close the drawing.

Chapter Review Questions

1. Which UCS do you use to return to the UCS home position?
   a. UCS, Face
   b. World UCS
   c. UCS, Named
   d. Dynamic UCS
2. UCS, Origin can change the location of the UCS in the Z-direction.
   a. True
   b. False
3. Which of the following holds true for **UCS** command and the **UCS Icon** command?
   a. **UCS Icon** controls the display of the icon.
   b. **UCS** controls the position and properties of the icon.
   c. **UCS** controls the display and position of the UCS.
   d. **UCS Icon** controls the display and orientation of the icon and UCS.
4. The UCS, X, Y, or Z options are typically used at what stage in the drawing process and why?
   a. Before the model is drawn, you want to draw on a different plane.
   b. After you finish the model and want to rotate the entire model to a different UCS.
   c. While you are working in the model and want to rotate the entire model to a different UCS.
5. How do you align the UCS icon and one of its axes?
   a. Select the square grip at the origin, move the cursor, select a new location, and rotate it along the axis.
   b. Select the square grip of the specific axis, move the cursor, and select a point to which to align it.
   c. Select the circle grip of the specific axis, move the cursor, and select a point to which to align it.
   d. Select the triangle grip, rotate it in the direction of alignment, and move it to the required location.

6. You can save a UCS by name.
   a. True
   b. False

Command Summary

All ribbon names reference the 3D Modeling workspace.

Button	Command	Location
	**Show UCS Icon at Origin**	• **Ribbon:** *Home* tab>Coordinates panel
	**UCS**	• **Ribbon:** *Home* tab>Coordinates panel or *View* tab>Viewport Tools panel
	**UCS Icon**	• **Ribbon:** *Home* tab>Coordinates panel
	**UCS Icon, Properties**	• **Ribbon:** *Home* tab>Coordinates panel
	**UCS Z-axis Vector**	• **Ribbon:** *Home* tab>Coordinates panel
	**UCS, 3 Point**	• **Ribbon:** *Home* tab>Coordinates panel
	**UCS, Face**	• **Ribbon:** *Home* tab>Coordinates panel
	**UCS, Named**	• **Ribbon:** *Home* tab>Coordinates panel
	**UCS, Object**	• **Ribbon:** *Home* tab>Coordinates panel
	**UCS, Origin**	• **Ribbon:** *Home* tab>Coordinates panel
	**UCS, Previous**	• **Ribbon:** *Home* tab>Coordinates panel
	**UCS, View**	• **Ribbon:** *Home* tab>Coordinates panel
	**UCS, World**	• **Ribbon:** *Home* tab>Coordinates panel
	**UCS, X**	• **Ribbon:** *Home* tab>Coordinates panel
	**UCS, Y**	• **Ribbon:** *Home* tab>Coordinates panel
	**UCS, Z**	• **Ribbon:** *Home* tab>Coordinates panel

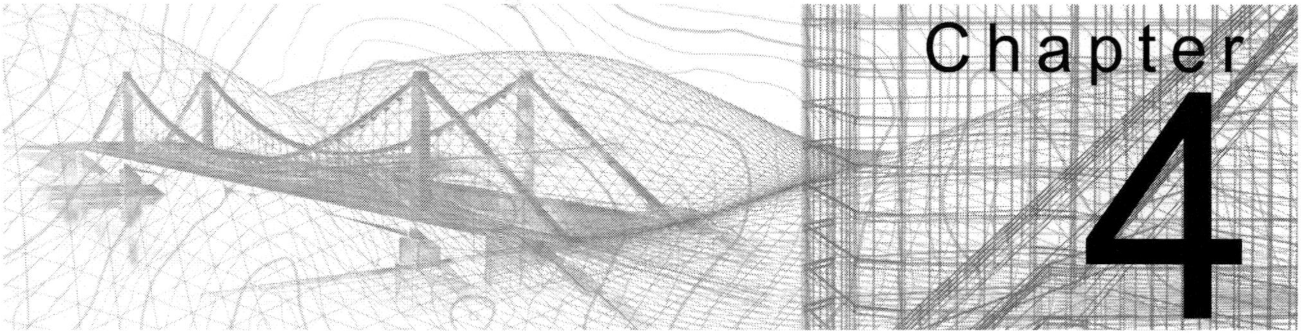

Creating Solids and Surfaces from 2D Objects

In this chapter, you learn how to create solids and surfaces from 2D objects, draw helixes and 3D polylines, and to create and modify 3D extrudes, sweeps, revolves, and lofts. You also learn how to create and edit NURBS surfaces.

Learning Objectives in This Chapter

- Create solid objects or surfaces from 2D objects.
- Extrude 2D linework to create a solid or surface.
- Create a 3D solid or surface by sweeping a 2D profile along a path.
- Create a solid or surface by revolving a profile around an axis.
- Create a smooth curved surface between two or more profiles in 3D space using the Loft command.
- Convert objects into NURBS surfaces that use fit points and control vertices.

4.1 Complex 3D Geometry

Rather than spending many hours creating objects with complex curves or intricate shapes using primitives and Boolean operations, you can quickly create solid objects from 2D objects. These objects, such as the plant stand and paper clip shown in Figure 4–1, can be created from polylines, polygons, circles, ellipses, splines, and bounded areas.

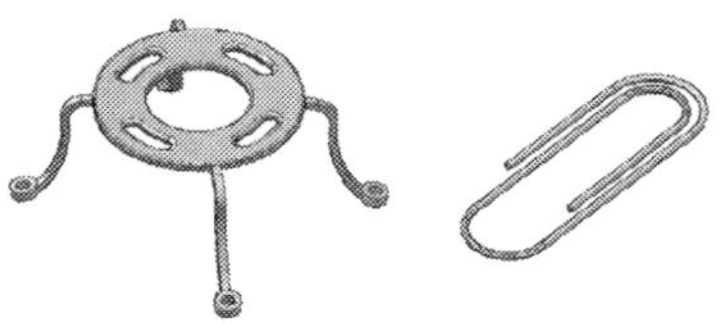

Figure 4–1

Creating Surfaces and Solids

You can create complex 3D geometry using one of four primary commands: (Extrude), (Revolve), (Sweep), and (Loft). In each case, you can create a solid or a surface depending on the type of defining geometry you use. These commands use profiles and paths.

A profile is a 2D object that defines the cross-section shape of a 3D object. If the profile is closed, the result is a solid and if the profile is open, the result is a surface, as shown in Figure 4–2.

*Complex solids (but not surfaces) can be modified using **Union**, **Intersect**, and **Subtract**.*

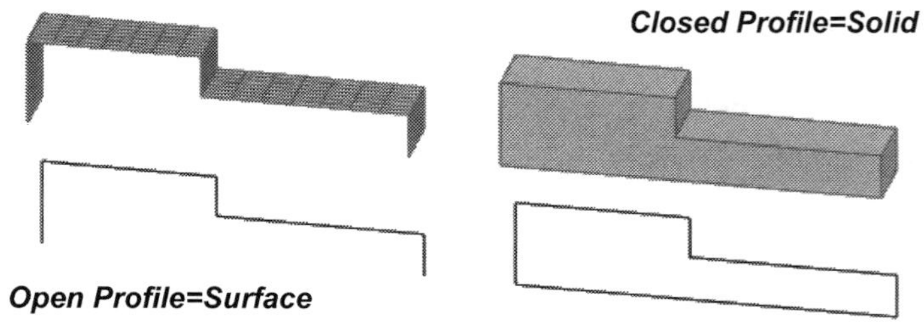

Figure 4–2

- A path is the guide that the profile follows as the solid or surface is created.
- Paths can be 2D or 3D objects.
- By default, profiles and paths are only deleted when a solid is created, not a surface. This can be modified in the Options dialog in the *3D Modeling* tab, in the *3D Objects* area, by selecting an option in the Deletion control while creating 3D objects drop-down list.

4.2 Extruded Solids and Surfaces

The **Extrude** command creates a solid or surface object that has a constant cross-section shape, as shown in Figure 4–3. Many different objects can be created with extrusions, from simple gears and plates to building concepts based on complex floor plans.

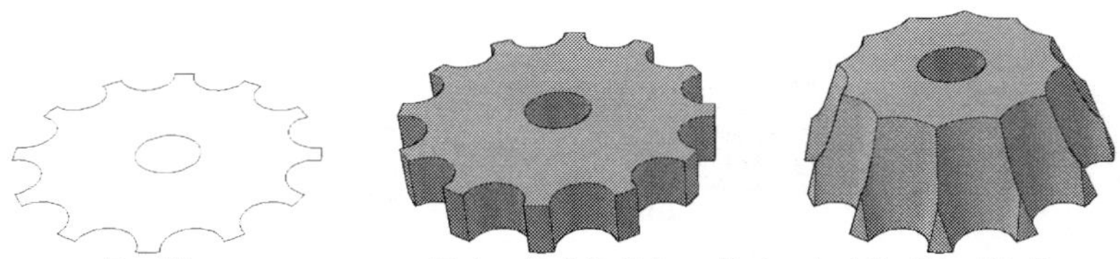

Profile ***Extruded Solid*** ***Extruded Solid with Taper***

Figure 4–3

- The extruded solid or surface is created on the current layer.

How To: Extrude an Object

1. In the *Home* tab>Modeling panel, click  (Extrude).
   - Alternatively, you can access the command on the *Solid* tab>Solid panel or type **extrude** at the command line.
2. Select the object(s) to be extruded and press <Enter>.
3. Specify the height of the extrusion by selecting a point in space or typing a distance.

- A line can be extruded to create a flat surface. An arc can be extruded to create a curved surface. Open 2D polylines or 2D splines become surfaces, while closed polylines, splines, and circles become solids.

Use  *(Selection Cycling) in the Status Bar to make it easier to select specific edges or faces.*

- You can select an edge or face of an existing 3D object to use as the profile or curve of the extrusion. Hold <Ctrl> to select the edge or face.
- You can extrude multiple objects in different directions and can also extrude non-planar profiles, such as splines.
- Use the **Mode** option to set the extrusion to be created as a surface or solid.

Extrude Options

Direction	Enables you to specify a start point and end point for the extrusion. Typically, the start point is a point on the profile and the end point is a different point in 3D space. Use object snaps or typed coordinates for the second point.
Path	Extrudes the profile along a previously drawn path. The path can consist of lines, circles, arcs, ellipses, elliptical arcs, 2D or 3D polylines, 2D or 3D splines, helixes, and edges of solids and surfaces.
Taper angle	Enables you to specify a tapered angle for the extrusion. A positive taper angles into the object, while a negative taper angles away form the object. The tapered angle cannot cause the solid to intersect itself. A preview of the taper displays.
Expression	Set the height using an equation or a formula.

Presspull

The **Presspull** command extrudes a shape based on a bounded area resulting in a single solid object. If you push the shape into a solid, it creates a void in the solid. If you pull the shape away from a solid, it adds the extruded shape to the solid. In both cases, the object still remains a single solid object. For example, draw a rectangle on a face, start the **PressPull** command, move the cursor over the bounded area, and push the bounded area away from the solid, as shown in Figure 4–4.

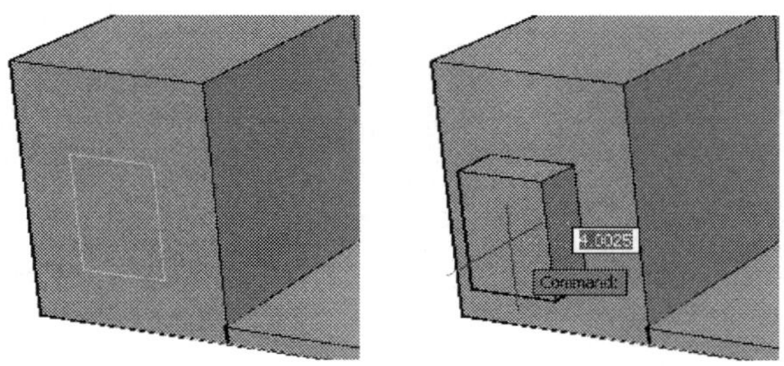

Figure 4–4

How To: Use the Presspull Command

1. On the *Home* tab>Modeling panel, click (Presspull).

   Alternatively, you can access the command in any of the following ways:

   - On the *Solid* tab>Solid panel.
   - Type **presspull** at the command line.
   - Press <Ctrl>+<Shift>+<E>.

2. Move the cursor inside a closed bounded area. The potential boundaries highlight as you move the cursor around. The objects do not need to be closed, but the boundary must be closed.
3. Click and *pull* the object up or *press* the object down to create the extruded solid.
4. The AutoCAD® software automatically extrudes the bounded area to the specified distance.
5. Continue to select other boundaries to extrude or press <Enter> to end the command.

- You can select 2D and 3D curves to create extrusions using the **Presspull** command.

- You can extrude a planer face and have it follow the angle of the adjacent sides, as shown in Figure 4–5. To do so, hold <Ctrl> when selecting the planer face.

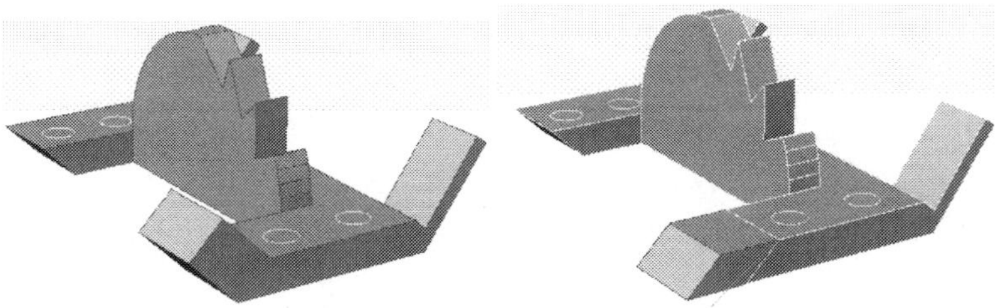

Without <Ctrl> ***With <Ctrl>***

Figure 4–5

Multiple

You can press or pull multiple objects at the same time, as shown in Figure 4–6. Press <Shift> while selecting multiple objects or select the **Multiple** option in the command, to press or pull multiple objects at the same time. Press <Enter> when finished selecting objects.

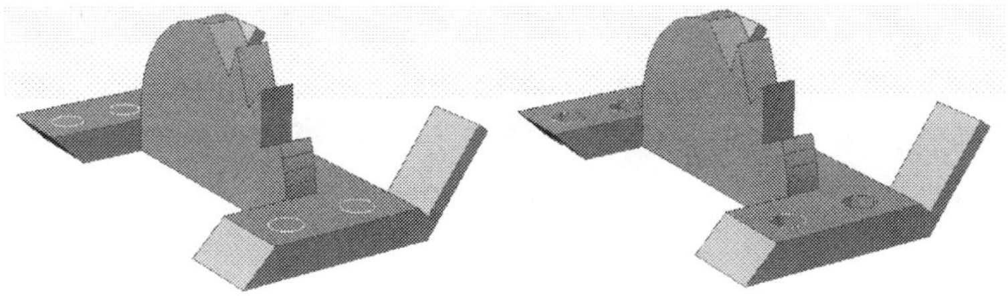

Figure 4–6

Move the cursor in the direction in which you want to press or pull the objects and either pick the location or type the distance value, as shown in Figure 4–7.

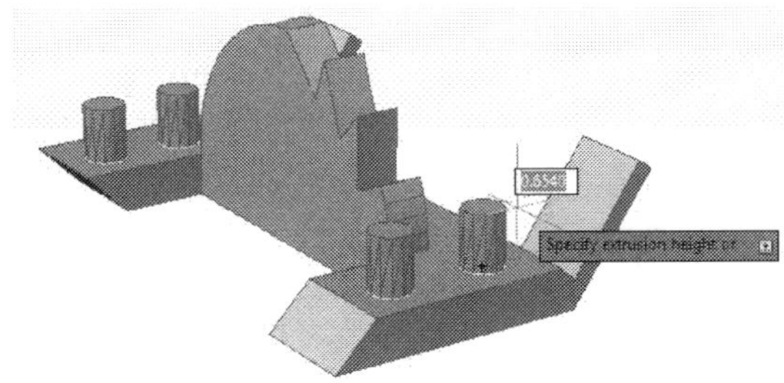

Figure 4–7

Modifying Extrusions

When working with extruded solids or surfaces, you can manipulate the vertices of the profile, and change the height of the extrusion with the arrow grip. It does not matter if the profile object is open (surface) or closed (solid) for the modification process. The height and taper angle can also be modified in Properties, as shown in Figure 4–8.

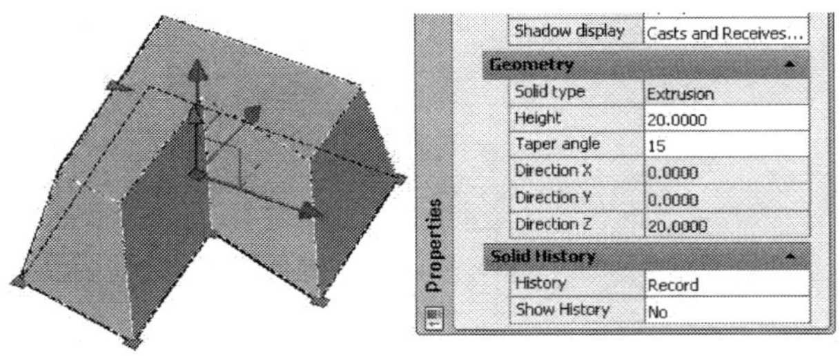

Figure 4–8

- If the extrusion uses a path, you can modify the profile and the path with grips.
- For an extrusion, you can use grips to change the profile, height, and taper. The tapered angle can also be modified in Properties.
- If the extrusion was created using the **Direction** option, only the height and profile can be modified, not the direction.
- Solids created with **Presspull** are considered extrusions. However, you cannot modify the vertices of the profile because they are created from a bounded area.
- If you do not know which type of solid or surface you are working with, select it and look in Properties. The type is listed in the *Geometry* area.

Practice 4a Creating an Extruded Solid

Practice Objective

- Create a composite 3D solid object by extruding 2D profiles and using Boolean operation tools.

In this practice, you will use **Extrude**, **Intersect**, and **Subtract** to create a solid, as shown in Figure 4–9.

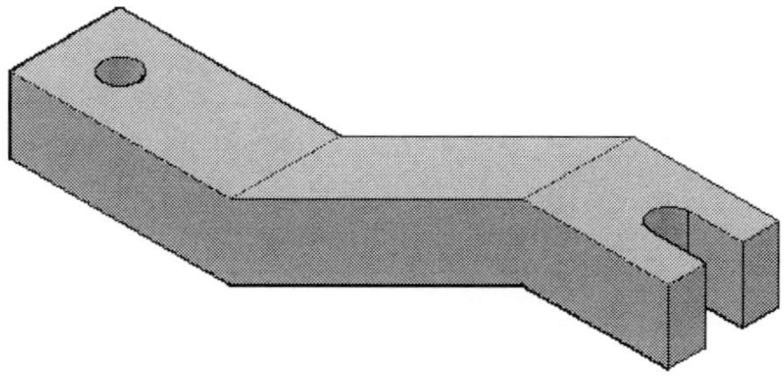

Figure 4–9

1. Open **Bar2.dwg**.
2. Switch to the **SE Isometric** view, if required.
3. On the *Solid* tab>Solid panel or *Home* tab>Modeling panel, click  (Extrude) and extrude the top view, as shown in Figure 4–10, upwards to a height of **3**.

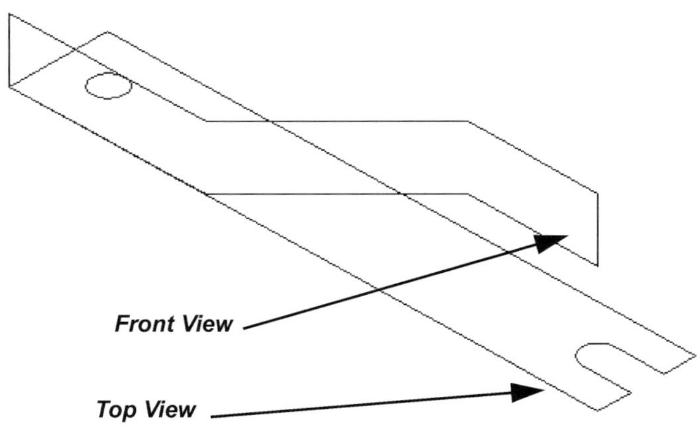

Figure 4–10

4. Click  (Extrude). Extrude the front view to a height of **3**, such that it overlaps the extruded top view.

5. Intersect the two extruded objects.
6. Extrude the small circle at the end of the part to a point above the other extrusions.
7. Subtract the resulting cylinder from the bar to create a hole.
8. Change the *Visual Style* to **Shades of Gray** and orbit around to check the created model.
9. Save and close the drawing.

Practice 4b

Extruding Along a Path

Practice Objective

- Create a solid by extruding a 2D profile along a path and subtracting it from an existing solid.

In this practice, you will extrude along a path to create a solid. You will then subtract the new solid from an existing solid to create a groove, as shown in Figure 4–11.

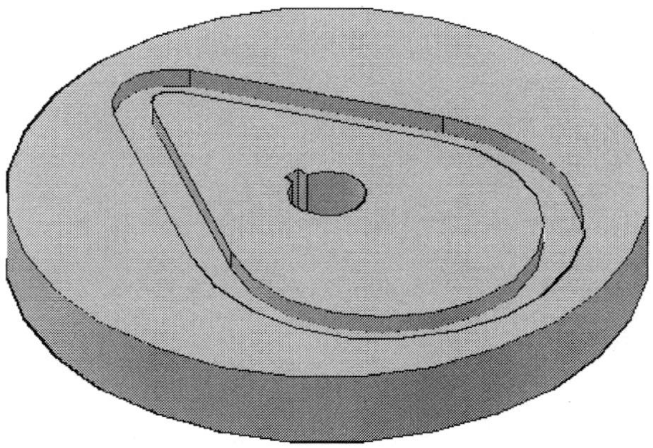

Figure 4–11

1. Open **Cam.dwg**.
2. Change the *Visual Style* to **Realistic** and then orbit around to familiarize yourself with the objects.
3. Change the *Visual Style* to **2D Wireframe**. Note that there is a gray polyline and a blue rectangle in addition to the 3D disk model.
4. Click  (Extrude) and select the blue rectangle as the object to extrude. Press <Enter>. At the *Specify height:* prompt, select **Path** and then select the gray polyline as the path.
5. Change the *Visual Style* to **Realistic** to view the results.
6. Subtract the extrusion from the disk.
7. Save and close the drawing.

4.3 Swept Solids and Surfaces

The **Sweep** command is similar to the **Extrude** command, with the exception of using a path along which to extrude. With **Extrude**, the profile object must be in the correct relationship with the path. **Sweep** does not require the profile to be aligned with the path. Sweeps can be used for roof lines, piping (as shown in Figure 4–12), ribs, and slot features.

An open profile produces a surface and a closed profile produces a solid. You can have more than one profile, but they must be in the same plane.

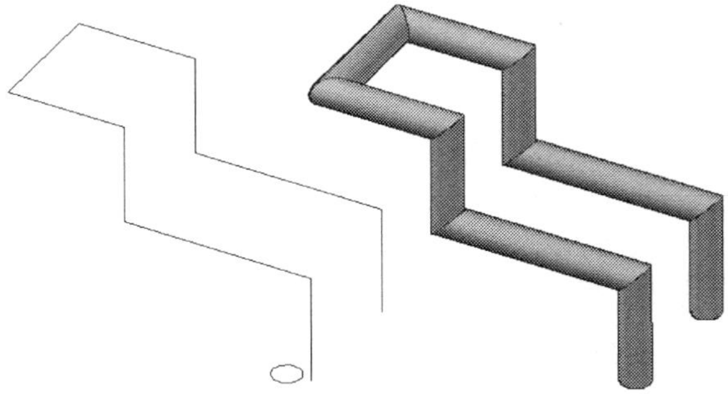

Figure 4–12

How To: Sweep Objects Along a Path

1. Draw the profile object.
2. Draw the path on which to sweep the object.
3. In the Home tab>Modeling panel, click  (Sweep).
4. Select the profile object(s) to be swept and press <Enter> to accept the selection set.
5. Select the path object.

- The AutoCAD software displays an alert in the Command Line if the software cannot create the sweep.

Sweep Options

Alignment	Aligns the object with the path before sweeping, as shown below. The default is **Yes**. If you select **No**, you can still create the sweep, but it is not aligned with the path. 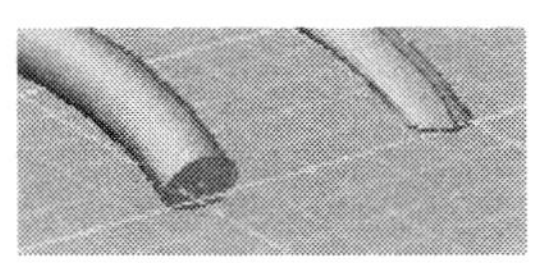 ***Aligned*** ***Not Aligned***

Base Point	Changes the location of the base point of the sweep.
Scale	Changes the size of the profile as it moves along the path. For example, a scale of 0.5 displays the start profile at full size, and the end profile at half size. The size changes equally along the path.
Twist/Bank	Specifies a twist angle or enables banking for a non-planer sweep path, such as a 3D polyline, 3D spline, or helix.

To select faces of a solid for a profile or edges of surfaces or solids for paths, hold <Ctrl> as you select them.

- Objects that can be profiles are lines, arcs and elliptical arcs, circles and ellipses, open or closed 2D polylines and splines, planar (flat) 2D faces, 2D solids, traces, regions, planar surfaces, and faces of solids.
- Objects that can be paths are arcs and elliptical arcs, circles and ellipses, open or closed 2D polylines and splines, 3D splines or polylines, helixes, and edges of surfaces or solids.

Modifying Sweeps

You can modify the profile and path of a sweep using grips or Properties, as shown in Figure 4–13. If the profile is aligned along the path, modify the profile in the path location.

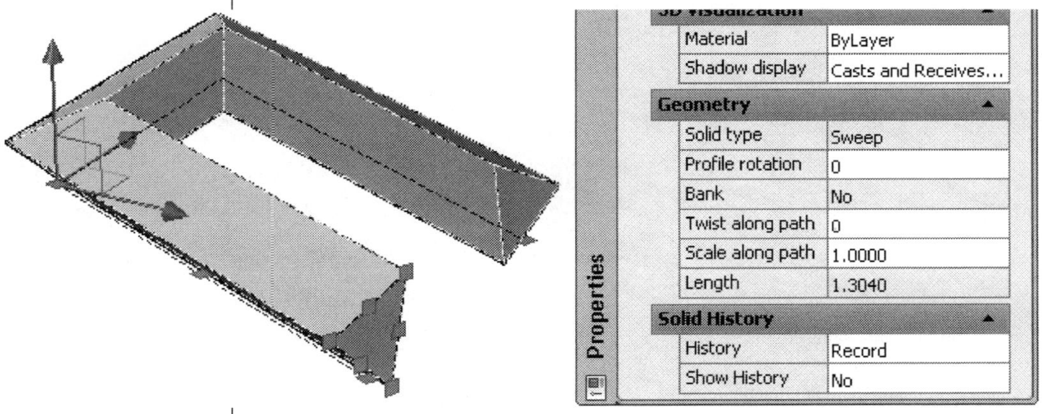

Figure 4–13

- You can change the **Profile rotation**, **Twist along path**, and **Scale along path** options in Properties.
- Modifying the profile changes it along the full path of the sweep.
- **Polysolids** are a type of sweep. Therefore, their profiles and paths can also be modified.

3D Paths

Several object types can be used as 3D paths, including **3D Polylines**, **Splines**, and **Helixes**.

3D Polyline

When using the **Polyline** command, you are restricted to the current XY plane. You can draw 2D polylines on various UCSs, but all points in the polyline must have the same Z-coordinate. A special command, **3D Polyline** (**3Dpoly**), enables you to construct polylines using various X, Y, and Z coordinates for each point, as shown in Figure 4–14.

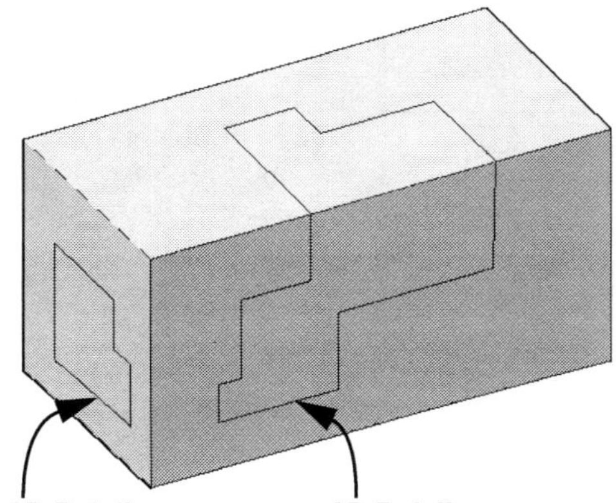

Figure 4–14

- A 3D polyline is similar to regular polylines, except that it does not have arc or width options. In the *Home* tab>Draw panel, click  (3D Polyline). You can edit 3D polylines with the **Polyline Edit** (**Pedit**) command.
- **Spline** objects in the AutoCAD software can be drawn in 2D or 3D space. Therefore, the points on the spline can have different Z-coordinates.

Helix

A helix is a complex 3D geometric object that spirals. It can be used as the basis of many different types of objects, such as the coils of a spring, a spiral staircase, or screw threads (shown in Figure 4–15).

The helix tool is not a solid or surface, but can be used to create solids or surfaces.

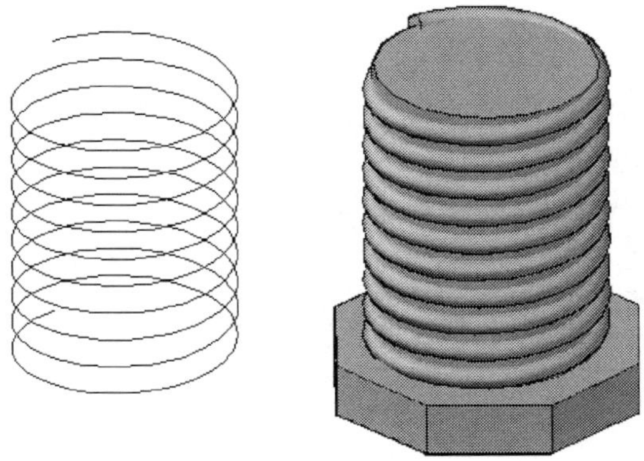

Figure 4–15

How To: Create a Helix

1. In the *Home* tab>expanded Draw panel, click  (Helix).
2. Specify a center point for the base.
3. Specify a radius for the base or select **Diameter** to specify the diameter.
4. Specify a top radius or diameter. A 2D spiral displays when you move the cursor.
5. Specify a height for the helix or select one of the options.

Helix Options

Axis endpoint	Enables you to select a point for the top of the helix. It can be at an angle from the original center point.
Turns	Sets the number of turns. You are prompted for the overall height. This selection also modifies the **Turn Height**.
turn Height	Specifies the distance between the turns. You are prompted for the overall height. This selection also modifies the number of **Turns**.
tWist	Sets the direction of the turn to be clockwise or counterclockwise.

Practice 4c Creating a Swept Solid

Practice Objective

- Create a solid object by sweeping a profile along a path and adjust the alignment and rotation of the profile.

In this practice, you will use **Sweep** to create a section of weatherstrip material, as shown in Figure 4–16. You will use the **Alignment** and **Twist** options to edit the profile with grips.

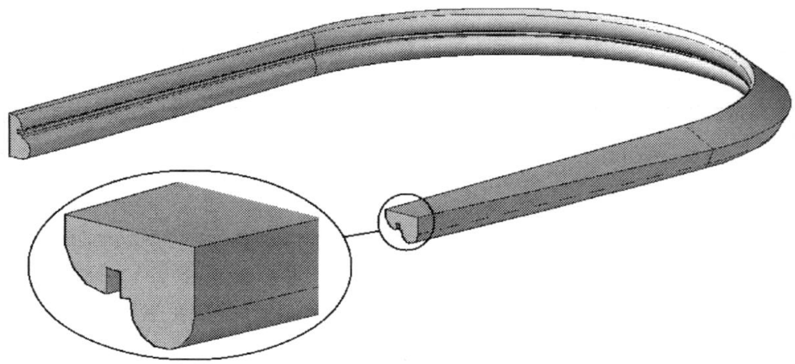

Figure 4–16

1. Open **Weatherstrip.dwg**. The profile and path of the weatherstrip is included in the drawing.
2. Switch to the **NW Isometric** view. The path and profile display.
3. In the *Home* tab>Modeling panel, expand (Extrude) and click (Sweep).
4. At the *Select objects to sweep* prompt, select the closed polyline as the profile and press <Enter>.
5. In the command options, select **Alignment**. At the *Align sweep object perpendicular to path before sweep* prompt, select **No**.
6. At the *Select sweep path* prompt, select the open polyline as the path.
7. Orbit around the model to display both ends of the sweep facing towards you. The starting point is not perpendicular to the path.

8. Undo the sweep.
9. Sweep the polyline along the path again using the **Twist** option with an angle of **90**. It automatically aligns itself to the path.
10. Zoom and orbit to display both ends. The end portion of the profile has been rotated.
11. Use grips to stretch one corner of the profile a small distance. It updates along the entire sweep.
12. Save and close the drawing.

Practice 4d Sweeping Along a Helix

Practice Objective

- Create a coil spring using a tapered helix and sweep.

In this practice, you will create a coil spring using a tapered helix and sweep, as shown in Figure 4–17.

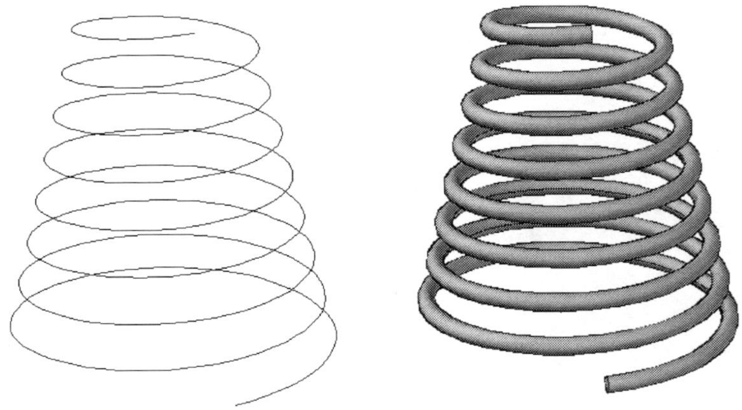

Figure 4–17

1. Start a new drawing based on **acad3D.dwt** and save it in your practice files folder as **Helix.dwg**.
2. In the *Home* tab>expanded Draw panel, click (Helix) and select a center point for the base. Set the *Base radius* to **2** and the *Top radius* to **1**.
3. Use the **Turns** option to set the *number of turns* to **8**.
4. Move your cursor above the base center point and set the *Height* of the helix to **4**.
5. Zoom in to the bottom portion of helix.
6. Using the bottom endpoint of the helix as the center point, draw a circle with a radius of **0.1** units.
7. In the *Solid* tab>Solid panel, click (Sweep).
8. At the *Select objects to sweep:* prompt, select the small circle and press <Enter>.
9. At the *Select sweep path:* prompt, select **Alignment**. At the *Align sweep object perpendicular to path before sweep* prompt, select **Yes**.

10. At the *Select sweep path:* prompt, select the helix.
11. Set the NW Isometric view and Shades of Gray visual style to display the coil spring model.
12. Save and close the drawing.

Practice 4e Sweeping Along a 3D Polyline

Practice Objectives

- Create a 3D polyline along the edge of an object and use it as the path for a sweep.
- Create a notch along the edge using the sweep.

In this practice, you will create a 3D polyline along the edge of an object and use it as the path for a sweep. You will then use **Subtract** to create a notch along the edge of a solid, as shown in Figure 4–18.

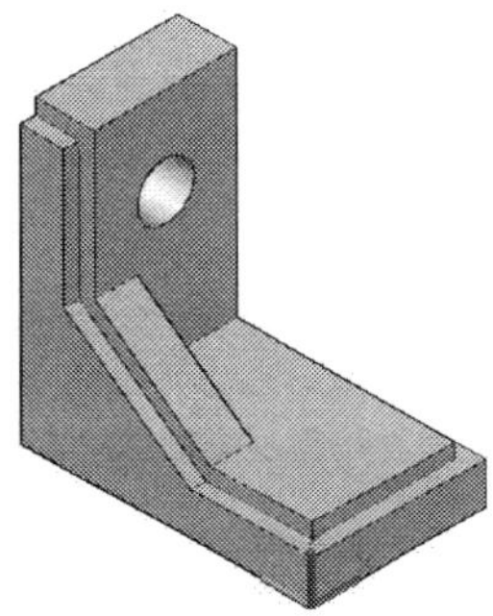

Figure 4–18

1. Open **Edge-Cut.dwg**.
2. Thaw the layer **Text**. The text displays similar to that shown in Figure 4–19.

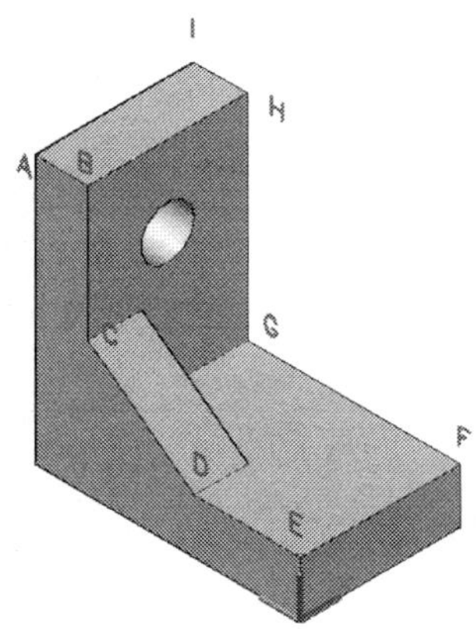

Figure 4–19

3. Make the layer **3DPolyline** current.

4. In the *Home* tab>Draw panel, click (3D Polyline).

*Use the 3D Object Snap set to **Vertex**.*

5. Draw a 3D polyline connecting points A through I, as shown in Figure 4–20.

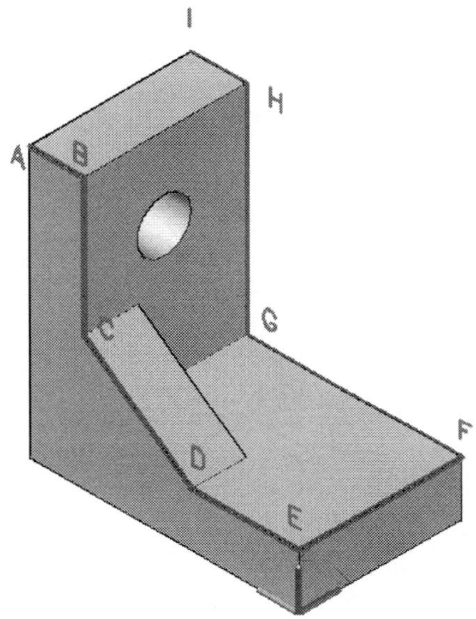

Figure 4–20

6. Freeze the layers **Text** and **0** and thaw the layer **Profile**. Only the red 3D polyline and the green rectangle are visible.
7. In the *Home* tab>Modeling panel, click (Sweep).
8. Select the small green rectangle on the layer **Profile** for the profile.
9. Select the 3D polyline as the path.
10. Thaw the layer **0**.
11. In the *Home* tab>Solid Editing panel, click (Subtract) and remove the new sweep from the original object.
12. Set layer **0** to be the current layer and freeze the layer **3DPolyline**.
13. View the model from different angles.
14. Save and close the drawing.

4.4 Revolved Solids and Surfaces

The **Revolve** command creates a solid or surface by revolving a profile around an axis. This command is useful for creating many cylindrical objects and for complex objects, such as the goblet shown in Figure 4–21.

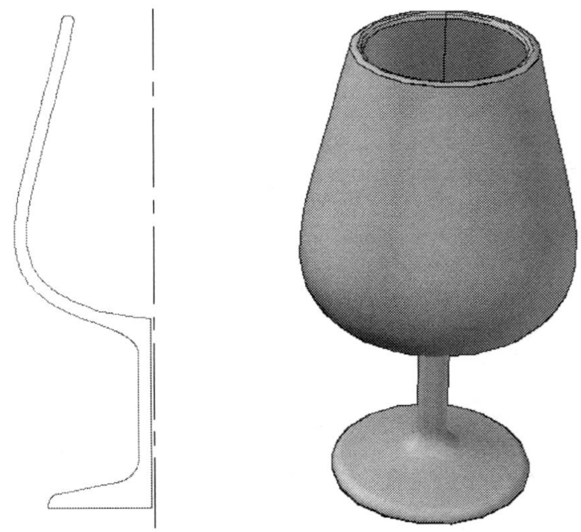

Figure 4–21

How To: Revolve Objects Around an Axis

1. In the *Home* tab>Modeling panel, click (Revolve).
2. Select the objects to revolve and press <Enter>.
3. Specify the axis using one of the options.
4. Specify the angle of rotation.

- You can select existing edges or faces as the profiles or curves to be revolved.

- You can revolve non-planar profiles.

Revolve Options

Object	Enables you to select an open object or edge to be revolved around the axis of revolution.
Mode	Enables you to select whether the revolve is created as a solid or surface.
X/Y/Z Axis	Rotates around the positive X-, Y-, or Z-axis.
Axis Start Point	Enables you to select a point to specify as the start point of the axis of revolution.
Axis End Point	Enables you to select a point to specify as the end point of the axis of revolution.
Start Angle	Enables you to specify the start angle for the revolution.
Angle of Revolution	Enables you to specify the angle of revolution.
Reverse	Enables you to reverse the direction of the revolve.
Expression	Enables you to use an expression or formula to control the revolve angle.

Modifying Revolves

You can use grips to modify the profile and location of a revolved solid's path in relation to its profile. You can change the *Angle of revolution* and the *Axis position* in Properties, as shown in Figure 4–22. It does not matter how the path was selected.

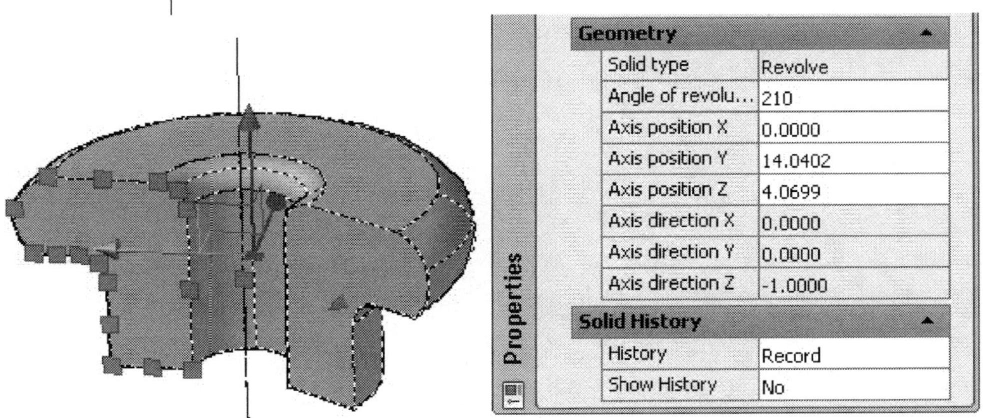

Figure 4–22

Practice 4f Creating Revolved Solids

Practice Objective

- Create two rings using the **Revolve** command with two closed polylines.

In this practice, you will use **Revolve** on two closed polylines to create the inner rings of the assembly shown in Figure 4–23.

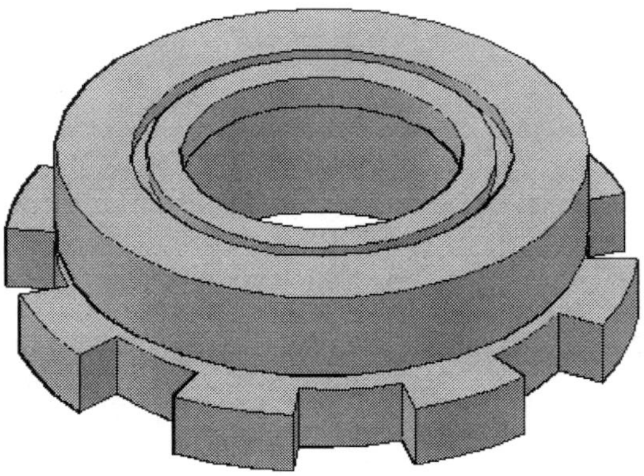

Figure 4–23

1. Open **Revolve.dwg**.

2. In the *Home* tab>Modeling panel, in the (Extrude) flyout, click (Revolve).

3. At the *Select objects to revolve* prompt, select the cyan polyline, as shown in Figure 4–24, and press <Enter>.

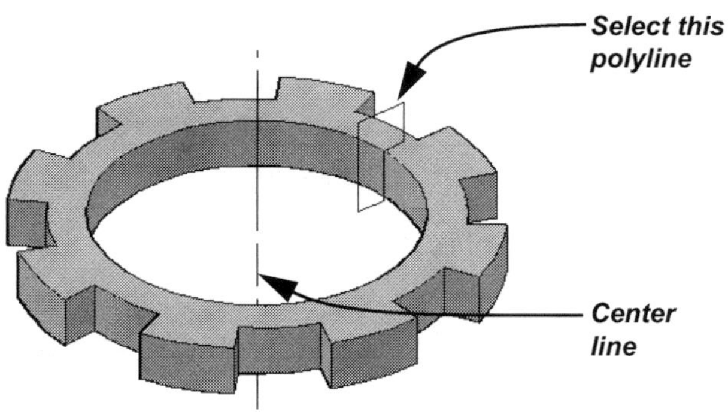

Figure 4–24

4. At the *Specify axis start point or define axis by* prompt, press <Enter> to select **Object**.

5. Select the yellow center line for the axis.

6. At the *Specify angle of revolution* prompt, press <Enter> to accept the default of **360** degrees.

7. Freeze the layer **Center**. Toggle on the layer **Top** and make it current.

8. Change the *Visual Style* to **2D Wireframe**.

9. In the *Solid* tab>Solid panel, click (Revolve). Select the green polyline as the object to revolve, as shown in Figure 4–25, and press <Enter>.

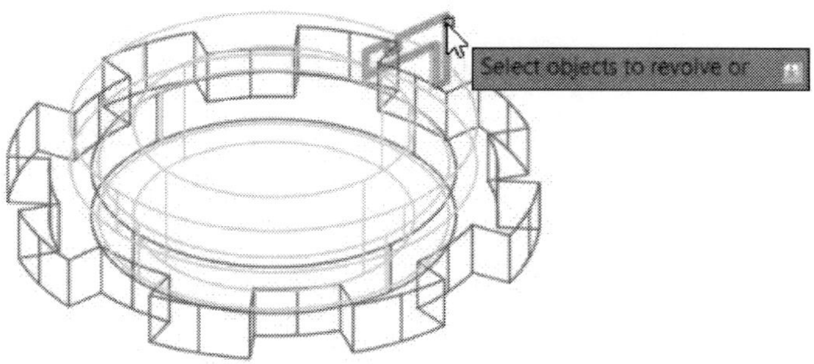

Figure 4–25

10. Snap to the center of the ring that you created earlier for the start point of the axis of revolution. Snap to the center of the red object (as shown in Figure 4–26) for the end point of the axis.

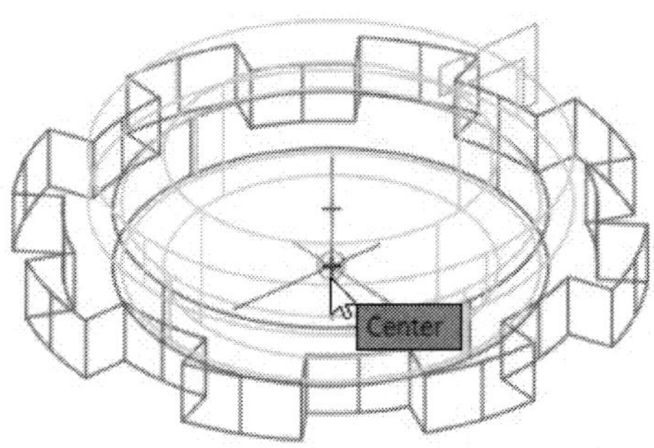

Figure 4–26

11. At the *Specify angle of revolution* prompt, press <Enter>.

12. Change the visual style to **Realistic** to display the result.

13. Save and close the drawing.

4.5 Lofted Solids and Surfaces

Lofts create a smooth curved surface between two or more profiles in 3D space. Lofts can be created from profiles (cross-sections) alone, and then you can use guides or a path to further define them, as shown in Figure 4–27. The profiles can be open or closed, but must all be one or the other. Open profiles create surfaces and closed profiles create solids.

- You can select existing edges or faces to use as profiles or curves when creating lofts.

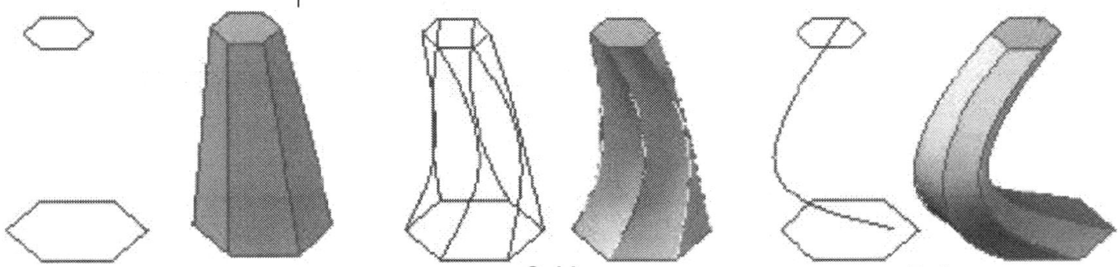

Figure 4–27

How To: Create a Loft

1. Create the cross-sections and then create the path or guides as required.
2. In the *Home* tab>Modeling panel, click  (Loft).
3. Select the cross-section profiles and press <Enter>. The order in which you select the cross-sections is important.
4. Select the option you want to use, as shown in Figure 4–28. The default is **Cross-sections only**.

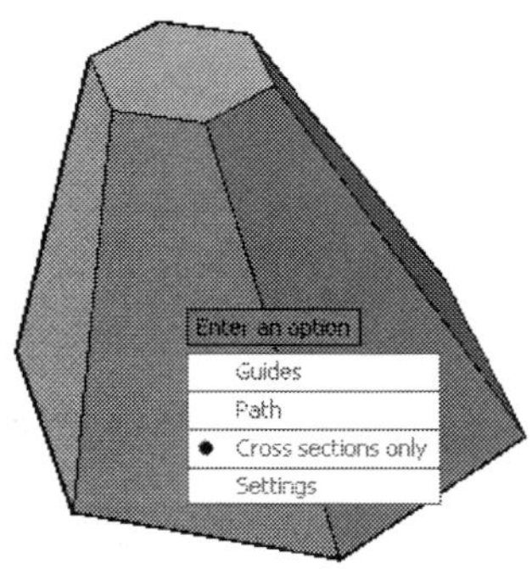

Figure 4–28

5. If you select **Guides** or **Path**, select the curves to be used to create the loft. The loft is created when you press <Enter>.

6. If you select **Settings**, the Loft Settings dialog box opens, as shown in Figure 4–29.

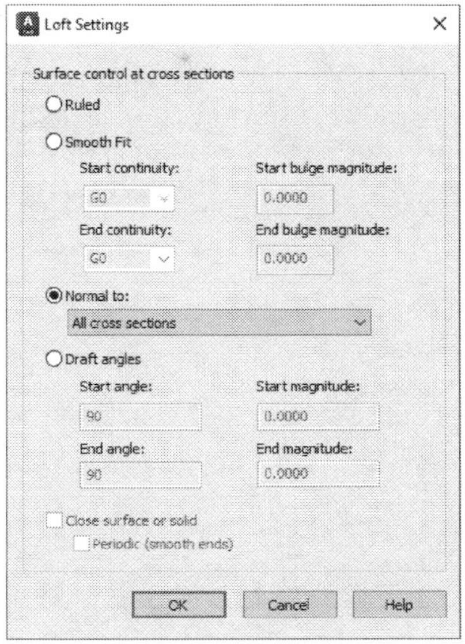

Figure 4–29

7. In the *Surface control at cross sections* area, set the options for controlling a loft created with cross-sections only.
8. Click **OK** to close the Loft Settings dialog box and create the loft.

- Examples of different loft settings are shown in Figure 4–30.

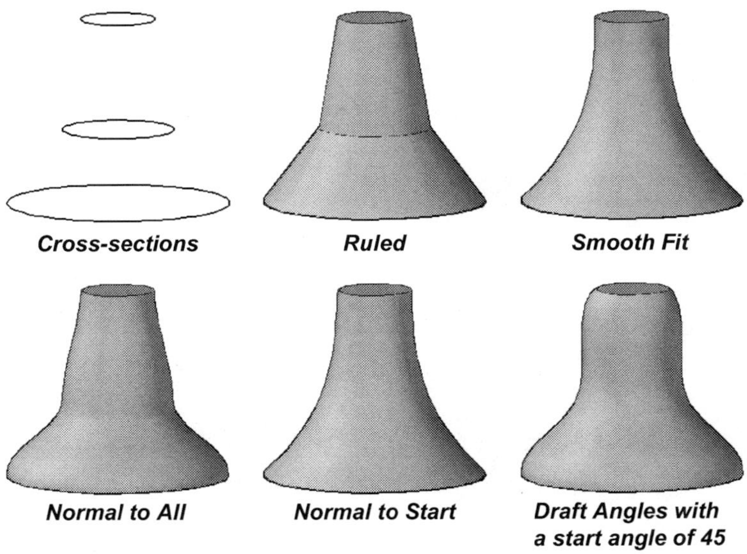

Figure 4–30

- If you select **Ruled** or **Smooth Fit**, you can also select the **Close surface or solid** option. This closes the surface between the first and last cross-section. If the cross-sections are closed objects, a thin solid shell is created.
- Another option for changing the Loft Settings is by using the heads up display, as shown in Figure 4–31.

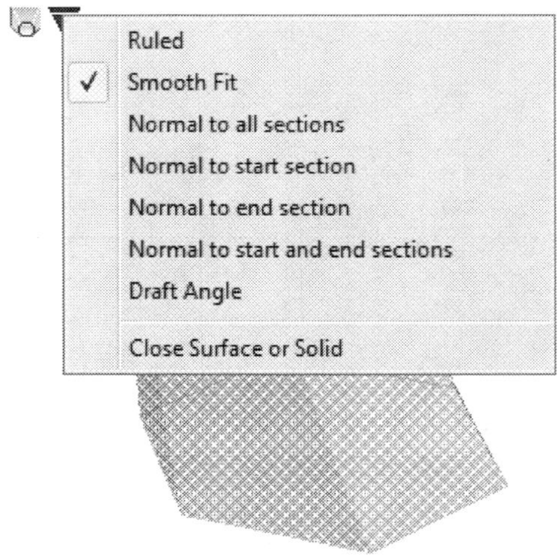

Figure 4–31

- While selecting the cross-section profiles, you can see a preview of the resulting loft, as shown in Figure 4–32.

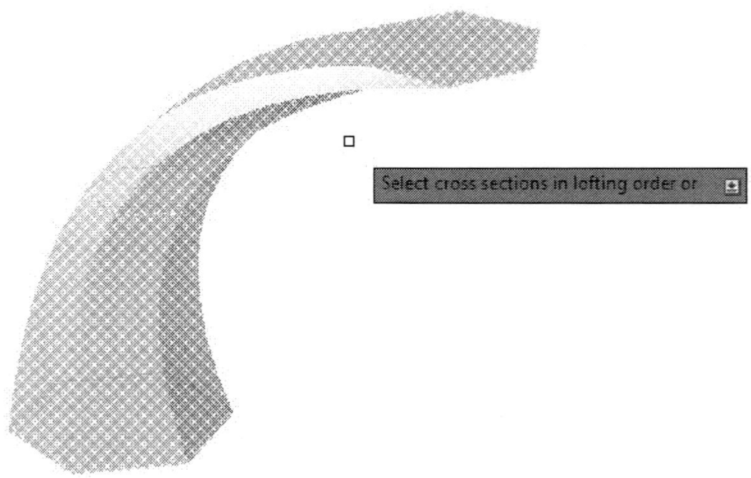

Figure 4–32

Modifying Lofts

Loft objects can be modified with grips at each cross-section. If the loft was created with a path or guides, you can also modify those objects. In Properties, you can only modify the *Surface Normals*. If it is set to **Use draft angles**, you can also modify the draft angles and magnitudes, as shown in Figure 4–33.

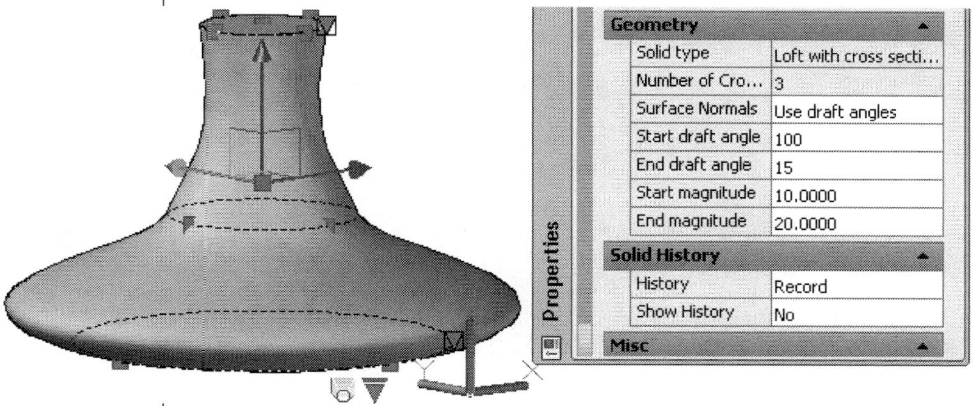

Figure 4–33

Practice 4g Creating a Lofted Solid

Practice Objective

- Create a 3D solid object from existing 2D profiles and a path using the **Loft** command.

In this practice, you will create a loft using the path and profiles provided in the drawing to create a faucet, as shown in Figure 4–34.

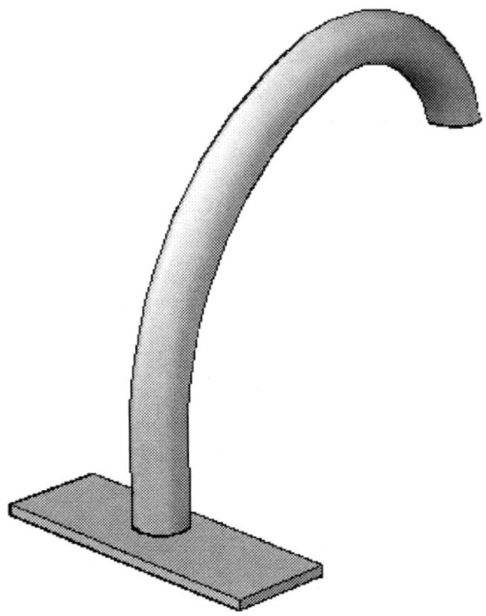

Figure 4–34

1. Open **Faucet-Path.dwg**.
2. In the *Solid* tab>Solid panel, in the (Sweep) flyout, click (Loft).
3. Select the six red cross-section circles in order from the base to the end and press <Enter>.
4. Select **Path** and select the blue polyline for the path.
5. View the faucet from several directions.
6. Save and close the drawing.

Practice 4h Basic Solid and Surface Editing

Practice Objective

- Modify 3D solid objects using grips and the Properties palette.

In this practice, you will use grips and Properties to modify revolves, primitives, extrusions, and sweeps, as shown in Figure 4–35.

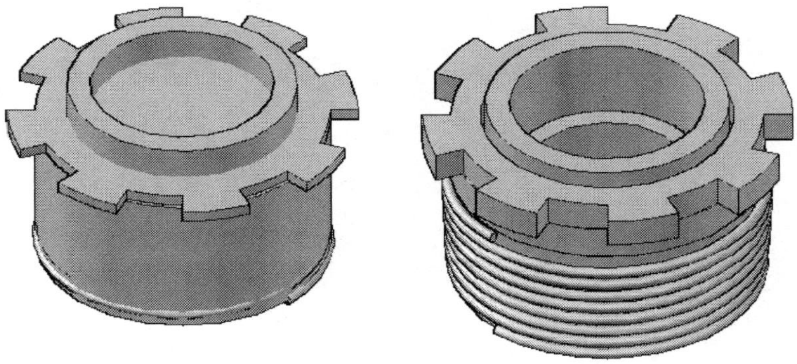

Before ***After***

Figure 4–35

1. Open **Assembly.dwg**.
2. View the various parts of the assembly. Each part is on a different layer in a different color. The objects include an extrusion (the gear), two revolves (the ring and the base), a sweep (the thread), and a solid primitive (the hole, whose layer is frozen).
3. Make the layer **Threads** the current layer and freeze all of the other layers.
4. Change the visual style to **2D Wireframe**.
5. Select the thread.
6. Select the grip at the starting point of the sweep and modify it so that the top radius and bottom radius are approximately the same.
7. Thaw the layer **Ring** and make it the current layer.
8. Freeze the layer **Threads**.
9. Select the ring and note that it is a revolve.

10. Move the center point of the revolve. This changes the radius. Undo the center point change.

11. Thaw all of the layers.

12. Select the red gear, which is an extrusion. Use middle upward arrow grips to change its height. Press <Esc> to clear the selection and then select the red gear again. Use Properties to change the *Height* to **0.3**.

13. In Properties, change the *Height* of the yellow cylinder (on the layer **Hole**) to **2**.

14. Change the visual style to **Realistic**. You can now see the portion of yellow cylinder above the gear.

15. Use the **Subtract** command to remove the yellow cylinder from the gear and create a hole.

16. Select the gear again. The grips have changed and you can no longer modify the extrusion.

17. Save and close the drawing.

4.6 NURBS Surfaces

NURBS (Non-Uniform Rational B-Splines) surfaces are another type of surface you can create. These types of surfaces are based on Bezier curves or splines, and therefore use similar settings, such as fit points and control vertices. Creating a NURBS surface is similar to creating any other procedural surface, using the same commands. However, there are specific editing tools and methods for NURBS surfaces. A NURBS surface with its control vertices displayed is shown in Figure 4–36.

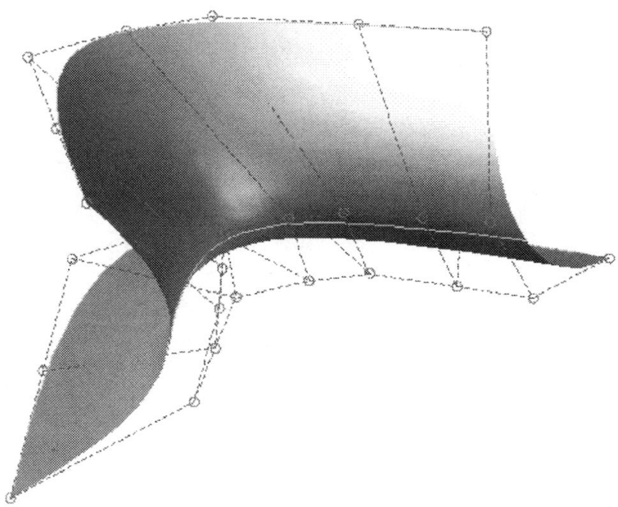

Figure 4–36

Creating NURBS Surfaces

All of the commands and methods used to create procedural surfaces (including **Extrude**, **Loft**, and **Sweep**) apply when creating NURBS surfaces. The only difference is the setting of a specific system variable during its creation. To create a NURBS surface, in the *Surface* tab>Create panel, click  (NURBS Creation).

- When  (NURBS Creation) is toggled on in the ribbon, (surfacemodelingmode = 1), any of the surface creation commands create a NURBS surface.
- When toggled off (surfacemodelingmode = 0), the surface creation commands create general procedural surfaces.

- Besides creating a NURBS surface from scratch, you can also convert a procedural surface into a NURBS surface.
- 3D solids can also be converted into NURBS surfaces. Each face of the 3D solid becomes a separate NURBS surface.

How To: Convert an Object into a NURBS Surface

1. In the *Surface* tab>Control Vertices panel, click  (Convert to NURBS).
2. Select a 3D solid or surface to convert.
3. Continue to select solid or surface objects to convert.
4. Press <Enter> to convert and exit the command.

- A procedural surface can be converted to a NURBS surface but a NURBS surface cannot be converted to a procedural surface.

Edit NURBS Surfaces

At first glance, a NURBS surface looks similar to a procedural surface. They both include and display their U and V isolines (the gridlines on a surface) when you select them, as shown in Figure 4–37. However, because a NURBS surface is actually sculpted from control vertices, you can also display the control vertices of the surface.

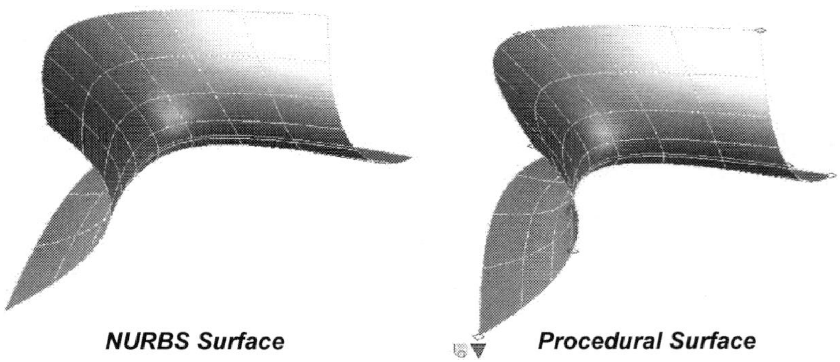

NURBS Surface ***Procedural Surface***

Figure 4–37

A NURBS surface can have its control vertices displayed or hidden, regardless of whether it is selected. A selected NURBS surface with its control vertices displayed is shown in Figure 4–38.

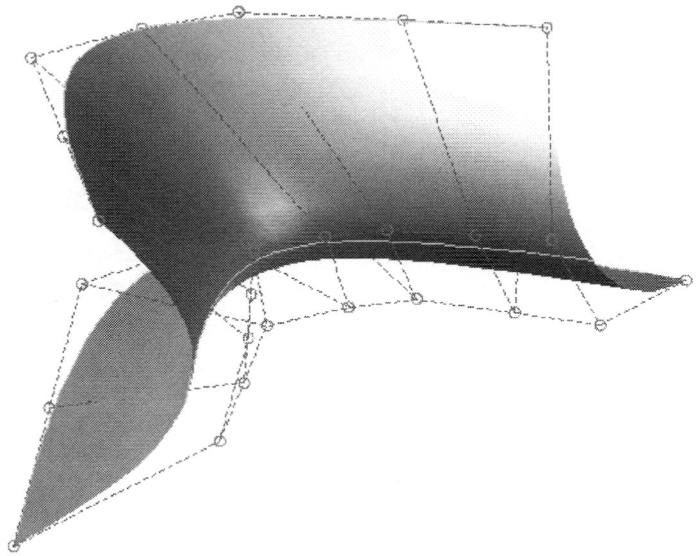

Figure 4–38

How To: Show the Control Vertices of a NURBS Surface

1. In the *Surface* tab>Control Vertices panel, click  (Show Control Vertices).
2. Select a NURBS surface.
3. Continue to select NURBS surfaces.
4. Press <Enter> to display the control vertices.

-  (Hide Control Vertices) hides all of the control vertices for every NURBS surface in the drawing.

Edit Control Vertice Points

When a NURBS surface has its control vertices displayed and the NURBS surface is also selected, both the U and V isolines display and the control vertices points become blue grips, as shown in Figure 4–39.

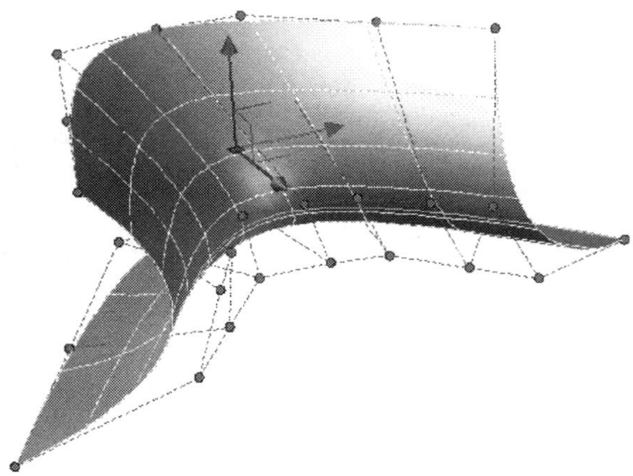

Figure 4–39

Each of the control vertices can individually be selected and moved to modify the shape of the NURBS surface. Dragging and editing control vertices gives you freedom to reshape the NURBS surface in free form.

How To: Edit a NURBS Surface Via a Control Vertice Point Grip

1. In the *Surface* tab>Control Vertices panel, click  (Show Control Vertices) and select the NURBS surface.
2. Press <Enter>.
3. Select the NURBS surface to make the control vertices turn into grips.
4. Select a control vertice point grip.
5. Move the cursor and select a new location to adjust the position of the control vertice point, thus modifying the shape of the NURBS surface.

- Hover the cursor over a control vertice point grip until the UCS icon and its origin display at the control vertice point. Then you can use the UCS icon to adjust the location of the control vertice point.
- Press and hold <Shift> to select multiple control vertices points.

Add Control Vertices

If you need to adjust a NURBS surface more precisely, you can add additional control vertices in the U- or V-directions. You can add control vertices anywhere along the NURBS surface.

How To: Add Additional Control Vertices to a NURBS Surface

1. In the *Surface* tab>Control Vertices panel, click (Add Control Vertice).
2. Select a NURBS surface.
3. Select a point on the surface to add the control vertice in the U-direction, as shown in Figure 4–40.
   - (Optional) Select **Direction** to add the control vertice in the V-direction.

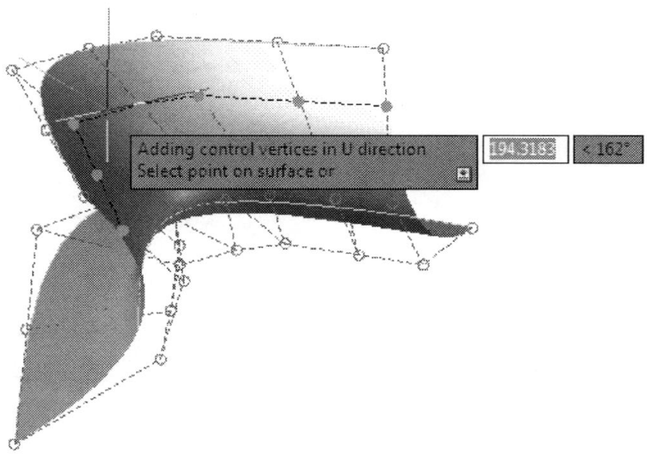

Figure 4–40

- You can edit the added control vertices as you would any other control vertices.
- You can add as many additional control vertices as required.
- A control vertice point is added at each intersecting (U or V) control vertice.

Remove Control Vertices

You can also remove control vertices in the U- or V-direction if it becomes too congested. This command removes the entire row (or column) of points along the specific control vertice set.

How To: Remove Control Vertices from a NURBS Surface

1. In the *Surface* tab>Control Vertices panel, click (Remove Control Vertice).
2. Select a NURBS surface.
3. Select a point on the NURBS surface to specify which set of control vertices in the U-direction to remove, as shown in Figure 4–41. The nearest set of control vertices to be removed highlights in red.
   - (Optional) Select **Direction** to remove a control vertice in the V-direction.

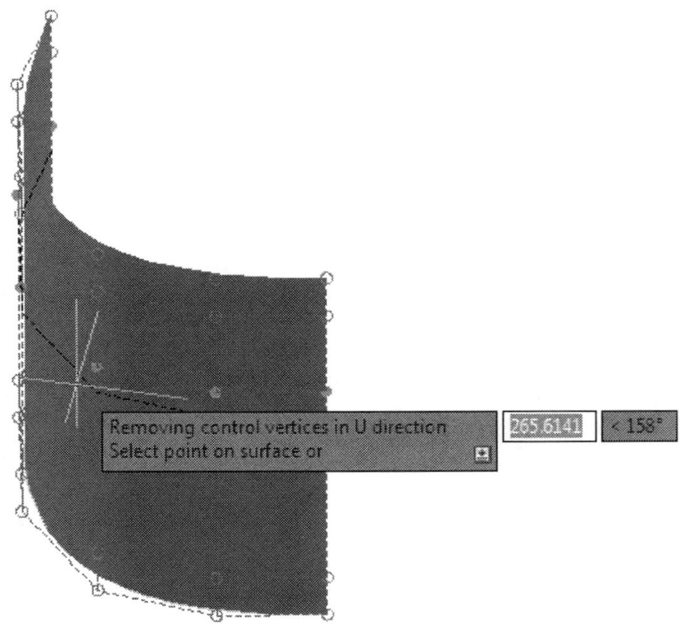

Figure 4–41

Control Vertice Edit Bar

When you want to modify the magnitude or direction of tangency at a specific point on a NURBS surface, you can use the **CV Edit Bar** command. It enables you to adjust a specific point on a NURBS surface, rather than adjusting a control vertice point of a NURBS surface.

How To: Modify a Point on a NURBS Surface

1. In the *Surface* tab>Control Vertices panel, click (CV Edit Bar).
2. Select a NURBS surface.
3. Select a point on the NURBS surface, as shown in Figure 4–42.

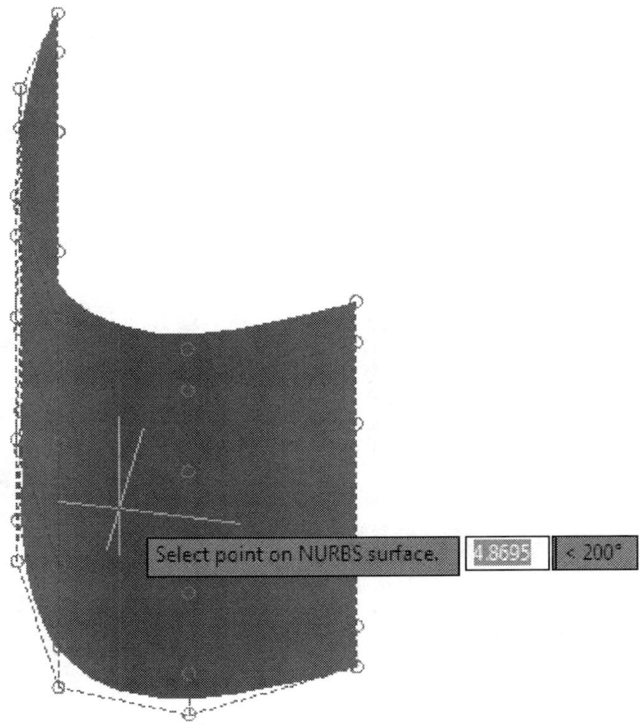

Figure 4–42

4. Select a grip on the edit bar, as shown in Figure 4–43, and modify the surface.

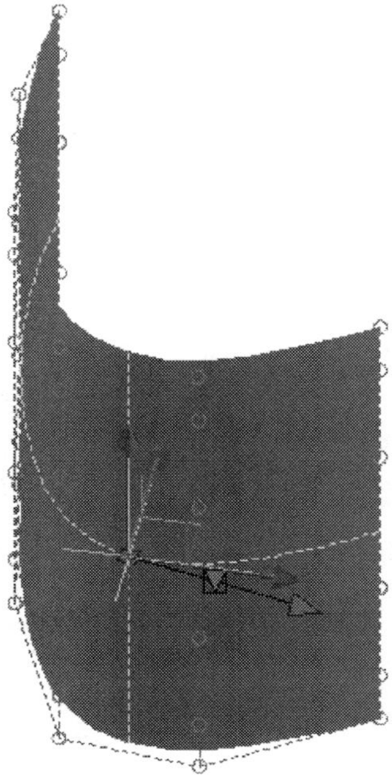

Figure 4–43

5. Press <Enter> to exit the command.

- The triangle grip enables you to switch between the options to move the point or adjust the tangent direction at the point, as shown in Figure 4–44.

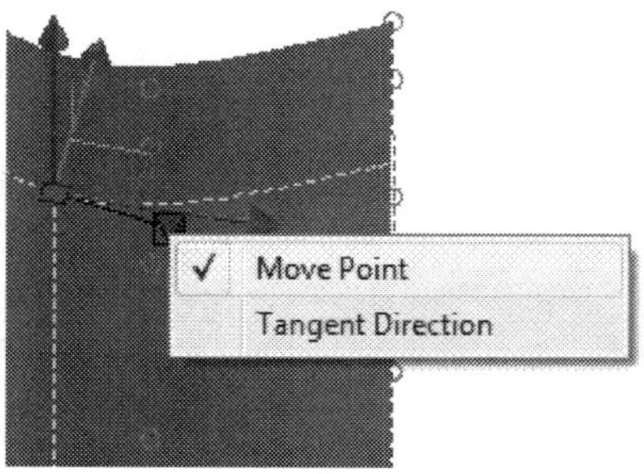

Figure 4–44

- The square grip at the origin of the temporary UCS icon adjusts either the location of the point or the tangent direction at the point.

- The tangent arrow grip adjusts the magnitude of the tangency at the point.

Practice 4i Create and Edit a NURBS Surface

Practice Objectives

- Create a NURBS surface using the **Loft** command.
- Edit a NURBS surface by adding control vertices, adjusting a control vertex point, and modifying a tangency point.

In this practice, you will create a NURBS surface using the **Loft** command. You will then add additional control vertices to the NURBS surface, and modify one of its points. Finally, you will use the **Control Vertices Edit Bar** command and modify a tangency point on the NURBS surface, as shown in Figure 4–45. Your final model might display differently because you might pick different points to modify.

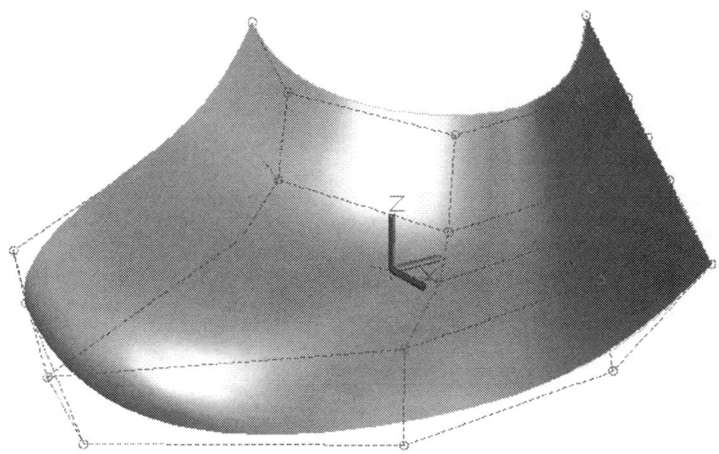

Figure 4–45

1. Open **NURBS.dwg**.
2. Select the two splines (which are at different Z elevations) and note their control vertices.
3. In the *Surface* tab>Create panel, toggle on 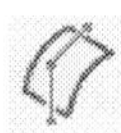 (NURBS Creation).
4. In the *Surface* tab>Create panel, click  (Loft). Select the two splines. A preview of the loft displays between the spline objects. Press <Enter> twice to create the NURBS surface.

5. Select the surface, and note the U and V isolines that display on it, as shown in Figure 4–46.

6. In the *Surface* tab>Control Vertices panel, click (Show CV). The control vertices of the NURBS surface display, as shown in Figure 4–47. Note that the top and bottom rows of control vertices match the control vertices of the splines used to create the surface.

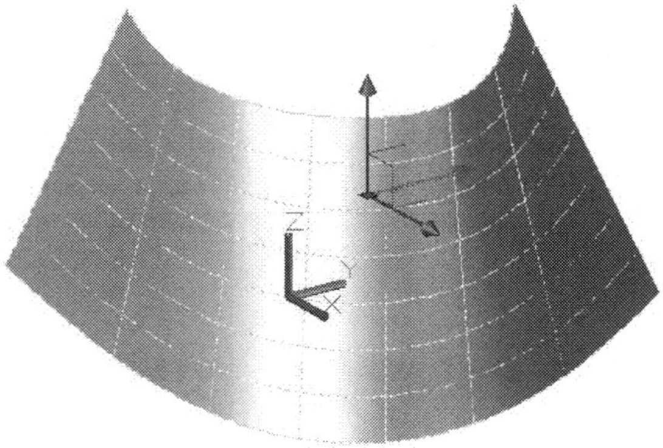

Figure 4–46

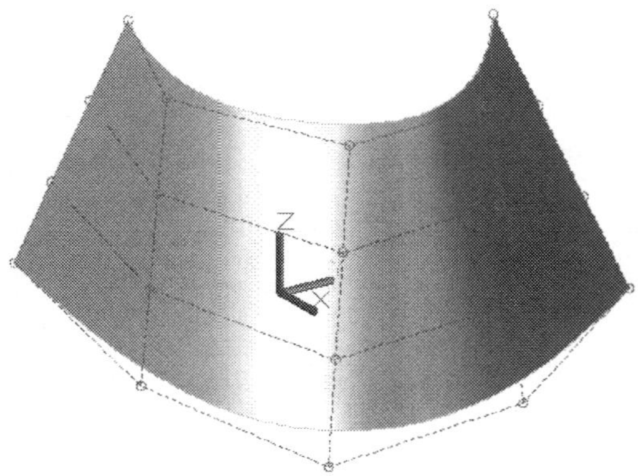

Figure 4–47

7. In the *Surface* tab>Control Vertices panel, click (Surface CV - Add).

8. At the *Select a NURBS surface* prompt, select the lofted surface that you created.

9. At the *Select point on surface* prompt, select a point near the center of the surface, as shown in Figure 4–48, to add control vertices in the U-direction.

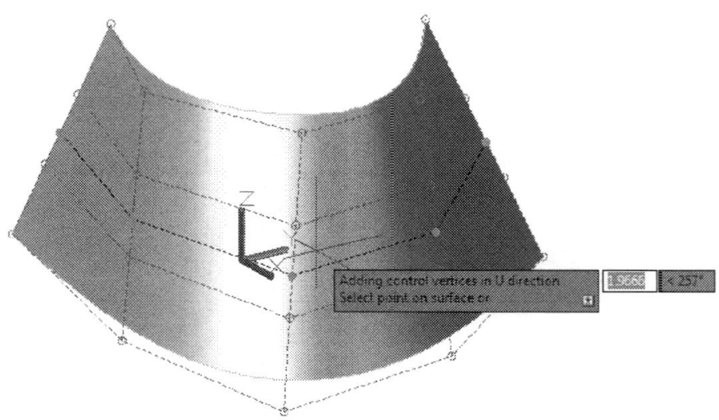

Figure 4–48

10. Select the NURBS surface to display the control vertice grips.

11. Select the control vertice grip that is next to the left bottom most edge grip, and move it away from the surface, as shown in Figure 4–49. Note that a portion of the surface that was near the control vertex also moved in the direction of the control vertex, but not all the way to it. It does not touch the control vertex point.

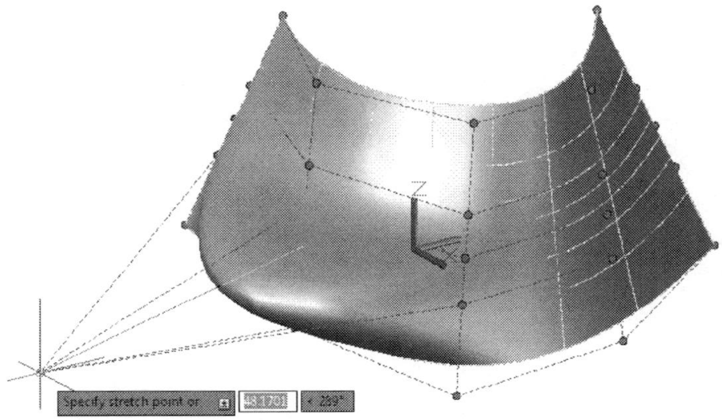

Figure 4–49

12. Press <Esc> to discard the move or undo the previous control vertex modification if you moved the control vertex out.

13. In the *Surface* tab>Control Vertices panel, click (CV Edit Bar) and select the NURBS surface.

14. At the *Select point on NURBS surface* prompt, select a point near the same control vertice point that you just modified, near the bottom left of the surface, as shown in Figure 4–50.

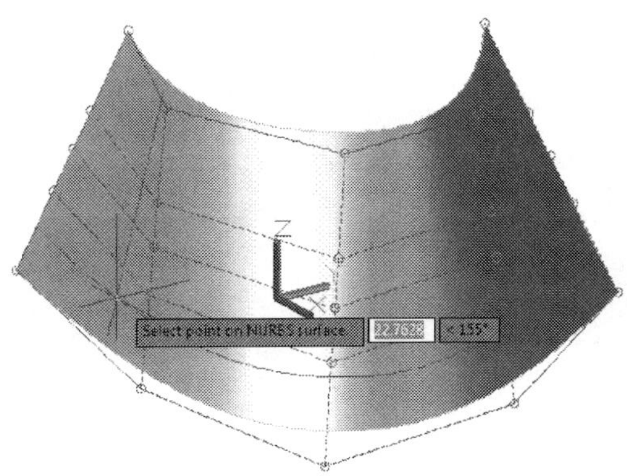

Figure 4–50

15. At the *Select a grip on the edit bar* prompt, select the square grip at the control vertex point's UCS origin point, move the cursor out away from the surface, as shown in Figure 4–51, and select a point. Note that the surface touches the point.

16. At the *Select a grip on the edit bar* prompt, select the triangle grip 9 (downward pointing arrow), and select **Tangent Direction**, as shown in Figure 4–52.

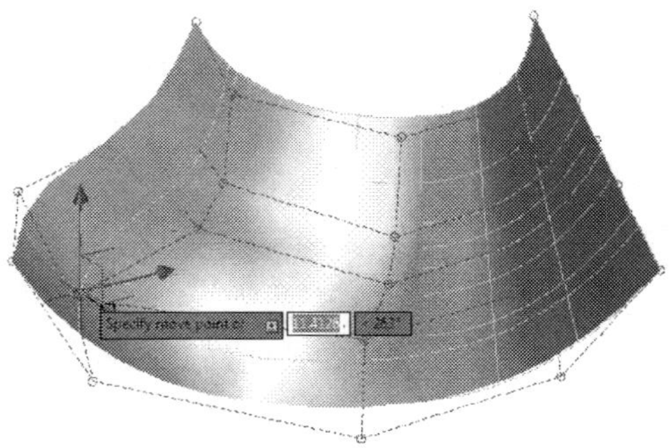

Figure 4–51

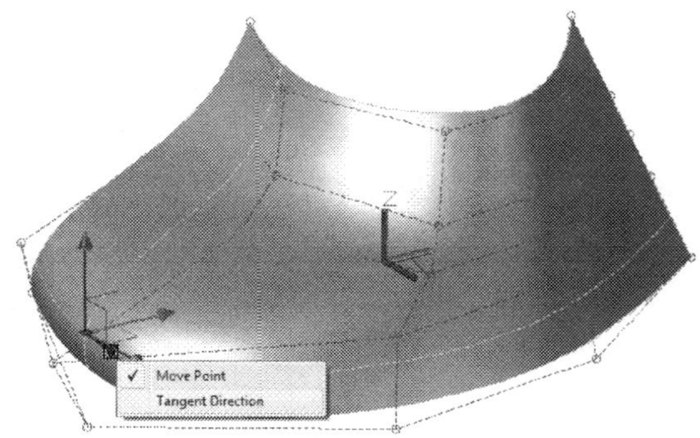

Figure 4–52

17. Select the square grip at the tangent point's UCS origin point, and move the cursor around to display real time previews of the surface at different tangencies at that point. Do not select a point. Press <Esc> to cancel the change in tangency direction.

18. Select the magnitude arrow grip (upward pointing), and move the cursor back and forth along the tangency axis to display real time previews of the surface at different degrees of magnitude of tangencies at that point. Do not select a point. Press <Esc> to cancel the change in tangency magnitude.

19. Press <Enter> to exit the command.

20. Save and close the file.

Chapter Review Questions

1. Which of the following enables you to create a loft?
    a. Cross-sections (profiles) only
    b. Guides only
    c. Paths only
    d. A mix of Guides and Paths
2. Which of the following correctly describes the procedure for creating a helix?
    a. Select a center point for the base, specify its radius, specify the height, and specify the top radius.
    b. Select a center point for the base, specify its radius, specify the top radius, and specify the height.
    c. Specify its radius, specify the top radius, specify the height, and select the center point for the base.
3. How do you specify the axis using the **Revolve** command? (Select all that apply.)
    a. Select an edge of the profile.
    b. Pick start and end points for the axis.
    c. Specify the X-, Y-, or Z axis.
4. When creating an extrusion, which of the following object types creates a surface?
    a. Region
    b. Circle
    c. Line
    d. Face
5. What type of object is created using the **Presspull** command?
    a. Bounded Area
    b. Mesh
    c. Surface
    d. Solid

6. You cannot modify sweep objects with grips.
    a. True
    b. False

Command Summary

All ribbon names reference the 3D Modeling workspace.

Button	Command	Location
	**3D Polyline**	• **Ribbon:** *Home* tab>Draw panel
	**Add Control Vertices**	• **Ribbon:** *Surface* tab>Control Vertices panel
	**Control Vertices Edit Bar**	• **Ribbon:** *Surface* tab>Control Vertices panel
	**Extrude**	• **Ribbon:** *Home* tab>Modeling panel or *Solid* tab>Solid panel
	**Helix**	• **Ribbon:** *Home* tab>expanded Draw panel
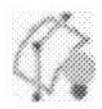	**Hide Control Vertices**	• **Ribbon:** *Surface* tab>Control Vertices panel
	**Loft**	• **Ribbon:** *Home* tab>Modeling panel or *Solid* tab>Solid panel
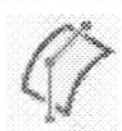	**NURBS Creation**	• **Ribbon:** *Surface* tab>Create panel
	**Presspull**	• **Ribbon:** *Home* tab>Modeling panel or *Solid* tab>Solid panel
	**Remove Control Vertices**	• **Ribbon:** *Surface* tab>Control Vertices panel
	**Revolve**	• **Ribbon:** *Home* tab>Modeling panel or *Solid* tab>Solid panel
	**Show Control Vertices**	• **Ribbon:** *Surface* tab>Control Vertices panel
	**Sweep**	• **Ribbon:** *Home* tab>Modeling panel or *Solid* tab>Solid panel

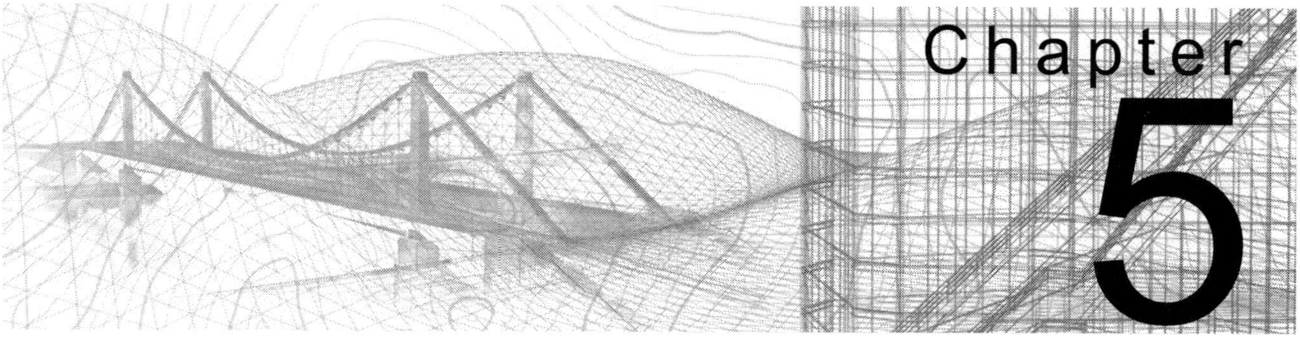

Modifying in 3D Space

In this chapter, you learn how to use the 3D Gizmo tools to move and rotate in 3D space, to use Align and 3D Align, and to use 3D Move, 3D Rotate, 3D Mirror, and 3D Array on objects in 3D space.

Learning Objectives in This Chapter

- Modify objects in 3D using the Gizmo tool.
- Align objects in 3D space by selecting points on other objects to move and rotate them at the same time.
- Modify 3D objects using 3D modify commands.

5.1 3D Gizmo Tools

3D Gizmos can be used with both 2D and 3D objects.

You can use grips to move and rotate objects in 2D space without starting a specific command. In 3D, there is a powerful 3D tool called a Gizmo that works in the 2D work plane and in 3D. It can be used to move, rotate, and scale objects, as shown in Figure 5–1.

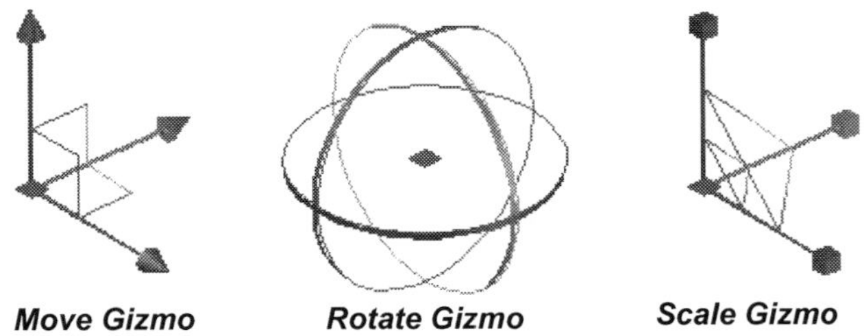

Figure 5–1

- When you select objects in a 3D view, the UCS icon turns into the **Gizmo** tool. This enables you to limit the movement of objects along an axis or plane and to rotate in 3D space. When you hover the cursor over a Gizmo, it automatically jumps to a location or vertex grip. It can also be used as a grip without being moved to another grip.
- The color-coded icon displays in the current UCS. Red indicates the X-axis, green the Y-axis, and blue the Z-axis.
- As you move the cursor over one of the axes on the **Gizmo** tool, the active axis highlights in gold and displays a guideline in the axis color. If you move the cursor over a plane, the plane highlights in gold, as shown in Figure 5–2.

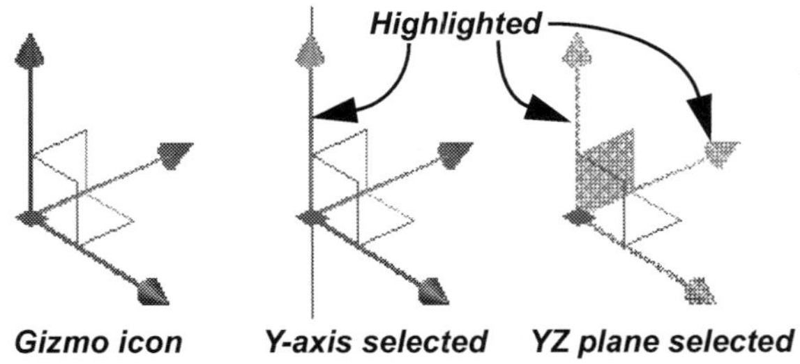

Figure 5–2

How To: Move, Rotate, or Scale Using the Gizmo Tool

*When a **Gizmo** operation is in progress and you need to switch to a different Gizmo, press <Spacebar> or <Enter> to cycle through the options.*

1. In a 3D view, select the objects you want to modify.
2. Move the **Gizmo** tool to a base point if required.
3. Select an axis or plane on the **Gizmo** tool.
   - To move an object, move the cursor along the axis or in the plane. You can type coordinates or select a point to end the command.
   - To rotate an object, move the cursor along the axis, as shown in Figure 5–3. Type an angle value or select a point to finish the command.
   - To scale an object, select the center triangular plane between the three axes in the **Gizmo** tool, and move the cursor towards or away from the center of the Gizmo.

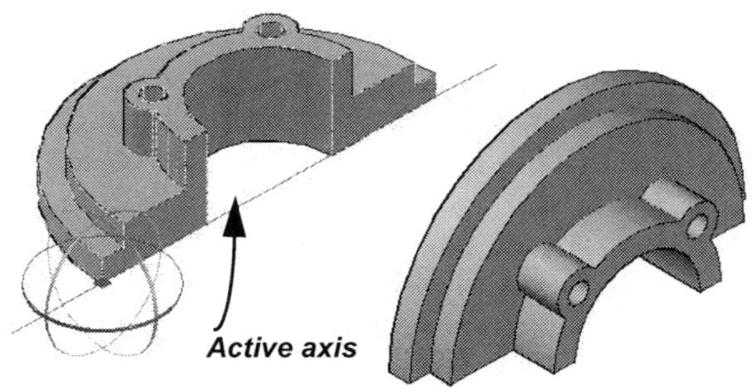

Figure 5–3

If you hover the cursor over a location grip on solid primitives, or vertex grips on paths and profiles, the **Gizmo** tool automatically jumps to that point.

If you want to set the base for the **Gizmo** tool before selecting an axis or plane, click on the center box of the **Gizmo** tool. It moves freely and can be placed anywhere in the drawing, as shown in Figure 5–4.

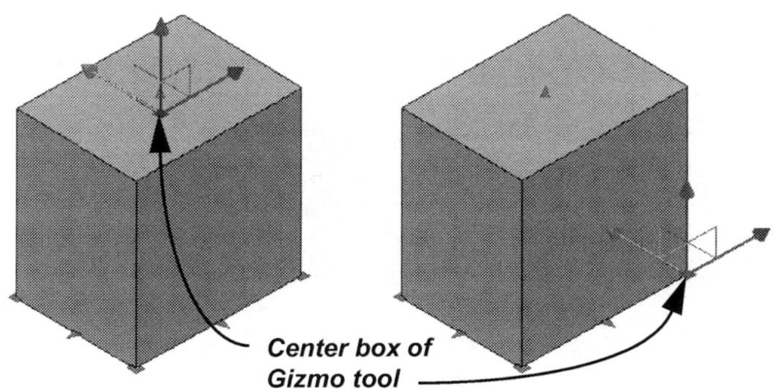

Figure 5–4

While you are using **Gizmo** tools, the options **Base point**, **Copy**, **Undo**, and **Exit** are available at the Command Line. If you are using the **Rotate Gizmo**, you can use the **Reference** option to set the rotation angle.

Right-click on a Gizmo to switch to a different Gizmo, relocate the Gizmo, align the Gizmo with a specific UCS, create a custom Gizmo, and reselect the Dynamic UCS, as shown in Figure 5–5.

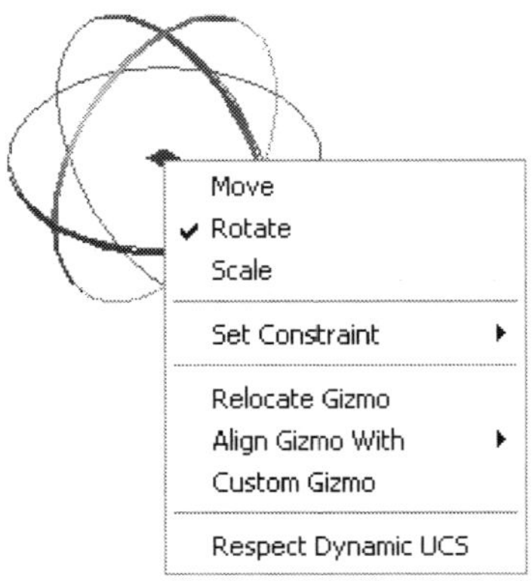

Figure 5–5

You can control which default gizmo displays when you select an object's grip. In the *Home* tab>Selection panel, expand

 (Move Gizmo) and select an option, as shown in Figure 5–6. The Selection panel is also available in the *Solid* and *Mesh* tabs.

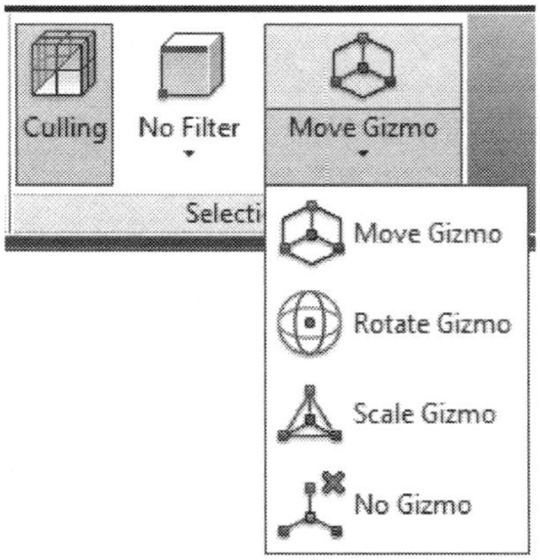

Figure 5–6

Practice 5a

3D Gizmo Tools

Practice Objective

- Rotate various 3D parts in correct orientation using the 3D Gizmo tool.

In this practice, you will use the **3D Gizmo** tools to move, rotate, and assemble some parts, as shown in Figure 5–7.

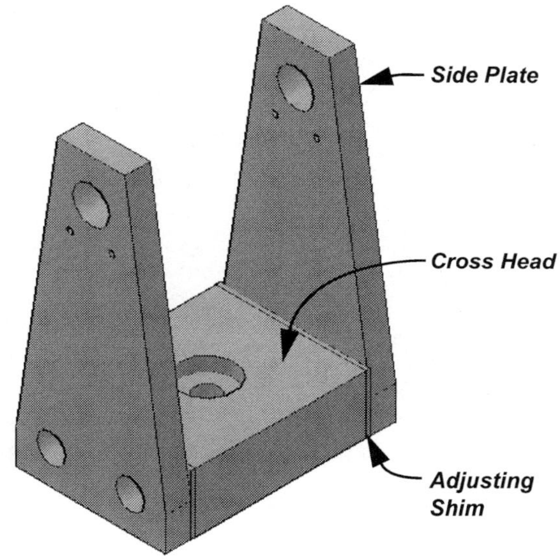

Figure 5–7

1. Open **Trolley-Assembly.dwg**.

*The Visual Style has been changed to **Realistic**.*

2. Select the adjusting shim and hover your cursor over the right corner square grip, as shown in Figure 5–8. The **Gizmo** tool moves to this location.

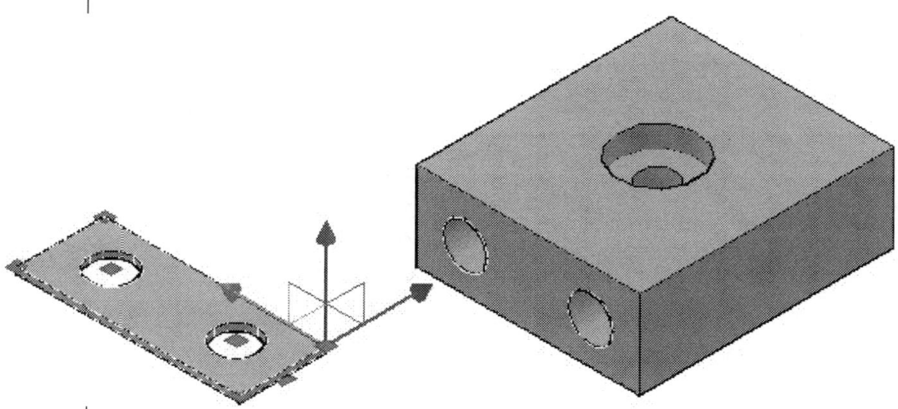

Figure 5–8

3. Move the cursor to the green Y-axis and select it.
4. Press the <Spacebar> to change to the **Rotate Gizmo**.
5. Rotate the shim **270** degrees around the axis, as shown in Figure 5–9.

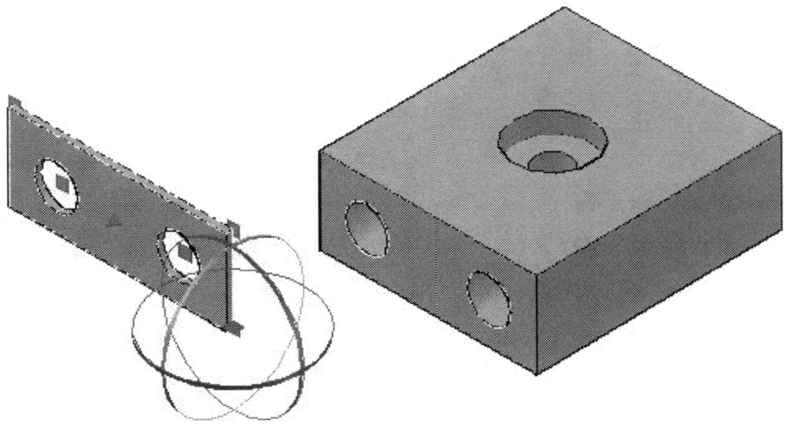

Figure 5–9

6. Use the standard **Move** command to place the shim against the cross head as shown in Figure 5–10. Make a copy of the shim on the other side of the cross head.

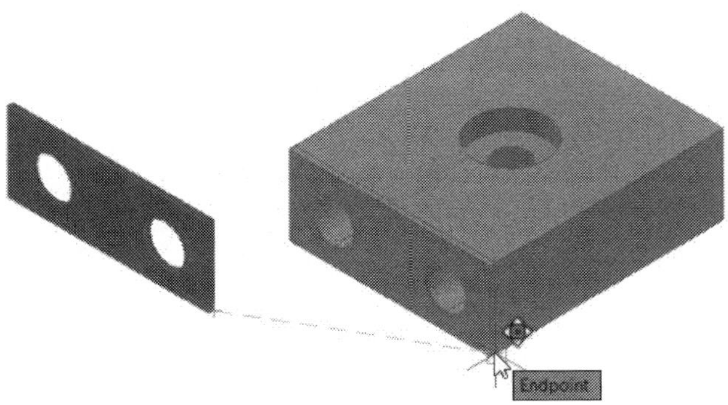

Figure 5–10

7. Select the side plate. It has a single grip because it is a composite solid.
8. In the **Gizmo** tool, select its square grip and drag it to the bottom (middle) of the side plate, as shown in Figure 5–11.

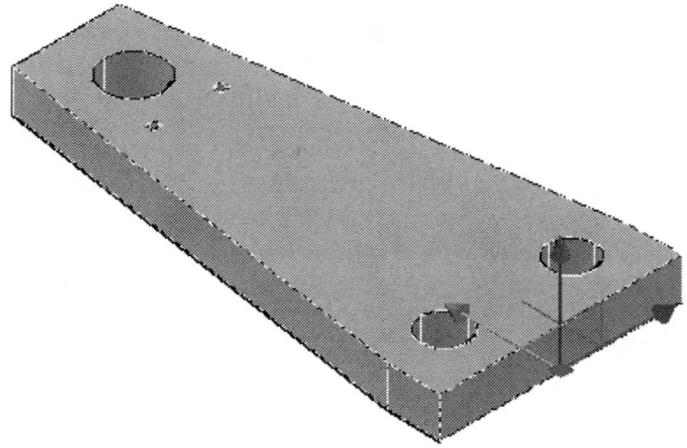

Figure 5–11

9. Select the red X-axis and press the <Spacebar> to change to the **Rotate Gizmo**.

The rotation direction depends on the movement of your cursor.

10. Rotate the object by **90** degrees in the upward direction, as shown in Figure 5–12.

11. Select the blue ring of the Rotate Gizmo and rotate the object by **90** or **270** degrees, as shown in Figure 5–12.

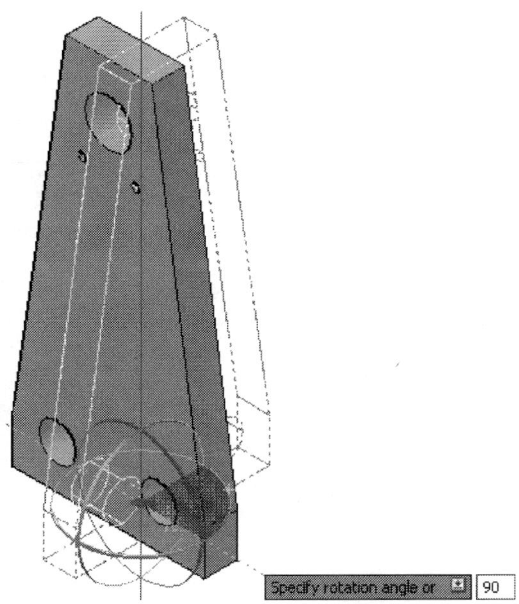

Figure 5–12

12. Move and copy the side plate to each side of the cross head on the outside of the adjusting shims.

13. Save and close the drawing.

5.2 Aligning Objects in 3D Space

The **Align** and **3D Align** commands enable you to move and rotate objects in 3D space by selecting points on other objects. They both adjust objects so that they are oriented correctly, as shown with the table top in Figure 5–13. However, they use different methods and have potentially different outcomes, so you should understand the benefits of each.

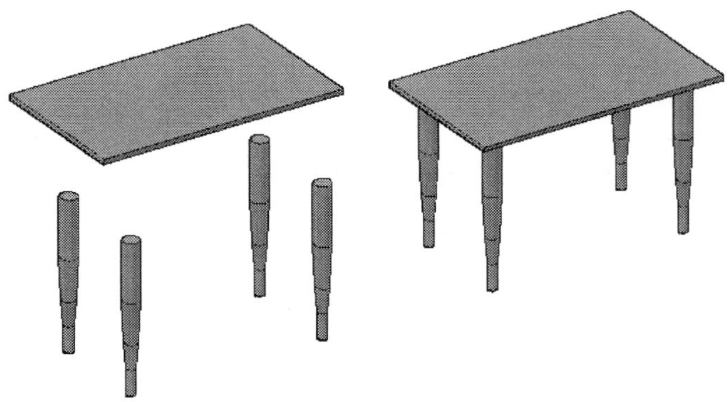

Figure 5–13

Align	Select a point on the source object and then select a point on the destination object, for up to three sets of points. It is not displayed until all of the selections have been completed. You can scale the source object.
3D Align	Align the source object to a face on the destination object or select up to three points on a source object and then three points on a destination object. Objects move dynamically, but you cannot scale the source object.

Align Command

The **Align** command enables you to move and rotate objects in 3D space with a single command, regardless of the placement of the current UCS. The move is defined by one, two, or three source and destination points. The command prompts you to select the objects to move and then prompts you to select three source and three destination points.

How To: Align Objects with Alignment Points

1. In the *Home* tab>expanded Modify panel, click (Align).
2. Select the object(s) to be aligned/moved and press <Enter>.
3. Specify the first source point and then select the first destination point.
   - If you press <Enter> the object is moved from the source point to the destination point, as shown in Figure 5–14.

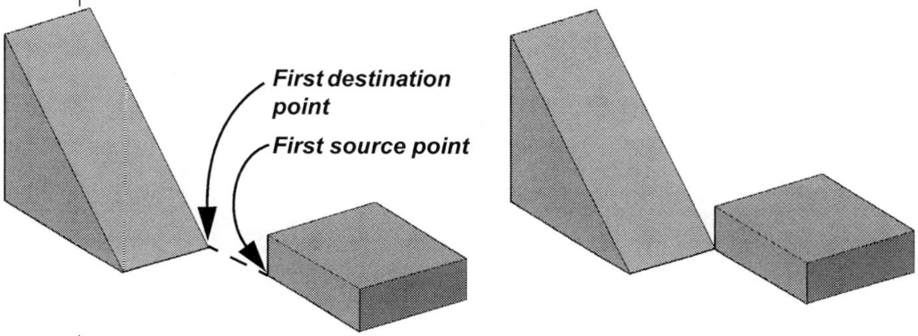

Figure 5–14

4. Specify the second source point and the second destination point.
   - If you press <Enter> at this time, the object is moved and rotated, as shown in Figure 5–15. You are also prompted to decide whether you want to scale the object based on the alignment points.

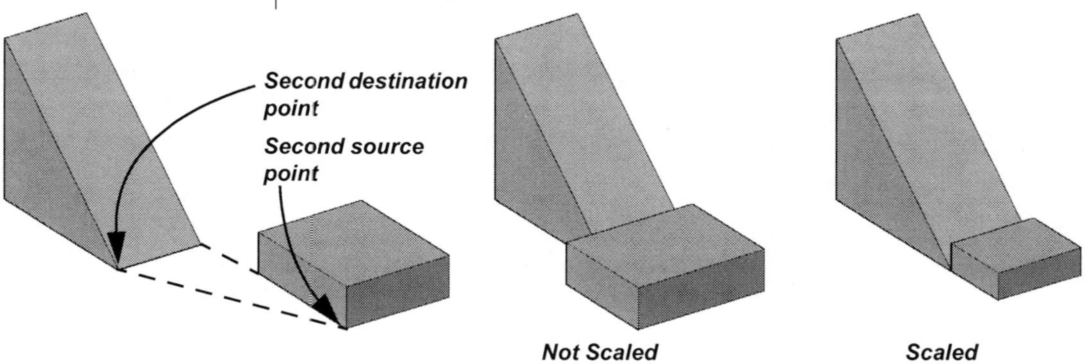

Figure 5–15

5. Specify the third source point and the third destination point and press <Enter>.
   - When you select the third set of points, the object is moved and rotated in two directions based on the plane specified by the points, as shown in Figure 5–16.

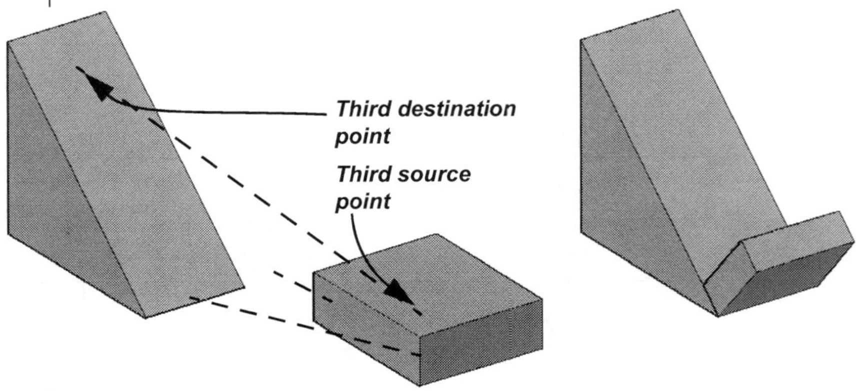

Figure 5–16

3D Align Command

The **3D Align** command enables you to mate surfaces and align edges in three dimensions. You can align objects to a face or by points. Any combination of one source point and one, two, or three destination points can be selected.

How To: Align Objects to a Face

1. In the *Home* tab>Modify panel, click (3D Align).
2. Select the object(s) to be aligned/moved and press <Enter>.
3. Select the point(s) on the source object and press <Enter>.
   - You can select one, two, or three points to define the plane on the source object.

4. Hover the cursor over the destination object. The source object moves dynamically with the cursor. As you cross a face, the source object automatically aligns with the face, as shown in Figure 5–17.

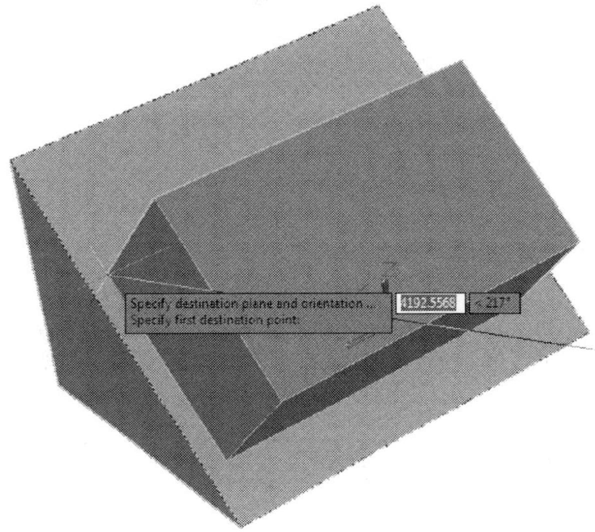

Figure 5–17

5. Click to place the object.

How To: Align Objects with Points

1. In the *Home* tab>Modify panel, click (3D Align).
2. Select the object(s) to align and press <Enter>.
3. Select point(s) on the source object and press <Enter>. You can select one, two, or three points to define the plane on the source object.
4. Select the first, second, and third destination points. The source objects move dynamically as you select the points.

Practice 5b

Aligning Objects in 3D

Practice Objective

- Move and rotate 3D objects to correctly align them using the **Align** and **3D Align** commands.

*10*In this practice, you will use **Align** and **3D Align** to complete the bracket part, as shown in Figure 5–18.

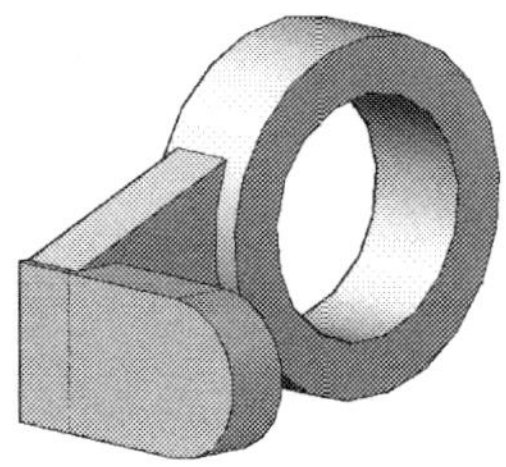

Figure 5–18

1. Open **Bracket.dwg**.
2. On the *Home* tab>expanded Modify panel, click (Align). Select the gray cylinder and press <Enter>.

*To access the quadrants of the cylinder, type **QUAD** or toggle on the **Quadrant** object snap.*

- For the first source and destination points, use the left side quadrant point of the cylinder and top corner endpoint of the cube, as shown in Figure 5–19.
- For the second source and destination points, use the right side quadrant point of the cylinder and bottom corner endpoint of the cube, as shown in Figure 5–19.
- For the third source and destination points, use the center of the cylinder and midpoint of the cube, as shown in Figure 5–19.
- The cylinder and the cube are placed as shown in Figure 5–19.

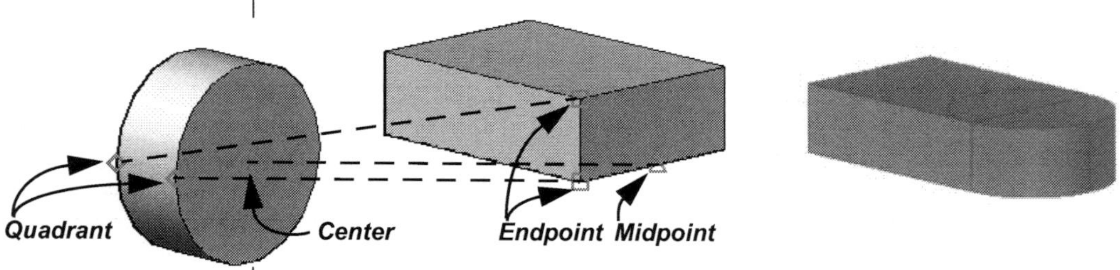

Figure 5–19

3. Union the two gray objects.

If the wireframe is hard to see against the white background, change the color of the layer 0 to a darker color.

4. Change *Visual style* to **2D Wireframe**.

Toggle on Polar Tracking.

5. On the *Home* tab> Modify panel, click (3D Align) and align the object that you created in Step 3 to the unfinished bracket, as shown in Figure 5–18. (**Hint:** Select the object (union) and use two source points on this object as shown in Figure 5–20. Press <Enter>. Select three destination points on the unfinished bracket as shown in Figure 5–20. Select the last two destination points along the respective Polar Tracking lines.)

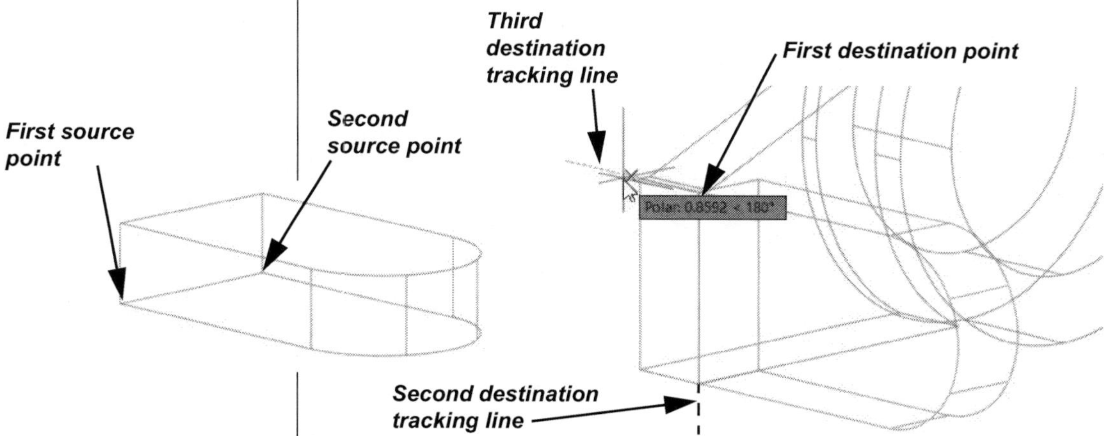

Figure 5–20

6. Change *Visual style* to **Shades of Gray**.

7. Save and close the drawing.

5.3 3D Modify Commands

Just as **Align** has a corresponding **3D Align** tool, several other modify commands have related 3D versions: **3D Move**, **3D Rotate**, **3D Scale**, **3D Mirror**, and **3D Array**. In many cases, you can use the standard commands with Dynamic UCS, but these commands provide an alternative method.

3D Move and 3D Rotate

You can use the **3D Gizmo** tool or the **3D Move** and **3D Rotate** commands to move and rotate objects.

How To: Move Objects in 3D Space

1. In the *Home* tab>Modify panel, click (3D Move).
2. Select the objects to be moved and press <Enter>.
3. Specify a base point.
4. Specify the second point.

How To: Rotate Objects in 3D Space

1. In the *Home* tab>Modify panel, click (3D Rotate).
2. Select the objects to be rotated and press <Enter>.
3. Specify a base point about which to rotate. The **Gizmo** tool moves to this location.
4. Select the axis or plane about which you want to rotate.

Type an angle value or specify an angle start point. When selecting the start point, you must also select an end point to freely rotate the object.

Hint: Additional Methods for Moving in 3D

To move objects up or down in the Z-direction, use the standard **Move** command with Polar Tracking or Ortho on. When you are prompted for the second point, move the cursor in the Z-axis and type the height value.

To move an object to a specific coordinate point, use the standard **Move** command and select the base point. When you are prompted for the second point, type the number (#) sign in front of the coordinate (**#0,0,0**). By default, Dynamic Input assumes you are using a relative coordinate, which does not move if you type **0,0,0**.

3D Scale

You can use the **3D Gizmo** tool or the **3D Scale** command to scale objects.

How To: Scale Objects in 3D Space

1. In the *Home* tab>Modify panel, click (3D Scale).
2. Select the objects to scale and press <Enter>.
3. Specify a base point. The **Gizmo** tool moves to this point.
4. Select the axis or plane along which you want to scale.
5. Specify the scale factor.

Mirroring Objects in 3D

The **Mirror** command works with 3D objects. The **3D Mirror** command enables you to mirror a selected object about a 3D plane, as shown in Figure 5–21, rather than about 2D points. You can mirror about the XY, YZ, and XZ planes, a 2D object, the view plane, or three points that you select to define a plane.

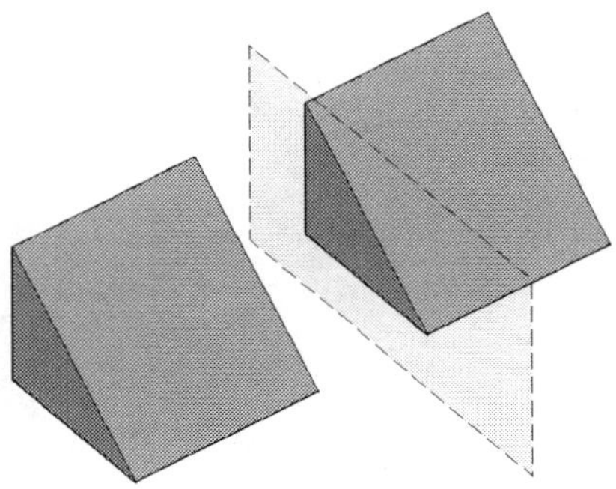

Figure 5–21

How To: Mirror Objects in 3D Space

1. In the *Home* tab>Modify panel, click (3D Mirror).
2. Select the object(s) to be mirrored and press <Enter>.
3. Define the mirror plane using the mirror plane options.
4. Select whether or not you want to delete the source objects.

Mirror Plane Options

Object	Prompts you to select an object. The mirroring plane is aligned with the plane of the selected object. Valid objects include: • **Circle:** The plane of the circle. • **Arc:** The plane of the arc. • **Pline:** The plane containing the 2D polyline.

Last	Uses the last mirroring plane that you defined.
Zaxis	Prompts you to select two points. The mirroring plane is the plane specified by a point on the plane and a point on the plane's normal (perpendicular to the plane).
View	Prompts you to select a point. The mirroring plane is created perpendicular to the view direction and passes through the selected point.
XY/YZ/ZX Plane	Prompts you to select a point. The mirroring plane is created parallel to the selected standard plane (XY/YZ/ZX) of the current UCS and passes through the selected point.
3points	Prompts you to select three points. The mirroring plane passes through the selected points.

Arraying Objects in 3D

You might want to draw a polar array with its center axis at an angle other than the Z-direction, or draw a rectangular array that includes the third dimension. For example, 3D polar arrays can be used to draw a turbine or a bolt circle and 3D rectangular arrays can be used to draw a series of columns and stacks of boxes, as shown in Figure 5–22.

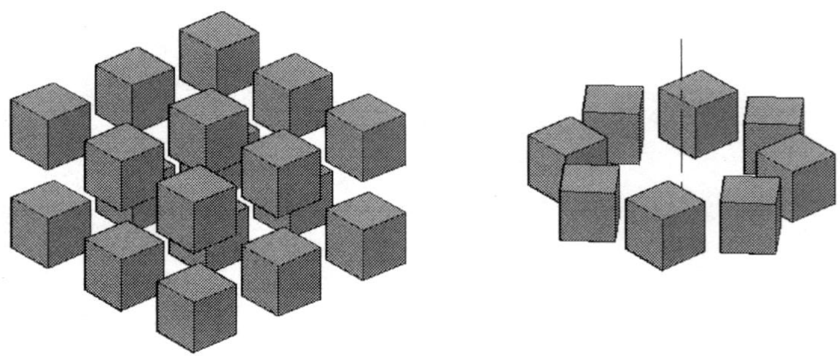

Figure 5–22

How To: Create a Rectangular 3D Array

1. At the Command Line, type **3D Array**.
2. Select the objects to be arrayed.
3. When prompted for the type of array, select **Rectangular**.
4. Enter the number of rows, number of columns, and number of levels. Rows are in the Y-direction, columns are in the X-direction, and levels are in the Z-direction.
5. Specify the distance between the rows, columns, and levels. You can do this by typing the coordinate values or selecting two points.

How To: Create a Polar 3D Array

The **Polar** option in the **3D Array** command enables you to select two points to define the axis of rotation for the array. The AutoCAD® software automatically changes the UCS based on those points, creates a regular polar array, and then changes back to the previous UCS.

- It might be easier to change the UCS and create a normal polar array.

1. Start the **3D Array** command.
2. Select the objects to be arrayed.
3. When prompted for the type of array, select **Polar**.
4. Specify the number of objects in the array and the angle to fill.
5. Specify whether or not you want to rotate the arrayed objects.
6. Specify the center point of the array and a second point on the axis of rotation.

Hint: Enhanced Associative Array

Use the enhanced Array commands (**arrayrect**, **arraypolar**, and **arraypath** in the *Home* tab>Modify panel) for creating associative 2D or 3D rectangular, polar, or path arrays respectively.

- Levels indicate the number of objects of the array in the Z-direction.
- The entire enhanced array selection set is treated as a single element.
- Selecting the single enhanced array selection set displays the *Array* contextual tab, as shown in Figure 5–23, enabling various types of editing.

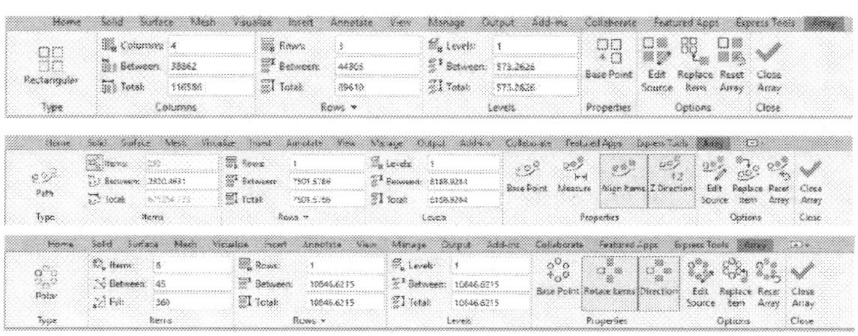

Figure 5–23

Practice 5c

Working with 3D Modify Commands

Practice Objectives

- Duplicate objects around two origin planes using the **3D Mirror** command.
- Create an array of 3D columns.

*10*In this practice, you will use (3D Mirror) to duplicate parts around the YZ plane and ZX plane, as shown in Figure 5–24. You will also use **3D Array** to create columns in a 3D building plan.

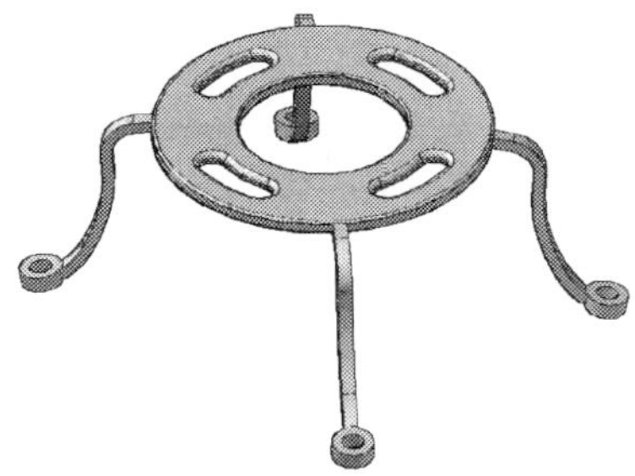

Figure 5–24

Task 1 - Work with 3D Mirror.

1. Open **Plant-Stand.dwg**.
2. In the *Home* tab>Modify panel, click (3D Mirror).
3. Select the cyan plate and magenta leg as the objects to mirror and press <Enter>.
4. Right-click and select **YZ**. Accept the default base point of **0,0,0**. Do not delete the source objects.
5. Click (3D Mirror), select all of the objects, and mirror them about the **ZX** plane. Accept the default base point of **0,0,0**. Do not delete the source objects.
6. Union the four pieces of the circular plate. Do not include the legs in the union.
7. Save and close the drawing.

Task 2 - Work with 3D Array.

1. Open **Bldg.dwg**.

Draw the box in Top view.

2. Click (Box) and create a **100' x 80' x 1'** solid box. This represents a floor slab.
3. Zoom Extents and Orbit around to display the thickness of the slab.
4. Click (Cylinder) and draw a column with a *radius* of **8"** and *height* of **8'-0"**. Center it **10'** over and **10'** up from the lower left corner of the slab.
5. In the *Home* tab>Modify panel, click (Rectangular Array). Select the cylinder and press <Enter>. In the *Array Creation* contextual tab, enter *Columns* as **9** and *Between* as **10'**; *Rows* as **7** and *Between* as **10'**; *Levels* as **2** and *Between* as **9'**, as shown in Figure 5–25. Click **Close Array** to complete the command.

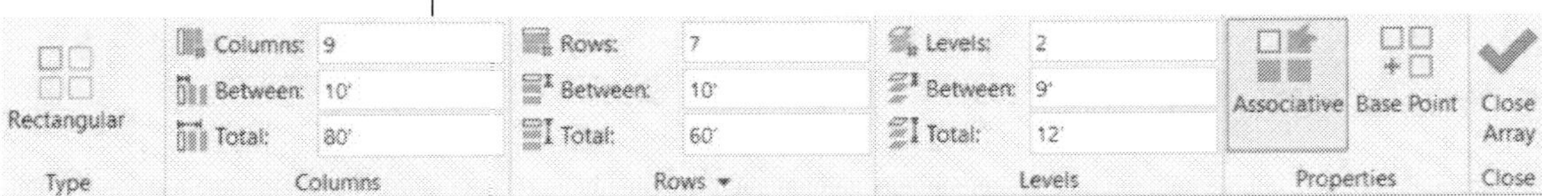

Figure 5–25

6. Copy the slab twice to create new floors above the original, **9'-0"** up from each other, as shown in Figure 5–26.

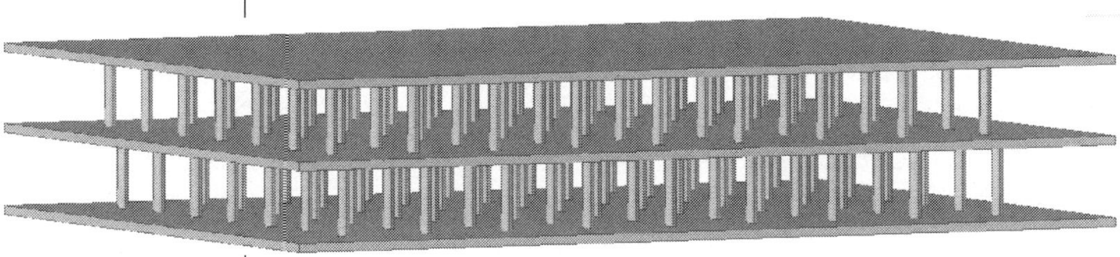

Figure 5–26

7. Orbit around to view both layers of columns.
8. Save and close the drawing.

Practice 5d Architectural Project - Gallery

Practice Objective

- Assemble a building using 3D objects created with a variety of 3D tools.

In this practice, you will create a massing study using solids built from profiles and paths, as shown in Figure 5–27. You can also use 3D modify tools to place the objects in the correct locations.

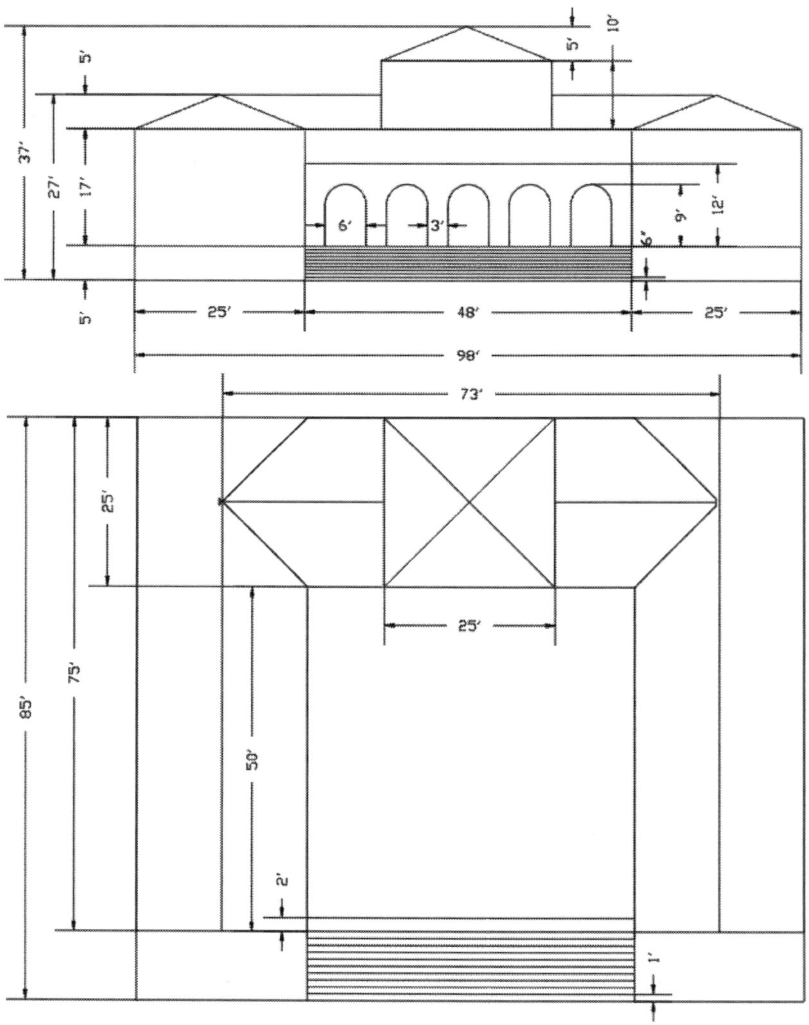

Figure 5–27

This is an empty drawing that uses architectural units.

1. Open **Gallery.dwg**. Use solids, profiles, and paths to construct the building. An isometric view is shown in Figure 5–28 to help you visualize the design.

Construction Tips

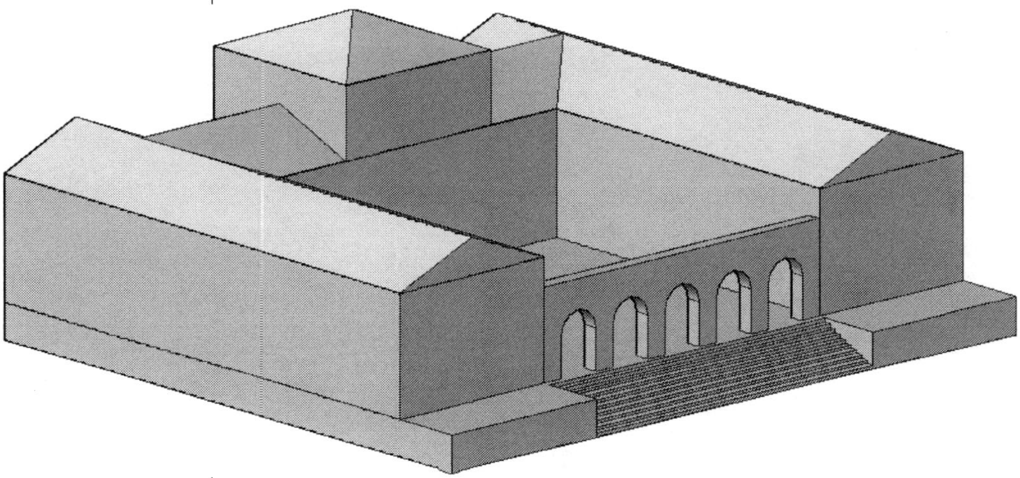

Figure 5–28

- The stairs are **1' wide** and **6" high**. One way to construct them is to create a 2D polyline of the side view and extrude it.
- You can create the arcade in the top view and then use **3D Rotate** to set it to the correct orientation.

Chapter Review Questions

1. Which of the following is one way in which the **Gizmo** tool can be used to modify an object?
    a. Stretch
    b. Array
    c. Scale
    d. Mirror
2. What is a difference between the **Align** and **3D Align** commands?
    a. The **3D Align** command enables you to scale the source object.
    b. The **Align** command enables you to align 2D objects only.
    c. The **3D Align** command enables you to mate surfaces and align edges in three dimensions.
    d. There is no difference between them.
3. You can use the **Move** command to move objects in the Z-direction.
    a. True
    b. False
4. When creating a Polar array, which of the following options is available only with the **3D Array** command?
    a. The angle to fill
    b. The number of objects in the array
    c. The axis of rotation
    d. The center point
5. In the **3D Mirror** command, which option do you use to mirror an object about a mirroring plane that is created parallel to the selected plane?
    a. Last
    b. View
    c. Object
    d. XY/YZ/ZX Plane

6. When using the Gizmo, which key enables you to switch between the Move, Rotate, and Scale gizmos?
   a. <Ctrl>
   b. <Shift>
   c. <Spacebar>
   d. <Esc>

Command Summary

All ribbon names reference the 3D Modeling workspace.

Button	Command	Location
	**3D Align**	• **Ribbon:** *Home* tab>Modify panel
NA	**3D Array**	• **Command Prompt:** 3darray
	**3D Mirror**	• **Ribbon:** *Home* tab>Modify panel
	**3D Move**	• **Ribbon:** *Home* tab>Modify panel
	**3D Rotate**	• **Ribbon:** *Home* tab>Modify panel
	**3D Scale**	• **Ribbon:** *Home* tab>Modify panel
	**Align**	• **Ribbon:** *Home tab*>expanded Modify panel

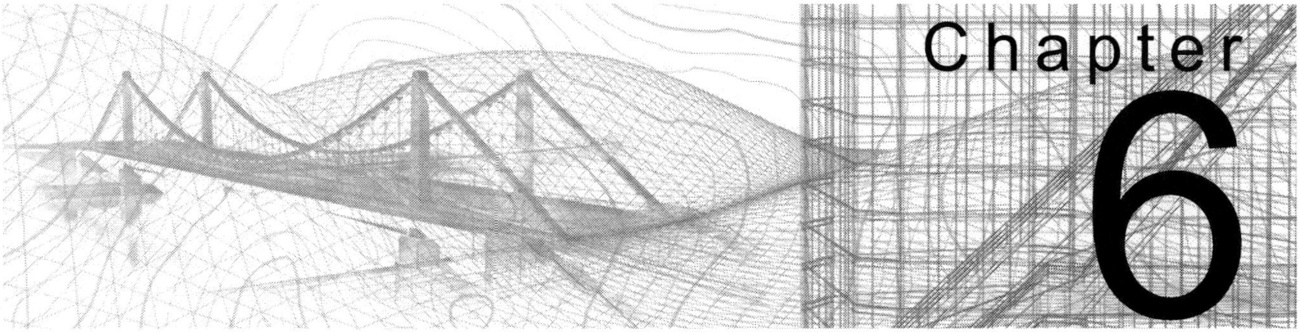

Advanced Solid Editing

In this chapter, you learn how to edit components of solids using grips, edit faces of solids using the solid editing tools, and to place fillets and chamfers on solids.

Learning Objectives in This Chapter

- Edit individual edges, faces, vertices, and parts of composite solids using grips, Properties, and other editing commands.
- Edit the faces of solids using various editing commands.
- Create beveled or rounded edges on solids.

6.1 Editing Components of Solids

Moving and rotating entire solids in 3D space is helpful, but you can go further and edit edges, faces, vertices, and even parts of composite solids, as shown in Figure 6–1. Once you have selected the objects, you can use grips, Properties, and other editing commands to modify the objects.

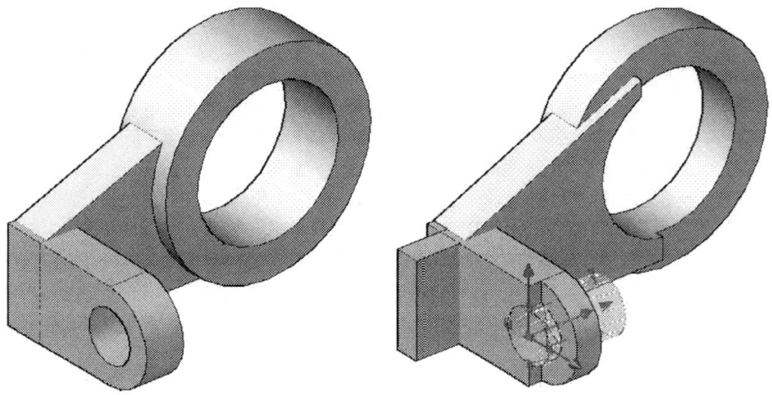

Figure 6–1

- If you edit parts of solid primitives, they do not retain their geometry information, such as length, width, or radius.
- Composite solids and their subobjects can also be modified to the face or edge level. Hold <Ctrl> and select the faces or edges after you have selected the subobject.
- Use the Subobject Selection Filter to select certain types of subobjects. Access it in the shortcut menu in an open area with no objects selected, or on the *Home* tab>Selection panel. The options available are No Filter, Vertex, Edge, Face, Solid History, and Drawing View Component.

How To: Select a Face, Edge, Vertex, or Sub-object of a Composite Solid

1. Hold <Ctrl> as you move the cursor over the solid. The various subobjects highlight as you move the cursor, as shown in Figure 6–2. While holding <Ctrl>, click to select the subobject(s).

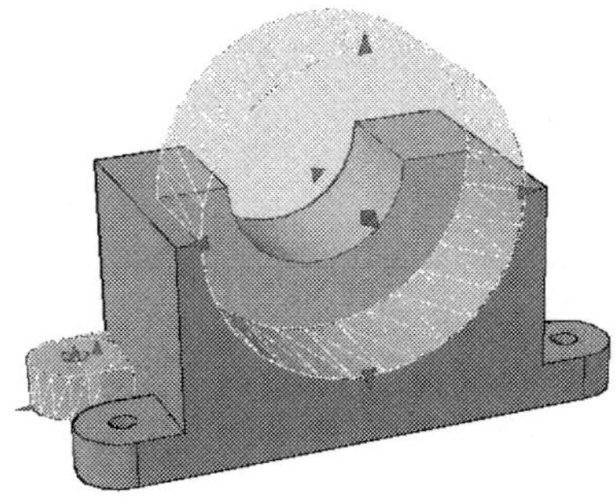

Figure 6–2

2. When the subobjects have been selected, hold <Ctrl> and select the faces and edges that you want to modify, as shown in Figure 6–3.

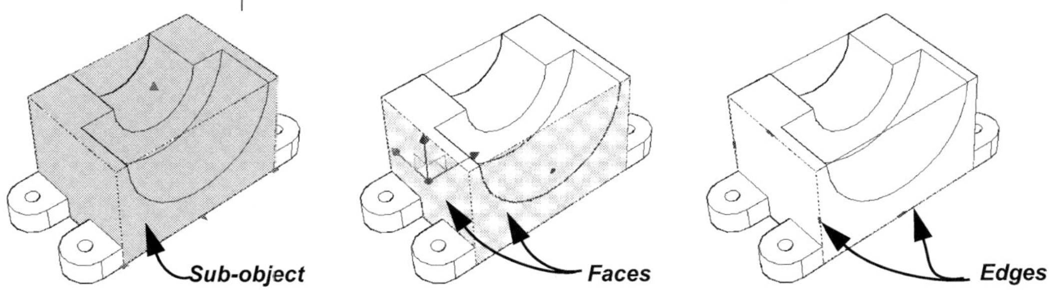

Figure 6–3

3. Modify the selected objects with their associated grips.

- To select a vertex, move the cursor over the vertex and click on it. The vertex does not highlight before you select it, as shown in Figure 6–4.

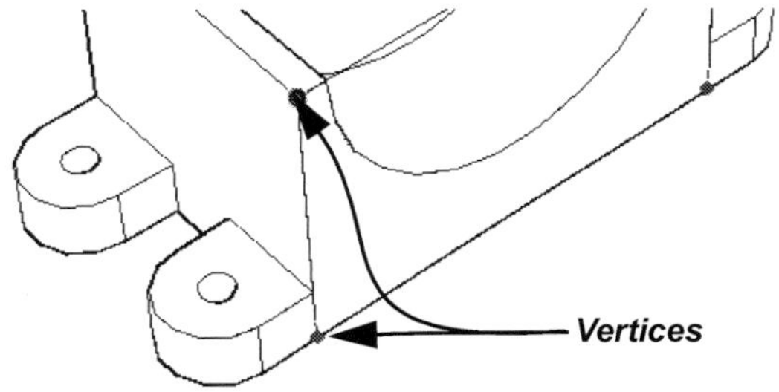

Figure 6–4

- You can select as many subobjects as required in one editing session.
- Use <Ctrl>+<Shift> to remove an object, face, vertex, or edge from the selection set.
- When individual subobjects of the solid, you can use the standard **Scale**, **Move**, **Erase**, and **Rotate** commands to edit them. For example, you might want to delete a hole in a composite solid, as shown in Figure 6–5. Hold <Ctrl>, select the subobject that creates the hole, and press <Delete> or start the **Erase** command. This process works with any face, vertex, or edge, as long as the gap can be filled.

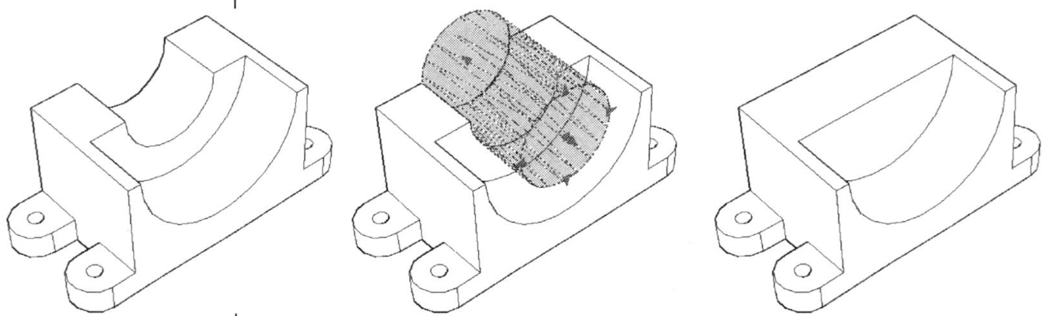

Figure 6–5

Hint: Solid History

If the Solid History is set to **Record** (SolidHist=1), it remembers the various component solids that make up the composite solid. This enables you to use <Ctrl> to select subobjects and manipulate them. If the Solid History is set to **None** (SolidHist=0), you cannot select subobjects, but you can edit the faces and edges of the composite solid.

- You can use Properties to modify the Solid History of solids once they have been created. If you set the *History* to **None**, you cannot restore the record on the existing solid. If you set the *History* back to **Record** and add other composite objects, those subobjects are accessible.

Editing Faces

Individual faces of solids can be modified with the ● grip, as shown in Figure 6–6. You can also use **PressPull**, **Extrude**, and **Revolve** on some faces.

Figure 6–6

- When you select the ● grip, you can stretch, rotate, and scale the face, or move and mirror the entire solid.
- If you select an axis or a plane of the grip tool, you can stretch, move, or rotate the face along the axis or plane.
- The **Presspull** command works on any planar (flat) face. It extrudes the face, keeping the object as one with the original solid. You can only extrude and revolve faces on solid primitives. The new extrusion or revolve is a separate object. You cannot extrude a sweep or a non-planar face (such as the curved section of a cylinder).

Editing Edges

Individual edges of solids can be modified with the ▬ grip and the grip tools. The process is similar to editing faces, except that the **Stretch** option only moves the selected edge while the rest of the edges stay in place, as shown in Figure 6–7.

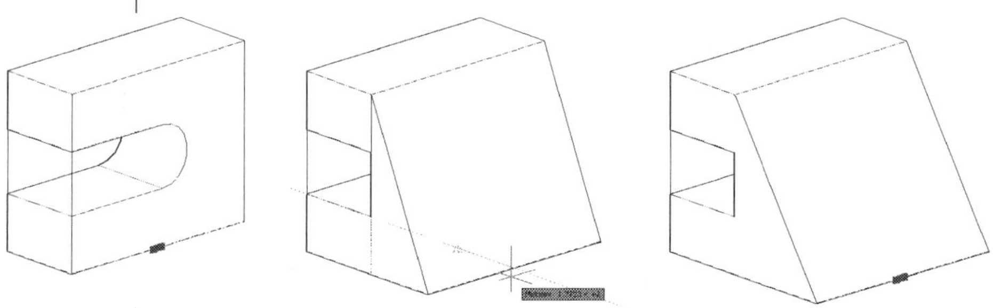

Figure 6–7

- When you select the grip, you can stretch, rotate, and scale the edge, or move and mirror the entire solid.
- If you select an axis or plane of the grip tool, you can stretch, move, or rotate the edge along the axis or plane.

Editing Vertices

The base point for the rotation and scale is the vertex grip you first selected.

When you select a vertex grip, you can stretch that point. You can also move and mirror the entire solid from that point. When you select two or more vertices, you can use the **Rotate** and **Scale** options, as shown in Figure 6–8.

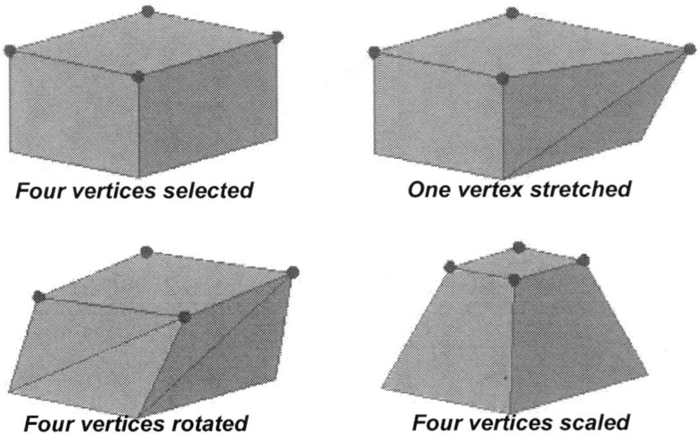

Figure 6–8

Modification Options

To help fine-tune the model adjustments, additional options are available when modifying a face, edge, or vertex. These options concern the parts themselves and their adjacent faces, including how they are affected based on the current modification scenario. The position, size, or shape of the selected portion can be maintained or modified, and its adjacent faces can also be maintained or modified. This includes being triangulated, which means being divided into two or more planar triangular faces.

The options might include **Extend Adjacent Faces**, **Move (selected portion)**, and **Allow Triangulation**.

To access these options, hover over the main grip for that portion and select the option in the multi-functional grip menu, as shown in Figure 6–9.

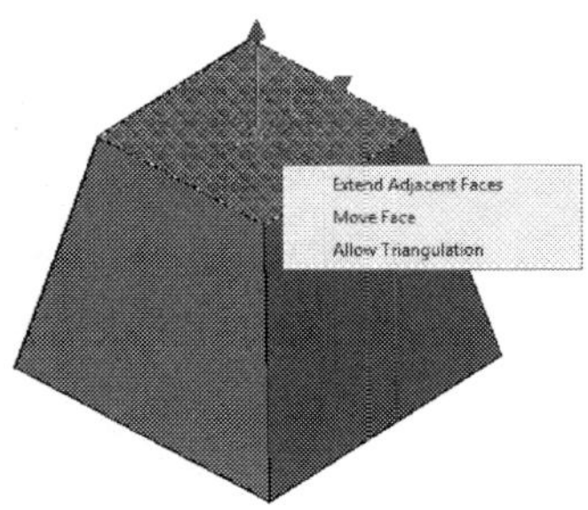

Figure 6–9

Practice 6a

Editing Components of Solids

Practice Objectives

- Create a conceptual design using Union, Subtract, and solid primitives.
- Modify various faces of 3D geometry.

In this practice, you will create a conceptual design of a hospital, as shown in Figure 6–10, using **Union**, **Subtract**, and solid primitives. You will use the face grip to adjust a solid face, add 2D objects onto faces, and then use **Presspull** to extrude them.

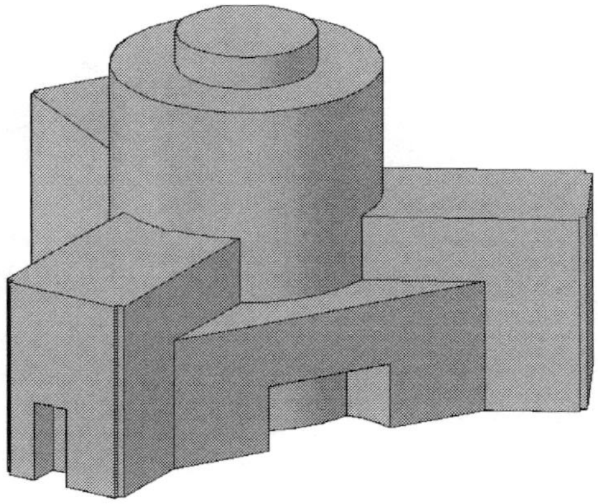

Figure 6–10

1. Open **Hospital.dwg**.
2. Union all of the solids except for the small cylinder at the front of the building.
3. Subtract the small cylinder from the front of the building.

*Use the **2D Array** command and clear the **Associative** option in the Array Creation contextual tab. If you created the array without clearing the **Associative** option, then you need to explode the array to turn the boxes into individual solids.*

4. Add two **10 x 10 x 300** boxes at the two corners of each wing.The box center should pass through corner edge, as shown in Figure 6–11. Use the **Center** option and snap to the corner.

   Create the two boxes on one wing and then create a **Polar Array** to add them to the other wings (use the center of the cylinder as the center point of the array).

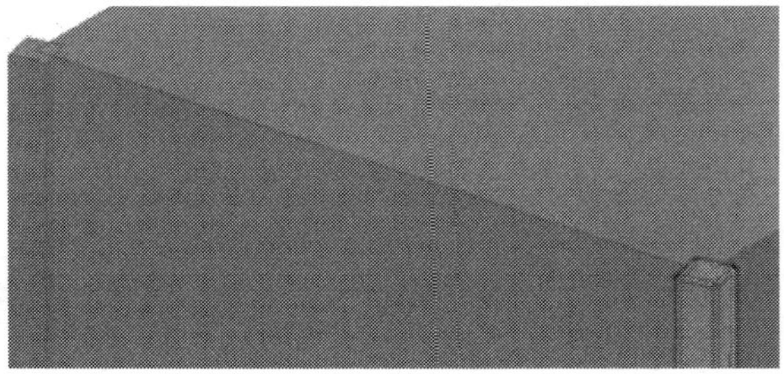

Figure 6–11

5. Subtract the boxes from the building to create ridges along the edges.

Change the radius in the Properties palette.

6. Press <Ctrl> and select the cylinder portion in the building. Increase its radius by **25** units(bringing it to a total of 225 units), as shown on the left in Figure 6–12.
7. Press <Ctrl> and click on the cylinder again until the top face of the cylinder is selected. Use the face grip to raise the face up by **100** units, as shown on the right in Figure 6–12.

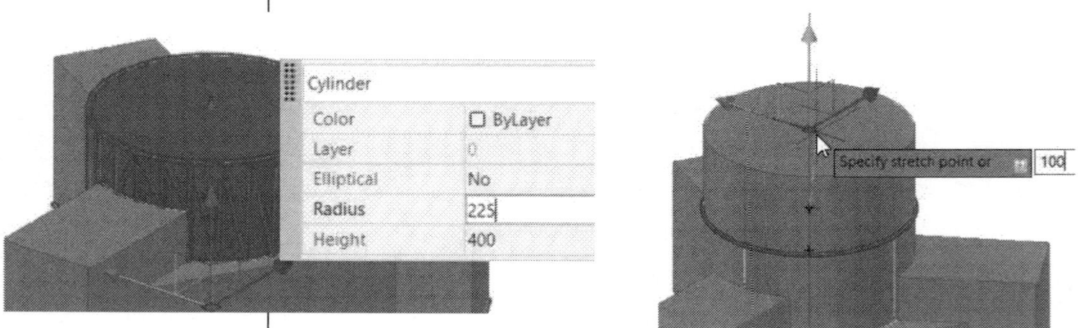

Figure 6–12

8. Draw a smaller radius circle on top of the main cylinder.Use  (Presspull) to create a raised tower with the circle. The height is up to you.

9. Add a 2D rectangle to the left end of the building and use **Presspull** to subtract it from the main building to create a recessed area for an entry. The depth is up to you.
10. Save and close the drawing.

6.2 Editing Faces of Solids

In some cases, you cannot edit solids as required using grips. Several other tools in the *Home* tab>Solid Editing panel, Extrude Faces flyout, enable you to edit the faces of solids, as shown in Figure 6–13.

Most of these commands are part of the ***Solidedit*** *command. You can type the command name, but you then need to follow many prompts to reach the correct options.*

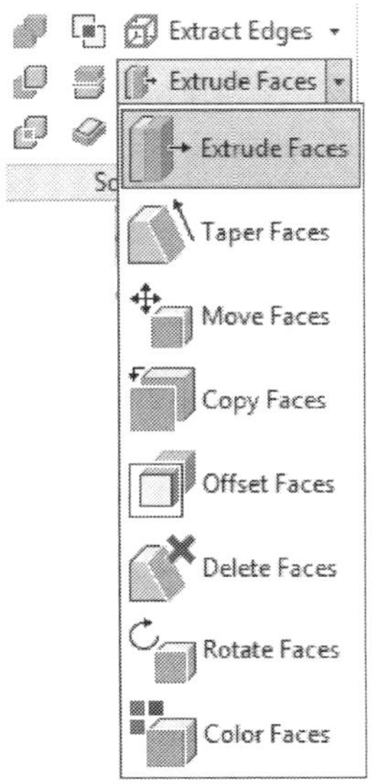

Figure 6–13

- **Taper Faces**, **Extrude Faces**, and **Offset Faces** are also located in the *Solid* tab>Solid Editing panel.
- These commands do not create a new object. They add or remove material to or from the existing object.

How To: Select Faces for Editing

1. Start the required **Solid Editing** command.
2. Select a face or edge of a solid. If you select an edge, the faces on either side of the edge are also selected.
    - To remove a face from the selection set, hold <Shift> and select the edge of one of the faces.
3. Continue to select faces as required.
4. Press <Enter> to finish selecting the faces and continue with the command.

- You can add faces and remove faces from the selection set using the **Add**, **Remove**, and **All** options.
- The **Undo** option undoes the last selection action.

Extruding Faces

*Running the **Solid Editing** commands removes the record of history on composite solids. As a result, you are no longer able to select individual solids in the composite.*

When you use the **Presspull** command to extrude a face on a solid, a separate solid is created and unioned to the original solid, as shown on the left in Figure 6–14. When you use **Extrude Faces**, the extrusion becomes part of the solid, not just a subobject.

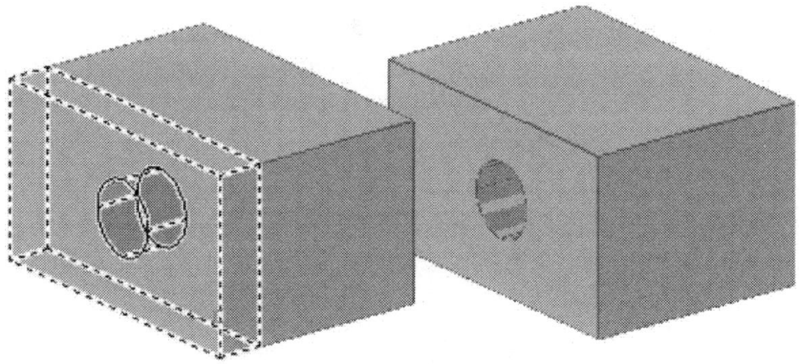

Extruded with Presspull ***Extruded with Extrude Face***

Figure 6–14

How To: Extrude Faces

1. In the *Home* tab>Solid Editing panel, click  (Extrude Faces).
    - Alternatively, you can access the command in the *Solid* tab>Solid Editing panel.
2. Select the face(s) that you want to extrude and press <Enter> to end the selection set.
3. Specify the height of the extrusion or identify a path.
4. Specify a taper angle, if required.
5. Press <Enter> twice to end the command.

- Only planar faces can be extruded. Use **Offset Faces** to extrude curved faces.

- A positive extrusion height adds mass to the solid. A negative extrusion height removes mass from the solid.

- A positive taper angle makes the new face smaller than the starting face. A negative taper angle makes the new face larger than the starting face.

- You can select a path along which to extrude the face. The path can be a line, arc, circle, 2D spline, or polyline.

- You can extrude multiple faces on the same object at the same time. However, the height and angle must be the same on all faces. If you extrude adjacent faces with the same command instance, the edges might be missing in the resulting solid. Use **Offset Faces** instead.

Offsetting Faces and Edges

While **Extrude Faces** only works on planar faces, **Offset Faces** can be used on curved faces, as shown in Figure 6–15. It also works well when multiple faces are selected.

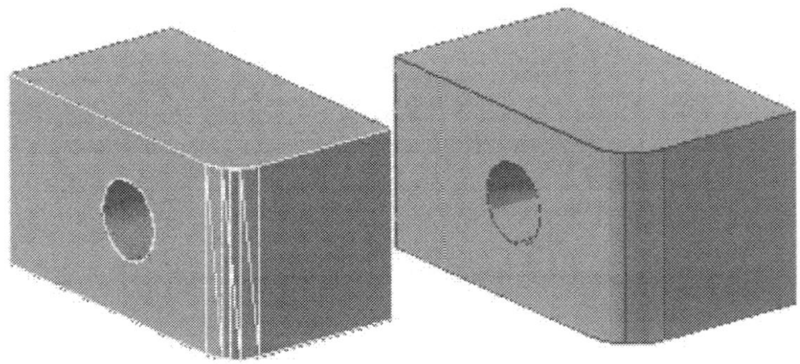

3 faces selected ***Faces offset***

Figure 6–15

How To: Offset Faces

1. In the *Home* tab>Solid Editing panel, Extrude Faces flyout, click (Offset Faces).
   - Alternatively, you can access the command in the *Solid* tab>Solid Editing panel.

*It is easier to select faces when you are in a Parallel view. Right-click on the ViewCube and select **Parallel**.*

2. Select the face(s) to be offset and press <Enter> to end the selection set.
3. Specify the offset distance.
4. Press <Enter> twice to end the command.

- You can offset more than one face at a time. Each face is offset parallel to itself.

- You cannot offset a face so that it is removed or so that two edges that did not meet, now do so.

- A positive offset distance adds mass to the solid. A negative offset distance removes mass from the solid. A positive distance increases the outside of a part, but decreases the size of a hole.

Offsetting Edges

You can also offset the edge of a planar face or planar surface, to create an offset curve, as shown in Figure 6–16.

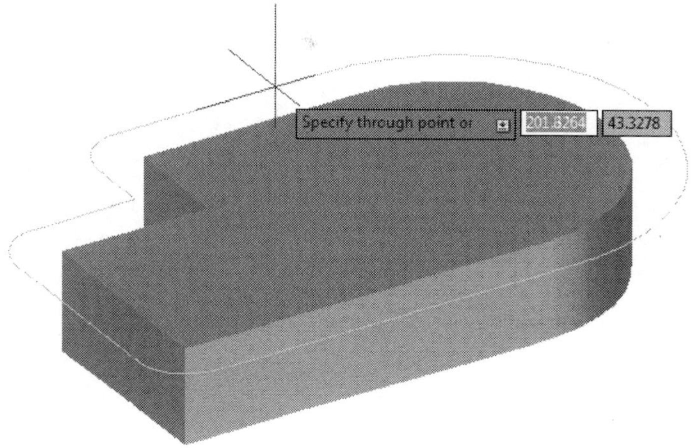

Figure 6–16

How To: Offset Edges

1. In the *Solid* tab>Solid Editing panel, Extrude Faces flyout, click (Offset Edge).
2. Select the face to be offset
3. Specify the point to go through (either inside or outside the boundary edge of the face).
4. Select another face to offset its edges, or press <Enter> to end the command.

- Options for the Offset Edge include specifying a distance for the offset and making the corners round or sharp.

Moving Faces

When designing with solids, you often need to move a hole or cutout from its current location, as shown in Figure 6–17. Rather than removing the hole and creating it again, you can use the **Move Faces** command.

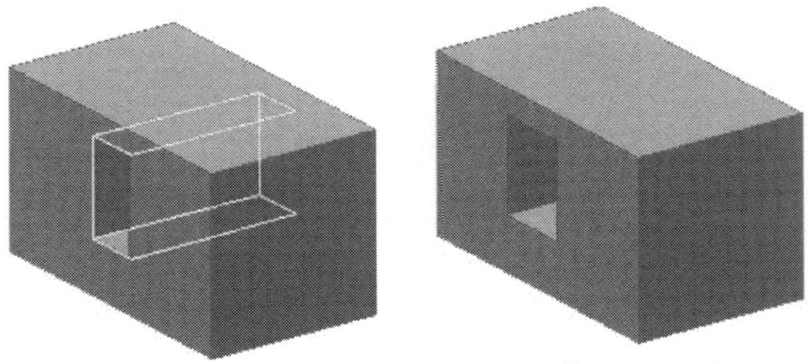

Faces selected ***Faces moved***

Figure 6–17

- To move or rotate a subtracted object, you only need to select the faces of the subtracted object and not the faces of the main solid. A good way to do this is to specify a crossing selection, select many faces, and then clear the selection of the ones you do not want.

How To: Move Faces

1. In the *Home* tab>Solid Editing panel, Extrude Faces flyout, click  (Move Faces).
2. Select the face(s) to be moved and press <Enter> to end the selection set.
3. Specify the base point of displacement and the second point of displacement, similar to the **Move** command.
4. Press <Enter> twice to end the command.

- You can also use the standard **Move** command or grips on a face. This moves the face and stretches any attached faces. Moving the face does not require that a new face be added or a new intersection created.

- You cannot move the base of a blind hole (a hole that does not pass through a part completely) to make it a through hole. However, you can use **Extrude Faces** to get that result.

Rotating Faces

If you want to change the orientation of a cutout in a solid, you can use the **Rotate Faces** command, as shown in Figure 6–18.

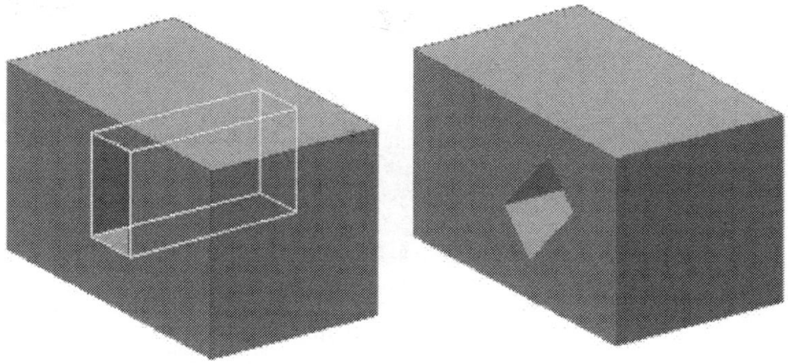

Faces selected ***Faces rotated***

Figure 6–18

How To: Rotate Faces

1. In the *Home* tab>Solid Editing panel, Extrude Faces flyout, click (Rotate Faces).
2. Select the face(s) to be rotated and press <Enter> to end the selection set.
3. Specify the axis of rotation.
4. Specify the rotation angle.
5. Press <Enter> twice to end the command.

- To rotate a face, select the face and an axis of rotation. The axis can be defined by two points, the X-, Y-, or Z-axis, a view, or an object.
- If you select an object as an axis, the axis used depends on the type of object selected. For a line, polyline, or spline, the AutoCAD® software uses the line between the start and end points as the axis. For a circle, arc, or ellipse, the AutoCAD software uses the line that passes though the center of the shape perpendicular to the plane of the shape.
- If you select a view to define the axis, the AutoCAD software uses the line of sight as the axis.
- You cannot rotate a face so that it causes a new cut to display in an existing face.
- You can rotate a single face, but tapering the face might be easier.

Tapering Faces

When you extrude a face, you have the option of applying a taper angle to the part. However, the taper angle affects all sides of the extruded section. If you only want to taper one face, you can use the **Taper Faces** command, as shown in Figure 6–19.

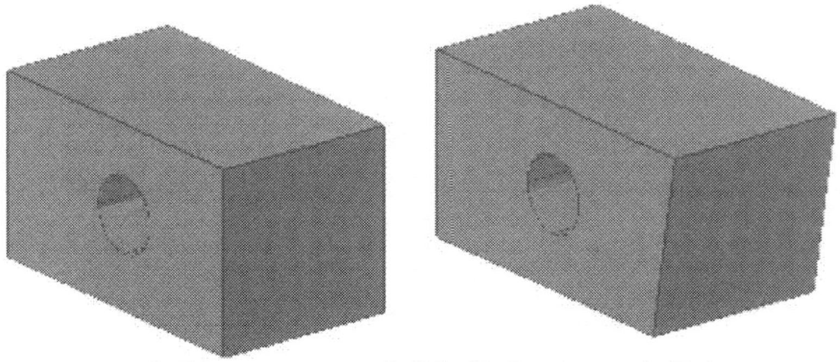

Solid ***Solid with face tapered -10 degrees***

Figure 6–19

How To: Taper Faces

1. In the *Home* tab>Solid Editing panel, Extrude Faces flyout, click  (Taper Faces).
    - Alternatively, you can access the command in the *Solid* tab>Solid Editing panel.
2. Select the face(s) you want to taper and press <Enter> to end the selection set.
3. Specify the base point and then another point along the axis to taper.
4. Specify the taper angle.
5. Press <Enter> twice to end the command.

- The two points of the axis are used to determine the axis about which the face rotates.

- A positive taper angle removes mass from the solid. A negative taper angle adds mass to the solid.

Removing Faces

To remove a fillet, chamfer, hole, or face from an object, as shown in Figure 6–20, use the **Delete Faces** command.

Solid with fillet ***Fillet face deleted***

Figure 6–20

How To: Delete Faces

1. In the *Home* tab>Solid Editing panel, Extrude Faces flyout, click (Delete Faces).
2. Select the face(s) that you want to delete.
3. Press <Enter> twice to end the command.

- You must select all faces to be deleted at the same time. For example, if you have a box with a V-shaped notch running along one side, you must select both sides of the V for the notch to be removed.

- You cannot delete a face if extending the existing faces cannot close the resulting shape.

Hint: Adding Color to Faces or Edges

You can use (Color Faces) or (Color Edges) in the *Home* tab>Solid Editing panel for emphasis or to change the look of a face in rendering.

- Colored edges are hidden in the **Conceptual** and **Realistic** visual styles.

- Colored edges or faces are not displayed if materials are applied and enabled.

Copying Faces

The **Copy Faces** command is used to copy existing geometry to create another 3D feature, such as the region shown in Figure 6–21. The region can then be used to create another solid or surface.

Figure 6–21

- If you copy a face, the resulting object is a region (if flat) or a surface (if curved).

How To: Copy Faces

1. In the *Home* tab>Solid Editing panel, Extrude Faces flyout, click (Copy Faces).
2. Select the face(s) you want to copy.
3. Specify the base point.
4. Specify a second point where the face is copied.
5. Press <Enter> twice to end the command.

Practice 6b Editing Faces of Solids

Practice Objective

- Modify faces of a 3D object by extruding, tapering, offsetting, moving, and rotating them.

In this practice, you will extrude, taper, offset, move, and rotate the faces of a solid model, as shown in Figure 6–22.

Figure 6–22

1. Open **Bracket1.dwg**.

The visual style used is Shades of Gray.

2. In the *Solid* tab>Solid Editing panel, Extrude Faces flyout, click  (Extrude Faces).

3. Extrude the small rectangular face at the left end of the part, as shown in Figure 6–23, by **1** unit with a *Taper Angle* of **10** degrees.

Hold <Ctrl> when selecting the individual faces. Press <Enter> twice to finish any Solid Editing command.

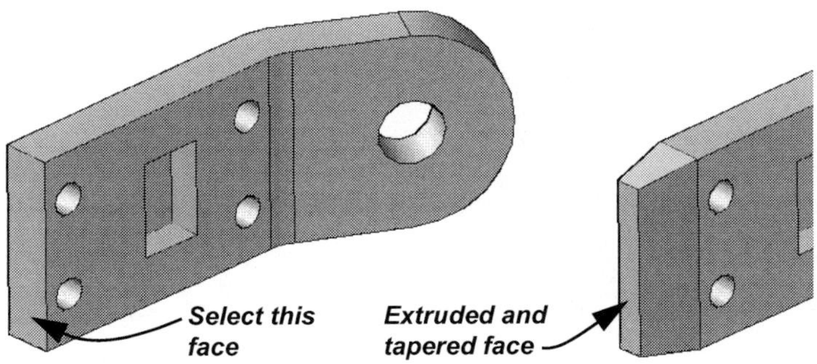

Figure 6–23

4. The rectangular hole has not been drilled completely through the object. In the *Solid* tab>Solid Editing panel, click (Extrude Faces) and select the face of the inner rectangle. Extrude the solid in a negative direction (**-1** unit) with no (**0** taper angle) taper to create an opening.

You must use a negative number to decrease the volume of the part.

5. In the *Solid* tab>Solid Editing panel, Extrude Faces flyout, click (Offset Faces) and make the large circular hole **0.25** units larger. Use **-0.25** as the *Offset distance*. Select only the hole and not the other faces.

6. In the *Solid* tab>Solid Editing panel, Extrude Faces flyout, click (Offset Faces) and offset the curved edge **0.5** units outside the part. The radius of the curve increases so that the curved edge is no longer tangent to the two adjacent sides, as shown in Figure 6–24.

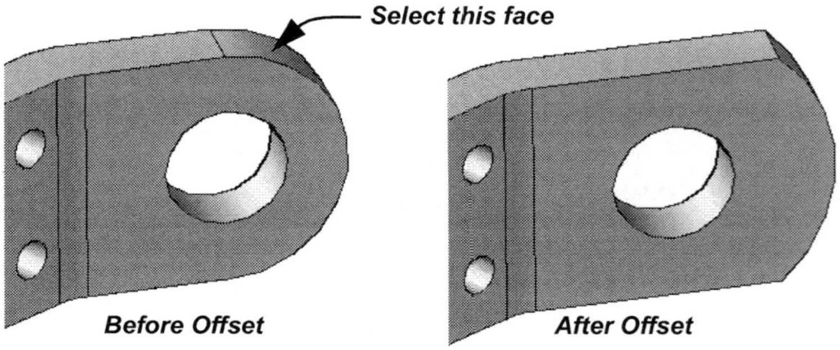

Figure 6–24

7. Toggle on **Osnap** with the **Midpoint** option selected.

To select the ***Mid Between 2 Points*** *object snap, hold <Ctrl> or <Shift> and right-click.*

8. In the *Home* tab>Solid Editing panel, Extrude Faces flyout, click (Rotate Faces). Select all four sides of the rectangular cutout. At *Specify an axis point*, select **Yaxis** from the down-arrow list (or the Command Line). At *Specify the origin of rotation*, press <Shift>, then right-click and select **Mid Between 2 Points**, as shown in Figure 6–25. Select the midpoints of the top and bottom horizontal edges of the cutout. Type **90** for the rotation angle. The cutout is rotated.

The visual style is changed to ***Conceptual****.*

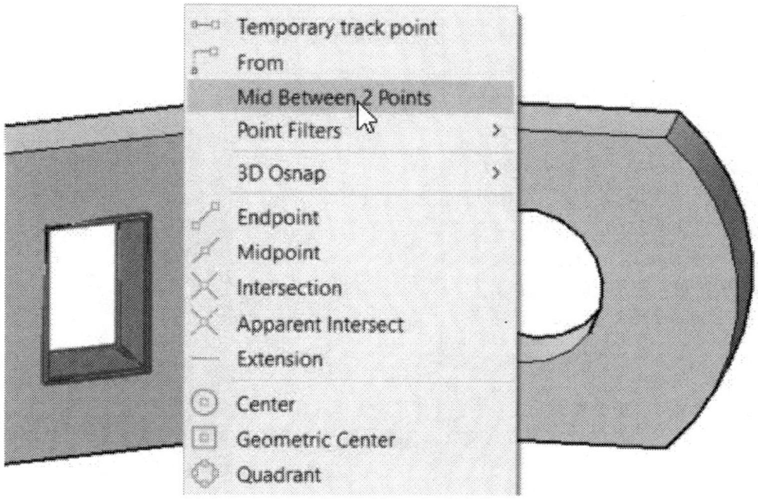

Figure 6–25

9. In the *Home* tab>Solid Editing panel, Extrude Faces flyout, click (Move Faces) and move the two holes on the outer tapered edge **0.5** units towards the cutout.

10. Save and close the drawing.

6.3 Fillets and Chamfers on Solids

Fillets and chamfers can be used in 2D and 3D work. The commands are the same, but they behave differently when used on a solid. **Fillet Edge** rounds edges and **Chamfer Edge** creates a bevel on the edge of a solid, as shown in Figure 6–26.

*If you use **Fillet** or **Chamfer**, the AutoCAD software assumes that you are filleting 2D lines until you select the first object. When you select the first object (an edge of a solid), the **Fillet** command changes to the solid version of the command.*

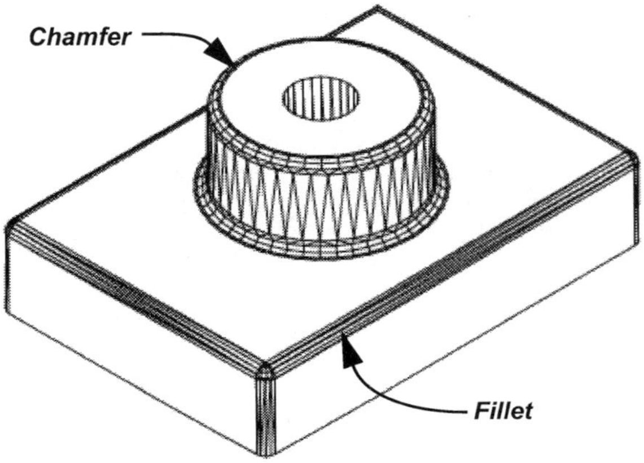

Figure 6–26

- When filleting multiple edges, you might need to create all of the fillets at the same time or perform a sequence of **Fillet** commands to get the required results.

How To: Add Fillets to Solids

1. In the *Solid* tab>Solid Editing panel, expand Fillet Edge flyout, click  (Fillet Edge).
2. Select an edge on the solid that you want to fillet. A preview of the fillet displays on the object.
3. Select additional edges to be filleted. You can also specify to fillet a chain or loop of edges.
4. Select the radius option and enter the fillet radius. The preview updates. Press <Enter>.
5. Press <Enter> twice to end the command.

- A chain enables you to select a group of edges with two clicks. The group of edges must be joined by fillets. At the *[Chain/Radius]:* prompt, select **Chain**. Select the line or fillet at one end of the chain and then select the line or fillet at the other end.

- Straight or curved edges can be filleted, as shown in Figure 6–27.

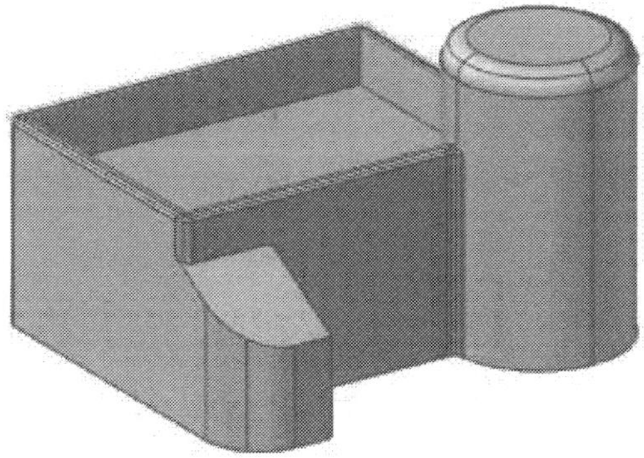

Figure 6–27

- If the fillets do not work at first, try creating them in a different way. Usually, if two or more fillets meet at a corner, you should apply the fillet with the smallest radius first. You cannot change the order in which edges are filleted.

- With the **Fillet** command, the AutoCAD software prompts you for an edge, enables you to change the radius, and then prompts for edges again. You do not have to select the same edge again. If you want to fillet more than one edge, select the other edges now. Selecting the same edge again does not change anything.

- You can also fillet surfaces using  (Fillet Surface) in the *Surface* tab>Edit panel. When you select the surfaces to fillet, a preview displays. Enter a radius value and the preview updates. Press <Enter> to end the command.

How To: Create 3D Chamfers

1. In the *Solid* tab>Solid Editing panel, expand Fillet Edge flyout, click  (Chamfer Edge).
2. Select the edge of the solid to be chamfered. A preview of the chamfer displays.
3. Select additional edges along the same face or select **Distance** to enter distance values for the chamfer.
4. Specify **Distance1** and then **Distance2**. The preview updates.
5. Press <Enter> to accept the chamfer and end the command.

You can also specify to chamfer a loop of edges.

- You can also use the **Chamfer** command, which prompts for distances after you select a 3D solid.
- When using the **Chamfer** command with solids, you cannot specify a distance and angle to define the chamfer, as you can when using the command with 2D objects.

You can use the **Loop** option to chamfer all edges of one face. At the *Select an edge loop or [Edge]:* prompt, select one edge of the base surface. The AutoCAD software selects all edges of that face and chamfers them when the face is accepted.

Hint: What Is the Base Surface?

In the **Chamfer** command, if you select an edge of a solid at the *Select first line* prompt, the AutoCAD software immediately prompts you to select a base surface and highlights one for you to accept or reject. The base surface is a plane that touches the edge you have selected. Every 3D edge has two possible base surfaces. The AutoCAD software suggests one by highlighting it. You can toggle between the two surfaces by using the **Next** option at the *Enter surface selection option* prompt.

- The Base surface chamfer distance is removed from the base surface. The other surface at the edge has the Other surface chamfer distance removed, as shown in Figure 6–28.

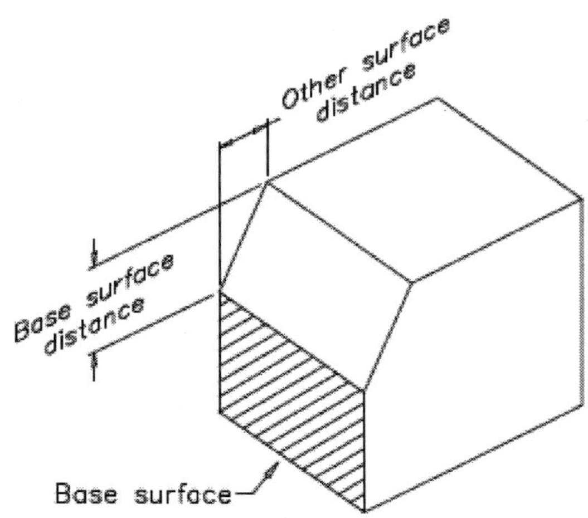

Figure 6–28

Practice 6c Fillets and Chamfers on Solids

Practice Objective

- Round and bevel the edges of a solid using the **Fillet Edge** and **Chamfer Edge** commands.

In this practice, you will use **Fillet Edge** and **Chamfer Edge** to finish the edges of an existing solid, as shown in Figure 6–29.

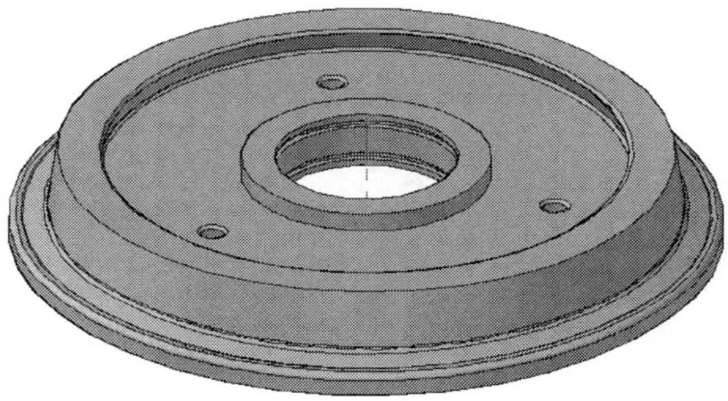

Figure 6–29

1. Open **Trolley-Wheel.dwg**.
2. In the *Solid* tab>Solid Editing panel, expand Fillet Edge flyout, click (Chamfer Edge). The cursor changes into a pick box with a 3D box. Select the edge as shown in Figure 6–30. A preview of the Chamfer displays. In the down-arrow list (or the Command line), select **Distance**.

*The visual style was changed to **Conceptual**.*

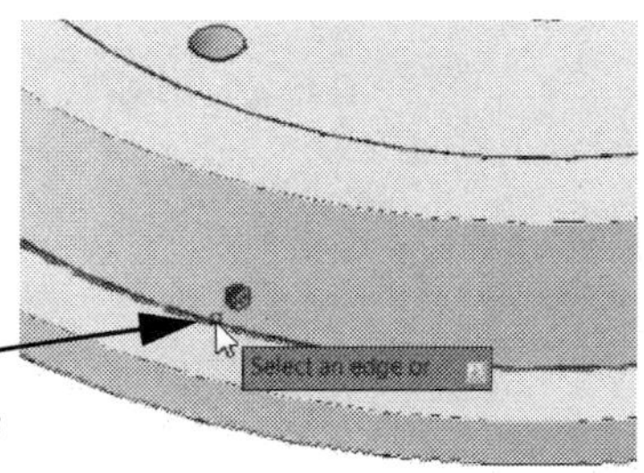

Select this edge first

Figure 6–30

3. At the *Specify Distance1* prompt, type **0.5**. The preview updates.
4. At the *Specify Distance2* prompt, type **0.125**. The preview updates again.
5. Press <Enter> twice to end the command.

6. Switch to the **Front** view to display the chamfer, as shown in Figure 6–31.

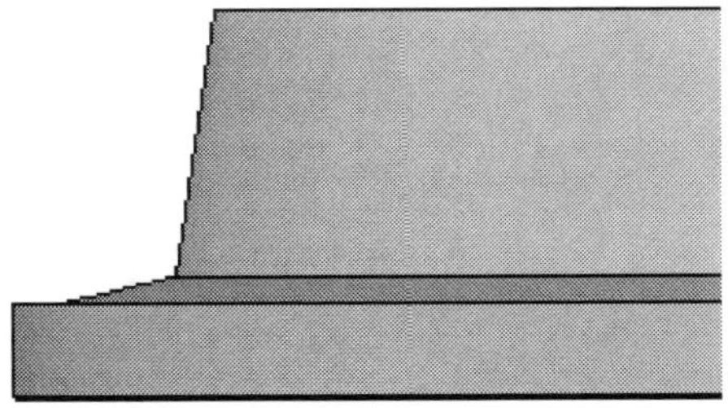

Figure 6–31

7. Orbit the object slightly to display the top edges of the trolley wheel.

A preview of the fillet displays.

8. In the *Solid* tab>Solid Editing panel, click (Fillet Edge) and select the outside edge of the wheel, as shown in Figure 6–32.

9. Enter a radius of **0.125**. Press <Enter> twice to end the command.

10. Repeat (Fillet Edge) and select the other edges, as shown on the left in Figure 6–32.

    - The filleted edges should look similar to that shown on the right in Figure 6–32. (The visual style was changed to **Conceptual**.)

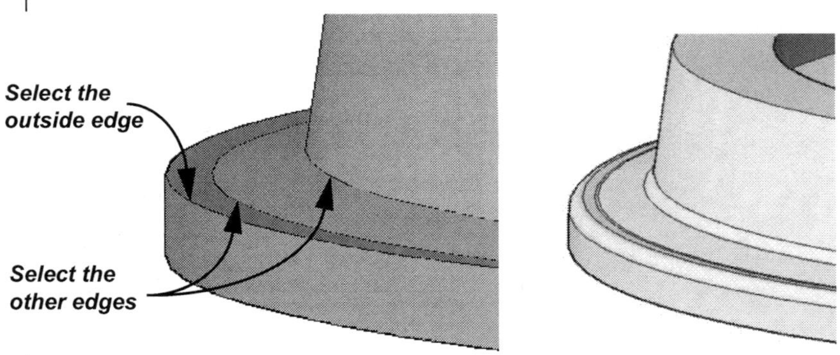

Figure 6–32

11. Fillet the top edges and the three small circles, as shown in Figure 6–33, with a radius of **0.0625**.

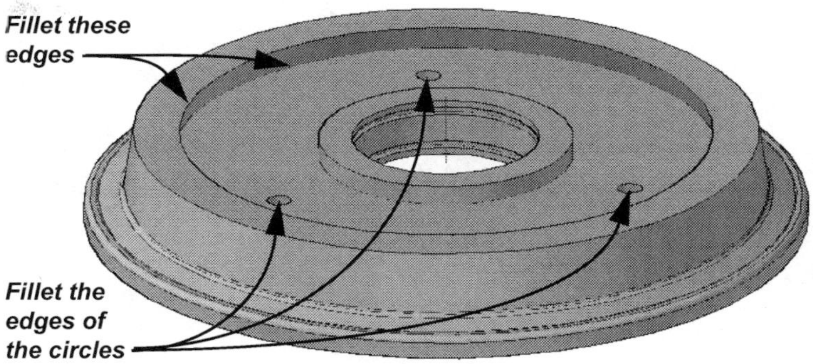

Figure 6–33

12. Fillet the bottom edges, as shown in Figure 6–34, with a fillet of **0.1875**.

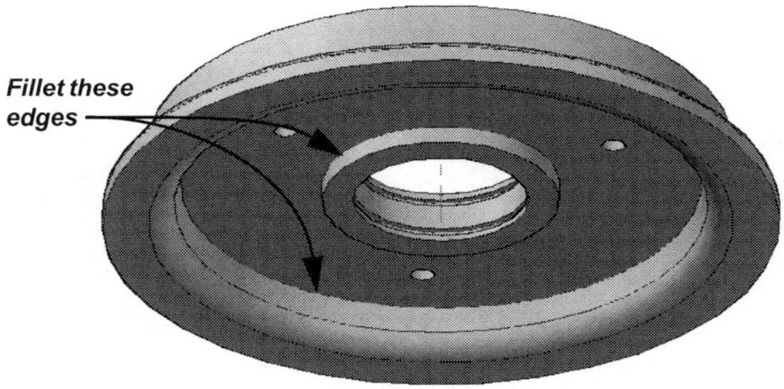

Figure 6–34

13. Save and close the drawing.

Practice 6d Mechanical Project: Bracket

Practice Objective

- Create a mechanical part using solids and solid editing tools.

In this practice, you will create the mechanical part shown in Figure 6–35 using solids and solid editing tools. The exact process is up to you.

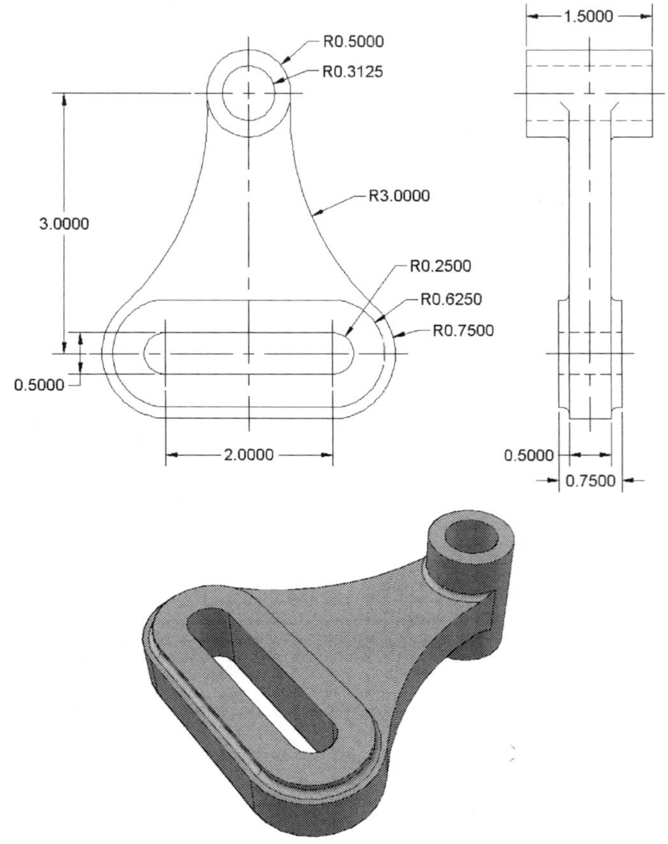

Figure 6–35

- Start a new drawing based on the **acad3D.dwt** template and save it as **Slotted-bracket.dwg**.

- Use solids to draw the object shown in Figure 6–35. Unless otherwise specified, all fillets are **0.1**.

Chapter Review Questions

1. How do you select a face or edge of a solid for editing?
    a. Hold <Tab> and select the face or edge.
    b. Hold <Ctrl> and select the face or edge.
    c. Click on the face or edge of the solid.
    d. Hold <Shift> and select the face or edge.
2. If you edit parts of solid primitives, they retain their geometry information, such as length, width, or radius.
    a. True
    b. False
3. When selecting the edge of a solid while using the **Fillet Edge** command, which of the following cannot be performed?
    a. Display a preview of the fillet.
    b. Select straight or curved edges to be filleted.
    c. Change the order in which edges are filleted.
    d. Use a chain to select a group of edges.
4. Which command changes the orientation of a cutout in a solid?
    a. **Rotate Faces**
    b. **Extrude Faces**
    c. **Offset Faces**
    d. **Move Faces**
5. What is the difference between the **Extrude Faces** and **Offset Faces** commands?
    a. **Extrude Faces** removes material but **Offset Faces** does not.
    b. **Extrude Faces** only works on curved faces whereas **Offset Faces** works on curved and planar faces.
    c. **Offset Faces** can be used on curved faces whereas **Extrude Faces** can be used on planar faces only.
    d. You cannot extrude multiple faces with **Extrude Faces** whereas **Offset Faces** extrudes multiple faces.

Command Summary

All ribbon names reference the 3D Modeling workspace.

Button	Command	Location
	**Chamfer**	• **Ribbon:** *Home* tab>Modify panel
	**Chamfer Edge**	• **Ribbon:** *Solid* tab>Solid Editing panel
	**Color Edge**	• **Ribbon:** *Home* tab>Solid Editing panel
	**Color Faces**	• **Ribbon:** *Home* tab>Solid Editing panel
	**Copy Faces**	• **Ribbon:** *Home* tab>Solid Editing panel
	**Delete Faces**	• **Ribbon:** *Home* tab>Solid Editing panel
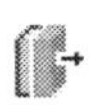	**Extrude Faces**	• **Ribbon:** *Home* tab>Solid Editing panel or *Solid* tab>Solid Editing panel
	**Fillet**	• **Ribbon:** *Home* tab>Modify panel
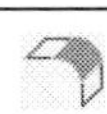	**Fillet (Surface)**	• **Ribbon:** *Surface* tab>Edit panel
	**Fillet Edge**	• **Ribbon:** *Solid* tab>Solid Editing panel
	**Move Faces**	• **Ribbon:** *Home* tab>Solid Editing panel
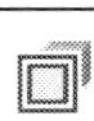	**Offset Edge**	• **Ribbon:** *Solid* tab>Solid Editing panel
	**Offset Faces**	• **Ribbon:** *Home* tab>Solid Editing panel or *Solid* tab>Solid Editing panel
	**Rotate Faces**	• **Ribbon:** *Home* tab>Solid Editing panel
	**Taper Faces**	• **Ribbon:** *Home* tab>Solid Editing panel or *Solid* tab>Solid Editing panel

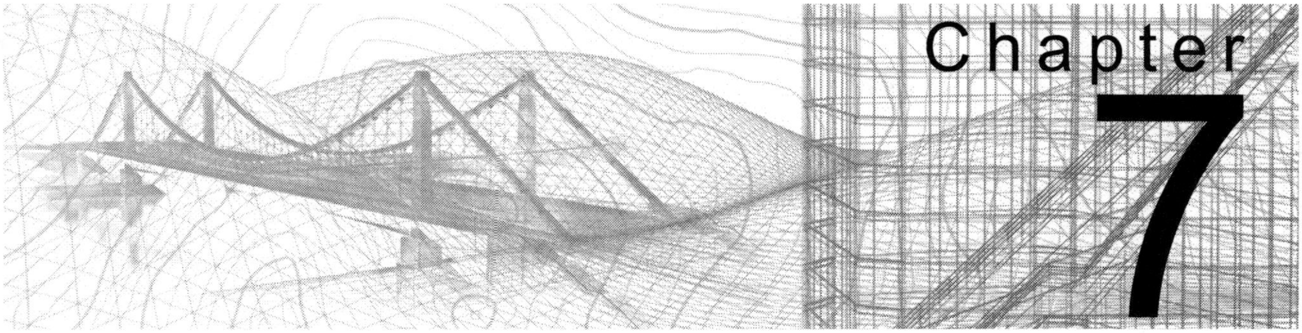

Additional Editing Tools

In this chapter, you learn how to create a shell of a solid, imprint edges on a solid, slice a solid, and convert objects to surface and solids.

Learning Objectives in This Chapter

- Create a shell at a specified thickness by hollowing out a 3D solid object.
- Imprint 2D objects on the faces of 3D solids to create and modify additional faces.
- Slice a solid to display the interior of an object, remove a portion of it, or create two mating parts.
- Compare solids to detect and display any overlapping volume areas.
- Update 3D-like objects to surface objects by converting them using the Planar Surface, Convert to Surface, and Explode commands.
- Create solids from circles or polylines that have a thickness or surface.

7.1 Creating a Shell

Plastic enclosures are often made of a thin shell of material as shown in the example in Figure 7–1. Many buildings can also start with a shell. The **Shell** command hollows out a solid and leaves a shell of a specified thickness.

*For ease in selecting faces, use the **Parallel** view rather than the **Perspective** view.*

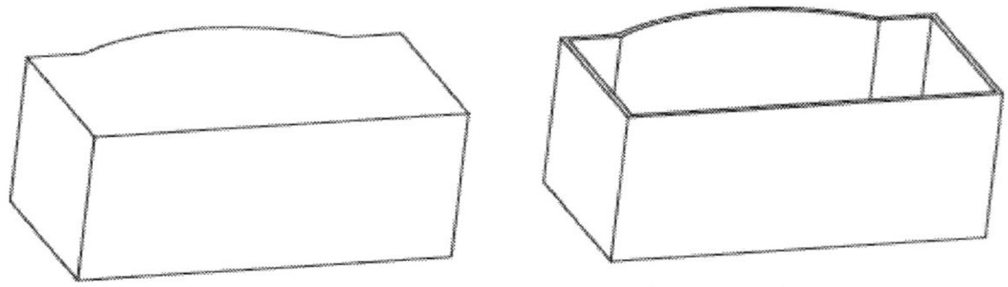

Figure 7–1

How To: Shell a Solid

1. In the *Home* tab>Solid Editing panel, click  (Shell).
   - Alternatively, you can access the command in the *Solid* tab>Solid Editing panel.
2. Select the 3D solid from which you want to create a shell.
3. Select any faces that you want to be removed after the shell process.
4. Enter a distance for the shell offset (specified thickness).
5. Press <Enter> twice to end the command.

- Use a negative offset distance to create the shell outside of the original solid (the original faces become the inside of the shelled object).

- Use a positive offset distance to create the shell inside the original solid (the original faces become the outside of the shelled object).You can remove faces from the selection set before completing the command. Faces that are removed do not offset and create an opening into the new solid.

- A solid object can only have one shell.

Practice 7a

Creating a Shell

Practice Objectives

- Create a 3D solid object using the **Loft** command.
- Hollow out a 3D solid object using the **Shell** command.

In this practice, you will draw a solid using the **Loft** command and then shell it to create a part, as shown in Figure 7–2.

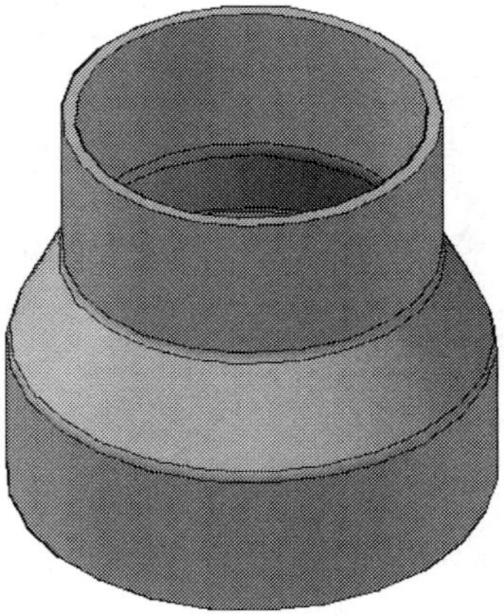

Figure 7–2

1. Start a new drawing based on **acad3D.dwt** and save it in your practice files folder as **Shell.dwg**.
2. Right-click on the ViewCube and select **Parallel**.
3. Draw four circles of specified diameters, along the same center at a distance specified as shown in Figure 7–3. Zoom in to the circles.

The vertical lines are a guide to help you locate the circles.

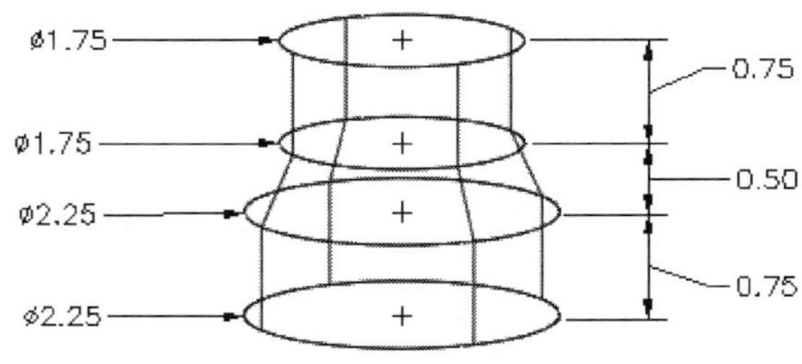

Figure 7–3

4. On the *Home* tab>Modeling panel, expand the Extrude flyout and click (Loft).
5. Select the four circles in order from the bottom to the top and press <Enter>.
6. Select **Settings**.

Instead of using the Loft Settings dialog box, you can select ***Ruled*** *in the drop-down list.*

If your object does not look similar, open and use ***Shell.dwg*** *for the remainder of this practice.*

7. In the Loft Settings dialog box, select **Ruled** and click **OK**. You should see an object similar to the one shown in Figure 7–4.

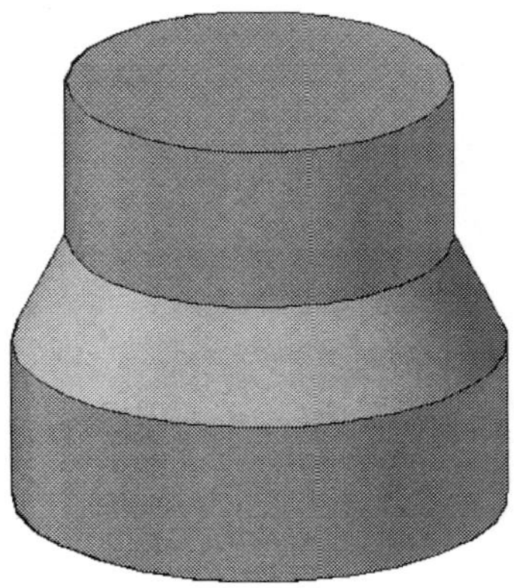

Figure 7–4

8. On the *Solid* tab>Solid Editing panel, click (Fillet Edge) and fillet the two inner circles with a radius of **0.125**.
9. On the *Solid* tab>Solid Editing panel, click (Shell).
10. Select the solid that you just created. At the *Remove faces* prompt, select the top and bottom face. Press <Enter>.
    - If you remove the sides, change the command to **Add** and add the sides to the solid.
11. At the Shell offset distance, enter **0.0625**.
12. Press <Enter> twice to end the command. The solid displays as shown in Figure 7–2.
13. Save and close the drawing.

7.2 Imprinting Edges of Solids

The imprinted object needs to intersect a face, but does not need to be completely on the face.

You can create additional faces and edges on solids by imprinting 2D objects on the faces, as shown in Figure 7–5. You can then modify these faces and edges as if they were created with the original solid.

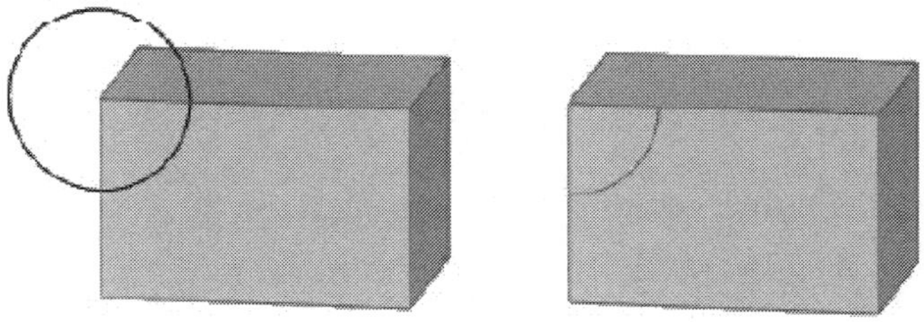

Figure 7–5

- You can imprint arcs, circles, lines, 2D and 3D polylines, ellipses, splines, regions, bodies, and 3D solids.
- You do not need to imprint objects if you are going to use **Presspull**, because it automatically creates a bounded area of any overlapping objects and then extrudes that bounded area into a solid or a void.

How To: Imprint Faces and Edges

1. Draw objects on the face of a solid, such as polylines, lines, or circles.
2. In the *Home* tab>Solid Editing panel, expand the Extract Edges flyout and click (Imprint).
   - Alternatively, you can access the command in the *Solid* tab>Solid Editing panel.
3. Select the solid on which you want to imprint.
4. Select the object to be imprinted.
5. At the *Delete the source object* prompt, select **Yes** or **No** to delete or keep the source object.
6. Select another object to imprint on the solid or press <Enter> to end the command.

__Copy Edges__ and __Color Edges__ are both located in the Home tab>Solid Editing panel.

- You can use (Copy Edges) to copy existing geometry to create another 3D feature. When you copy an edge, the resulting object is a line, arc, circle, spline, or ellipse. These edges can be imprinted on a solid.

- You can use (Color Edges) to change the color of selected edges to emphasize them.

Hint: Checking and Cleaning Solids

Two additional solid editing tools are located in the *Home* tab>Solid Editing panel>Separate flyout and *Solid* tab>Solid Editing panel>Shell flyout.

- (Check) is used to validate that the solid you are using is a valid 3D solid. If it is not, you cannot edit the solid with the Solid Editing tools.
- (Clean) removes all redundant edges, but does not remove imprinted edges. The entire solid is cleaned at the same time.

Practice 7b Imprinting Edges on a Solid

Practice Objective

- Create a 3D solid using commands to copy and imprint edges to be used as profiles.

In this practice, you will use **Shell**, **Copy Edge**, **Imprint**, and **Taper Faces** to create a solid casing, as shown in Figure 7–6. The change to the solid with each step is shown in Figure 7–6.

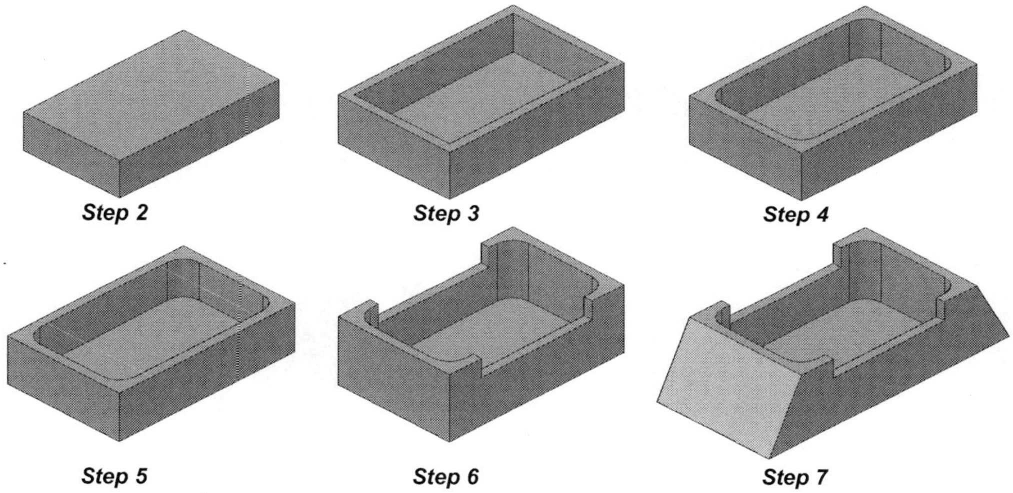

Figure 7–6

1. Start a new drawing using **acad3D.dwt** and save it in your practice files folder as **Casing.dwg**.
2. Create a **3 x 5 x 1** solid box.
3. **Shell** the solid, removing the top face to leave it open, and using an shell offset distance of **-0.25**.
4. **Fillet Edge** the inside corners (select vertical edges on the inside four corners) with a radius of **0.5**.
5. In the *Home* tab>Solid Editing panel, use the **Copy Edges** command to copy the shorter outside top edges from the ends of the box **one** unit inwards along the top.
6. In the *Home* tab>Solid Editing panel, expand the Extract Edges flyout and use (Imprint) to create an imprint of the two lines that were created in Step 5. Delete the copied lines. **Extrude** the two new faces at either end, upwards by **0.5**.

7. **Taper** the two outside faces at the ends of the part by **30°**.
   - In the *Home* tab>Solid Editing panel, expand the Extrude Faces flyout and click  (Taper Faces).
   - Select the shorter side outside face (as shown in Figure 7–7) and press <Enter>.
   - At the *Specify the base point* prompt, select the top endpoint of the vertical edge, as shown in Figure 7–7.
   - At the *Specify another point along the axis of tapering* prompt, select the bottom endpoint of the vertical edge, as shown in Figure 7–7.
   - At the *Specify the taper angle* prompt, enter **-30**.
   - Press <Enter> twice to exit the command.
   - Repeat for other side.

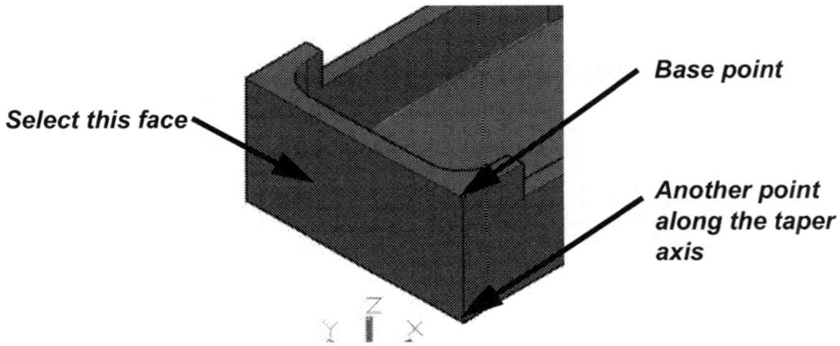

Figure 7–7

8. Save and close the drawing.

7.3 Slicing a Solid Along a Plane

Another way to create complex solids is to create the solid and then slice off part of the solid. You can use this technique to display the interior of an object (as shown in Figure 7–8), to remove a portion of the solid completely, or to create two mating parts.

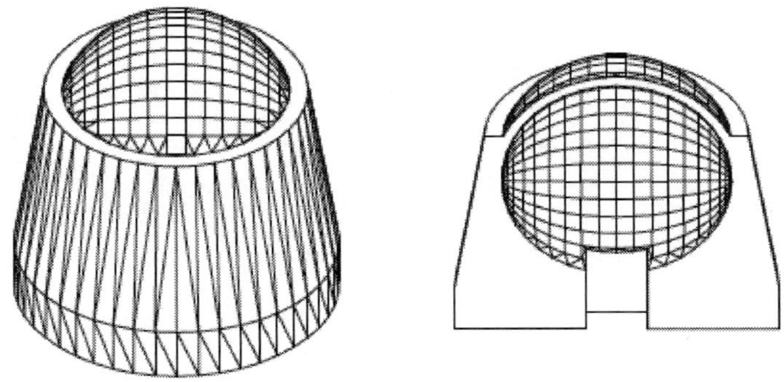

Figure 7–8

- The **Slice** command enables you to cut a solid along a defined plane, retaining either half or both halves.

How To: Slice a Solid

1. In the *Home* tab>Solid Editing panel, click (Slice).
    - Alternatively, you can access the command in the *Solid* tab>Solid Editing panel.
2. Select the solids to be sliced.
3. Use the slicing plane options to define the slicing plane.
4. Specify a point on the side of the object you want to keep or select **Both**.

Slicing Plane Options

Planar Object	Prompts you to select an object. The slicing plane is aligned with the plane of the selected object. Valid objects include circles, ellipses, arcs, 2D splines, and 2D polylines.
Surface	Prompts you to select a surface. The object is sliced along the plane of the surface, as shown in Figure 7–9.
Z Axis	Prompts you to select two points. The first point is on the cutting plane and the second point is on the Z-axis perpendicular (normal) to the plane.
View	Prompts you to select a point. The slicing plane is created perpendicular to the view direction and passes through the selected point.
XY/YZ/ZX Plane	Prompts you to select a point. The slicing plane is created parallel to the selected standard plane (XY/YZ/ZX) of the current UCS and passes through the selected point.
3points	Prompts you to select three points. The slicing plane passes through the selected points.

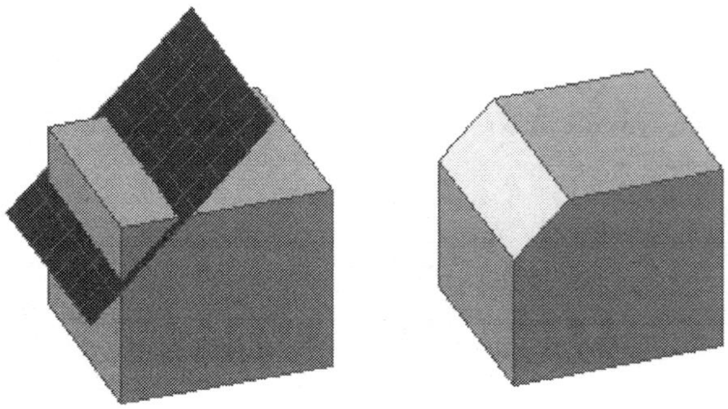

Slicing a solid with a plane

Figure 7–9

- 3D meshes created with surface tools in previous releases cannot be used with the **Slice** command.
- If you want to display the interior of a solid object but do not want to create a separate object, use the **Section Plane** command.

Practice 7c Slicing a Solid

Project Objective

- Cut off a portion of a block and split it into two parts using the **Slice** command.

In this practice, you will use **Slice** to cut off a portion of a block and split it into two parts, as shown in Figure 7–10.

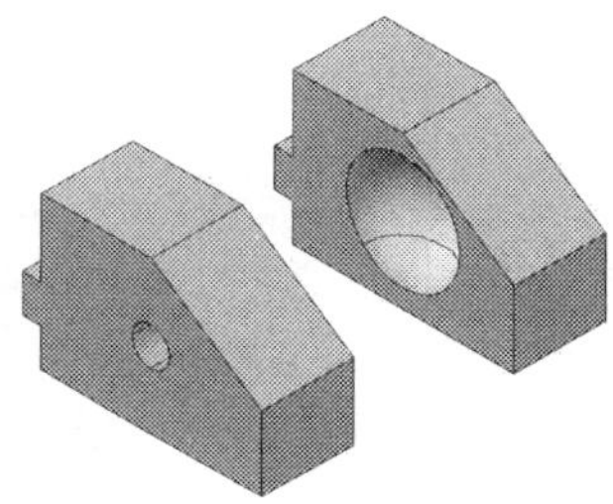

Figure 7–10

1. Open **Block.dwg** and switch to the **SE Isometric** view.
2. On the *Solid* tab>Solid Editing panel, click (Slice).
3. At the *Select objects to slice:* prompt, select the block. Press <Enter> to continue.
4. When prompted for the start point of the slicing plane, press <Enter> to select **3points**.
5. Select the midpoints at **A**, **B**, and **C**, as shown in Figure 7–11, as the three points on the slicing plane.

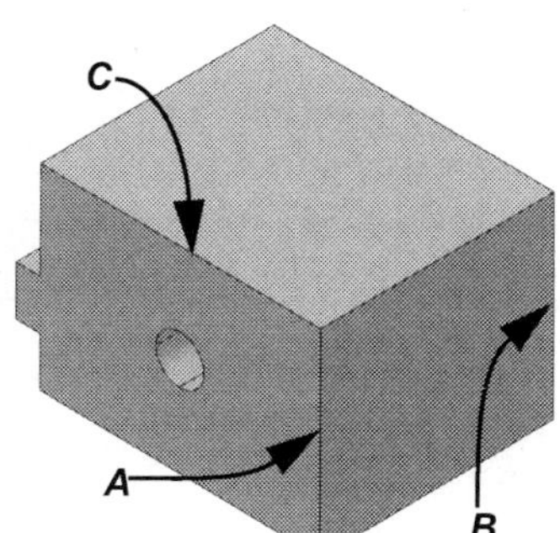

Figure 7–11

6. At the *Specify a point on the desired side* prompt, select a point anywhere on the lower half of the block. Note that the top portion above the slice line is removed.

7. On the *Solid* tab>Solid Editing panel, click (Slice), select the block, and press <Enter>.

8. When prompted for the start point of the slicing plane, select **ZX**. Specify the midpoint at the bottom right edge, as shown in Figure 7–12.

9. At the *Specify a point on the desired side* prompt, select the **keep Both sides** option to keep both sides of the object.

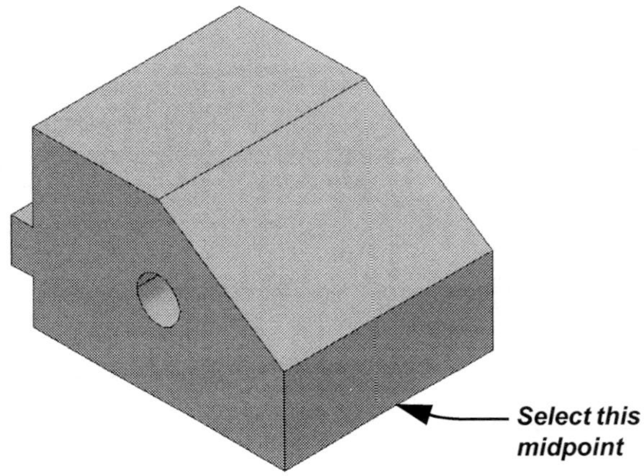

Figure 7–12

10. Move one of the sides away to display the interior, as shown in Figure 7–13. View it from several directions.

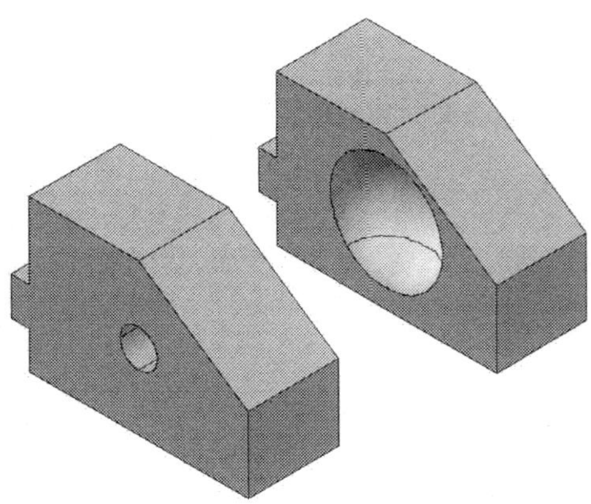

Figure 7–13

11. Save and close the drawing.

7.4 Interference Checking

The **Interfere** command creates temporary solid objects from any selection of two or more overlapping solids, as shown in Figure 7–14. The command displays the interference objects and enables you to investigate it further by highlighting various pairs of interferences and viewing the objects without creating them. When you have finished your investigation, you can discard or keep the temporary solids.

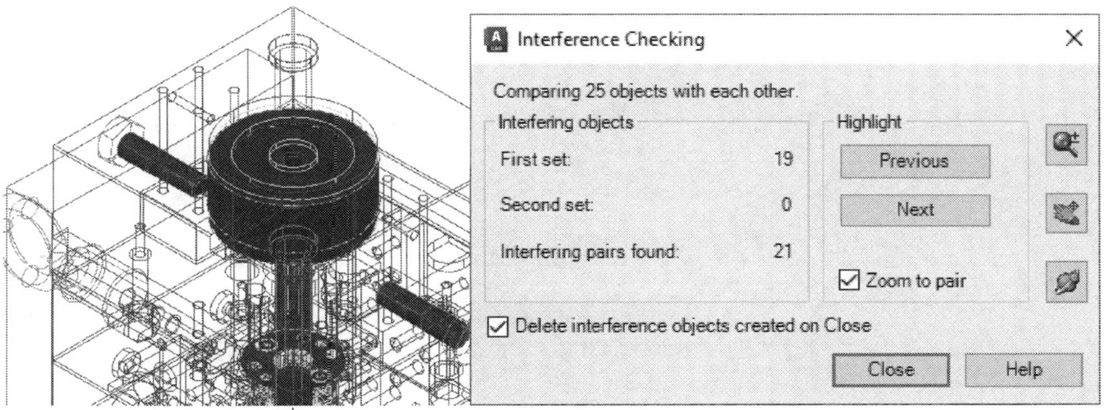

Figure 7–14

How To: Check Interferences Between Two or More Solids

You can specify one selection set of solids where each solid is checked against all others, or two selection sets where the entire set is checked against the other set.

1. In the *Home* tab>Solid Editing panel, click (Interfere).
   - Alternatively, you can access the command in the *Solid* tab>Solid Editing panel.
2. Select the first set of objects and press <Enter>.
3. For one selection set, press <Enter> to accept the **Check First Set** option without selecting other objects. For two selection sets, select the second set of objects, and press <Enter>.

4. The Interference Checking dialog box opens as shown in Figure 7–15. It displays information about the interferences and options for modifying the view to display the information more clearly.

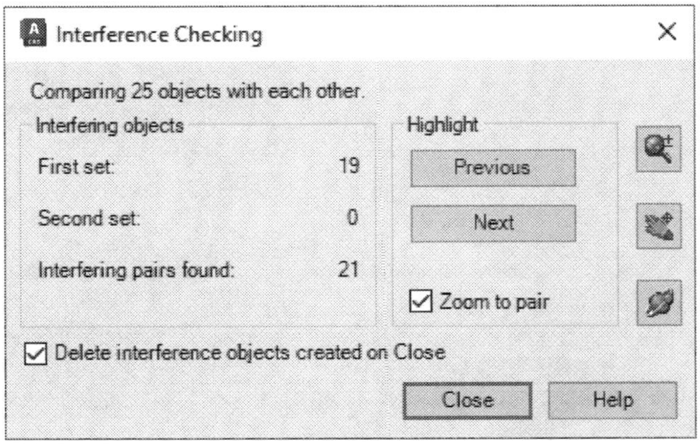

Figure 7–15

5. Click **Close** to close the Interference Checking dialog box.

- If you have more than one interfering pair, click **Previous** or **Next** to highlight the various pairs of objects.
- While using **Previous** or **Next**, if the **Zoom to pair** option is selected, the screen zooms in automatically to display the current pair of solids.
- To zoom, pan, or orbit while remaining in Interference Checking mode, click the icons in the Interference Checking dialog box. When you have finished navigating, press <Enter> or <Esc>, or right-click and select **Exit** to return to the dialog box.
- If the **Delete interference objects created on Close** option is selected, the interference objects are discarded. If you clear the option, new objects are created in your drawing.

Interference Check Options

Two additional options are available: **Nested Selection** and **Settings**. Select an option before selecting objects.

- The **Nested Selection** option enables you to select individual solid objects that are nested in blocks or reference files.

- The **Settings** option controls the display of the interference objects, as shown in Figure 7–16. By default, the *Visual style* of the interference objects is set to **Realistic** with the *Color* set to **Red**, while the *Viewport* is set to **Wireframe**. These settings enable you to see the interference options in the selected solids.

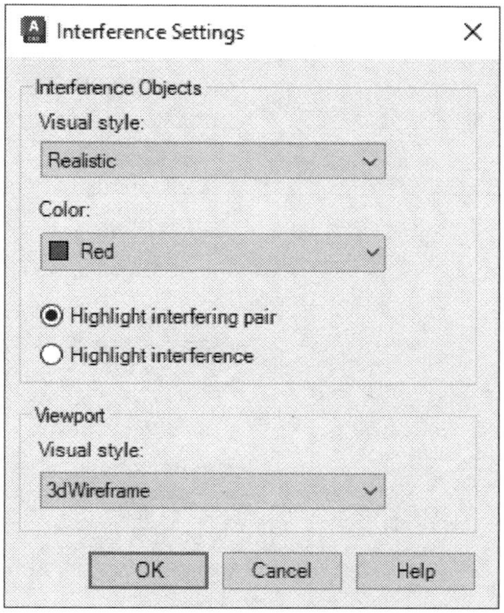

Figure 7–16

The **Highlight interfering pair** option in the Interference Settings dialog box highlights both the original objects and temporary interference objects when you toggle between interfering pairs. The **Highlight interference** option only highlights the interference objects when you toggle between pairs.

Hint: Getting Information About 3D Objects

The AutoCAD® software's standard Inquiry commands (**Distance**, **Area**, and **List**) work with 3D objects. In addition, the **Mass Properties** (**Massprop**) command is designed to give specific information about solids.

- All of the tools are available in the *Home* tab>Utilities panel in the Drafting & Annotation Workspace.
- Use the **measuregeom** command options to calculate the **Distance**, **Radius**, **Angle**, **Area**, or **Volume**.

(continued)

Hint: Getting Information About 3D Objects *(continued)*

(List) (in the *Home* tab>expanded Properties panel in the Drafting & Annotation workspace) displays information that is also found in Properties. However, in List, this information cannot be changed. What is listed varies with the type of 3D object and how it was created.

- If you list a solid primitive, the length, width, and height of the object display.
- If the solid is a composite, only the dimensions of the bounding box display (the smallest rectangular boundary into which the object fits).
- Extruded, revolved, swept, and lofted solids or surfaces list their associated information, while planar surfaces only display the bounding box.

(Area) with the **Object** option selected, displays the surface area of a 3D solid. For example, if you need to know how much paint is required to cover your 3D model or how long an object would take to dissolve, use **Area** to determine the model's area.

- Surfaces have an area.

The **Mass Properties** command calculates and displays the mass properties of a set of selected solids for mechanical designers who require more detailed information about 3D objects.

- All properties apply to the entire selection set. For example, if you select two objects, Mass Properties returns the combined mass of the objects.
- The AutoCAD software uses a *density* of **1**, so that the value of Mass is equal to the value of Volume.
- If you write the Mass Properties information to a file, the file is saved as <drawingname>.MPR.

Practice 7d Interference Checking

Practice Objective

- Check the interference between several parts of an assembly.

In this practice, you will check the interference between several parts of an assembly, as shown in Figure 7–17.

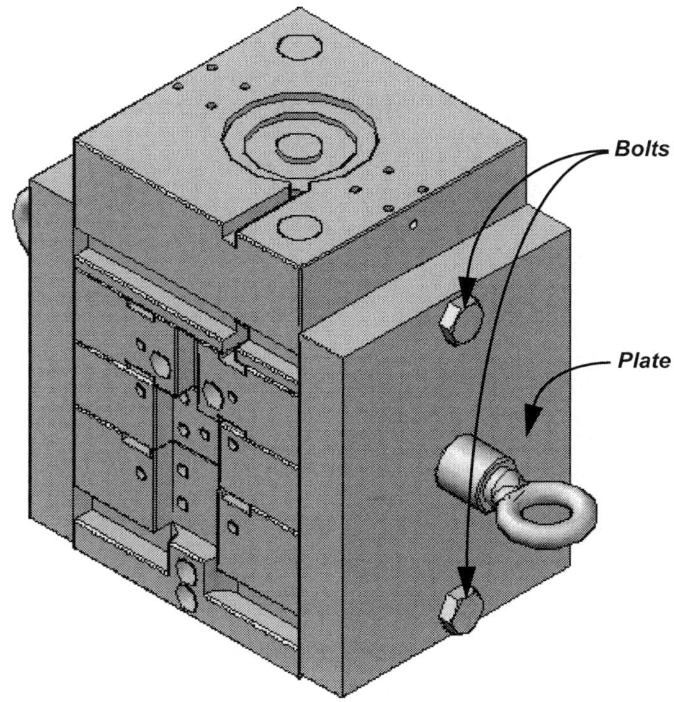

Figure 7–17

1. Open **Mold-Assembly.dwg**.

2. In the *Solid* tab>Solid Editing panel, click  (Interfere).

3. Select the two bolts on the red plate on the right side and press <Enter>.

4. For the second set of objects, select the red plate on the right side of the mold. Press <Enter>.

5. The highlighted areas display the interference, and the Interference Checking dialog box provides the various numbers, as shown in Figure 7–18.

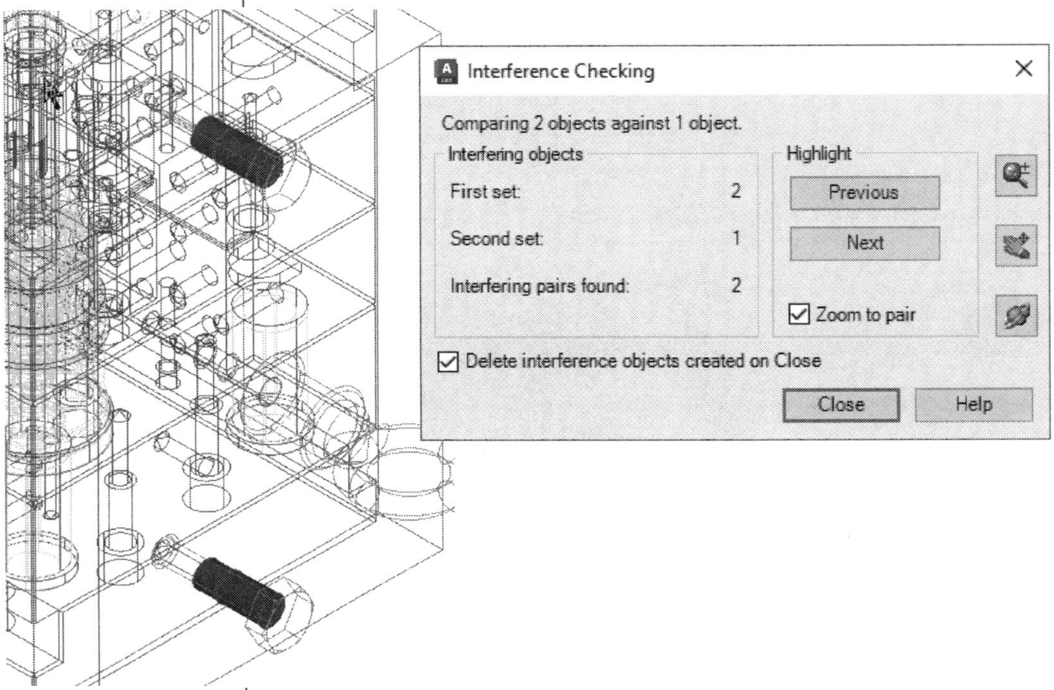

Figure 7–18

6. Click **Close** in the dialog box.

7. Click  (Interfere).

This is a quick method of highlighting all interfering geometry.

8. At the *Select first set of objects* prompt, type **All** and press <Enter> twice.

9. At the *Select second set of objects* prompt, press <Enter>.

10. In the Interference Checking dialog box, click **Next** to display each interference area.

11. Click **Close**.

12. Save and close the drawing.

7.5 Converting Objects to Surfaces

When working with legacy drawings, they might contain 3D-like objects. You can update them to the new surface objects using tools such as **Planar Surface**, **Convert to Surface**, and **Explode** to convert curved solids to surfaces.

Creating Planar Surfaces from 2D Objects

Planar surfaces are not solids, but they are the most basic type of surface. The **Planar Surface** command enables you to create flat rectangular surfaces or turn existing 2D closed objects into flat surfaces, as shown in Figure 7–19.

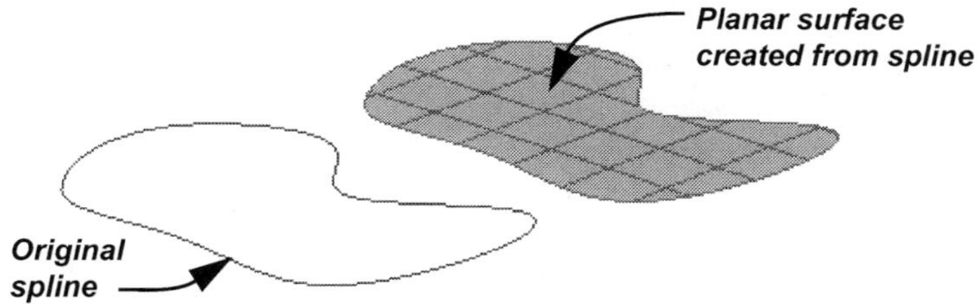

Figure 7–19

How To: Create Planar Surfaces from 2D Objects

1. Draw the closed 2D object(s), such as a polyline or a spline.
2. In the *Surface* tab>Create panel, click (Planar Surface).
3. Select **Object**.
4. Select the object(s) to convert.
5. Press <Enter>.

Converting 2D Objects to Surfaces

Lines, arcs, and polylines must have thickness before you convert them. Polylines cannot have a width.

The **Convert to Surface** command can change objects to surfaces. Objects can include circles, rectangles, other closed polylines, 2D solids, regions, planar 3D faces, 3D solids, and lines, open polylines, and arcs with thickness, as shown in Figure 7–20.

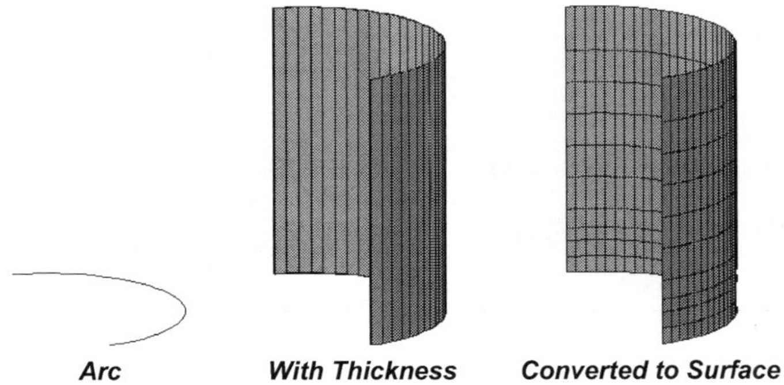

Figure 7–20

How To: Convert Objects to Surfaces

1. In the *Mesh* tab>Convert Mesh panel, click  (Convert to Surface).
   - Alternatively, you can access the command in the *Home* tab>expanded Solid Editing panel.
2. Select the objects you want to convert and press <Enter>.

Hint: Thickness

Thickness is a projection in the Z-direction of a 2D object that lies on the XY plane, as shown in Figure 7–21. Adding thickness to 2D objects can give the impression of 3D, but they are not actually 3D objects.

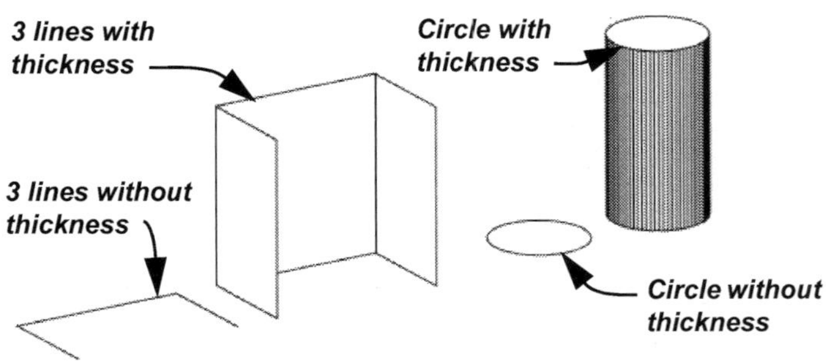

Figure 7–21

- You can change the thickness of existing objects in Properties.

Converting Solids to Surfaces

When you use (Explode) to explode curved solids, such as the cylinder shown in Figure 7–22, the curved portion of the solid becomes a surface. The flat portion of the solid becomes a region.

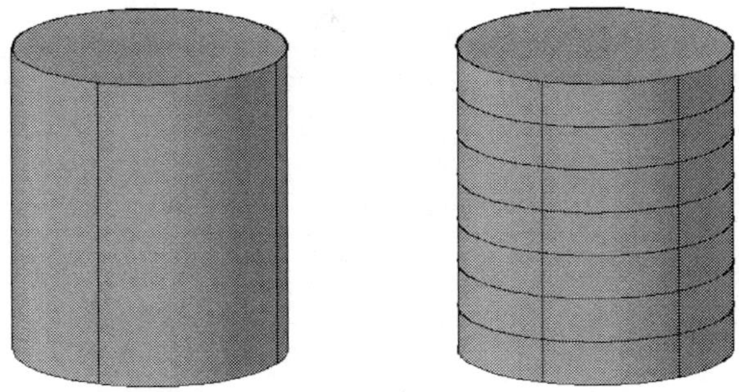

Solid ***Surface and Regions***

Figure 7–22

- Regions can be converted to surfaces with the **Convert to Surface** command.
- When you explode flat surfaces, they also become a region. Curved surfaces become arcs and lines.

> **Hint: Using Surfaces**
>
> A surface is a non-solid, zero-thickness feature that can define a contoured shape. Surfaces help capture the design intent of complex shapes that are not easily defined using solid features. Once defined, surfaces can be used as references to help create other features (solid and non-solid).

7.6 Converting Objects to Solids

The easiest way to convert 2D objects to a solid is to use **Presspull**. It automatically creates a region around the enclosed area and extrudes it. You cannot use **Presspull** on surfaces, but you might have some 2D objects with thickness in your drawing that can be converted, as shown in Figure 7–23. You can use **Convert to Solid** on some 2D elements and **Thicken** to convert surfaces to solids. If you need to create a wireframe diagram from a solid, use **Extract Edges**.

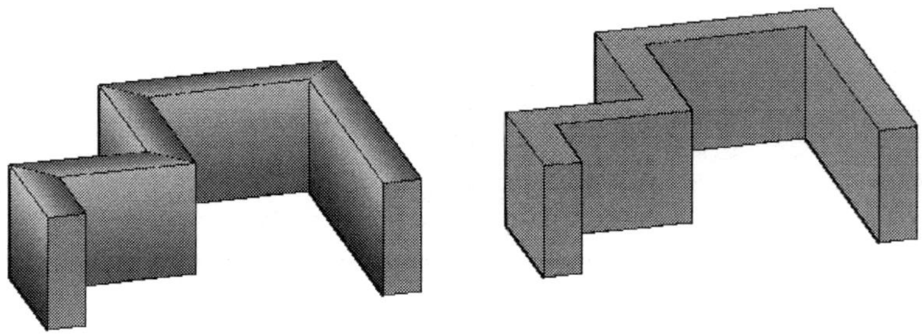

Polyline with width and thickness ***Converted to solid***

Figure 7–23

Converting 2D Objects to Solids

You can create solids from circles or polylines that have thickness by using **Convert to Solid**. A polyline can be open and have a uniform width or be closed without any width, as shown in Figure 7–24.

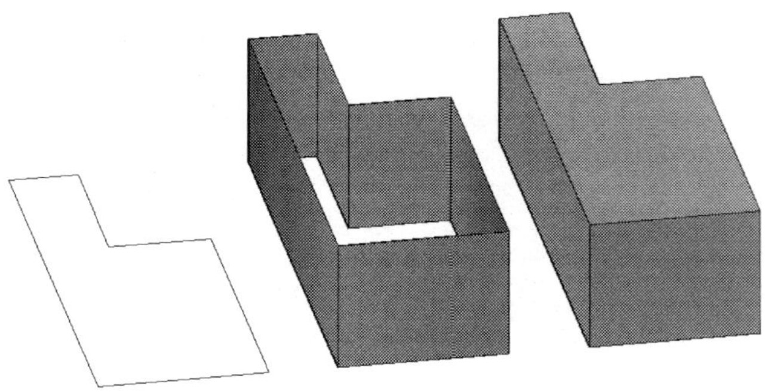

Closed polyline ***With thickness*** ***Converted to solid***

Figure 7–24

How To: Convert Objects to Solids

1. In the *Home* tab>expanded Solid Editing panel, click (Convert to Solid).
    - Alternatively, you can access the command in the *Home* tab>expanded Solid Editing panel.
2. Select the objects to be converted and press <Enter>.

- You can start the command and then select objects or select objects and then start the command.

Converting Surfaces to Solids

If you have surface objects in your drawing, you can convert them to solids using **Thicken**, as shown in Figure 7–25. The surface can be created with the **Planar Surface** command or any of the commands that use open profiles and paths, such as **Extrude**, **Sweep**, **Revolve**, and **Loft**. the **Planar Surface** command enables you to convert 2D closed objects into flat surfaces.

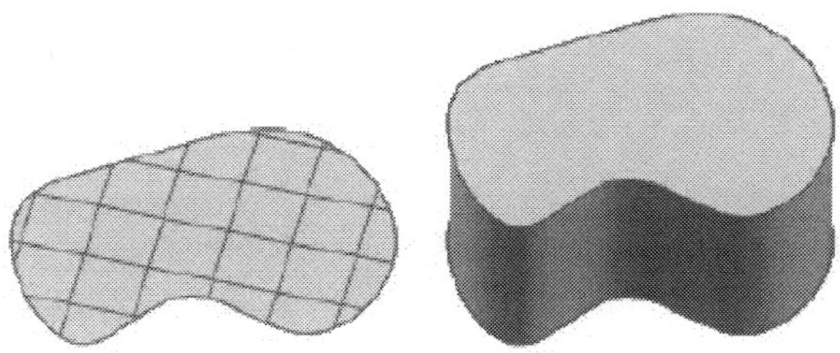

Figure 7–25

How To: Convert Surfaces to Solids

1. In the *Home* tab>Solid Editing panel, click (Thicken).
    - Alternatively, you can access the command in the *Solid* tab>Solid Editing panel.
2. Select the objects you want to convert and press <Enter>.
3. You are prompted for the thickness of the new solid.

- You can start the command and then select objects or select objects and then start the command.
- A positive thickness creates the solid in the positive axis of the plane. A negative thickness creates the solid in the opposite direction.

Converting Solids or Surfaces to Wireframe

You can extract edges from solids or surfaces to create wireframe drawings, as shown in Figure 7–26.

- The original object remains, but cannot be moved or erased.

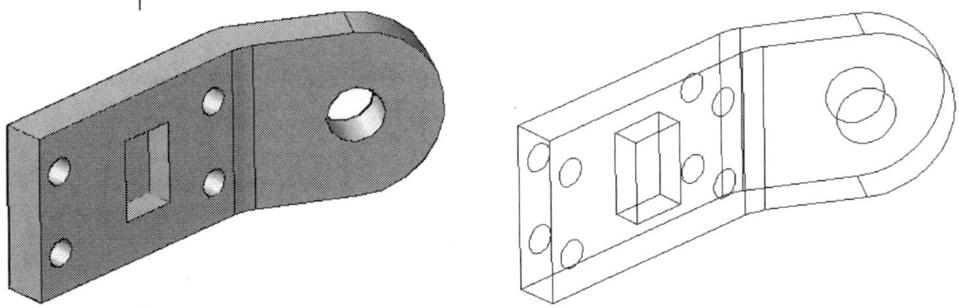

Figure 7–26

How To: Convert Solids or Surfaces to Wireframe

1. In the *Home* tab>Solid Editing panel, click 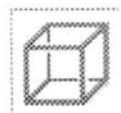 (Extract Edges).
    - Alternatively you can access the command in the *Solid* tab>Solid Editing panel.
2. Select the objects from which you want to extract edges and press <Enter>.

Practice 7e Converting Objects to Surfaces and Solids

Practice Objective

- Add thickness to a polyline profile and convert it into a surface and a solid.

In this practice, you will add a thickness to a polyline profile and copy it. You will then turn one copy into a surface, modify it, and convert it to a solid. You will also modify the other copy of the polyline and convert it to a solid. Both are shown in Figure 7–27.

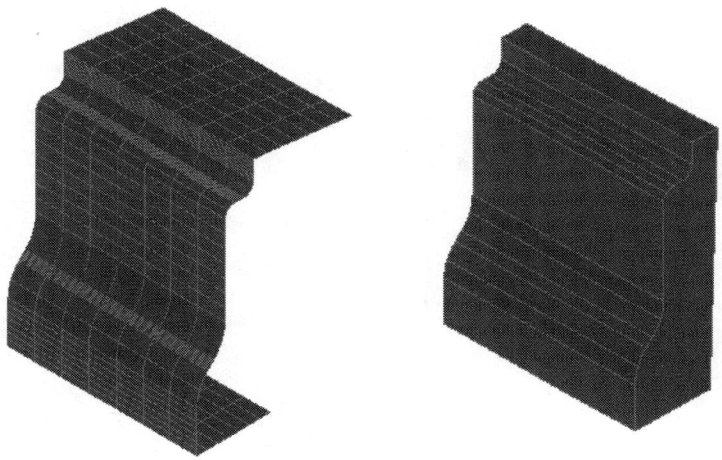

Figure 7–27

1. Open **Profile.dwg**.

2. Select the existing profile. In Properties, change the *Thickness* to **10**. The object now looks like a surface but is still a polyline, as shown in Figure 7–28.

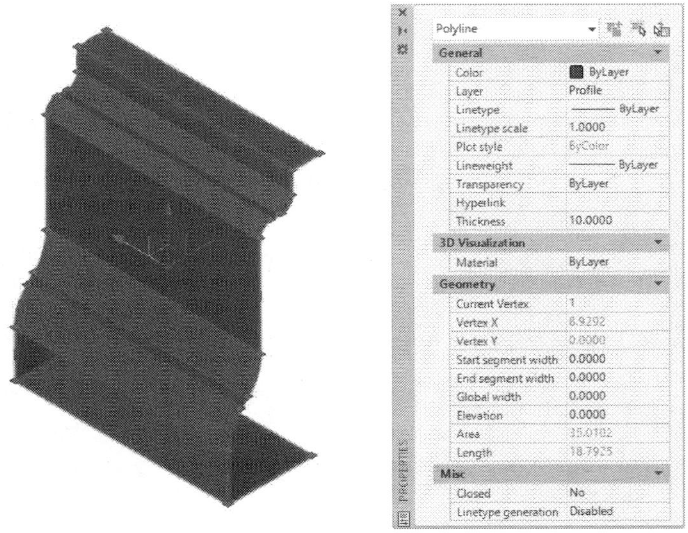

Figure 7–28

3. Make a copy of this polyline.

4. In the *Mesh* tab>Convert Mesh panel, click  (Convert to Surface). Select one of the polylines and press <Enter>. The polyline is now an extruded surface. Polyline and the newly converted extruded surface are overlapping each other. Use the **Move** command to move the extruded surface on the side, as shown in Figure 7–29. You will notice that the surface separates from the polyline.

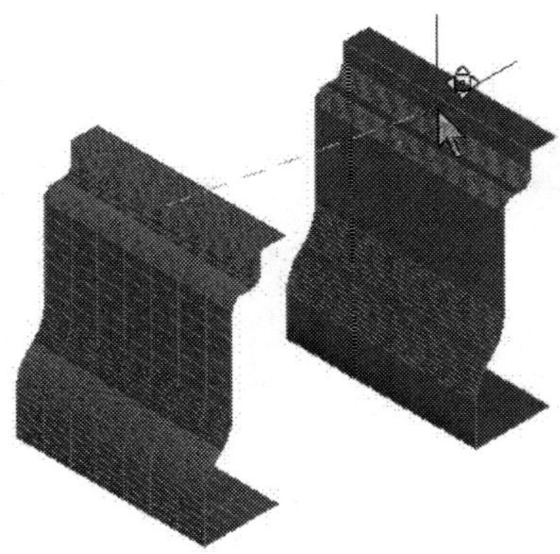

Figure 7–29

Each vertex of the surface profile can be modified.

5. Use the top corner grip to lengthen the top surface, similar to that shown in Figure 7–30.

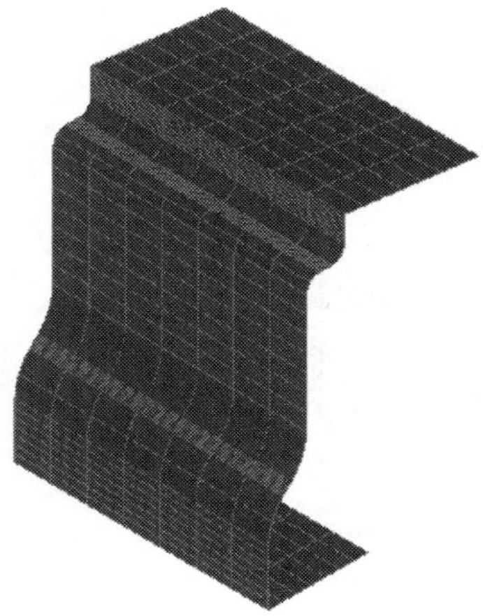

Figure 7–30

6. In the *Mesh* tab>Convert Mesh panel, click (Convert to Solid) and select the surface and press <Enter>. Note in the Command line that it cannot convert the surface into a solid.

You might have to change the draw order of the polyline and send it to the back to make selecting the surface easier.

7. In the *Home* tab>Solid Editing panel, click (Thicken). Select the surface and press <Enter>. Set the *Thickness* to **0.5**. The surface is converted to a solid, as shown in Figure 7–31.

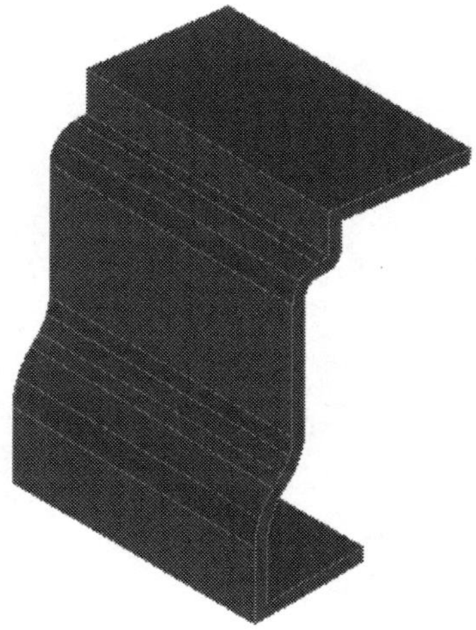

Figure 7–31

8. On the *Home* tab>expanded Solid Editing panel, click  (Convert to Solid) and select the other polyline with thickness and press <Enter>. This one cannot be converted because it is an open curve.

9. Select the polyline, right-click, expand Polyline, and select **Edit Polyline**. Select **Close.** Note that the polyline is closed.

10. On the *Home* tab>expanded Solid Editing panel, click  (Convert to Solid), select the closed polyline, and press <Enter>. The solid is created, as shown in Figure 7–32.

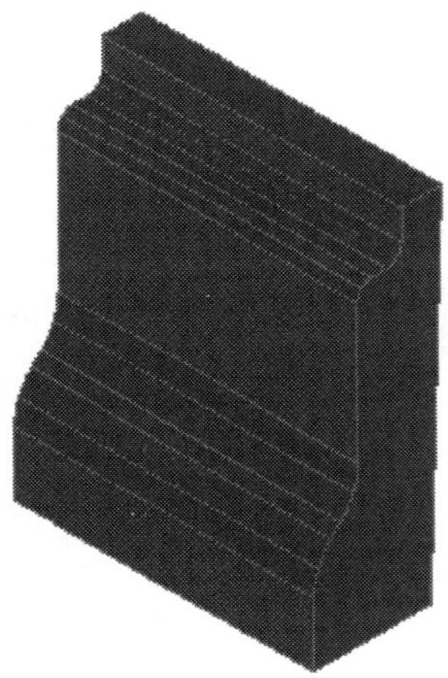

Figure 7–32

11. Save and close the drawing.

Practice 7f

Mechanical Project - Connector

Practice Objective

- Create a 3D solid model using various 3D modeling tools.

In this practice, you will create a solid model from the connector shown in Figure 7–33.

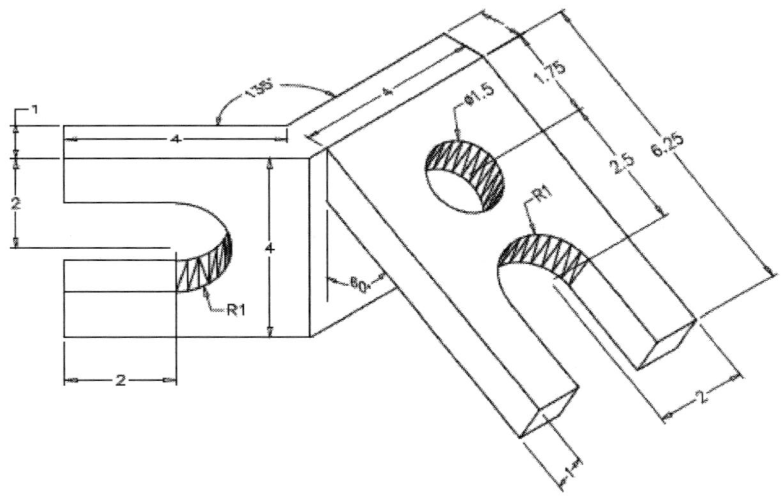

Figure 7–33

1. Start a new drawing based on **acad3D.dwt**. Save it in your practice files folder as **Connect.dwg**.

2. Draw a solid model of the connector shown in Figure 7–33. Do not include the dimensions.

- The volume of the part should be approximately **44.6** cubic units.

Chapter Review Questions

1. Which command enables you to hollow out a solid?
    a. **Union**
    b. **Subtract**
    c. **Shell**
    d. **Presspull**
2. You can imprint a 2D object on a solid and then modify the new faces or edges.
    a. True
    b. False
3. Which half remains when you cut a solid using the **Slice** command?
    a. Only the left half remains.
    b. Only the right half remains.
    c. Both halves always remain.
    d. It is your choice which half remains.
4. With the **Interference Check** command, which option do you specify to control the display of interference objects?
    a. **Settings**
    b. **Visual Styles**
    c. **Highlight Interference**
    d. **Nested Selection**
5. The **Extract Edges** command is used to create...
    a. Meshes
    b. Profiles
    c. Wireframes
    d. 2D objects
6. Which of the following commands do you use to convert 2D closed objects into flat surfaces?
    a. **Convert to Surface**
    b. **Extrude**
    c. **Planar Surface**
    d. **Explode**

Command Summary

All ribbon names reference the 3D Modeling workspace.

Button	Command	Location
	**Area**	• **Ribbon:** *Home* tab>Utilities panel (*in the 2D Drafting and Annotation workspace*)
	**Check**	• **Ribbon:** *Home* tab>Solid Editing panel>Separate flyout or *Solid* tab>Solid Editing panel>Shell flyout
	**Clean**	• **Ribbon:** *Home* tab>Solid Editing panel>Separate flyout or *Solid* tab>Solid Editing panel>Shell flyout
	**Convert to Solid**	• **Ribbon:** *Home* tab>expanded Solid Editing panel or *Mesh* tab>Convert Mesh panel
	**Convert to Surface**	• **Ribbon:** *Home* tab>expanded Solid Editing panel or *Mesh* tab>Convert Mesh panel
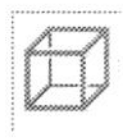	**Extract Edges**	• **Ribbon:** *Home* tab>Solid Editing panel or *Solid* tab>Solid Editing panel
	**Imprint**	• **Ribbon:** *Home* tab>Solid Editing panel>Extract Edges flyout or *Solid* tab>Solid Editing panel
	**Interfere**	• **Ribbon:** *Home* tab>Solid Editing panel or *Solid* tab>Solid Editing panel
	**List**	• **Ribbon:** *Home* tab>Utilities panel (*in the 2D Drafting and Annotation workspace*)
N/A	**Mass Properties**	• **Command Prompt:** massprop
	**Planar Surface**	• **Ribbon:** *Surface* tab>Create panel
	**Shell**	• **Ribbon:** *Home* tab>Solid Editing panel>Separate flyout or *Solid* tab> Solid Editing panel
	**Slice**	• **Ribbon:** *Home* tab>Solid Editing panel or *Solid* tab>Solid Editing panel
	**Thicken**	• **Ribbon:** *Home* tab>Solid Editing panel or *Solid* tab>Solid Editing panel

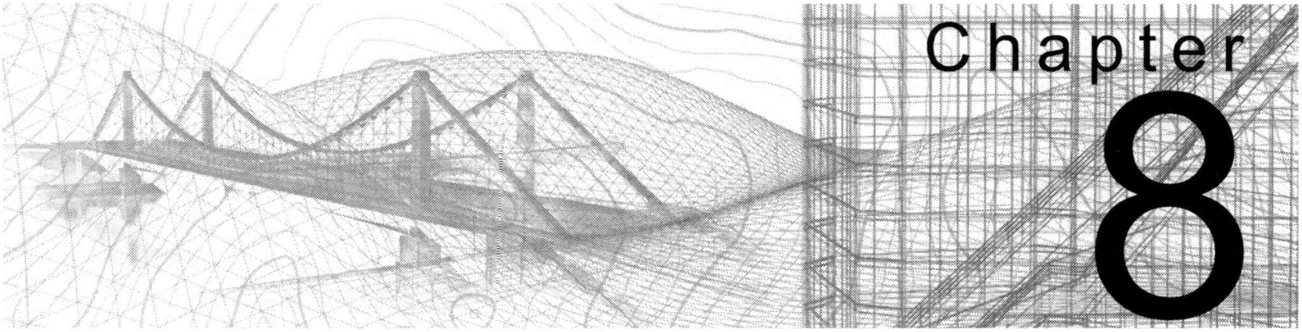

Refining the View

In this chapter, you learn how to create and view sections, create perspectives using cameras, manage views, and animate views using ShowMotion.

Learning Objectives in This Chapter

- Display slices of 3D objects without actually cutting the objects.
- Create precise pictures of objects with a specific camera location, target point, and lens length.
- Create new views that can easily be restored in the drawing window.
- Add backgrounds to views to add more realism and highlight designs.
- View movement and transitions between saved views.
- Create shots and view categories to be used for a ShowMotion animation.
- Create animation motion paths by assigning a camera and target to a path.

8.1 Working with Sections

The section commands enable you to display slices of 3D objects without actually cutting the objects, as shown in Figure 8–1. They can be considered design tools and drafting tools. Once you have created a section for working drawings, you can create a 2D section block from the live section or a 3D section block for further modification.

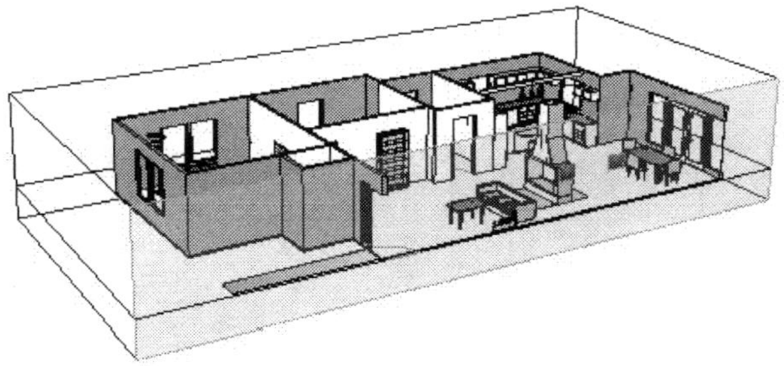

Figure 8–1

Working With Sections

Section planes work with drawing reference files (Xrefs).

There are several steps to creating and using sections as follows:

1. Place a **Section Plane** and modify it to display the most important information by setting the section type, moving grips, and setting jogs, as required.
2. View the objects with **Live Sectioning** activated.
3. Generate a **2D** or **3D section block** that can be dimensioned and used in working drawings, as shown in Figure 8–2.

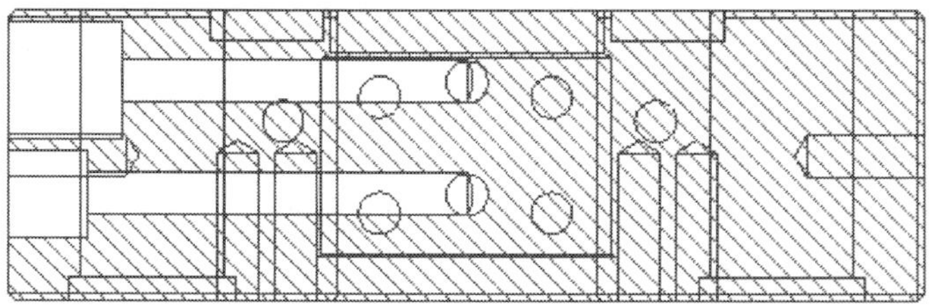

Figure 8–2

- A section plane impacts all objects in a drawing, regardless of the length, width, or height of the plane, boundary, or volume.

Setting the Section Plane

The first step in working with sections is to define the section plane and set it to work as required. You might need to modify the first placement of the plane using various section types, grips, and jogs, as shown in Figure 8–3.

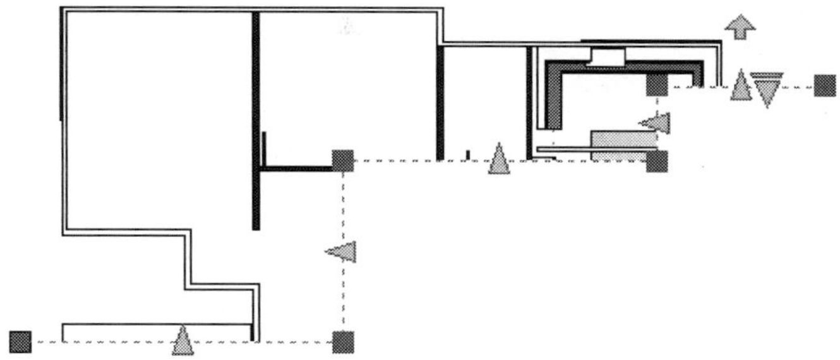

Figure 8–3

How To: Add a Section Plane

1. In the *Home* tab>Section panel, click (Section Plane).
2. Select a face or any two points to define the section. The two points must not touch any solid objects because if they do, the closest face is automatically selected.
3. The section is placed using the default settings.

- When you select two points to place a section plane, the objects do not display the cut-away view. If you use a face to place the plane, the objects display in the cut-away view. You can change this setting by right-clicking and selecting or clearing **Live Sections**.
- Object snaps, Dynamic UCS (**ducs**), and the selection of faces, edges, and sub-objects of composite solids are disabled when a section plane is in the drawing. If you freeze the layer in which the section plane is located, you can access these objects.
- While creating a **Section Plane**, select **Draw Section** to immediately create jogs, or select **Orthographic** to align the plane to the Front, Back, Top, Bottom, Left, or Right sides.

Section Plane Types

When working with a section plane object, you can view and modify the boundary in three ways, as shown in Figure 8–4.

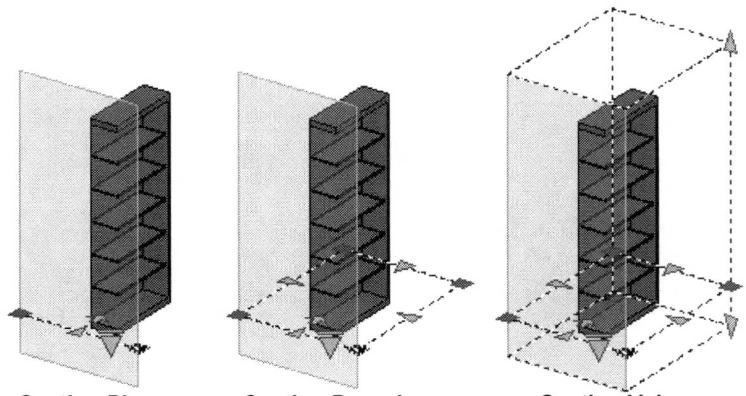

Section Plane ***Section Boundary*** ***Section Volume***

Figure 8–4

- **Section Plane:** Only displays the cut through the solid.
- **Section Boundary:** Displays the plane and the base of the boundary that the plane impacts.
- **Section Volume:** Displays the boundary and height of the plane.

Section Plane Grips

	Menu grip switches between section types, as shown in Figure 8–5.
	Arrow grips move back and forth in a defined direction.
	Standard square grips can be moved independent to other grips, similar to a vertex in solids.
	Flip arrow grip mirrors cut of section.

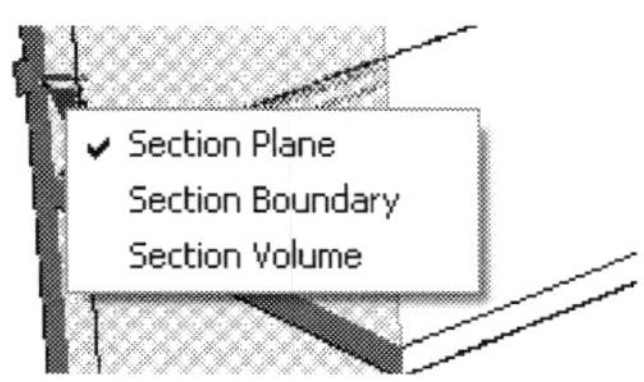

Figure 8–5

How To: Add a Jog to a Section

1. Select a section object (set the type to **Plane** for ease of manipulation).
2. Right-click and select **Add jog to section**.
3. Select a point on the section line to add the jog. The **Nearest** object snap is on automatically, enabling you to easily select a point on the section line.
4. A jog is placed automatically. Use grips to modify it as required.

- If you are working with a complex architectural model, switch to a parallel top view with the **2D Wireframe** visual style. Then use the **Layer Isolate** command to isolate only those layers that help you to place the section, as shown in Figure 8–6. Switch to a 3D view to finish creating the section.

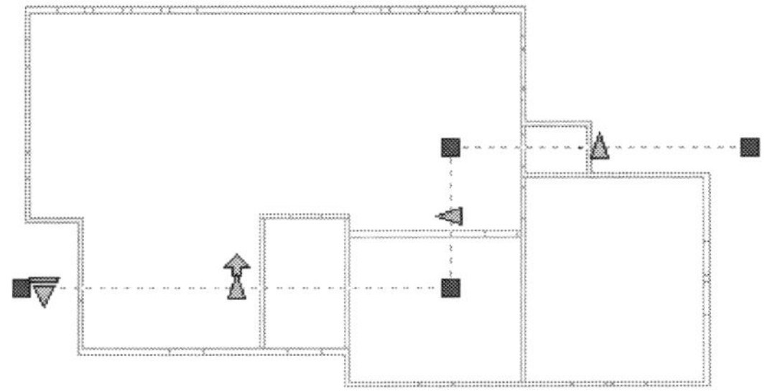

Figure 8–6

Working with Live Sections

Live Sections display a cut-away view of the object, as shown in Figure 8–7. They are on by default when you create a section by face, but off when you create a section by selecting points. You can toggle **Live Sections** on and off in the shortcut menu, in Properties, or by double-clicking on the section plane.

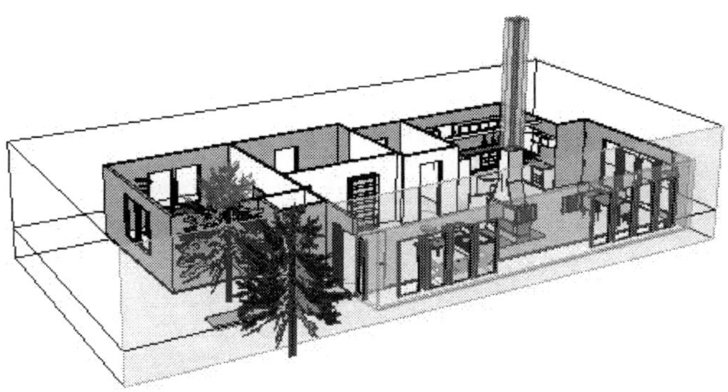

Live Section activated with cut-away geometry displayed

Figure 8–7

- If **Live Sections** is on, you can display the full model with the cut-away section highlighted. Right-click and select **Show cut-away geometry**, as shown in Figure 8–8.

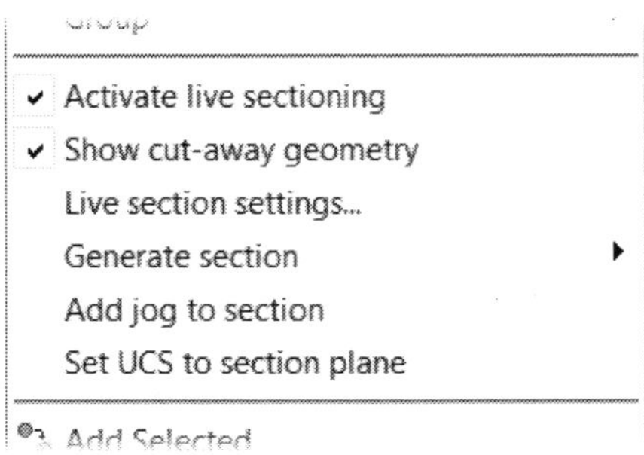

Figure 8–8

- You can use **Live sections settings…** in the shortcut menu to modify the way in which Live Sections and cut-away geometry display. The Section Settings dialog box opens as shown in Figure 8–9.

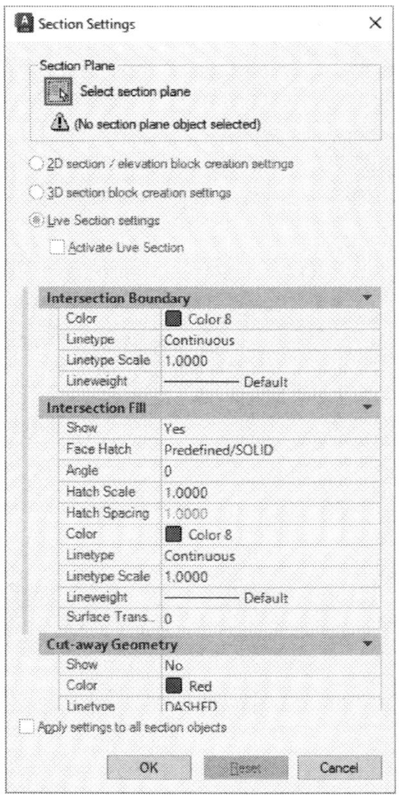

Figure 8–9

Generating Sections from Section Planes

When you generate a section, you can create a 2D or 3D object. In both cases, the objects are inserted into the current drawing as a block by default. Both objects can be scaled and rotated as you insert them, just like any other block. Neither object is linked to the original solids. A 2D section of a building is shown in Figure 8–10.

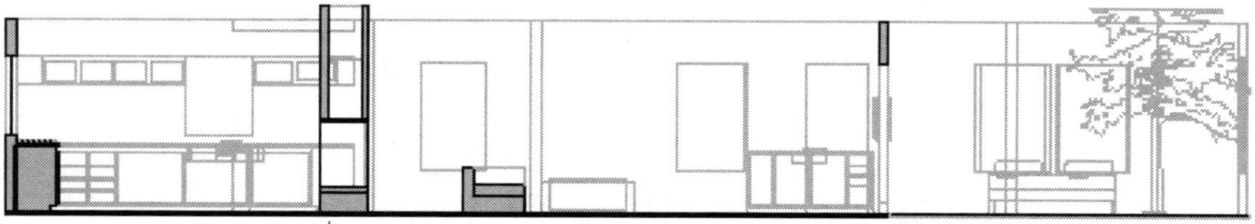

Figure 8–10

- 2D Section/Elevation objects can be used in working drawings to dimension or diagram.
- 3D Sections are full 3D objects that are cut at the section plane. A hatch also displays at the face where the 3D object was cut. 3D Sections can also be used in working drawings or as the base of another object.

How To: Generate a 2D or 3D Section

1. Select the section plane.
2. Right-click, expand **Generate section** and select **2D/3D block...**.
3. In the Generate Section/Elevation dialog box, select **2D Section/Elevation** or **3D Section**, as shown in Figure 8–11.

If you explode a 2D section, it consists of lines, arcs, etc. with hatches on the section cut. When you explode a 3D section, the objects are still solids.

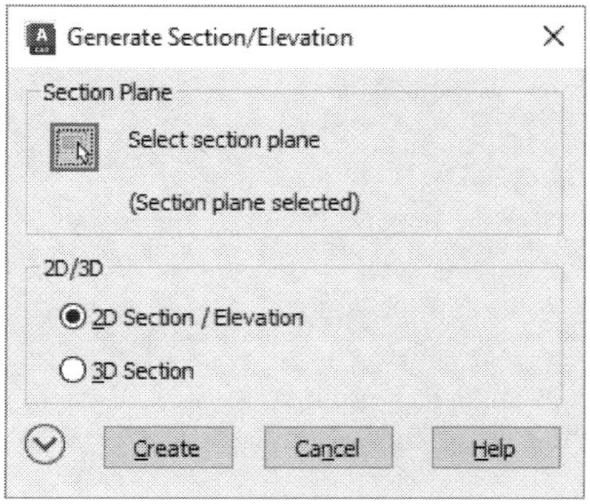

Figure 8–11

4. Click **Create**.
5. Specify the insertion point, the X- and Y-scale factors, and the rotation for the block.

- By default, all objects in the drawing are included in the section object. If you want to select specific objects to include, update an existing section block in the drawing or export the section to a new file. Click  to expand the Generate Section/Elevation dialog box.

Hint: Section Plane Properties

You can modify section planes in Properties, as shown in Figure 8–12.

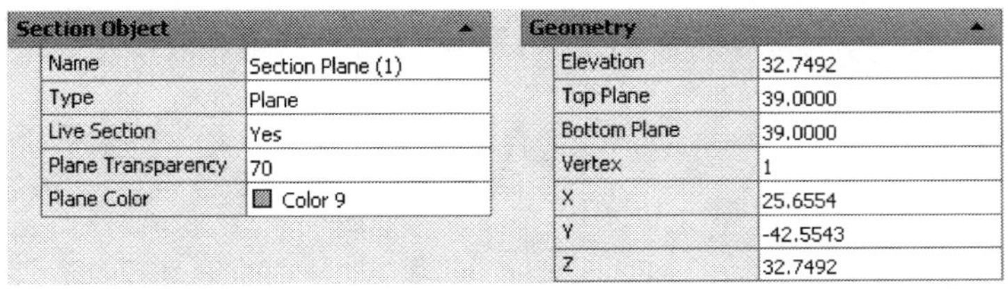

Figure 8–12

You can change the *Type* and *Live Section* settings instead of using grips, and set the geometry of the plane. You can also modify the *Name* of each section object in a drawing and change its *Plane Color* and *Plane Transparency*.

Practice 8a Working with Sections

Practice Objective

- Create a section plane of a 3D solid and create a copy of the remaining section using the section commands.

In this practice, you will create a section plane and then view the section and cut-away portion using Live Sections, as shown on the left in Figure 8–13. You will then create a 3D section, as shown on the right in Figure 8–13.

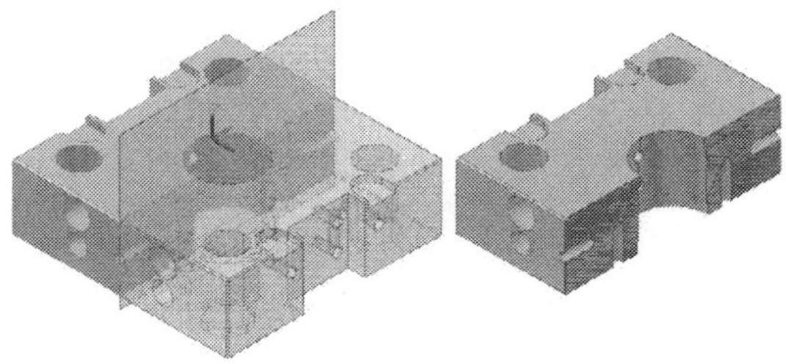

Figure 8–13

1. Open **Bottom-Plate.dwg** and switch to the **SE Isometric** view.

2. In the *Home* tab>Section panel, click  (Section Plane).

Ensure you select the center of the hole and not the face of the solid.

3. Click the center of the small hole on the left side of the mold plate. For the second point of the section, orbit around the model, and select the center of the similar hole on the other side to create a section plane through the plate, as shown in Figure 8–14. Only half of the model is displayed as solid.

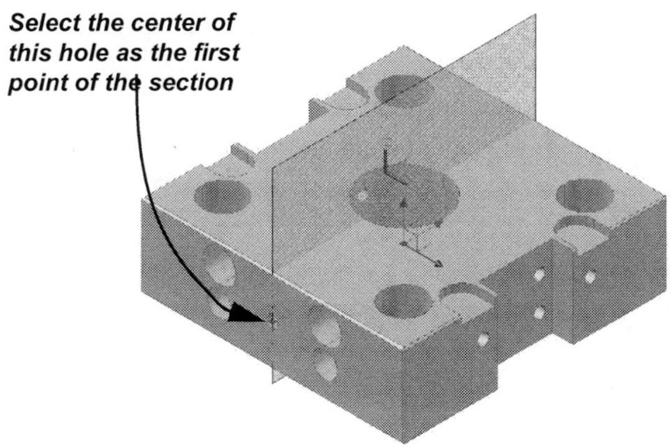

Figure 8–14

4. Select the new section plane. Right-click and ensure that **Activate live sectioning** is checked. Press <Esc> to clear the selection and view the sectioned object, as shown in Figure 8–15. Note that the cut -away geometry is not visible.
5. Select the section plane again, right-click, and select **Show cut-away geometry**. Press <Esc> to clear the selection. The cut-away geometry of the solid displays in red.
6. To make the cut-away section display more clearly, select the section plane, right-click, and select **Live section settings**.
7. In the Section Settings dialog box, scroll to the *Cut-away Geometry* area and set the *Color* to **yellow**. Click **OK**. Press <Esc> to clear the selection. The cut-away geometry displays as yellow, as shown in Figure 8–16.

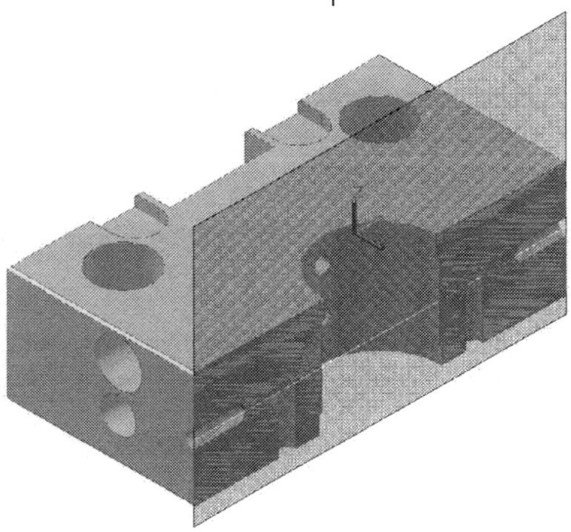

Figure 8–15

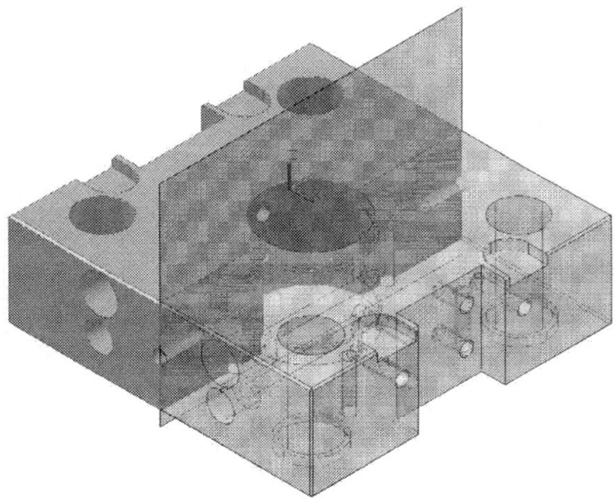

Figure 8–16

8. Select the section plane, right-click, and select **Generate section>2D/3D block**.
9. In the Generate Section/Elevation dialog box, select **3D section** and click **Create**.
10. Place the section next to the existing solid at the default scale and rotation.
11. To remove the section plane, select and erase it.
12. Save and close the drawing.

8.2 Working with Cameras

To show a design to clients and others, you need to display it in a way that enables them to clearly understand what the final design is going to look like. Perspectives give the most realistic view of buildings and other large objects by displaying them as the eye would actually see them from a particular viewpoint. Figure 8–17 displays the Camera Preview on the left, and the location and direction of the camera in the **Top** view on the right.

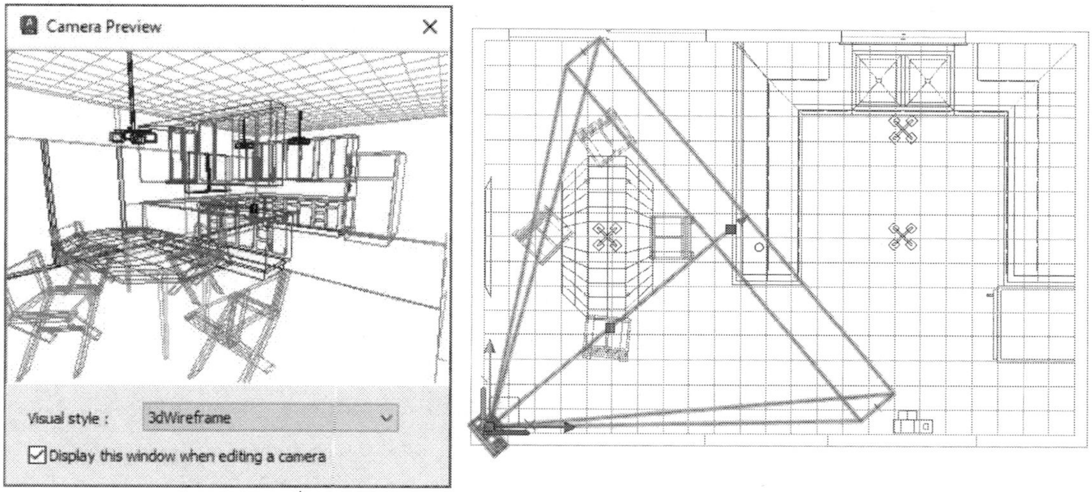

Figure 8–17

By placing a camera, you can create precise pictures of objects with a specific camera location, target point, and lens length. You can also clip the views to *cut away* objects in front of or behind the target.

You might need to toggle on the visibility of the Camera panel on the ribbon, as it might not be on by default.

- The camera enables you to create basic perspectives and specify visual styles for the view. For more sophisticated rendered views, use a software such as 3ds Max.

How To: Add a Camera

*The easiest method of adding a camera is often to do so in the **Top** (plan) view.*

1. While in a **Top** (plan) view, in the *Visualize* tab>Camera panel, click  (Create Camera).
2. Specify the camera location and the target location (what the camera is pointing at), as shown in Figure 8–18.

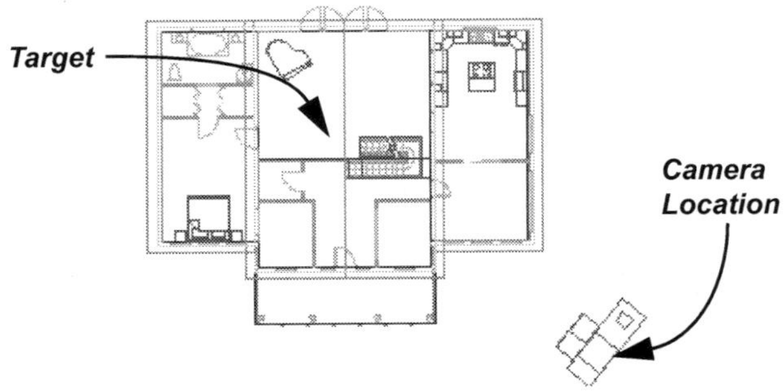

Figure 8–18

3. Specify the options as required or press <Enter> to complete the command. These options can be adjusted after the camera is placed.

> **Hint: Cameras on the Tool Palette**
>
> You can access cameras with some preset options in the Cameras tool palette, as shown in Figure 8–19.
>
> 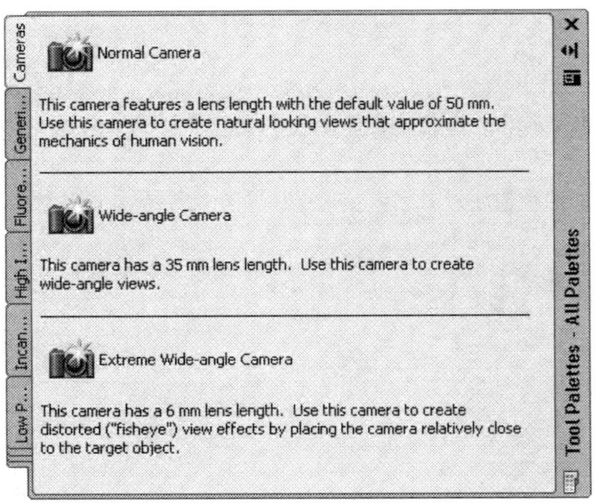
>
>
> **Figure 8–19**

Adjusting a Camera

To modify a camera, click on the camera icon. The Camera Preview opens and grips display on the camera icon. The various grips allow you to modify those camera and target settings. Grip options include the Camera and Target locations, Target distance, and Lens length/FOV (Field of view). The same information can be modified more precisely in Properties, as shown in Figure 8–20.

To open the Properties palette, right-click on the camera and select ***Properties****. The Properties palette can remain open at all times. Dock and hide it to one side of the drawing window.*

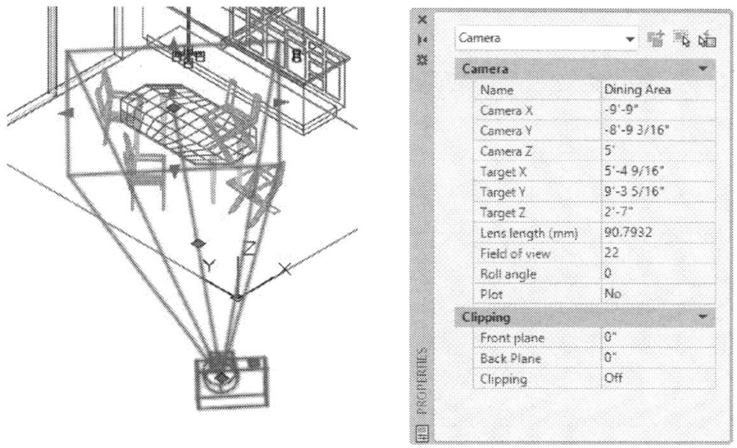

Figure 8–20

- In Properties, you can also name the camera and create clipping planes.
- The Camera Preview opens an additional window that displays the picture the camera is taking. You can set the visual style for this view.
- If you do not want to use the additional Camera Preview window, clear the **Display this window when editing a camera** option.
- When a camera has been added to the drawing, you can apply the view to Model Space or to a Paper Space layout by selecting its name in the 3D Navigation Control in the *Home* tab>View panel, as shown in Figure 8–21.

You can also view the picture created by the camera by right-clicking on the camera icon and selecting ***Set Camera View****.*

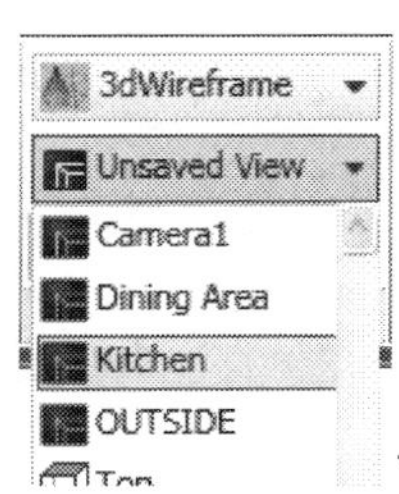

Figure 8–21

- You can change the Lens length using the slider, and the Camera and Target locations by changing the X-, Y-, and Z-coordinates in the *Home* tab>expanded View panel, as shown in Figure 8–22.

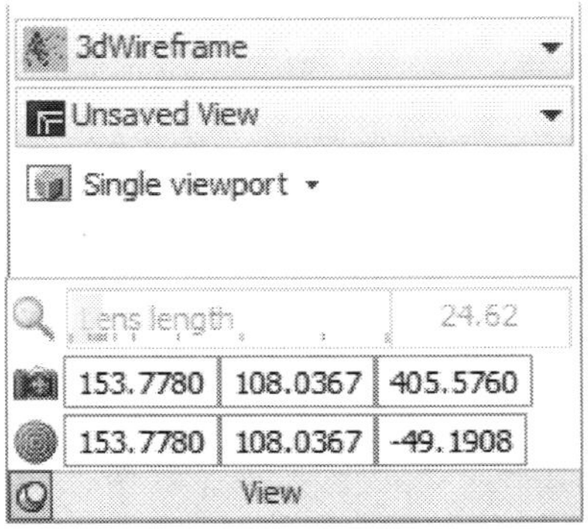

Figure 8–22

Clipping Camera Views

When laying out a drawing for presentation, you might want to display a cut-away view. The most precise way to do this is to create a section plane in the drawing. However, you can also use camera clip planes that enable you to view a model with the sections removed, as shown in Figure 8–23.

Figure 8–23

- Drawings have two clip planes: front and back. Both are perpendicular to the line of sight or parallel to the screen. The front clip plane removes the portion of the design in front of the plane (that is, closer to the viewer) and the back clip plane removes the portion of the design behind the plane.
- It is easiest to work on clip planes in the **Top** view with the visual style set to **2D Wireframe**. You can see the camera view in the Camera Preview window with any visual style.

How To: Create Clip Planes

1. Once you have a camera in your drawing, switch to the **Top** view and set the *visual style* to **2D Wireframe**.
2. Click on the camera and open Properties.
3. In Properties, change *Clipping* to **Front on**, **Back on**, or **Front and Back on**, as shown in Figure 8–24.

Clipping	
Front plane	1'-5"
Back Plane	0"
Clipping	Front on

Figure 8–24

4. Set the *Front plane* or *Back Plane* to a number other than **0**.
5. You can modify the clip plane(s) in the drawing using grips, as shown in Figure 8–25.

When you use grips, ensure you select the correct grip to move the clip plane rather than the target. Hover the cursor over the grips to see their tooltips.

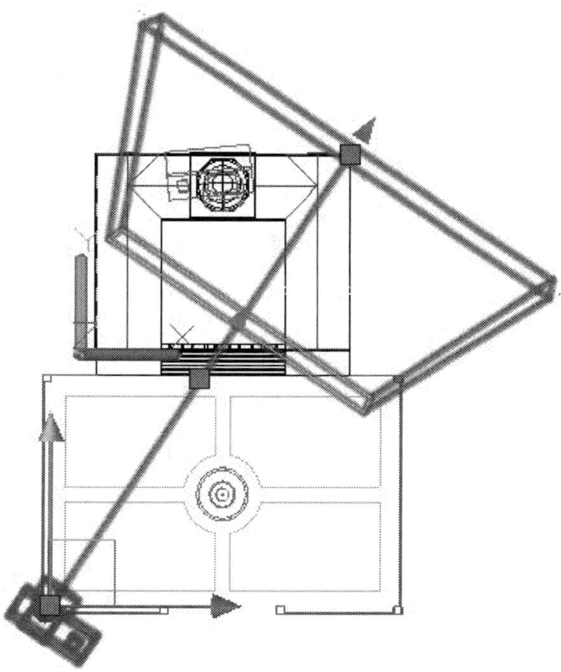

Figure 8–25

6. Move the clip planes as required until you have the required view.

Practice 8b Working with Cameras

Practice Objective

- Set up views by creating a camera and use clipping planes to view it with portions removed.

In this practice, you will set up views by creating cameras, as shown in Figure 8–26, and then use clipping planes to view a design with portions removed.

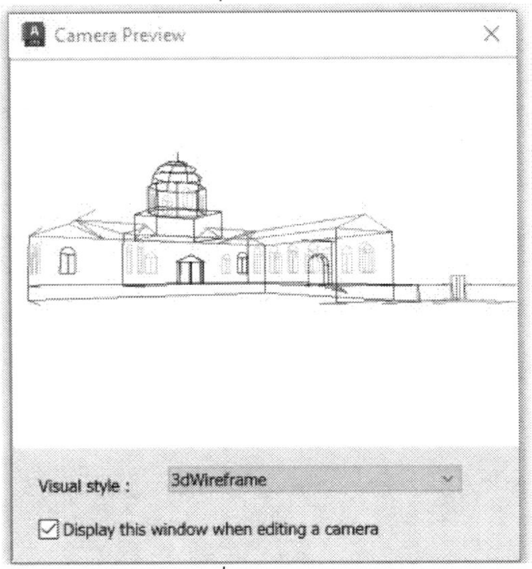

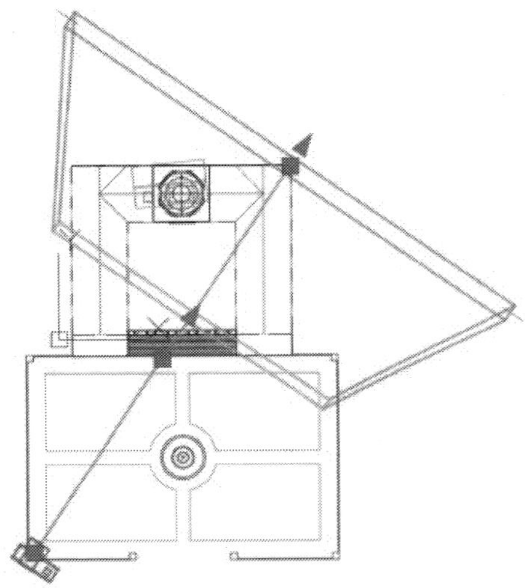

Figure 8–26

Task 1 - Create camera views.

1. Open **Museum-Perspectives.dwg**.
2. Switch to the **SW Isometric** view, if required.
3. In the *Visualize* tab>Camera panel, click (Create Camera).

*If the Camera panel is not displayed, switch to the Visualize tab, right-click on the ribbon, expand Show Panels and select **Camera**.*

4. For the camera position, select the end of the lightning rod at the top of the dome.
5. For the target, drag your cursor and select the center point at the top of the fountain. The view lines up through these two points.

6. Press <Enter> to exit the command. Hover your cursor over the camera to highlight the camera and the target as shown in Figure 8–27.

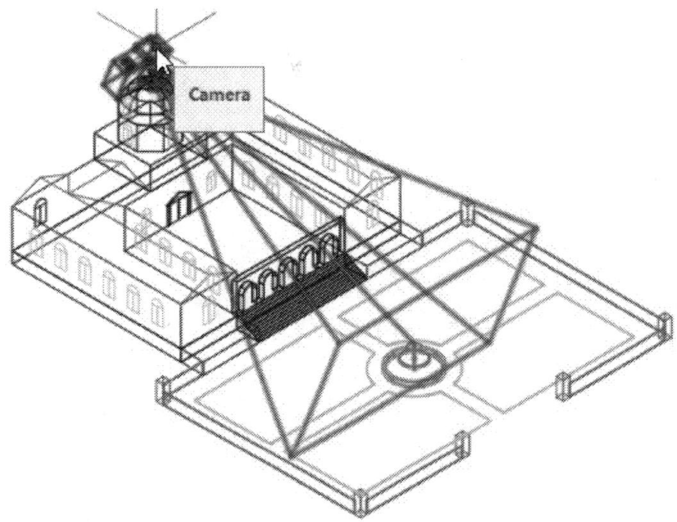

Figure 8–27

7. Click the **Camera** icon in the drawing window to open the Camera Preview dialog box. Open the Properties for the camera.

8. In Properties, change the *Name* of the camera to **Birds Eye** and change the *Lens length* (mm) to **25**.

9. Press <Esc> to clear the selection of the camera.

10. In the *Visualize* tab>Camera panel, click  (Create Camera).

11. For the camera location, select an end point at the top of the red column closest to you in the south west corner of the garden wall.

12. For the target, select the center of the middle archway at the front of the building.

13. Select **Name** from the options and enter **Front** as the *Name*. Press <Enter> twice to exit the command.

14. Click the **Front** camera icon in the drawing window to open the Camera Preview dialog box.

As you move any of the grips, the changes to the view can be seen in the Camera Preview dialog box.

15. Use the **Lens Length/FOV** and **Target** grips to adjust the view to display the entire building (you might need to toggle off object snaps and 3D object snaps temporarily to move the target grip).

16. Press <Esc> to clear the selection of the camera.

17. In the *Home* tab>View panel, expand the 3D Navigation Control and select the new **Birds Eye** camera view and note this view.

Task 2 - Work with clipping planes.

1. Switch to the **Top** view and switch to **Parallel** view, if required.

2. Select the camera (Front) on the lower left corner of the garden wall.

3. In Properties, set *Clipping* to **Front on** and set the *Front plane* to **80'-0"**.

4. Use grips to move the Target Distance behind the building. You should see part of the clipping plane start to cut some of the garden wall, portion of stairs, fountain etc, similar to that shown in Figure 8–28.

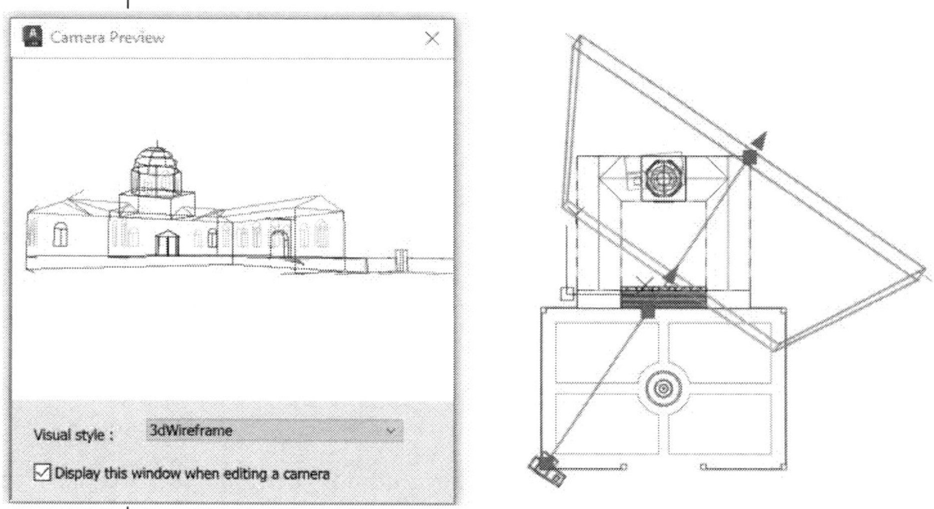

Figure 8–28

5. In Properties, set *Clipping* to **Off**.

6. Save and close the drawing.

8.3 Managing Views in 3D

Named views store still camera shots of a drawing under specified names that can easily be restored in the drawing window. The views not only keep track of camera and target locations, but also options such as the layers and UCS associated with the view. You can also create new views that do not use cameras.

Existing named views are available in the 3D Navigation Control in the *Visualize* tab>Views panel (or *Home* tab>View panel), in which you can also find preset orthographic and isometric views, as shown in Figure 8–29.

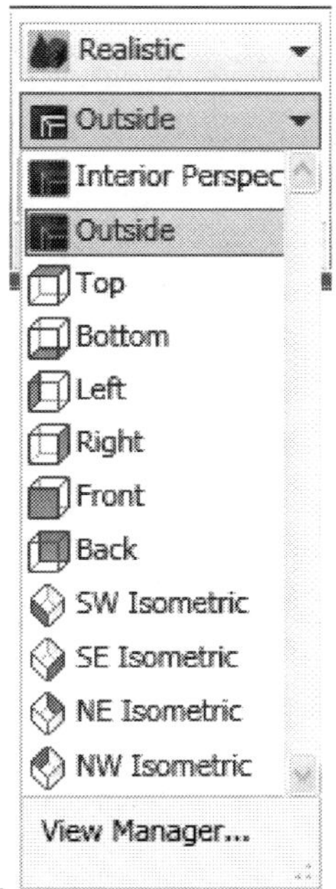

Figure 8–29

- You can easily access the named views by expanding the 3D Navigation Control and selecting it from the list. It also sets it as the current view.
- Named views can be used in Model Space or in an active layout viewport.
- The View Manager dialog box sets, creates, deletes, modifies, and renames named views. It also manages model views, layout views, preset views, and camera views. You can select a named view and click **Set Current** to make it the current view.

- To open the View Manager dialog box, select **View Manager** at the bottom of the 3D Navigation Control drop-down list in the ribbon, or click  (View Manager) in the *Visualize* tab> Named Views panel.

How To: Create a New Named View

1. Set up the view as you want it to be saved.
2. In the *Home* tab>View panel, expand the 3D Navigation Control and select **View Manager...**.
3. In the View Manager, click **New**, as shown in Figure 8–30.

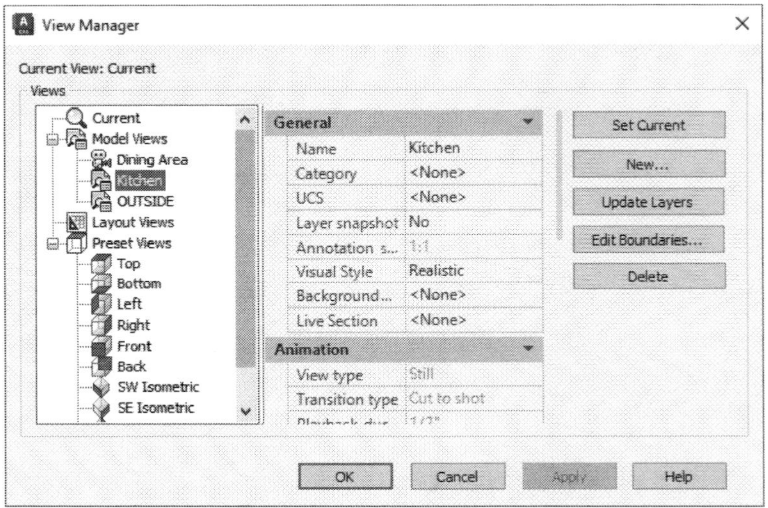

Figure 8–30

4. Fill out the New View/Shot Properties dialog box, as shown in Figure 8–31, including the *View name*, *Boundary*, *Settings*, and *Background* areas.

*The **View category** option refers to views that are used in sheet sets, such as plans and elevations. The categories are created in the Sheet Set Manager.*

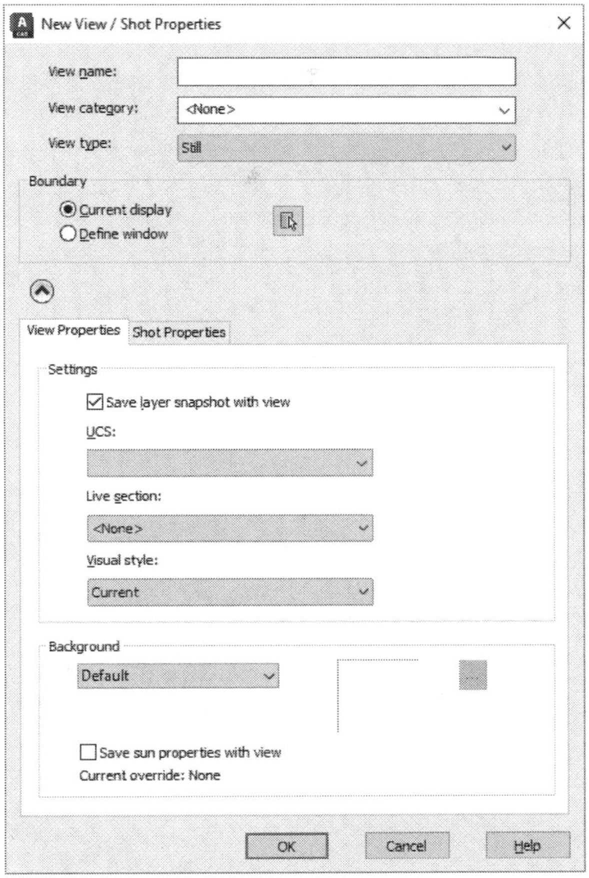

Figure 8–31

5. Click **OK**.

New View Options

Save layer snapshot with view	Enables the view to retain the layer states that are set when the view is saved.
UCS	Sets a UCS to be saved with the view.
Live section	Enables you to activate a section plane, if one is available in the drawing. Once a Live Section is on, it stays on until you deactivate it through the **Section Plane** shortcut menu option.
Visual style	Sets a visual style to be saved with the view.

Adding Backgrounds to Views

To add more realism or to highlight your design in the drawing window, you can add backgrounds to views. These backgrounds can be a solid, gradient, image, or Sun & Sky, as shown in Figure 8–32.

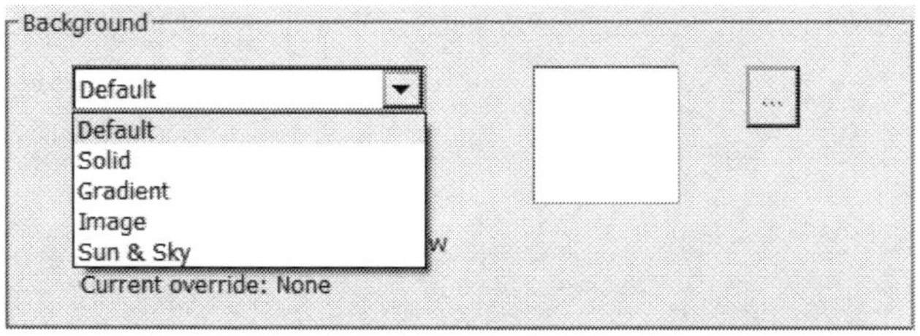

Figure 8–32

- Solid backgrounds can be any single color, while gradient backgrounds can be a mix of two or three colors.

- Images can be any of the standard image files that the AutoCAD® software can view. In the Background dialog box shown in Figure 8–33, click **Browse** to select an image and then click **Adjust Image** to modify the image as required.

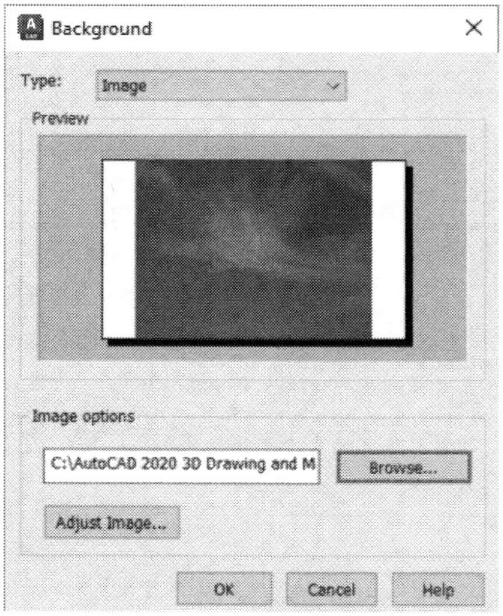

Figure 8–33

*Lighting Units are set in the Drawing Units dialog box. They are not available if the Insertion Scale is set to **Unitless**.*

- The Sun & Sky setting mimics the effects of sunlight in your drawing. The position of the sun is determined by the geographic location and the time settings. The Sun & Sky setting is only available when using **American** or **International** lighting units.

- To remove a background, select a view in which a background has not been set. Preset views do not remove a background.

Modifying Views

Once a view has been defined, you can modify its properties in the View Manager, as shown in Figure 8–34. In the *Visualize* tab>Views panel, click  (View Manager) to open the View Manager dialog box. In the View Manager, you can do the following:

- Rename views
- Change the UCS
- Change layers
- Change the visual style stored with the view
- Add a Background or Live Section
- Change the boundary of the view.

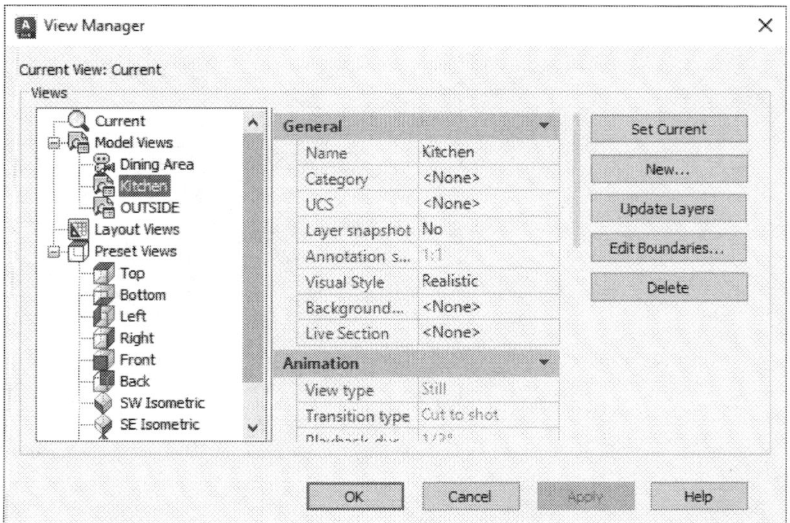

Figure 8–34

Layer Snapshot

Views that store layer settings have the *Layer snapshot* set to **Yes** in the View Manager. You can select a view in the list and then click **Update Layers** to save the current layer settings with the view.

Editing View Boundaries

Once a view has been defined, you can modify its boundaries by selecting it in the list and clicking **Edit Boundaries**. The current boundary area highlights on the view, as shown in Figure 8–35.

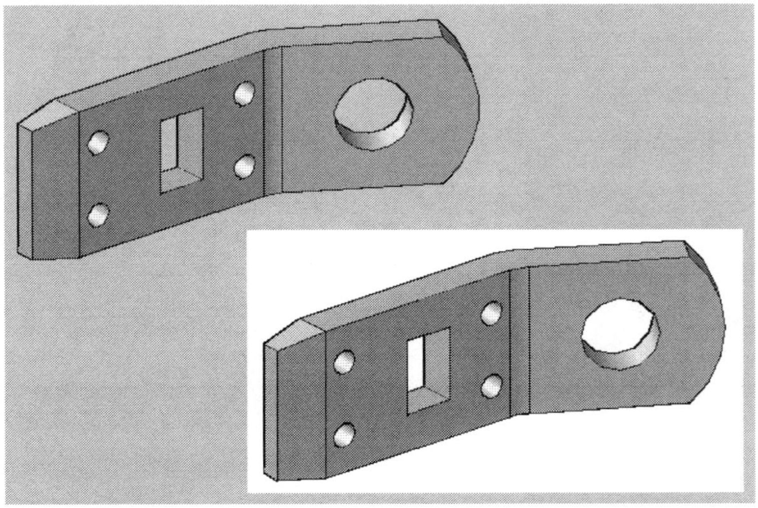

Figure 8–35

Select two points on the screen to define a new area, as shown in Figure 8–36, and press <Enter>.

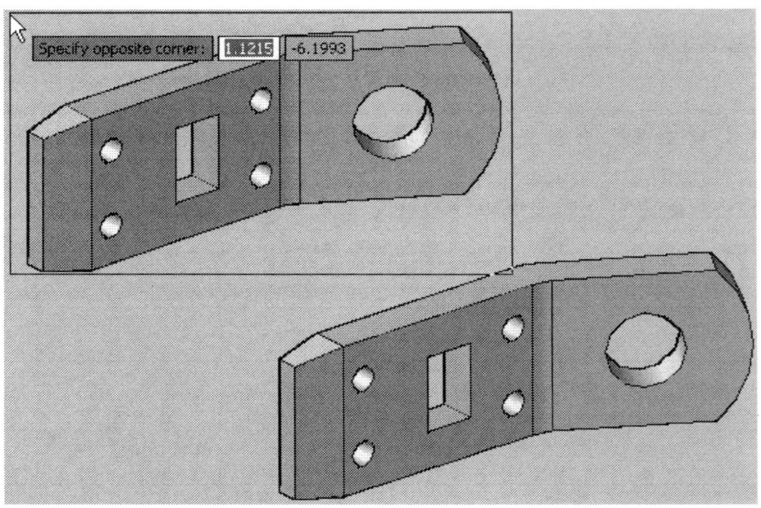

Figure 8–36

Practice 8c

Managing Views in 3D

Practice Objective

- Modify the visual styles and backgrounds of existing views using the View Manager.

In this practice, you will modify existing views, update them with visual styles and backgrounds in the View Manager, and add an image as a background, as shown in Figure 8–37 for the **Dining Area** view.

Figure 8–37

Task 1 - Update a view with the Sun and Sky background.

1. Open **Kitchen-Views.dwg**.
2. In the *Home* tab>View panel, expand the 3D Navigation Control and select the **Kitchen** view. The view uses the visual style **3dWireframe** and is not easy to figure out the details.
3. In the *Home* tab>View panel, expand the 3D Navigation Control and select **View Manager...**
4. In the View Manager, expand Model Views (if required) and select **Kitchen**. Click **Set Current**.

5. In the *General* area, set the *Visual Style* to **Realistic** (as shown in Figure 8–38) and click **Apply**. The view updates.

6. Expand the *Background override* edit box (down arrow) and note that it does not have an option for **Sun and Sky** (as shown in Figure 8–38).

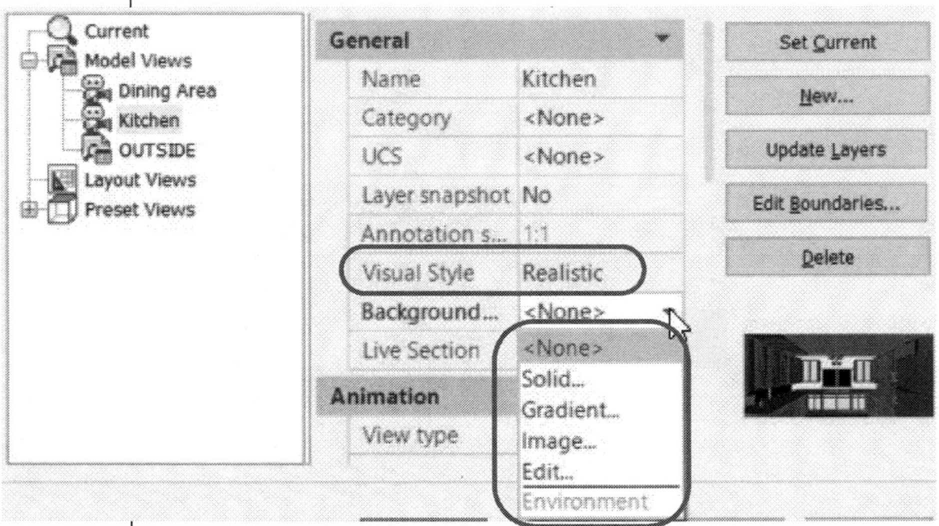

Figure 8–38

7. Click **OK** to close the View Manager.

8. Type **Units** to open the Drawing Units dialog box.

9. Set the *Insertion scale* to **Inches** and the *Lighting* to **American**. Click **OK**.

10. Open the View Manager again.

11. Select the **Kitchen** view and click **Set Current**.

12. Expand the *Background override* edit box and note that **Sun & Sky** is listed.

13. Click **OK** to close the View Manager. The model displays as shown in Figure 8–39.

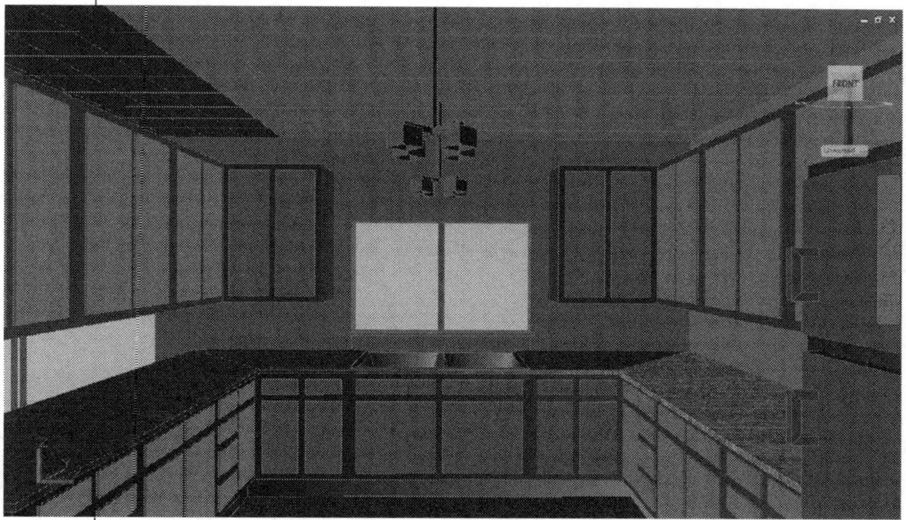

Figure 8–39

Task 2 - Update a view with an image background.

1. Switch to the **Dining Area** view. In this case, the visual style is not set by the view so it displays in the current visual style.
2. Open the View Manager.
3. Select the **Dining Area** view and set the *Visual Style* to **Realistic**.
4. Set the *Background Override* to **Image**.
5. In the Background dialog box, in *Image options* area, click **Browse** and select one of the images in your practice files folder (**Mare's-Tail.jpg**, **Sunset.jpg**, or **Sunset2.jpg**).

6. Click **Adjust Image** and modify the *Image position* to **Stretch** to fill the window, as shown for **Mare's-Tail.jpg** in Figure 8–40. Click **OK**.

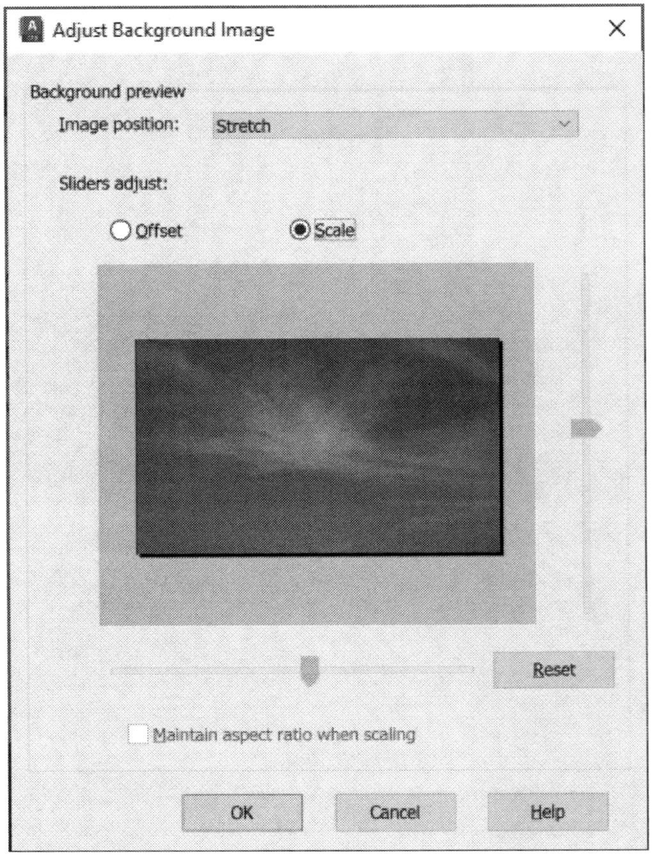

Figure 8–40

7. Click **OK** to accept the image. In the View Manager, click **Apply**.

*You might need to switch to a different saved view and then switch back to the **Dining Area** view, for the drawing window to update.*

8. Set the **Dining Area** view to be current and click **OK**. The image should display in the windows.

9. Save and close the drawing.

8.4 Animating with ShowMotion

ShowMotion enables you to capture movement and transitions between saved views. With ShowMotion, saved views are referred to as shots and a sequence of shots can be saved in a view category. When the **ShowMotion** command is active, thumbnails of the available view categories and shots display, along with a toolbar containing the ShowMotion commands, as shown in Figure 8–41.

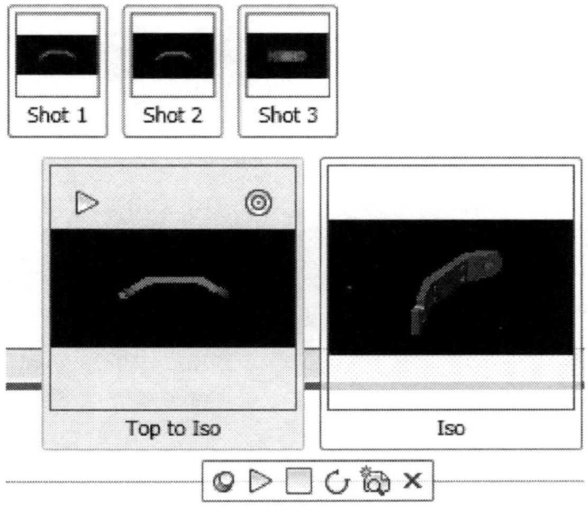

Figure 8–41

View categories display at the bottom of the drawing window. If you hover the cursor over a view category, its associated views display above. If you roll over a view, it expands in size and the view category display gets smaller.

How To: Play a ShowMotion Animation

1. In the *View* tab>expanded Viewport Tools panel, click (ShowMotion).
   - Alternatively, you can access the command in the Navigation bar.
2. Hover the cursor over the view category that you want to play.
3. In the view category, click (Play) to start an animation.

- If you want to jump directly to a view without playing its animation, click (Go) in the view thumbnail.

ShowMotion Options

The ShowMotion toolbar ( ) displays below the thumbnails of the view categories.

	Unpin: If ShowMotion is pinned, it remains active until you click (Close). If unpinned, ShowMotion is terminated when you click anywhere in the drawing window.
	Play: Displays the shots in the order in which they are played. When you click (Play), the icon changes to (Pause) while the animation is played.
	Stop: Ends the animation of the shots.
	Turn on Looping: If active, repeats the animation until it is stopped.
	New Shot: Opens the New View/Shot Properties dialog box to create a new shot.
	Close: Ends the **ShowMotion** command and closes the thumbnails and control panel.

8.5 Creating ShowMotion Shots

To use ShowMotion, shots and view categories must be created using the New View/Shot Properties dialog box.

How To: Create a Shot

1. In the *View* tab>expanded Viewport Tools panel or In the Navigation Bar, click (ShowMotion).
2. Set up the view that you want to use.
3. In the ShowMotion Toolbar, click (New Shot).
4. In the New View/Shot Properties dialog box, enter a name for the view and then specify a *View category* and *View type*, as shown in Figure 8–42. If the *View category* you want to use does not exist, type a new name. The *View type* can be **Cinematic**, **Still**, or **Recorded Walk**.

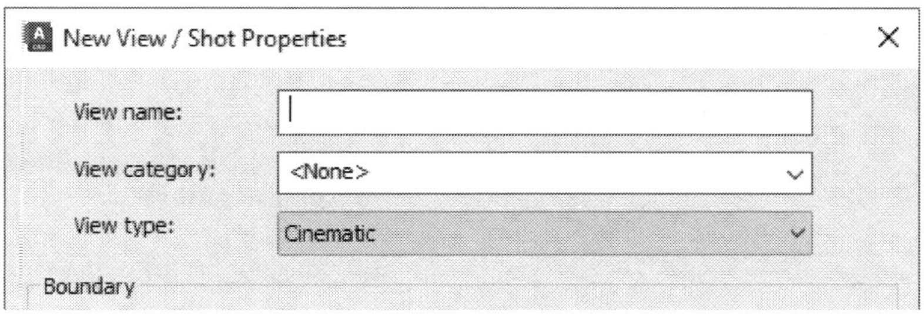

Figure 8–42

5. Specify the *Transition type*, as shown in Figure 8–43. Transition types include **Fade from black into this shot**, **Fade from white into this shot**, and **Cut to Shot**.

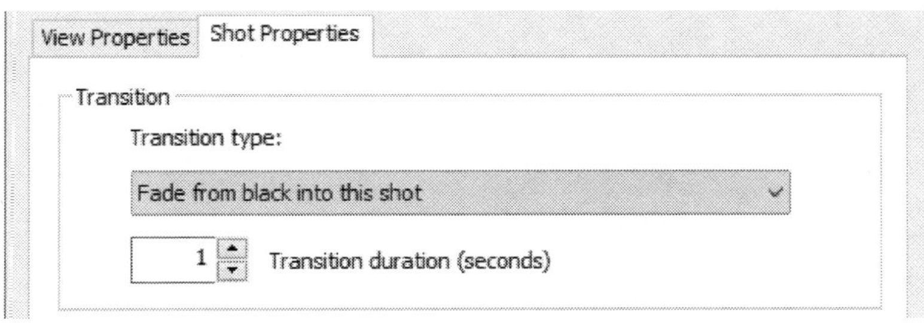

Figure 8–43

6. Set the required motion, as shown in Figure 8–44. This includes the *Movement type* and *Duration*. Other options vary by the selected *Movement type*. In each case, you set the current position of the camera from the **Starting point**, **Ending point**, or **Half-way point** using the drop-down list below the thumbnail view.

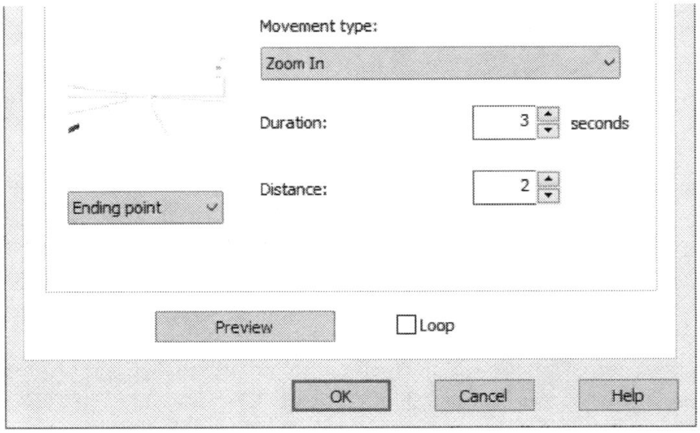

Figure 8–44

7. Click **Preview** to test the animation before it is saved.
8. Click **OK** to close the New View/Shot Properties dialog box and create the shot.

- To edit an existing shot, hover the cursor over the shot, right-click, and select **Properties**.

- If you are creating a series of shots to run together, first add a view category to contain the views. Then, as you create each shot, start it at the end of the previous shot.

Shot Properties

View name	Specifies the name of the view.
View category	Specifies the category to which to assign the view. Select in the drop-down list of existing categories or enter a name to create a new category.
View type	Select the type of view in the drop-down list. • **Cinematic:** Uses a single camera with added animation of the camera movement. • **Still:** Stores a single stationary camera. • **Recorded Walk:** Click and drag in the application window to define the camera path. Only available for Model Space views.
Transition	Defines the transition type and duration of the transition. Options include: • **Fade from black into this shot** • **Fade from white into this shot** • **Cut to shot**
Motion	Defines the motion for the view. The options vary depending on the selected view type: • For Cinematic shots, options include **Movement type (Zoom In/out, Track left/right, Crane up/down**, **Look**, and **Orbit**), **Duration**, **Distance**, and **Current camera position**. • For Still shots, the option is **Duration**. • For Recorded Walk shots, the option is **Start Recording**.
Preview	Previews the animation.
Loop	Continuously plays the animation.

- The *View Properties* tab is used to set the boundary, setting, and background properties of the view.
- Shots and named views can also be modified in the View Manager dialog box.
- The order in which the shots are played can be modified by right-clicking on a shot and selecting **Move Left** or **Move Right**.

Practice 8d

Animating with ShowMotion

Practice Objective

- Review an existing ShowMotion animation and create a new one by adding new shots and adjusting its Motion options.

In this practice, you will investigate an existing ShowMotion animation, as shown in Figure 8–45, and create a new ShowMotion animation.

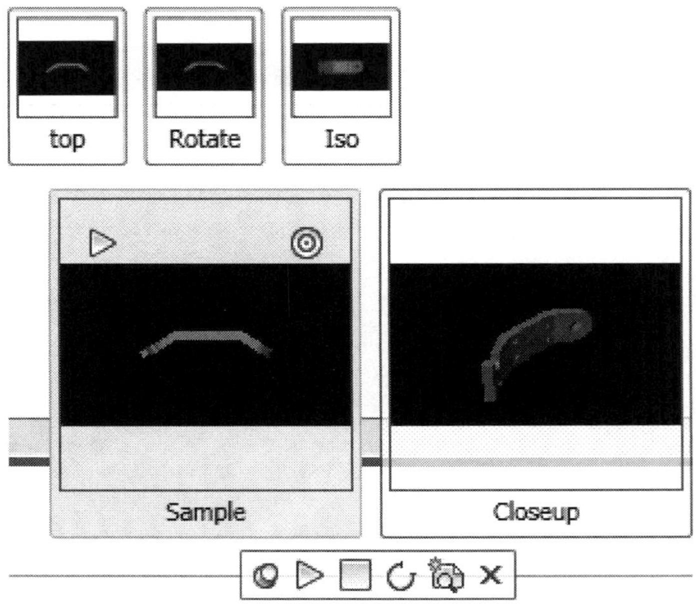

Figure 8–45

Task 1 - Review an existing ShowMotion animation.

1. Open **3D-Solid.dwg**.
2. In the Navigation Bar, click 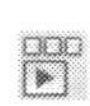 (ShowMotion).

The display of the Sample view category thumbnail and the ShowMotion toolbar might be dependent on your display monitor.

3. A *Sample* view category thumbnail along with the ShowMotion toolbar displays near the bottom of the drawing window. Hover the cursor over the *Sample* view category thumbnail. Several shot thumbnails display, as shown in Figure 8–46.

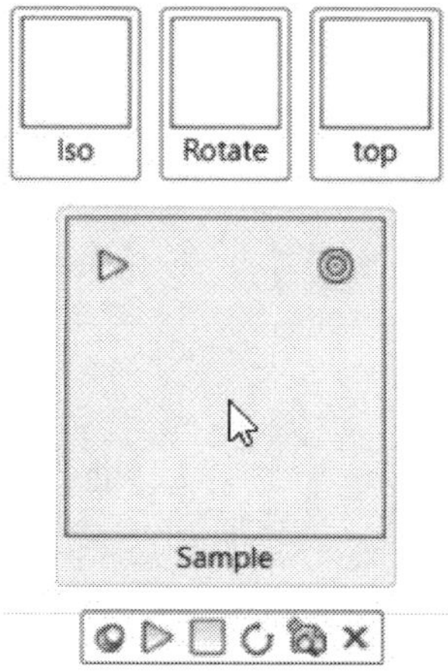

Figure 8–46

4. In the Sample view category thumbnail, click 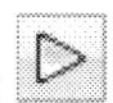 (Play). The animation plays the set of shots.

5. Hover the cursor over one of the shot thumbnails and click 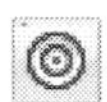 (Go), as shown in Figure 8–47. The view displays without animation.

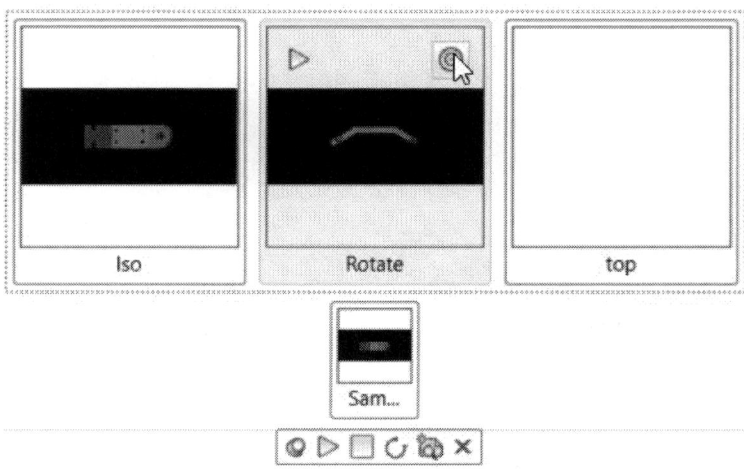

Figure 8–47

Task 2 - Create a ShowMotion Animation.

1. In the ViewCube, click (Home).
2. In the ShowMotion toolbar, click (New Shot).
3. In the New View/Shot Properties dialog box, for the *View name*, type **Start**.
4. In the *View category*, type **Closeup** to create a new view category.
5. Set the *View type* to **Cinematic**.
6. Set the *Movement type* to **Zoom In** and change the current position of the camera to **Starting point**.
7. Click **Preview** and set the *Distance* to **20** to obtain a useful closeup view of the model.
8. Click **OK**.
9. In the Closeup view category, select the shot you just made and click (Play).
10. In the ShowMotion toolbar, click (New Shot).
11. Name the new shot **Crane** and set the *View category* to **Closeup**.
12. Set the *Movement type* to **Crane down** from the **Starting point** of the camera. Select **Always look at camera pivot point**.
13. Click **Preview** and adjust the distances and duration as required to obtain a useful closeup view of the model.
14. Create some more shots in this view category. Remember to play the last shot to get to the new starting point for your next shot.
15. Play the entire category.
16. Save the drawing.

If you forget to put a shot in a category, right-click on the shot and select ***Properties*** *to open the View/Shot Properties dialog box.*

8.6 Creating Animations

Camera views are static pictures of a drawing, but in many cases, moving around the objects in 3D space helps when explaining a design concept. The AutoCAD software includes commands that enable you to create animation motion paths, and to walk through, and fly around your drawings. The navigation tools are similar to those used in video games. Once you learn to navigate through your drawings, animations can be a very effective way of displaying your design, as shown in Figure 8–48.

Figure 8–48

- Animation Motion Paths, Walk, and Fly are the methods used to navigate through a drawing. Animation Motion Paths assign a camera and a target to a path that guides them through the drawing. When you walk, you stay on the XY plane. However, when you fly, you are not limited to the XY plane.
- You might need to toggle on the visibility of the Animation panel on the ribbon as it is not on by default.

Using Walk and Fly

In the *Visualize* tab>Animations panel, (Walk) and (Fly) enable you to use the mouse and keyboard to interactively move around the objects in your drawing. Use the keyboard to move up, back, and side to side. At the same time, drag the cursor in the direction in which you want to look.

For example, you might want to walk through the open door of a building, but are not facing it directly. In the *Visualize* tab>

Animations panel, click (Walk), and then press and hold **Move Forward** (<Up Arrow> or <W>). At the same time, hold the mouse button and drag the cursor toward the open door.

- A green cross displays at the target location on the screen.
- It is useful to have a view saved at a good starting point so that if you get lost, you can return to the original location.

Walk and Fly Navigation Mappings

<Up Arrow> or <W>	Move up.
<Down Arrow> or <S>	Move down.
<Left Arrow> or <A>	Move left.
<Right Arrow> or <D>	Move right.
<F>	Toggle on Fly mode.

- Drag the mouse to turn and use the <W>, <A>, <S>, and <D> keys if the cursor is on your right and the <Up>, <Down>, <Left>, and <Right> arrow keys if the cursor is on the left.
- Scrolling the mouse wheel zooms in and out, moving the location of the camera without changing the lens length or field of view.

Position Locator and Shortcut Menu

By default, the Position Locator opens when you first start to walk or fly. It displays a bird's eye view of the objects in your drawing, along with the camera and its lens length and field of view, as shown in Figure 8–49. You can change the location of the camera in the Position Locator, but other walk and fly properties are modified in the Walk and Fly Settings dialog box.

The shortcut menu indicates the current mode and enables you to change it as required. Other navigation modes include the **Free Orbit**, **Swivel**, and **Zoom** commands, as shown in Figure 8–50. Each mode also has a numbered shortcut key.

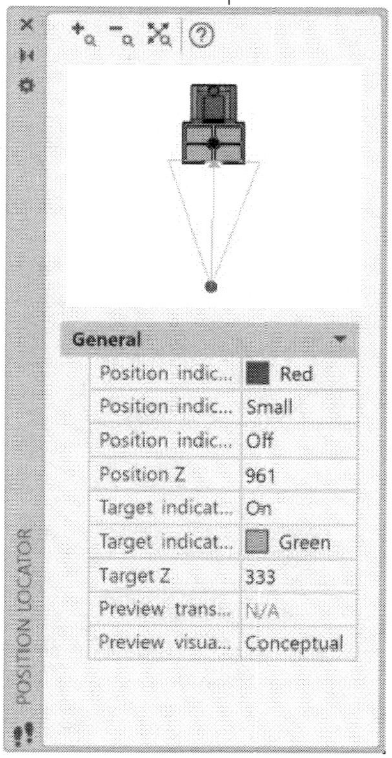

Figure 8–49

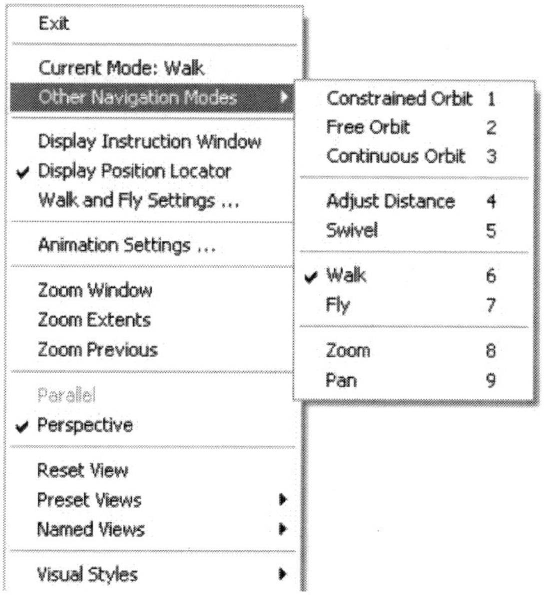

Figure 8–50

- You can use the Walk and Fly Settings dialog box to control the display of the instruction balloon and the Position Locator window, and to modify the step sizing and number of steps per second.

Modifying Walk and Fly Settings

You can easily change the camera, target, and step information in the *Home* tab>View panel and in the Walk and Fly Settings dialog box.

- In the *Home* tab>expanded View panel, you can change the *Lens Length* and *Field of View* using the slider bar or by typing values in the edit fields, as shown in Figure 8–51.
- In the *Home* tab>expanded View panel, you can see the change in the *Camera Position* and *Target Position* fields (as shown in Figure 8–51) and can modify them as required.
- In the *Visualize* tab>Animations panel, click  (Walk and Fly Settings) to open the Walk and Fly Settings dialog box,where you can enter values for the *Walk/fly step size* and *Steps per second*, as shown in Figure 8–51. When you are far away from the objects in your drawing, you can have a larger step size and more steps per second. However, when you get closer to the objects, you need to slow down. For example, if you want to fly over a building, you need to go fairly quickly with longer steps. However, when you are inside the building, you need to have shorter steps and fewer steps per second.

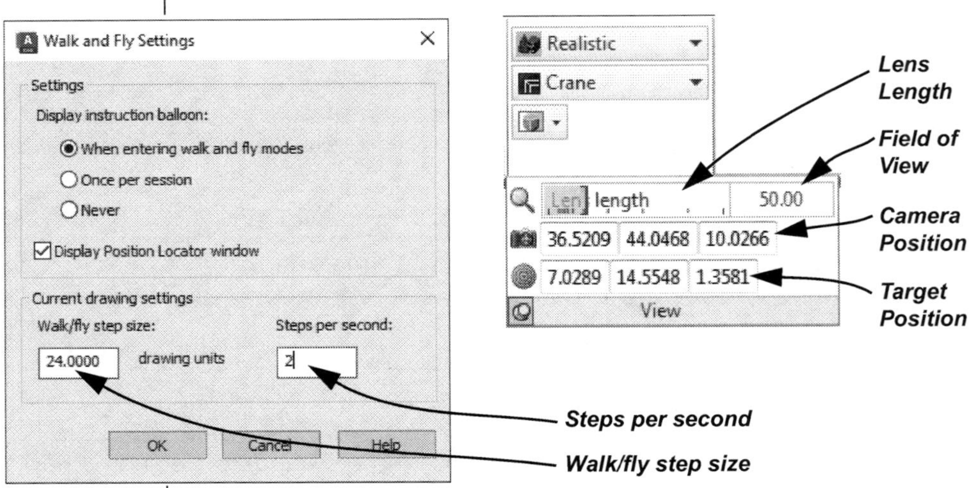

Figure 8–51

> **Hint: Displaying Cameras and Light Glyphs**
>
> Toggle off any cameras and light glyphs before you work with Walk and Fly, especially if you are far away from the model. The glyphs resize to the screen and not the actual objects.
>
> (Show Cameras) is located in the *Visualize* tab>Camera panel. (Light glyph display) is located in the *Visualize* tab> expanded Lights panel. These tools do not toggle off the cameras or lights, only their glyphs.

Animating a Walkthough

Walking and flying are useful when explaining your model to others. However, to display the most important features of the design, you might want to create animations as shown in Figure 8–52.

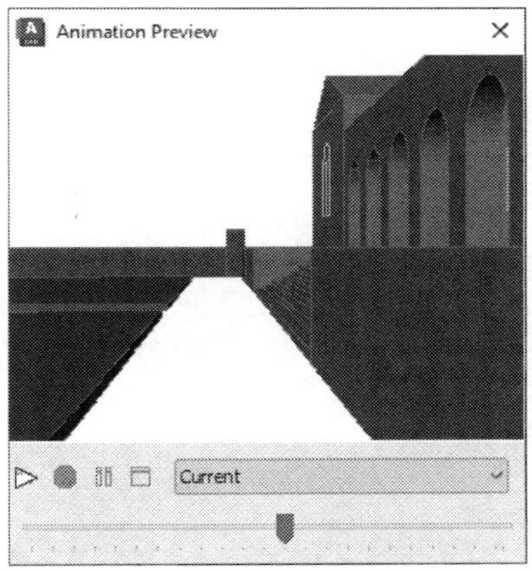

Figure 8–52

There are two ways of creating animations:

- You can create an animation while you are in any 3D Navigation command.
- You can create an animation path and then save the animation with the camera following the path.

How To: Record a 3D Navigation Animation

You can record animations while you are in any 3D Navigation command. These include **3D Orbit**, **Walk**, **Fly**, **Pan**, and **Zoom**. You must be in the full 3D Navigation command because this does not work with transparent commands. You can right-click, expand Other Navigation Modes, and select a different mode while you are in the animation.

If the Animations panel is not displayed, right-click on the ribbon and select ***Animations*** *from the Show Panels list.*

1. Start a 3D Navigation command.
2. In the *Visualize* tab>Animations panel, (Record) is no longer grayed out. Click (Record).
3. Use the 3D Navigation commands as required.
4. In the *Visualize* tab>Animations panel, click (Pause).
5. To review the animation, click (Play Animation).
6. The Animation Preview dialog box opens. Verify that the animation is correct.
7. In the Animation Preview dialog box, click (Save) to save the animation. Alternatively, in the *Visualize* tab>Animations panel, you can click (Save Animation).
8. When the animation has been saved, you can review it again using the software in which it was designed to be viewed.

- You can control the animation process in the Animation Settings dialog box, as shown in Figure 8–53. You can set the *Visual Style*, *Resolution*, *Frame rate*, and *Format* for the animation. In the *Visualize* tab>Animations panel, click (Save Animation). In the Save As dialog box, click **Animation settings**.

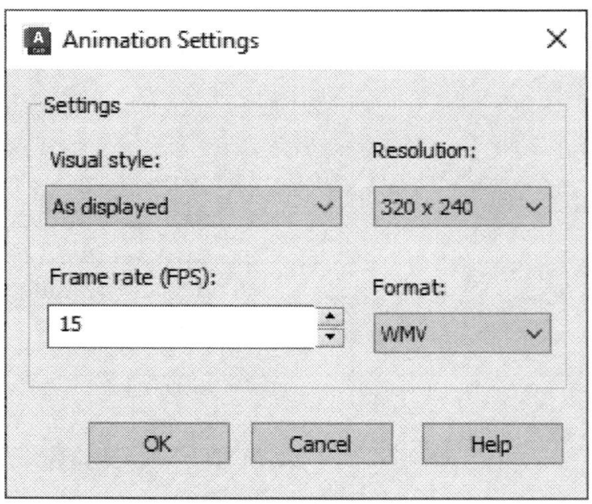

Figure 8–53

- Animations can use a lot of computer power. If you want shadows to display in your animation, toggle off all other softwares that might currently be running.

Animation Motion Paths

In the *Visualize* tab>Animations panel, clicking (Animation Motion Path) enables you to create a camera and follow a path to display a series of frames that move smoothly through your 3D design. This is different from recording animations. It can be smoother and more precise than using **3D Navigation** commands.

A camera is automatically created when you start this command. You can use the camera and its target to create an animation based on one of them traveling along a specified path. Link either the camera or the target to a point if you want it to remain still, or to a path if you want it to move. Only one can be linked to a point at a time. The path must be created before the animation is created, as shown in Figure 8–54.

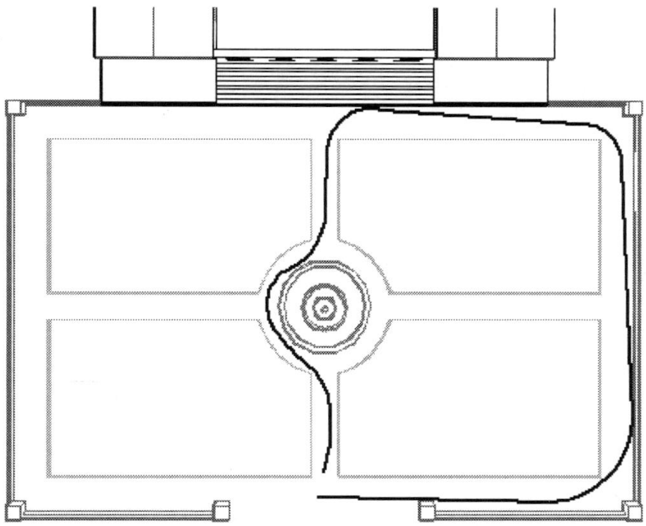

Figure 8–54

- Create a path using **Polyline**, **Line**, **Circle**, **Arc**, **Ellipse**, **Spline**, **3D Polyline**, or **Elliptical Arc**. The path does not display when the animation is played.

How To: Create an Animation Motion Path

1. Draw a path (polyline, line, circle, arc, ellipse, spline, 3D polyline, or elliptical arc) to be followed by the camera or the target.
2. Start the **Animation Motion Path** command.

3. In the Motion Path Animation dialog box, in the *Camera* area, select **Path** or **Point**, as shown in Figure 8–55.

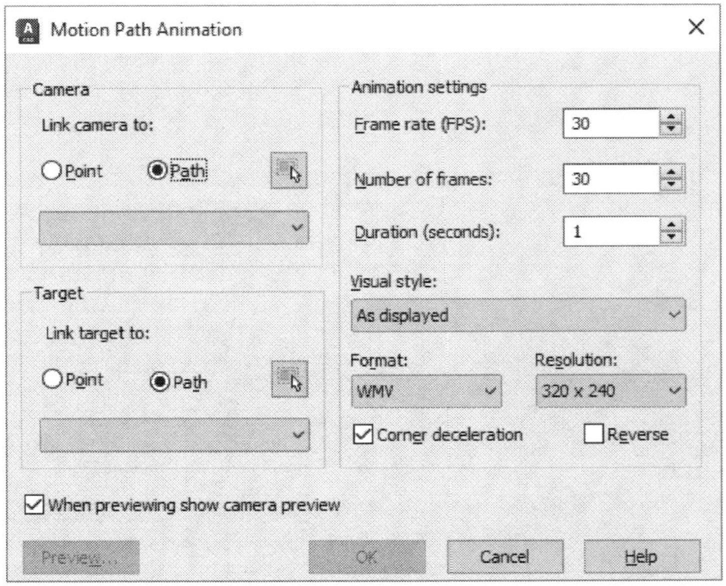

Figure 8–55

- **New camera point:** Click  (Pick Point). In the drawing window, select a location for the point. In the Point Name dialog box, enter a name and click **OK**.

*You need to create the path before starting the **Animation Motion Path** command.*

- **New camera path:** Click  (Select Path). In the drawing window, select a path. In the Path Name dialog box, enter a name and click **OK**.
- **Existing camera path or point:** Expand the drop-down list and select a saved path or point.

4. In the *Target* area, select **Path** or **Point**.

- **New target point:** Click  (Pick Point). In the drawing window, select a location for the point. In the Point Name dialog box, enter a name and click **OK**.

*You need to create the path before starting the **Animation Motion Path** command.*

- **New target path:** Click  (Select Path). In the drawing window, select a path. In the Path Name dialog box, enter a name and click **OK**.
- **Existing target path or point:** Expand the drop-down list and select a saved path or point.

5. In the *Animation Settings* area, set the options as required.
6. Click **Preview** to display the animation or click **OK** to end the command and save the animation.

Practice 8e Walking and Flying Through Models

Practice Objective

- Create a walk through of a model and then animate a walk through of a defined path.

In this practice, you will walk through a model and then animate a walk through of a defined path, as shown in Figure 8–56.

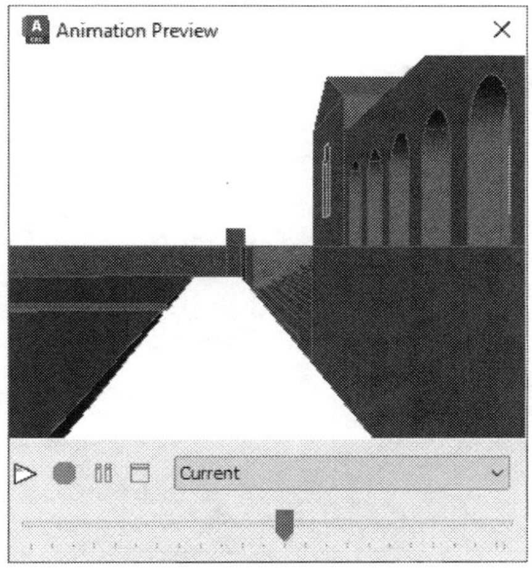

Figure 8–56

*If the Animations panel is not displayed, in the Visualize tab, right-click on the ribbon, expand Show Panels, and select **Animations**.*

1. Open **Walk-Through.dwg**.
2. In the *Visualize* tab>Animations panel, in the Walk flyout, click (Walk and Fly Settings).
3. In the Walk and Fly Settings dialog box, set the *Walk/fly step size* to **24** drawing units and click **OK**.
4. In the *Visualize* tab>Animations panel, click (Walk).

You can also use different arrow keys on the keyboard to walk in their respective directions.

5. Using the keyboard and mouse, begin walking through the model. (Use <W> to walk up and <S> to walk right). Press <Esc> to end the command.
6. Switch to the **Top** view.
7. Toggle on the layer **Path**. Note that a red path line is displayed.
8. In the *Visualize* tab>Animations panel, click (Animation Motion Path).

9. In the Motion Path Animation dialog box, verify that *Link camera to* is set to **Path**. Click (Select Path) and select the red polyline. Name it **Outside Path2** and click **OK**.

10. In the *Target* area, verify that *Link target to* is set to **Path**. Click (Select Path) and select the red polyline. Name it as **Path2** and click **OK**.

11. In the *Animation settings* area, set the *Frame rate* to **15** FPS, *Number of frames* to **150** frames, *Duration* to **15** seconds and *Resolution* to **320 x 240**.

12. Click **Preview** to preview the animation. Once the animation is created, the Animation Preview dialog box opens. Click (Play) to play the animation. Close the Animation Preview dialog box.

13. In the Motion Path Animation dialog box, click **OK**.

14. In the Save As dialog box, set the *File name* to **Walk-Through.wmv**, set the *Save in* location to your practice files folder, and click **Save**. It will create a video of the animation.

15. Save and close the drawing.

16. In the Windows Explorer, locate the **Walk-Through.wmv** and play it.

Chapter Review Questions

1. How do you access a saved view and make it current? (Select all that apply.)
   a. Expand the 3D Navigate Control and select a named view.
   b. In the View Manager, select the named view, and select **Set Current**.
   c. Start the **Named View** command, select the view, and make it current.
2. Live Sections are on by default when you create a section by selecting points.
   a. True
   b. False
3. In which of the following locations can you modify the target location of a camera? (Select all that apply.)
   a. The grips on the camera itself.
   b. The Properties palette.
   c. The Camera Settings dialog box.
4. In the New View/Shot Properties dialog box, which of the following are the type of background that can be added to view? (Select all that apply.)
   a. Image
   b. Gradient
   c. Cinematic
   d. Sun & Sky
5. For Shot Properties, which of the following is a type of ShowMotion Movement?
   a. Pan
   b. Zoom Extents
   c. Walk
   d. Crane Up

6. What can you modify in the Position Locator window that opens when you start to walk or fly?
   a. Walk/Fly step size
   b. Walk/Fly steps per second
   c. Location of the camera
   d. All of the above

Command Summary

All ribbon names reference the 3D Modeling workspace.

Button	Command	Location
	**Animation Motion Path**	• **Ribbon:** *Visualize* tab>Animations panel
	**Create Camera**	• **Ribbon:** *Visualize* tab>Camera panel
	**Fly**	• **Ribbon:** *Visualize* tab>Animations panel
	**New Shot**	• **ShowMotion Toolbar**
	**Section Plane**	• **Ribbon:** *Home* tab>Section panel
	**ShowMotion**	• **Ribbon:** *View* tab>expanded Viewport Tools panel • **Navigation Bar**
	**View Manager**	• **Ribbon:** *Visualize* tab>Views panel or *Home* tab>View panel>expanded 3D Navigation Control
	**Walk**	• **Ribbon:** *Visualize* tab>Animations panel
	**Walk and Fly Settings**	• **Ribbon:** *Visualize* tab>Animations panel

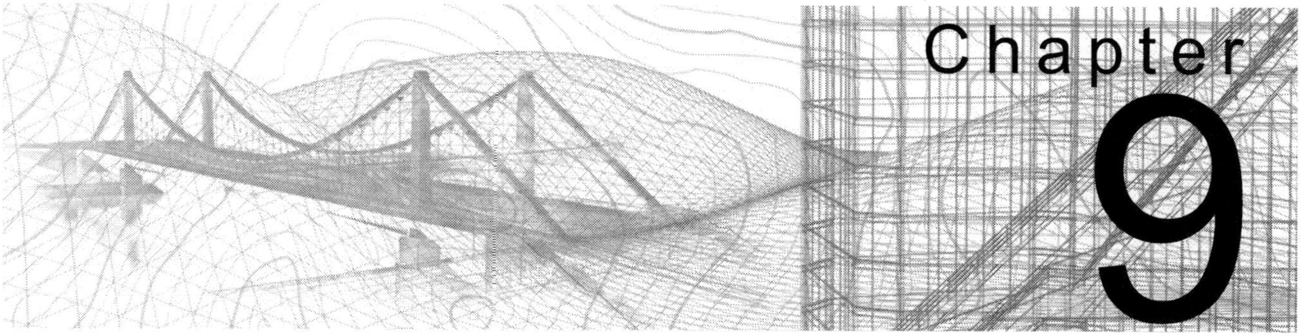

Point Clouds

In this chapter, you learn how to attach and manage point cloud data, and how to automatically create 2D documentation from point clouds,

Learning Objective in This Chapter

- Attach and manage point clouds.

9.1 Point Clouds

Point Clouds are dense groupings of points created by 3D scanners. You then save the point clouds as .RCP or .RCS file formats. They are faster and more efficient than the previous file formats. In the *Insert* tab>Reference panel, use (Attach) or **POINTCLOUDATTACH** command to insert the point cloud into the drawing file.

- As with xrefs, images, and other externally referenced files, you can attach and manage point clouds using the External References Manager.
- Point cloud object snaps have been added to the *3D Object Snap* tab in the Drafting Settings dialog box and the 3D Object Snap options in the Status Bar.
- In a point cloud, you can use the **Object** option in the **UCS** command to align the active UCS to a plane.
- Dynamic UCS aligns to a point cloud plane according to point density and alignment.
- Once you attach a point cloud to a drawing, select it to display the *Point Cloud* contextual tab, as shown in as shown in Figure 9–1.

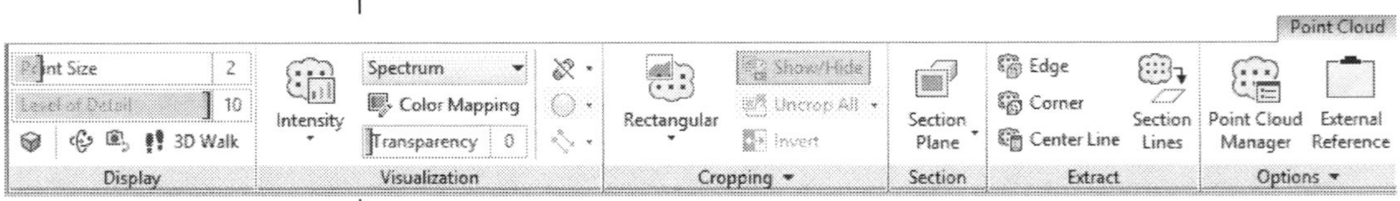

Figure 9–1

Attach Point Cloud

In the Attach Point Cloud dialog box, you can preview a point cloud and its detailed information (such as its classification and segmentation data) before attaching it, as shown in Figure 9–2. You can also use a geographic location for the attachment location (only available if the point cloud includes it).

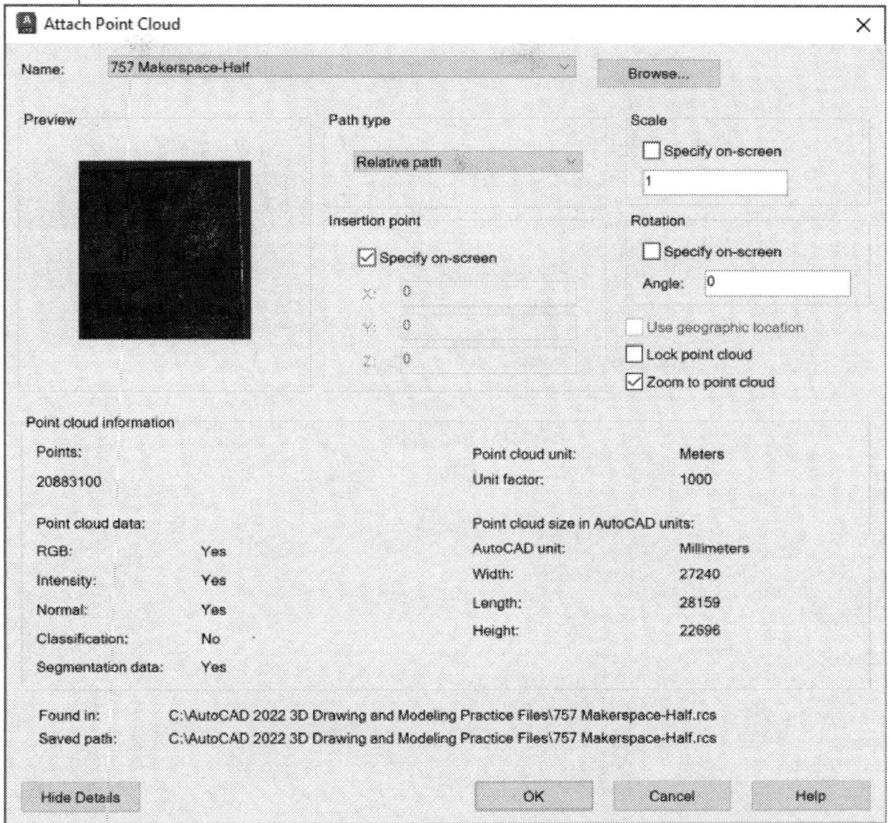

Figure 9–2

How To: Attach a Point Cloud

1. In the *Insert* tab>Reference panel, click  (Attach).
2. In the Select Reference File dialog box, expand the Files of type drop-down list and select the **Autodesk Point Cloud (*.rcp; *.rcs)** file format. Select a file and click **Open**.
    - The AutoCAD software can attach Point Cloud Project (RCP) and Scan (RCS) files (which are produced by the Autodesk ReCap software).
    - The Autodesk ReCap software enables the creation of a point cloud project file (RCP) that references multiple indexed scan files (RCS). It converts scan file data into a point cloud format that can then be viewed and modified in other products.
3. In the Attach Point Cloud dialog box, click **Show Details** to display the point cloud information.

4. In the *Path type*, *Insertion point*, *Scale*, and *Rotation* areas, set the options that you want to use to attach the point cloud, as shown in . Click **OK**.

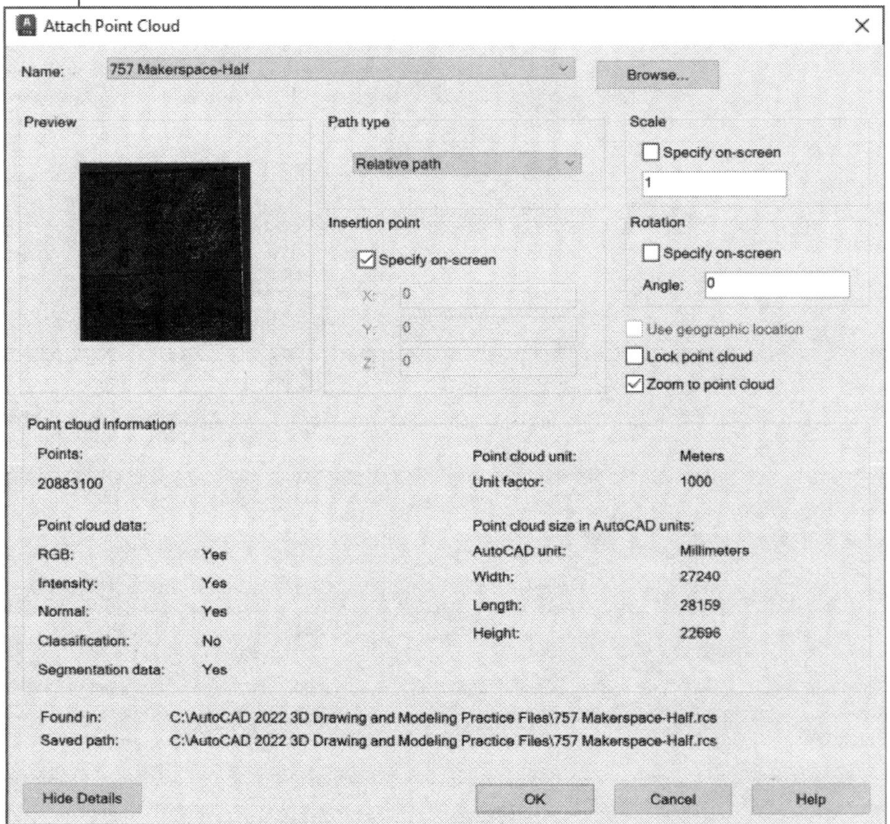

Figure 9–3

5. At the *Specify insertion point* prompt, click in the drawing to locate the point cloud.

Point Cloud Contextual Tab

When the point cloud has been attached, select it to display the *Point Cloud* contextual tab, as shown in Figure 9–4.

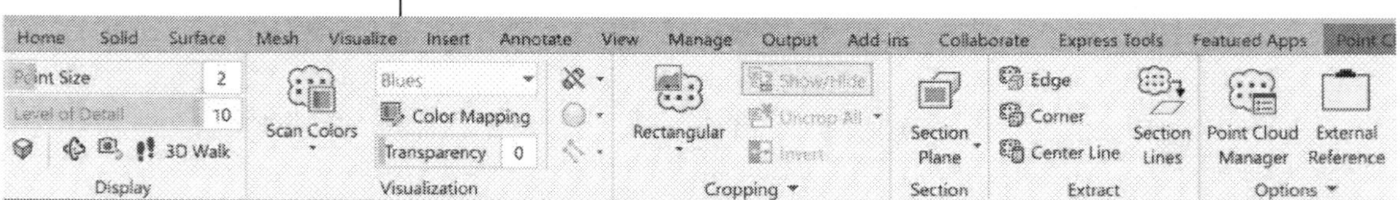

Figure 9–4

Display Panel

The Display panel enables you to control the size of the points in the point cloud using the Point Size slider, and the density of the points in all of the point clouds in the drawing using the Level of Detail slider, as shown in Figure 9–5. You can also access (Perspective), (3D Orbit), (3D Swivel), and (3D Walk).

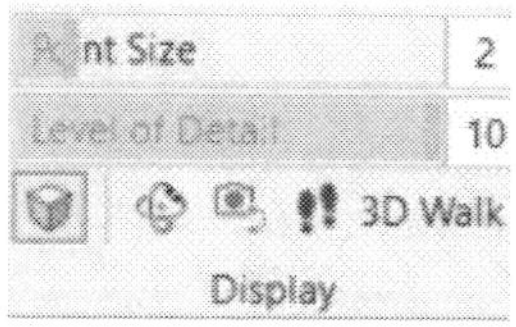

Figure 9–5

Visualization Panel

In the Visualization panel, the options in the expanded Stylization drop-down list enable you to colorize the point cloud based on the **Scan Colors**, **Object Color**, **Normal** direction of a point, **Intensity** (reflectivity), **Elevation**, or **Classification**. The Point Cloud Color Map dialog box (shown in Figure 9–6) enables you to customize the colorization using the options in the *Intensity*, *Elevation*, and *Classification* tabs. You can also use the lighting tools to apply lighting effects to the point cloud.

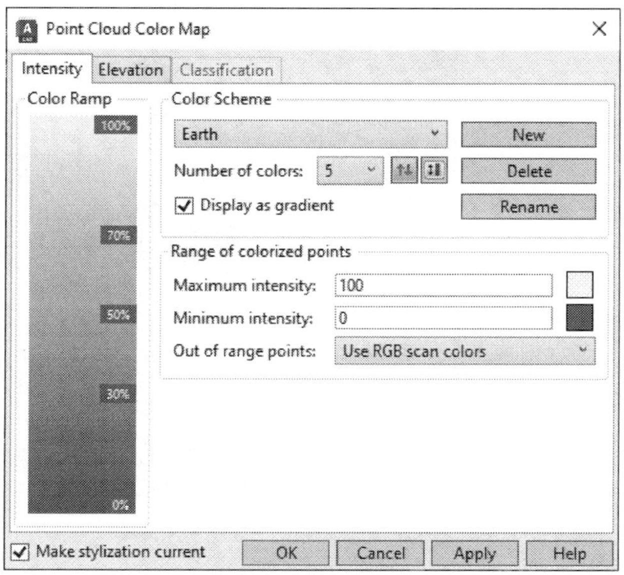

Figure 9–6

Point Cloud Transparency

When point clouds exist in a drawing with other geometry, it can be difficult to see anything behind the point cloud. The **Transparency** tool in the *Point Cloud* contextual tab> Visualization panel enables you to adjusts the transparency of the point cloud, as shown in Figure 9–7. Alternatively, you can adjust the point cloud transparency in the Properties palette, as shown in Figure 9–7.

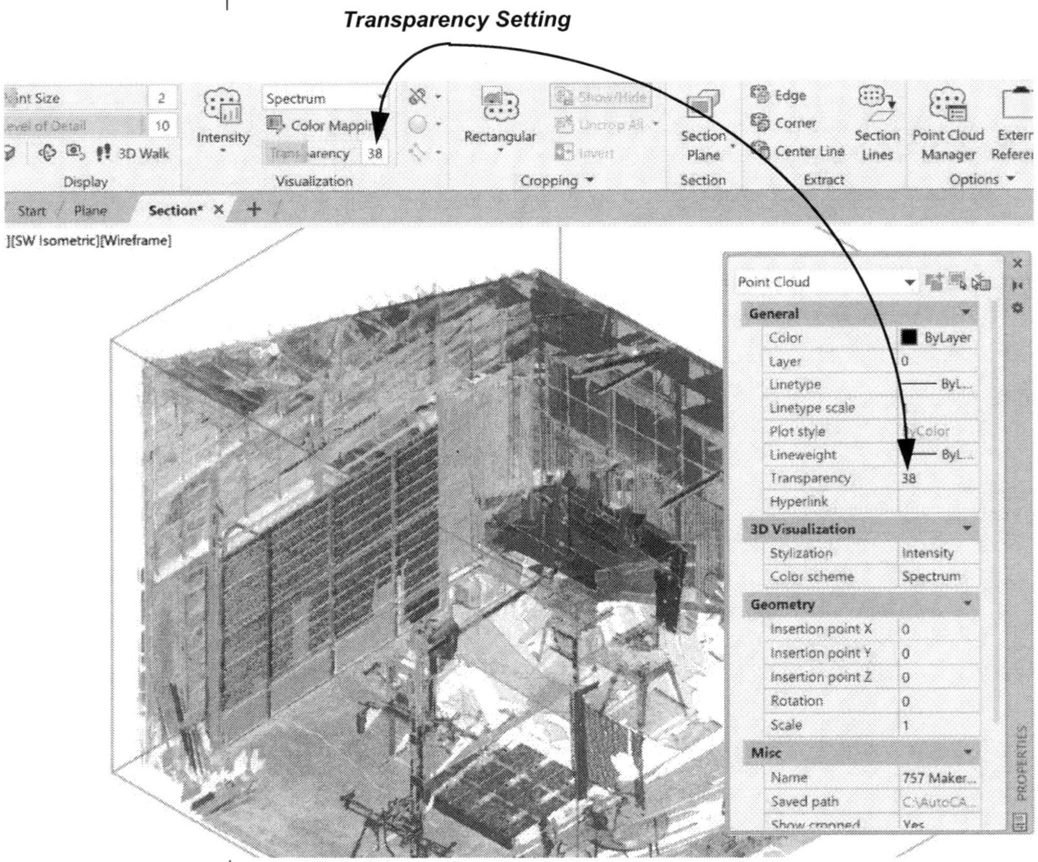

Figure 9–7

Cropping Panel

Displaying the bounding box around the point cloud data enables you to determine its position in 3D space relative to the other objects in the drawing. The cropping tools in the Cropping panel enable you to display only the information that is required for your project, as shown in Figure 9–8. The cropping boundary can be rectangular, circular, or polygonal and is normal to the screen. You can use (Invert) to reverse the displayed points from inside to outside the boundary.

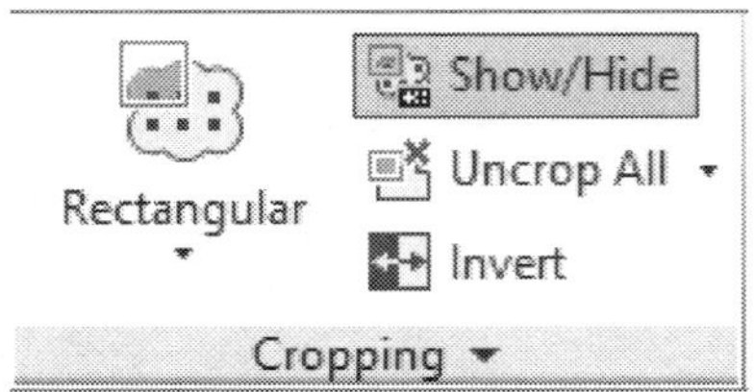

Figure 9–8

In the expanded Cropping panel, there is a tool that enables you to save and restore named cropping states. Both the visibility of the scans and regions as they display and the cropping boundary are maintained in named cropping states, as shown in Figure 9–9.

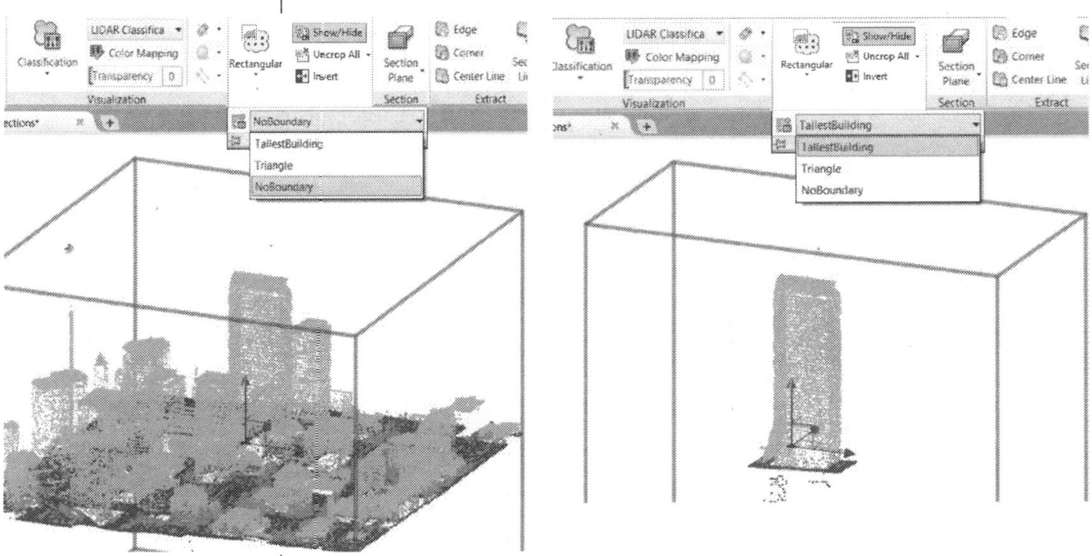

Figure 9–9

Hint: List Crop States

The new command **POINTCLOUDCROPSTATE** can be used to **S**ave, **R**estore, and **D**elete crop states, as shown in Figure 9–10. Using the **?** option will list all of the available crop states.

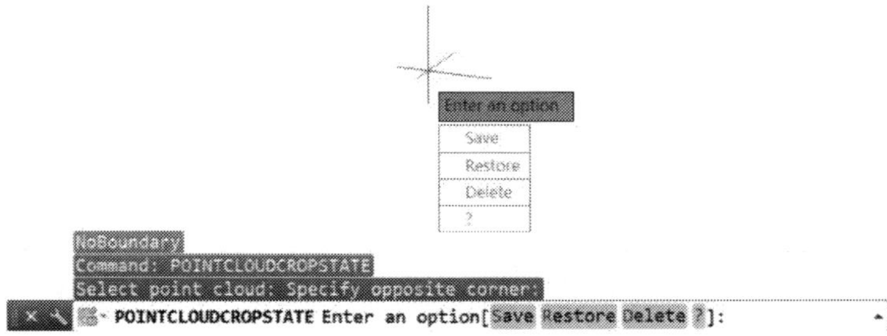

Figure 9–10

How To: Save a Named Crop State

1. Once a point cloud has been attached, select it in the model.
2. In the *Point Cloud* contextual tab>Cropping panel, select an appropriate crop boundary, as shown in Figure 9–11.

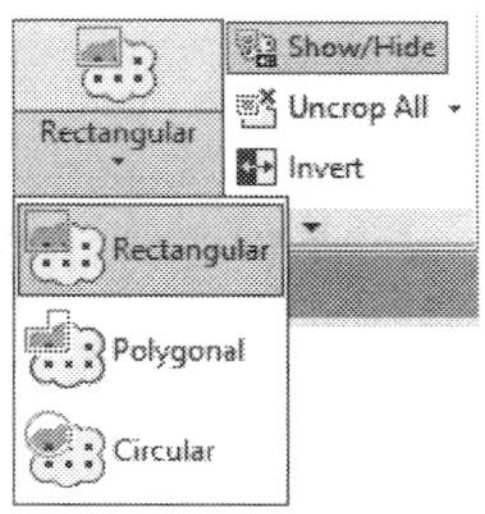

Figure 9–11

3. In the model, pick points to draw the boundary. If a Polygonal boundary was selected, press <Enter> when done.
4. At the cursor, select either **Inside** or **Outside** to indicate which points to keep.
5. Expand the *Point Cloud* contextual tab>Cropping panel, click  (New Crop State).
6. Enter a name for the new crop state.

Section Panel

The Section Plane flyout is located in the Section panel of the contextual *Point Cloud* tab in the ribbon. It enables you to create section objects for the selected point cloud. Section objects can be created by specifying points or for different orthogonal orientations, as shown in Figure 9–12.

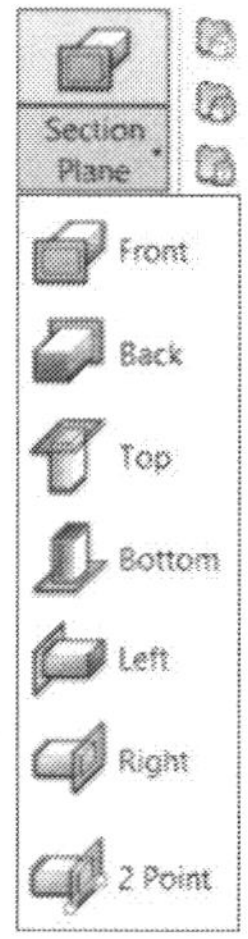

Figure 9–12

How To: Create a Point Cloud Section

1. Attach a point cloud, and select the point cloud in the model.
2. In the *Point Cloud* contextual tab>Section panel, click the down-arrow in the  (Section Plane).
3. Select the section orientation required.
4. Press <Esc> to release the point cloud selection.

Extract Panel

The Extract panel (shown in Figure 9–13) enables you to create section lines from point clouds when live sectioning is toggled on.

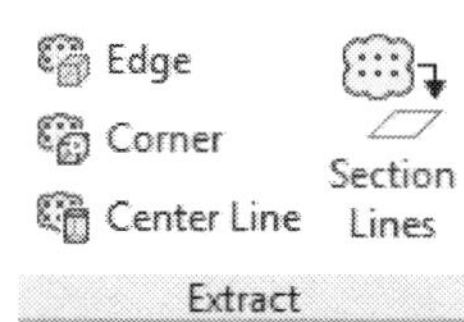

Figure 9–13

When using the  (Section Lines) command, linework can be extracted for the entire cross section or just for the perimeter. When creating section lines, settings can be adjusted to either speed up the creation process or make section line creation more accurate. The Extract Section Lines from Point Cloud dialog box is shown in Figure 9–14. The linework created from sections can be created on the active layer or a specific layer. Tolerances can be set to ensure lines meet a minimum length or have a specific connection and angle tolerance.

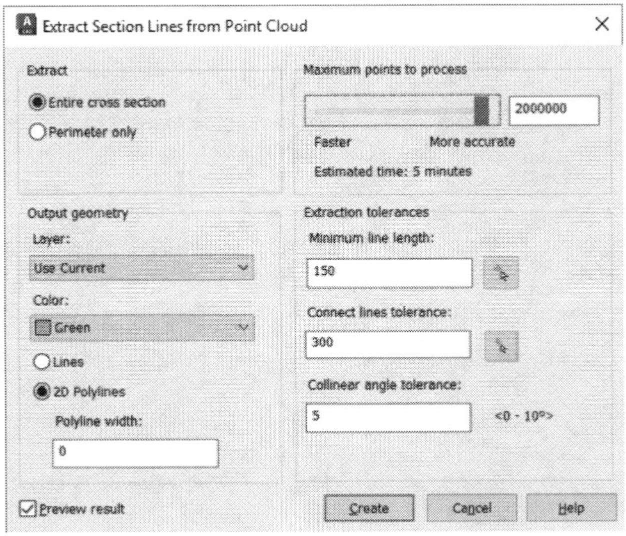

Figure 9–14

A process bar displays in the status bar, which indicates how much of the section generation process is complete, as shown in Figure 9–15.

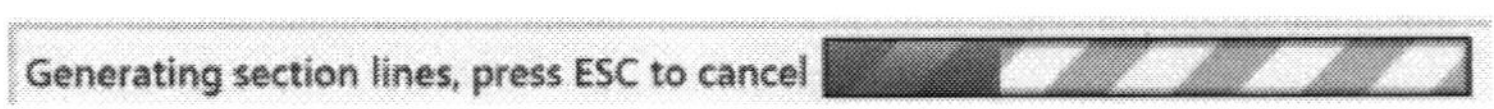

Figure 9–15

Other tools in the Extract panel enable you to create one line at a time, as follows:

Icon	Command	Description
	Edge	Creates a line where two point cloud planer segments intersect.
	Corner	Extracts a point where three point cloud planer segments intersect.
	Centerline	Creates a line at the center of a cylindrical segment of a point cloud.

How To: Create Section Lines from Point Clouds

1. In the model, select the point cloud section line. In the contextual *Section Plane* tab>Display panel, verify that **Live Section** is toggled on, as shown in Figure 9–16.

Figure 9–16

2. Press <Esc> to release the section line.
3. In the model, select a point cloud that has a section already created.
4. In the *Point Cloud* contextual tab>Extract panel, click  (Section Lines).
5. In the Extract Section Lines from Point Cloud dialog box, set the appropriate settings, as shown in Figure 9–17.

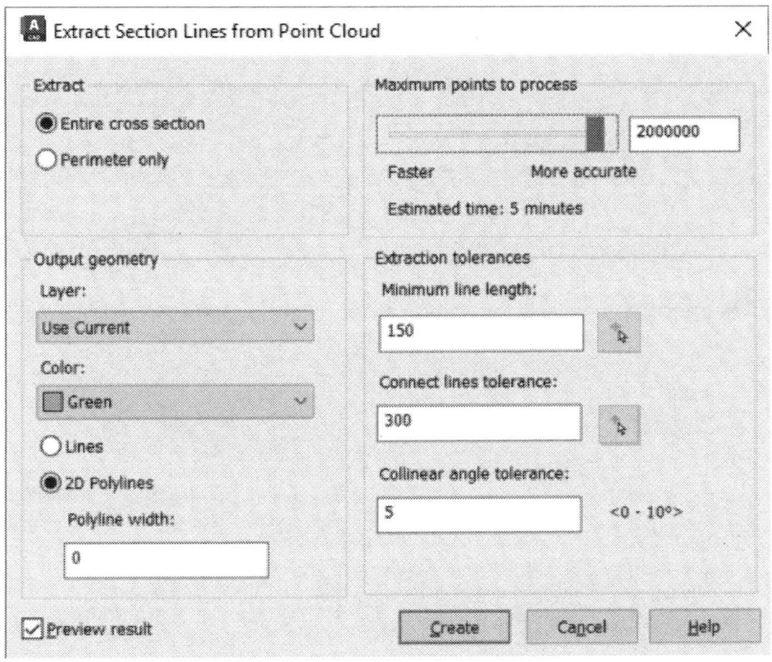

Figure 9–17

6. Click **Create**.

Options Panel

The Options panel (shown in Figure 9–18) enables you to access the Point Cloud Manager and External References Manager. You can use the Point Cloud Manager to modify multiple point clouds at the same time. A list of all of the point clouds in the drawing and their regions, unassigned points, and scans display. You can toggle the objects on/off, rename, isolate, and highlight them in the drawing.

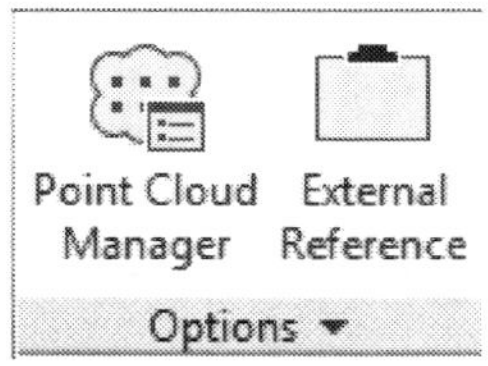

Figure 9–18

The Point Cloud Manager now includes on/off buttons for scans and regions, as shown in Figure 9–19. Tooltips will always display the full name of the scans and regions, since they can be truncated in order to display the new on/off button.

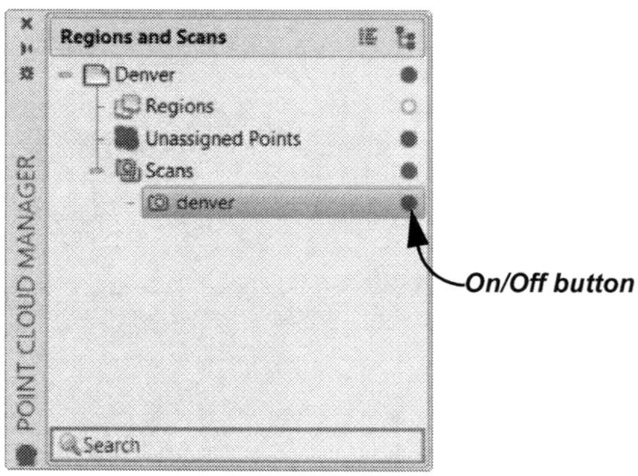

Figure 9–19

Object Snap

Point Cloud object snap modes have been added to the *3D Object Snap* tab of the Drafting Settings dialog box, as shown in Figure 9–20. They interpret faces and edges according to the point density and alignment.

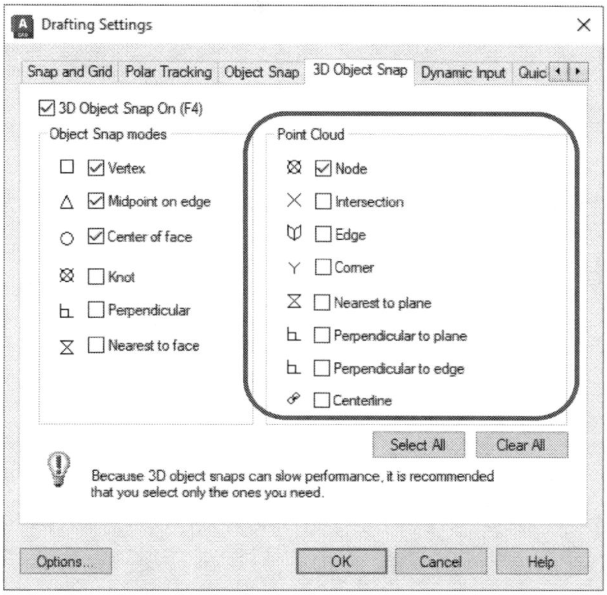

Figure 9–20

The point cloud object snaps are described as follows:

Icon	OSnap	Description
	Node	Snaps to a point in a point cloud.
	Intersection	Snaps to the apparent intersection of 2 lines of a sectioned point cloud.
	Edge	Snaps to the edge of two intersection planes.
	Corner	Snaps to the corner of 3 intersecting planes.
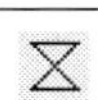	Nearest to plane	Snaps to any point in a plane.
	Perpendicular to plane	Enables you to draw perpendicular to a plane.
	Perpendicular to edge	Enables you to draw perpendicular to the edge of two intersecting planes.
	Centerline	Snaps to the centerline of a cylindrical shape.

Dynamic UCS

 (Dynamic UCS) (located in the Status Bar) is a powerful tool that can help you draw using objects that are already in your model when drawing objects on temporary planes. Dynamic UCS now recognizes point cloud planes if the file includes segmentation data. The Properties palette indicates if the point cloud includes segmentation data, as shown in Figure 9–21.

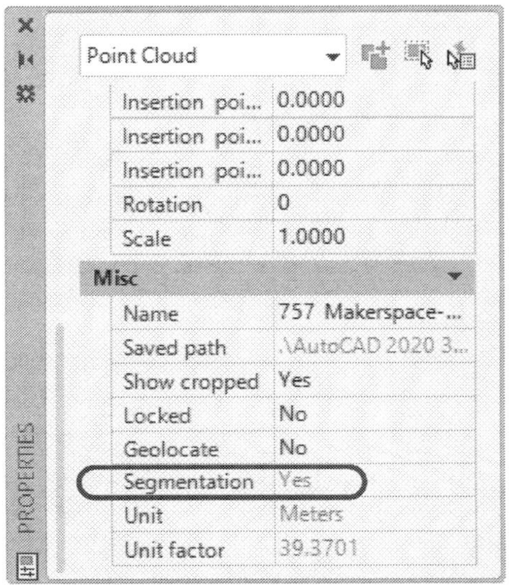

Figure 9–21

How To: Use Dynamic UCS with Point Clouds

1. Verify that the point cloud file includes segmentation data in the Properties palette.
2. In the Status Bar, toggle on 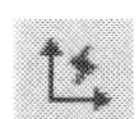 (Dynamic UCS).
3. In the Status Bar, toggle off all point cloud object snaps.
4. Start a draw command (circle, line, etc.).
5. Move the cursor over a point cloud face to highlight a plane and start drawing.

Practice 9a

Attach a Point Cloud

Practice Objectives

- Attach a point cloud when no other model exists for your project.
- Use the options in the Point Cloud contextual panel to modify the point cloud.

In this practice, you will attach a point cloud to a new drawing file, as shown in Figure 9–22. You will then analyze it by changing the intensity color mapping.

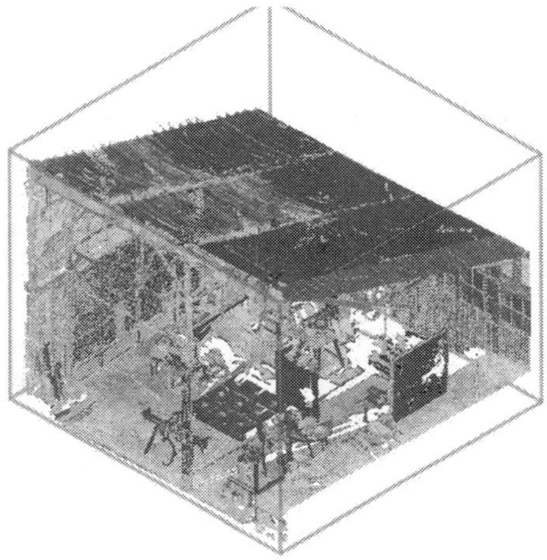

Figure 9–22

Task 1 - Attach a point cloud.

1. Start a new drawing based on **acad3D.dwt**.
2. In the *Insert* tab>Reference panel, click  (Attach).
3. In the Select Reference File dialog box, expand the Files of type drop-down list and note the available file formats. Select the **Autodesk Point Cloud (*.rcp; *.rcs)** file format.
4. Navigate to your practice files folder and select **757 Makerspace-Half.rcs** and click **Open**.
5. Accept the default options in the Attach Point Cloud dialog box and click **OK**. Press <Enter> to use an insertion point of **0,0**.
6. Save the file as a **757 Makerspace-Half.dwg** in your practice files folder.

Task 2 - Analyze the point cloud.

1. Change the active view to **SW Isometric** view.
2. In the drawing window, select the point cloud. The *Point Cloud* contextual tab displays.
3. In the Visualization panel, expand the Stylization drop-down list and click  (Intensity).
4. The color scheme should display in multiple colors, as shown in Figure 9–23.

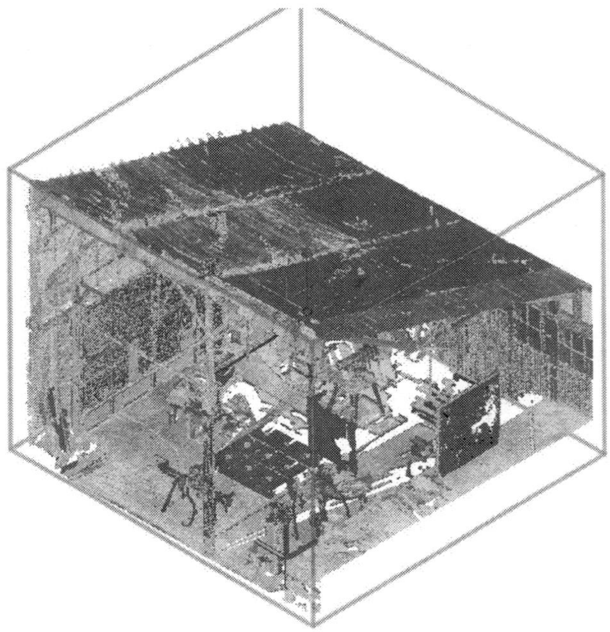

Figure 9–23

5. Save and close the file.

Practice 9b Working with Sections

Practice Objective

- Create a section plane of a point cloud using the section commands.

In this practice, you will create a section plane and then view the section of a point cloud. Next you will create section lines. The finished point cloud should look as shown in Figure 9–24.

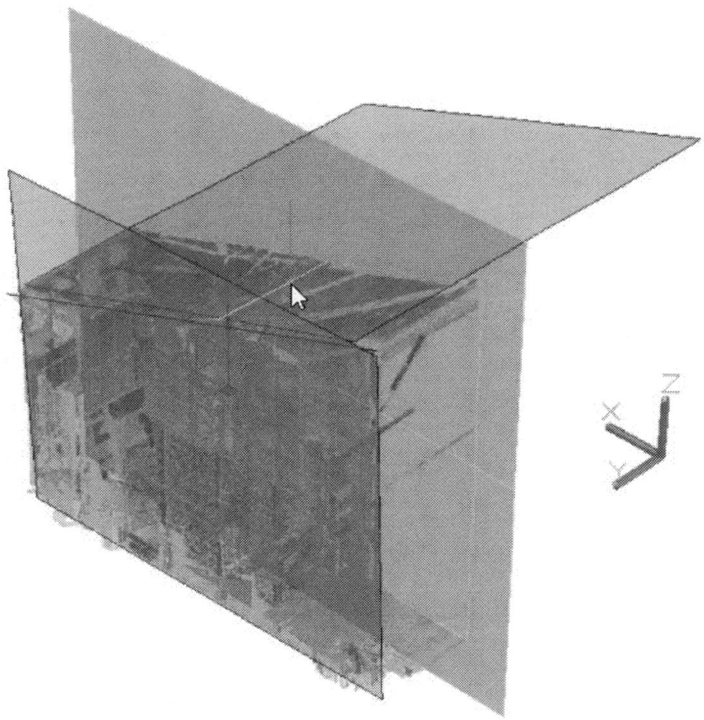

Figure 9–24

Task 1 - Create a section plane.

1. Open **Sections.dwg** and switch to the **SW Isometric** view.
2. In the drawing window, select the point cloud.
3. In the *Point Cloud* contextual tab>Section panel, expand Section Plane flyout and select  (Front).
   - The centroid of the point cloud is selected as a default, as shown in Figure 9–25.

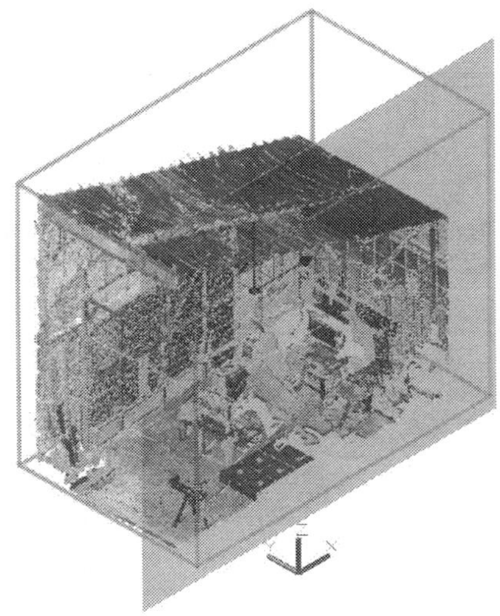

Figure 9–25

4. Press <Esc> to release the point cloud.
5. Select the new section planethat was added to the front. Right-click and verify that **Activate live sectioning** is checked.

6. Use the Y-Gizmo (green arrow pointing towards the back side) to move the section plane **200** to the north so that it cuts a section in the water heater, as shown in Figure 9–26. Press <Esc> to clear the selection and view the sectioned point cloud.

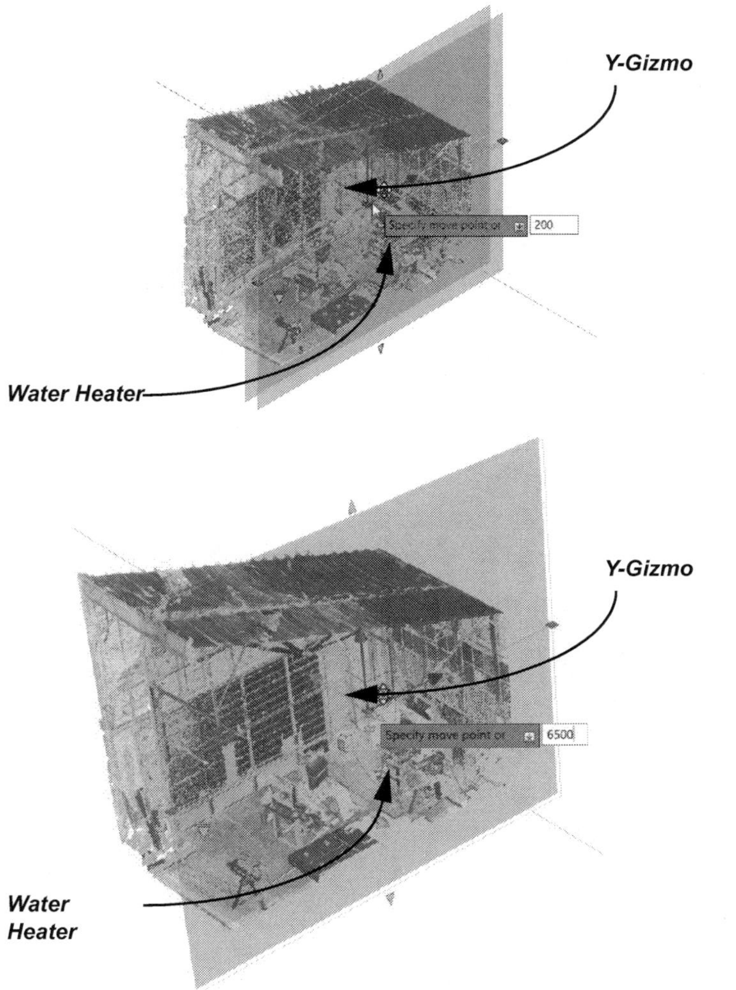

Figure 9–26

Task 2 - Extract linework from a point cloud.

1. In the drawing window, select the point cloud.
2. In the *Point Cloud* contextual tab>Extract panel, click (Section Lines).

3. In the Extract Section Lines from Point Cloud dialog box, verify that the *Output geometry Color* is set to **Green**. Change the *Maximum points to process* to **2,000,000** (move the slider to the right most end), as shown in Figure 9–27. Leave all other settings to their default and click **Create**.

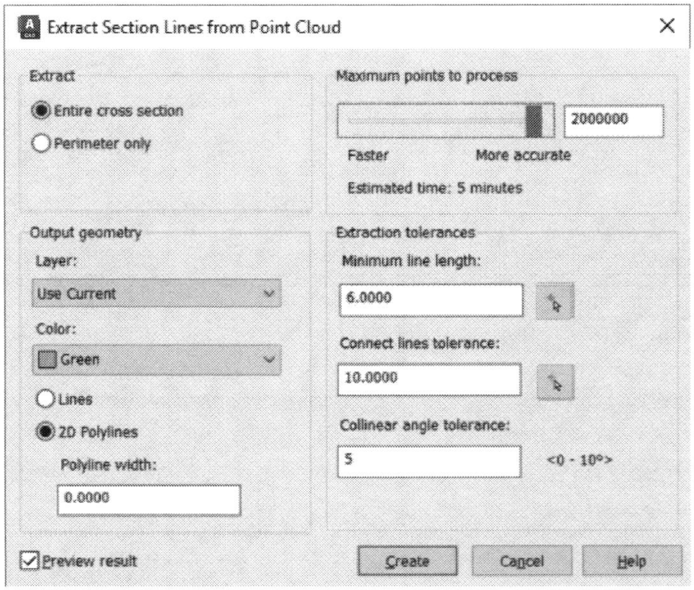

Figure 9–27

It might take a few minutes to complete the creation.

4. A process bar displays in the status bar. After the process is complete, at the command line, select **Accept**.

5. With the Point Cloud still selected, in the *Point Cloud* contextual tab>Visualization panel, change the Transparency to about **50%** to make it easier to see the new linework.

6. Change the view to the **NW Isometric** view.

7. Select the point cloud again, if it is no longer selected.

8. In the *Point Cloud* contextual tab>Extract panel, click  (Edge).

9. In the model, click the north wall as the first plane and the roof for the second plane to create an edge from, as shown in Figure 9–28.

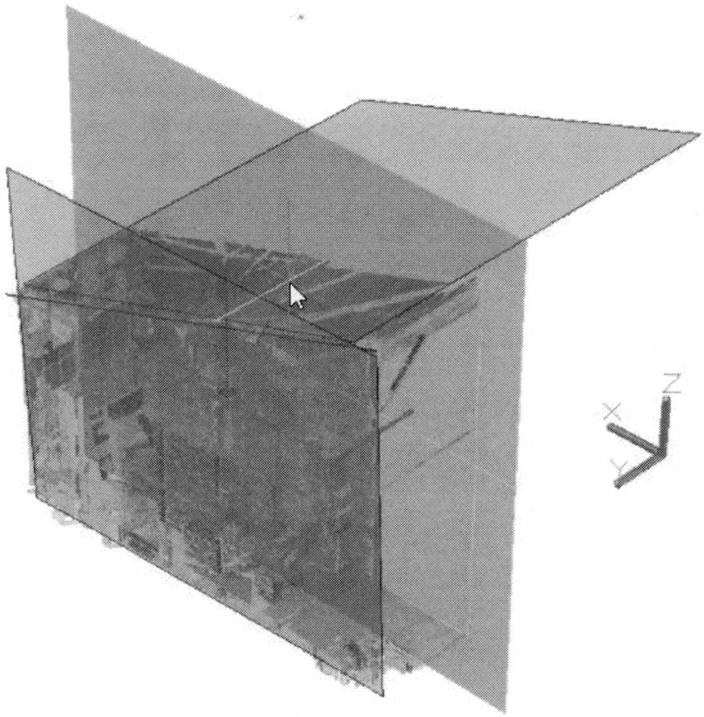

Figure 9–28

10. If time permits, try drawing linework using the point cloud object snap options.

11. Save and close the drawing.

Chapter Review Questions

1. The AutoCAD software cannot insert Point Cloud Project (RCP) and Scan (RCS) files.
   a. True
   b. False
2. Where are the Point Cloud Object Snap modes found?
   a. Drafting Settings dialog box>*Snap and Grid* tab
   b. Drafting Settings dialog box>*Object Snap* tab
   c. Drafting Settings dialog box>*3D Object Snap* tab
   d. *Point Cloud* contextual tab>Object Snap panel
3. You can extract a linework for which portion when using the  (Section Lines) command? (Select all that apply.)
   a. Entire cross section
   b. Edge
   c. Perimeter
   d. Point

Command Summary

Button	Command	Location
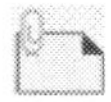	**Attach Point Cloud**	• **Ribbon:** *Insert* tab>Reference panel • **Command Prompt:** pointcloudattach
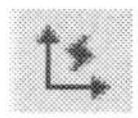	**Dynamic UCS**	• Status Bar
	**Extract Centerline**	• **Ribbon:** *Point Cloud* contextual tab> Extract panel • Command Prompt: pcextractcenterline
	**Extract Corner**	• **Ribbon:** *Point Cloud* contextual tab> Extract panel • **Command Prompt:** pcextractcorner
	**Extract Edge**	• **Ribbon:** *Point Cloud* contextual tab> Extract panel • **Command Prompt:** pcextractedge
	**Extract Section**	• **Ribbon:** *Point Cloud* contextual tab> Extract panel • **Command Prompt:** pcextractsection

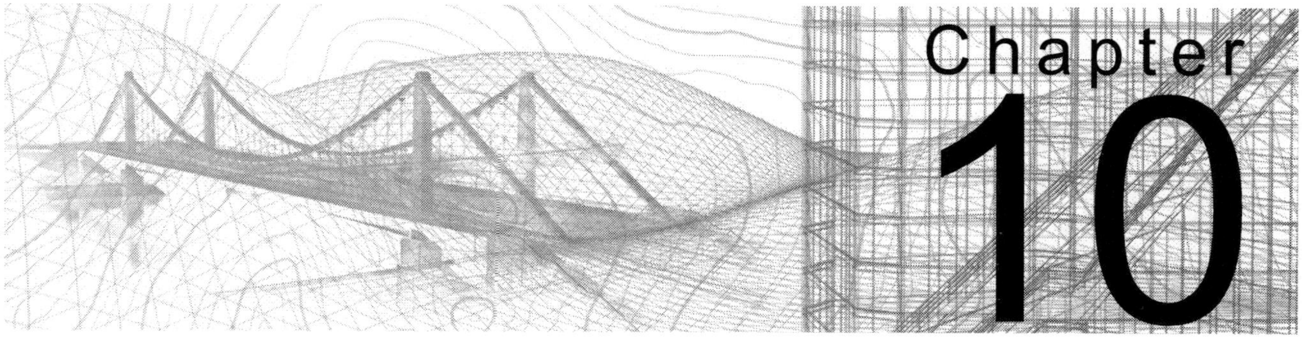

Visualization

In this chapter, you learn how to create visual styles, add materials to objects, do sun studies, set up lights, and render using basic tools.

Learning Objectives in This Chapter

- Customize visual styles by creating a new style in the Visual Styles Manager and adjusting the settings.
- Attach materials to objects using the Materials Browser.
- Specify light sources to cast shadows and create realistic views.
- Create a rendered image of a 3D solid model to be used for presentations.

10.1 Creating Visual Styles

Visual styles provide a variety of ways in which to view models as you work on them. The visual style options include Hidden, Conceptual, Realistic, and Sketchy, as shown in Figure 10–1. You can also customize visual styles by changing the hidden lines to dashed or by adding jitter and overhang to lines to make them look sketched.

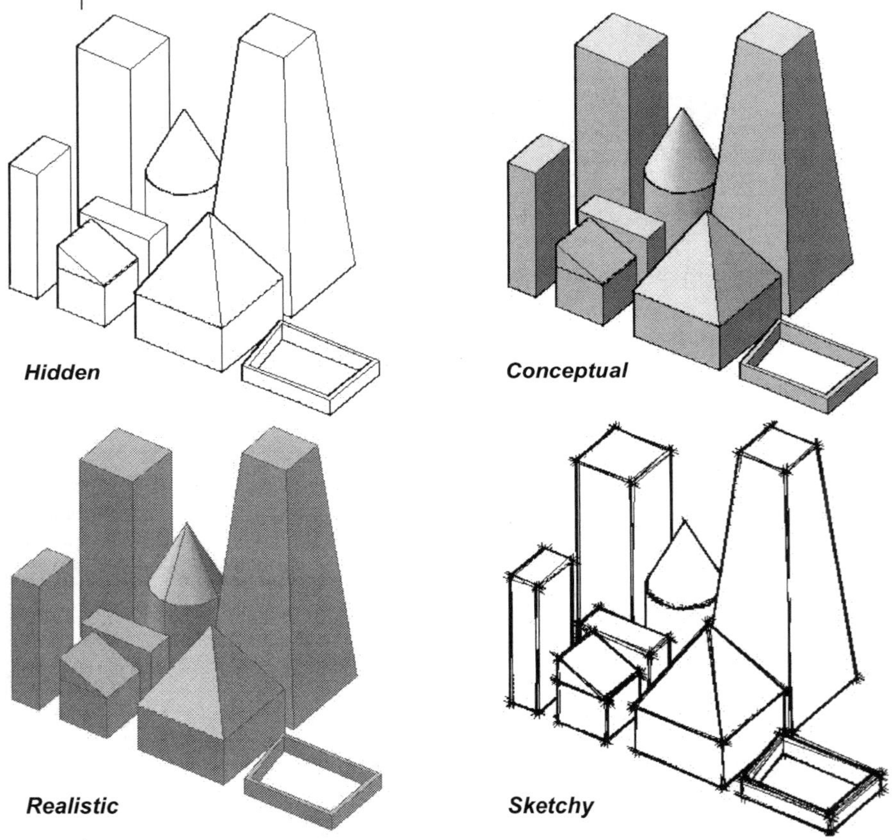

Figure 10–1

The Visual Styles Control in the *Home* tab>View panel contains a number of visual styles, as shown in Figure 10–2. You can also create custom visual styles by selecting **Save as a New Visual Style** or **Visual Styles Manager...**.

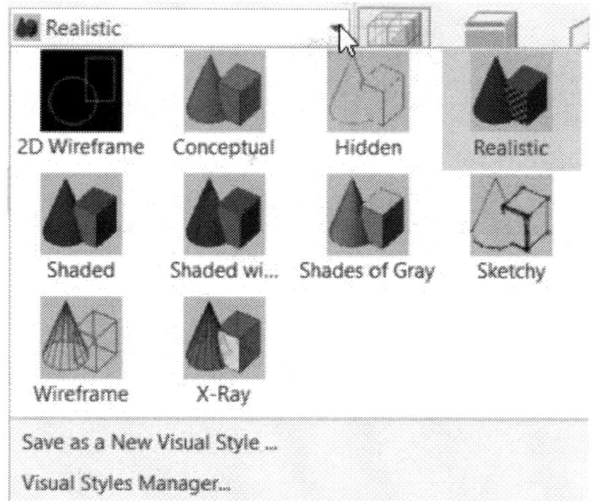

Figure 10–2

- Visual styles are saved in a drawing. If you want to use them in other drawings, you should create them in a template.

How To: Create a Custom Visual Style

1. In the *Home* tab>View panel, expand Visual Styles and select **Visual Styles Manager**. Figure 10–3 shows the Visual Styles Manager.

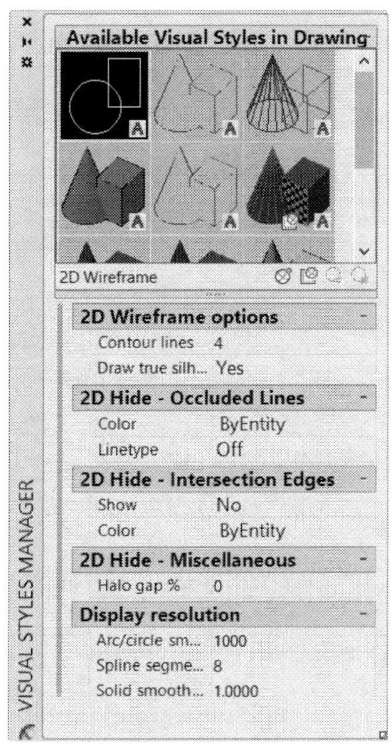

Figure 10–3

2. Click (Create New Visual Style) or right-click anywhere in the *Available Visual Styles in Drawing* area and select **Create New Visual Style....**
3. In the Create New Visual Style dialog box, enter a *Name* and *Description* and click **OK**.
4. Modify the options in the *Face Settings*, *Lighting*, *Environment Settings*, and *Edge Settings* areas as required. Note the changes to the icon in the *Available Visual Styles in Drawing* area as you modify the visual style.
5. Click (Apply Selected Visual Style to Current Viewport) to apply the custom style to the drawing.

Additional Options

	Export the Selected Visual Style to the Tool Palette: Adds a visual style to a custom tool palette.
	Delete the Selected Visual Style: Removes the selected visual style from your drawing. You can only delete custom visual styles.

Visual Style Settings

Visual styles have four main groups of settings:

- **Face Settings:** Control how 3D faces display. For example, whether they are transparent or solid and whether they display materials or colors.
- **Lighting:** Controls the effect of lighting in a viewport. By default, shadows are toggled off in all existing visual styles, because they can take a lot of time to generate.
- **Environment Settings:** Control shadows and backgrounds.
- **Edge Settings:** Control the visual look of edges on a model, including the overhang and jitter in the silhouette around the objects.

When you modify the settings in the Visual Styles Manager, it creates a specific style. If you modify the settings using the tools in the ribbon, a temporary override is created.

Face Settings

The primary face setting in a visual style is the *Face style*. You can also set the *Lighting quality*, *Color*, *Opacity*, and *Material display,* as shown in Figure 10–4.

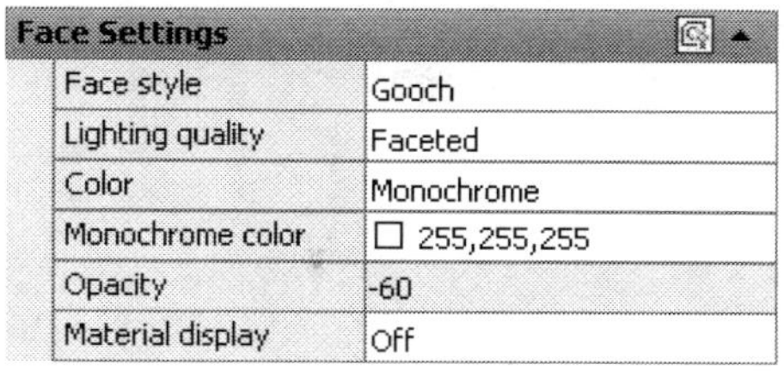

Figure 10–4

There are three different types of Face styles: **Realistic**, **Gooch**, and **None**, as shown in Figure 10–5.

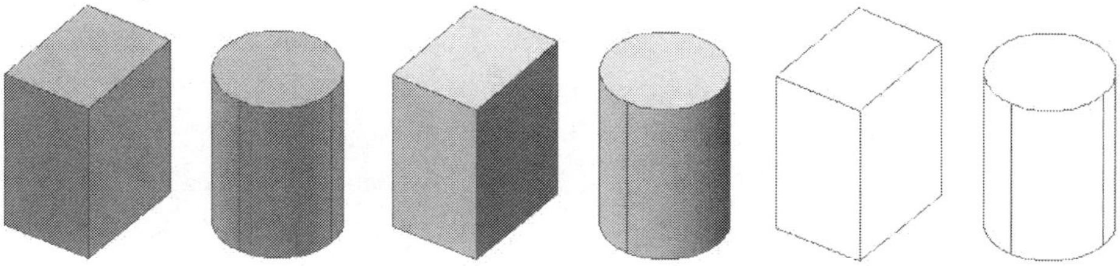

Realistic *Gooch* *None*

Figure 10–5

Face style	**Realistic:** Displays a realistic look with sharp differences between light and shadows. The Realistic visual style uses the Realistic face style, as shown in Figure 10–5. **Gooch:** Displays a cartoon-like look with a softer contrast between light and shadows. Lighted areas use warm tones, while darkened areas use cool tones as shown in Figure 10–5. The Conceptual visual style uses the Gooch face style. **None:** Only edges display, not faces, as shown in Figure 10–5. Both Hidden and Wireframe are examples that do not have a specified face style.
Lighting quality	Select from **Faceted**, **Smooth**, and **Smoothest**.
Color	Controls the display of colors on faces. **Normal:** Uses the colors of the object in the drawing. **Monochrome:** Shades all faces of the objects using the color specified by the **Monochrome color** option. **Tint:** Shades all faces of the objects by changing the hue and saturation values. Uses the color specified by the **Tint color** option. **Desaturate:** Softens the normal colors of faces in the drawing.

Opacity	Controls the transparency of objects. A higher number creates a more transparent object. Click (Opacity) in the *Face Settings* area title bar to toggle between positive and negative numbers. You can also temporarily override the Opacity in the *View* tab>Visual Style panel using (X-Ray Effect).
Material display	Controls the display of materials and textures on the faces of objects to which materials have been applied. **Materials and Textures:** Toggles on both Materials and Textures. Materials display color and translucency, while textures map an image file to the surface, giving the object a realistic look. In the *Visualize* tab>Materials panel, click (Materials / Textures On). **Materials:** Toggles Materials on and Textures off. In the *Visualize* tab>Materials panel, click (Materials On / Textures Off). **Off:** Toggles off both Materials and Textures. In the *Visualize* tab>Materials panel, click (Materials / Textures Off).

Lighting

Shadows can use a lot of computer memory and should only be toggled on when required.

There are two settings for Lighting as shown in Figure 10–6. The shadows display as you create new 3D objects and move with the objects when they are modified.

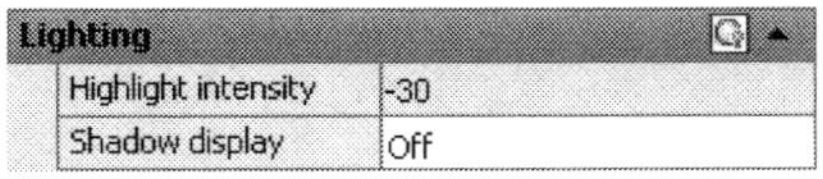

Figure 10–6

Highlight intensity	Controls the shininess of objects in the drawing. A lower number intensifies the highlights and makes the objects shine. Click (Highlight intensity) in the *Lighting* area title bar to toggle between positive and negative numbers. This option is not available when Materials are toggled on.
Shadow display	Controls the display of shadows. **Mapped Object shadows:** Displays full shadows (shadows cast by objects on the ground and on other objects). **Ground shadow:** Displays shadows cast by objects on the ground. **Off:** Toggles off any shadows in visual styles.

In the *Visualize* tab>Lights panel, there are two types of shadows: **Full Shadows** and **Ground Shadows**, as shown in Figure 10–7.

Full Shadows ***Ground Shadows***

Figure 10–7

- The sun or user-defined lights must be toggled on in the drawing for the shadows to be displayed. Full Shadows are only available when you have Hardware Acceleration toggled on.
- Additional options are available for shadows when you prepare objects for rendering.

Environment Settings

Environment settings (shown in Figure 10–8) control the use of backgrounds. Backgrounds are set in views, but can be toggled on or off in a visual style.

Figure 10–8

Edge Settings

Edge settings vary according to the type of Edge that displays. Edge Settings include *Occluded Edges*, *Intersection Edges*, *Silhouette Edges*, and *Edge Modifiers*, as shown in Figure 10–9.

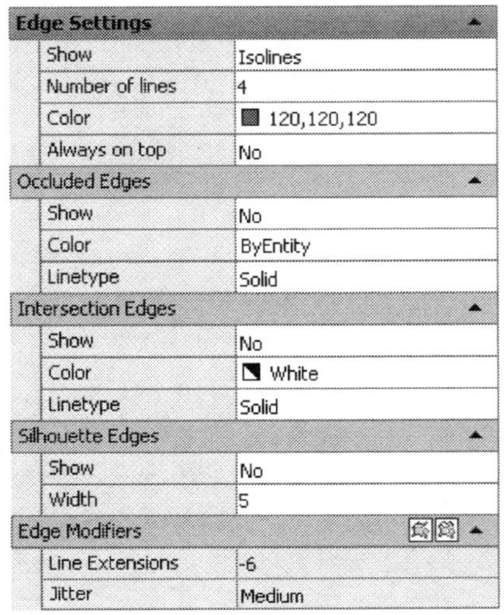

Figure 10–9

You can add overhanging lines and jitter to make the objects look as if they have been sketched, as shown in Figure 10–10. You can also use the Sketchy visual style to display objects with a sketched appearance. Some Edge settings control the look of silhouette edges and occluded edges, as shown in Figure 10–11.

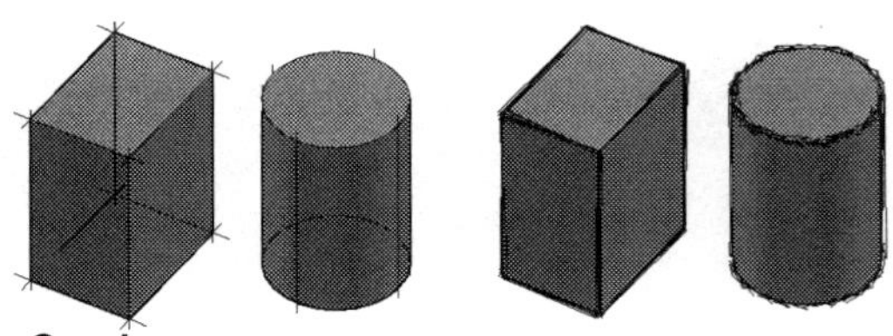

Overhang ***Jitter***

Figure 10–10

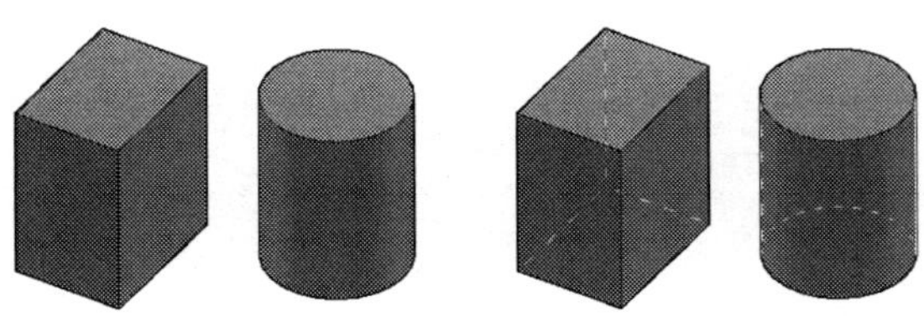

Silhouette Edges On ***Occluded Edges On***

Figure 10–11

Show

In addition to toggling edges off, Edge Mode can be set to either **Facet Edges** or **Isolines**, as shown in Figure 10–12.

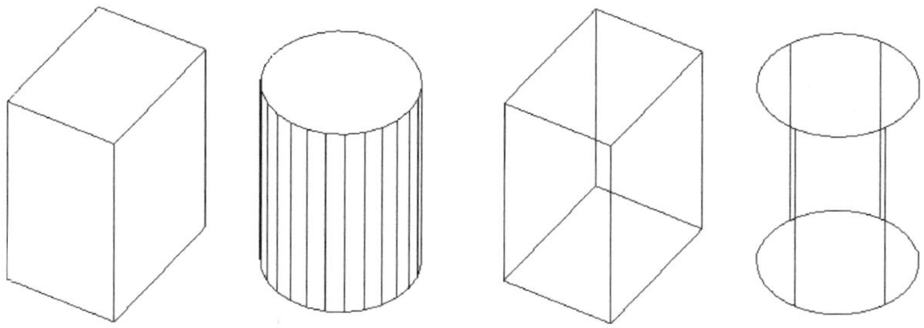

Facet Edges *Isolines (4)*

Figure 10–12

Facet Edges	Displays edges at each facet.
Isolines	Displays edges according to the number of Isolines.
None	Removes all edges from the visual style. This can only be used if face styles are set to **Realistic** or **Gooch**.

- **Number of lines:** Specifies the number of Isolines displayed on the object. If you do not see a change, regenerate the view (**Regen**) to update it.
- **Color:** Specifies the color displayed on the edges.
- **Always on top:** Specifies whether or not Isolines are always displayed on top of the solid.

Occluded Edges

Controls the settings for obscured (or hidden) edges.

Show	Controls whether occluded (obscured) edges display.
Color	Specifies the color of occluded edges.
Linetype	Specifies the linetype of occluded edges.

Intersection Edges

Controls the settings for lines where objects overlap, but are not joined together.

Show	Controls whether intersection edges display.
Color	Specifies the color of intersection edges.
Linetype	Specifies the linetype of intersection edges.

Silhouette Edges

Silhouette Edges control the visibility and width of the outline around solid objects.

Show	Controls whether silhouette edges display.
Width	Specifies the width of silhouette edges.

Edge Modifiers

*If the Edge mode is set to **Isolines**, no options are available for modifying the **Crease angle** and **Halo gap %**.*

Use Edge Modifiers to display the objects in a hand-drawn or sketched manner.

Line Extensions	Specifies the overhang length, forcing the lines to extend beyond their intersections. Click (Line Extension Edges) in the Edge Modifiers title bar to toggle the Line Extensions on or off.
Jitter	Sets the Jitter level to **Off**, **Low**, **Medium**, or **High**, controlling the sketched appearance of the objects. Click (Jitter Edges) in the Edge Modifiers title bar to toggle the Jitter on or off.
Crease angle	Creates a smooth effect by specifying the angle at which the facet edges in a face are not displayed.
Halo gap %	Specifies the gap size when an object is hidden by another object.

Practice 10a Creating Visual Styles

Practice Objective

- Create a new visual style using the Visual Styles Manager.

In this practice, you will create a new visual style that would be used for typical presentations at your company, such as the sketched look shown in Figure 10–13.

Figure 10–13

1. Open **Skyline.dwg**.
2. In the *Home* tab>View panel, expand Visual Styles and select **Visual Styles Manager**.
3. Click  (Create New Visual Style). Enter **Sketch** for the name and leave the description blank. Click **OK**.
4. Modify the various options in the Visual Styles Manager as follows for the new style:
   - Under *Face Settings*, in the Color drop-down list, select **Tint**. In the Tint Color list, select **Select Color** and in the dialog box, click the *Index Color* tab and select color **161** (a light blueish purple color), then select **OK**. Turn the *Face style* to **Gooch**.
   - In the *Edge Modifiers* section, click  (Line Extension edges) and  (Jitter edges).

5. With your new style selected, click (Apply Selected Visual Style to Current Viewport). The objects display in a sketched look similar to that shown in Figure 10–13.

6. Save and close the drawing.

10.2 Working with Materials

Many materials display as you work in visual styles, while others only display when you render a view.

When you look at an object, you do not only see its shape. You also gather information about it by its material. The same is true when you view a 3D drawing, as shown in Figure 10–14. Materials help you to understand the purpose and qualities of the objects. For example, if you see box made of wood, you would have a different sense of its probable weight and durability than a box made of glass.

Figure 10–14

You can attach materials to objects using the Materials Browser or by attaching materials by layer. Materials are stored in libraries. The Autodesk Library contains a variety of standard materials. You can also create and edit custom libraries and custom materials and textures.

- Most of the materials that are supplied with the AutoCAD® software, such as masonry, wood, and flooring, are designed for use in architectural drawings. If you place them on small objects, the materials do not display at the expected scale, as shown in Figure 10–15.

Figure 10–15

Using the Materials Browser

The Materials Browser is the primary way of adding materials to drawings. It is used to view and apply existing materials to your drawing and to create, modify, and manage new and existing materials. You can drag-and-drop materials directly onto objects.

You can use the Materials Browser to manage, search for, sort, select and organize your materials. They can be saved in custom libraries. You can also display all available materials or only the ones used in the current drawing. The materials include preview images, to help when selecting them. In the *Visualize* tab>

Materials panel, click (Material Browser).

The Materials Browser contains the *Document Materials:* area, which displays previews of all of the materials that have been added to the drawing. It also contains the *Libraries:* area, which contains two panels. The panel on the left in Figure 10–16 displays the names of all of the libraries in the drawing. When you expand a library, it displays a list of categories. Select a category to display all the materials in that category, in the panel on the right, as shown in Figure 10–16.

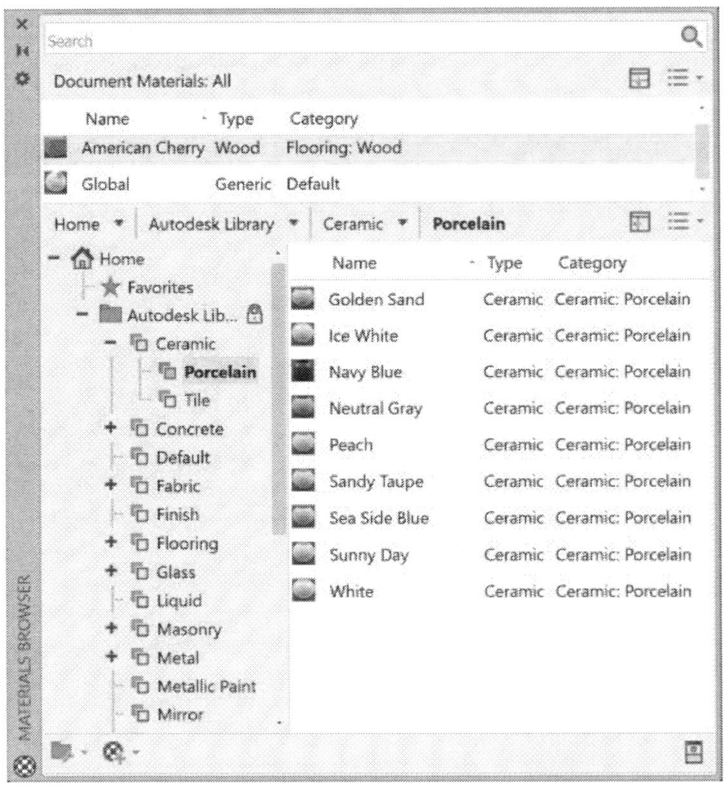

Figure 10–16

- You can change how the materials are previewed in the panel by clicking (icon) and selecting the required *View Type*, as shown in Figure 10–17. They can be displayed as a list, thumbnails, or text only.

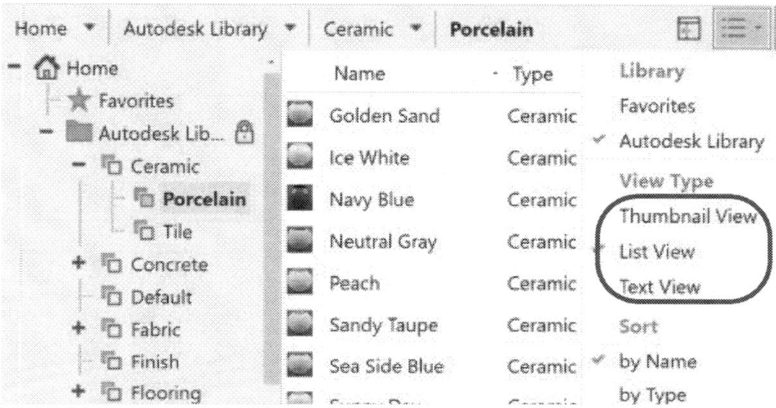

Figure 10–17

- Type a material name in the *Search* field to search for materials with that name in all open libraries. The *Document Materials* and *Libraries* areas display the search results.

Libraries

To add materials to a drawing you need to open the library in which they are located. By default, the standard Autodesk Library is open. To open a custom library, expand (Libraries) at the bottom of the Materials Browser and select **Open Existing Library**. In the Add Library dialog box, navigate to the location in which the custom library has been saved, select its name and click **Open**. Library files are saved with an .ADSKLIB file extension.

You can also create custom libraries. These can be useful for organizing commonly used materials, custom materials, job specific materials, etc.

How To: Create a New Custom Library

1. In the Materials Browser, expand (Libraries) and select **Create New Library**, as shown in Figure 10–18.

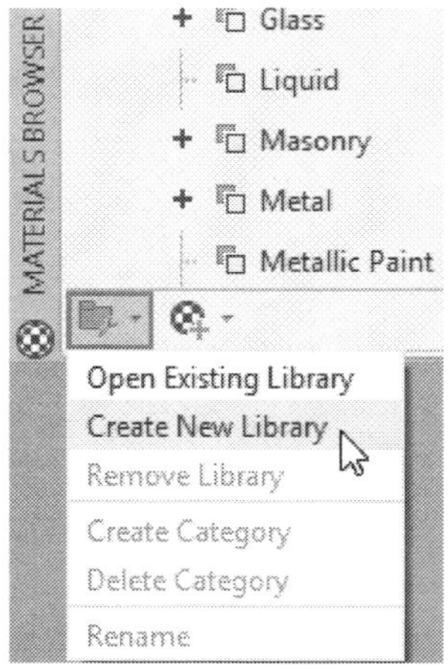

Figure 10–18

2. In the Create Library dialog box, navigate to the location in which you want to store the library, type a name, and click **Save**.
3. In the *Libraries* area, the new library displays under Home.
4. In the Materials Browser, drag-and-drop materials from the *Document Materials* area to the new library.
5. Right-click on the library name and select **Create Category** to create categories in the library. You can also expand (Libraries) and select **Create Category**.
6. Create categories and drag-and-drop materials to them as required, as shown in Figure 10–19.

You might require permissions to modify the material library.

*The selected View Type is **Thumbnail View**.*

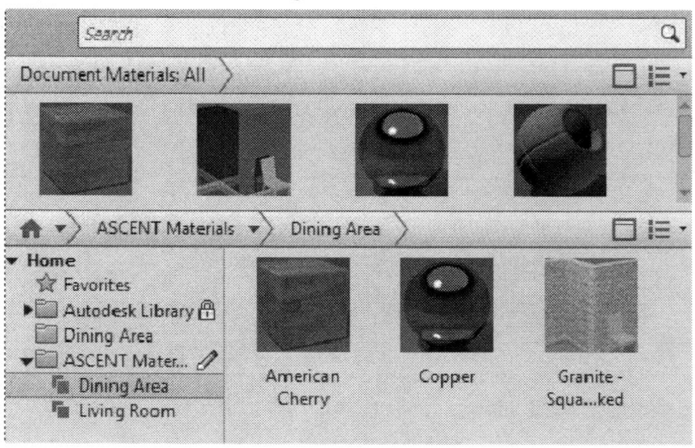

Figure 10–19

- To delete a library, select it in the *Libraries* area, expand (Libraries) and select **Remove Library**. You can also right-click on the library's name and select **Remove Library**.

Adding Materials

Once you have created a library or when you are ready to add materials to objects, you need to load materials into the drawing. This is done by selecting a category in a library, then hovering over the material swatch that you want to add to the drawing, and selecting one of the **Apply** buttons.

How To: Load Materials

It might be necessary to expand a library category first.

1. Open the Materials Browser.
2. In the *Libraries* area, expand a library.
3. In the Library, select a category to display previews of the materials stored in that category.
4. Hover over the material that you want to use and click (Add material to document). It is added to the *Drawing Materials* and loaded into the drawing.
5. The materials can then be added to objects or layers.

How To: Attach Materials from the Materials Browser

1. Open the Materials Browser.
2. In the *Drawing Materials* area, select a material or load one from the library as required.
3. Drag-and-drop the material onto an object.

- To attach a material to multiple objects, select the objects so that they display their grips, then right-click on the material in the *Document Materials* area in the Materials Browser and select **Assign to Selection**. The material is applied to all of the selected objects.
- To delete materials from an object, click (Remove Materials) in the *Visualize* tab>expanded Materials panel. At the *Select objects* prompt, select the objects from which you want to remove the materials.

Applying, Displaying, and Removing Materials

You can apply a material to individual faces. If you only apply materials to displayed faces, it saves rendering time later. To attach a material to a single face, hold <Ctrl> as you drag-and-drop the material.

You can also assign a material to the full solid. In Figure 10–20, the glass material is assigned to the full solid of the object on the left and only to the outside face of the object on the right. The transparency is limited if the entire solid is not selected.

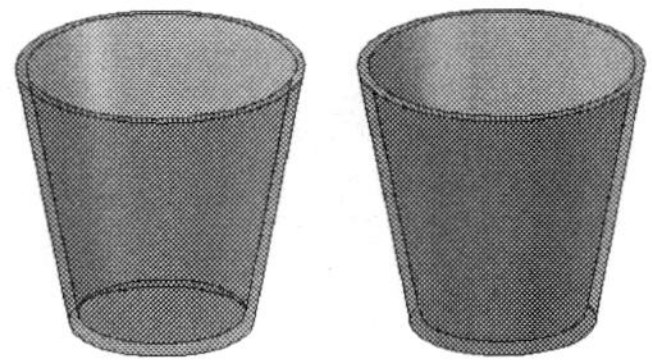

Figure 10–20

You can independently control various display options in the *Document Materials* and *Library* areas by expanding the Display Options drop-down list and selecting an option, as shown in Figure 10–21.

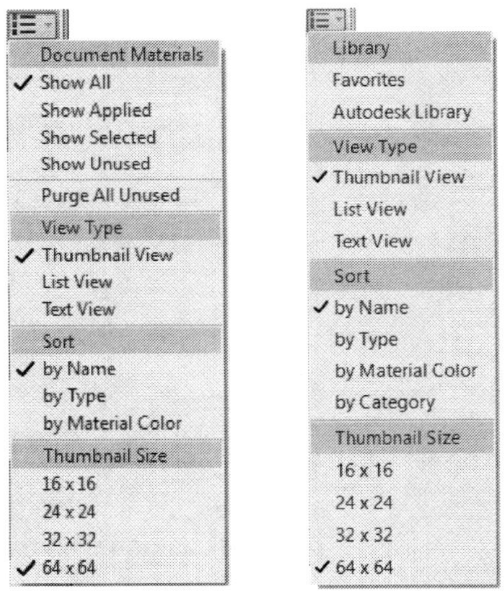

Figure 10–21

- In the *Document Materials* area, you can display all materials in the drawing, only those applied to objects or faces, only those applied to selected objects, or only those that are not being used.
- To remove unused materials from the drawing, you can select **Purge All Unused** in the Document Materials Display Options drop-down list, or in the shortcut menu in the *Drawing Materials* area in the Materials Browser.

You can also set the View Type (from thumbnails to lists), Sort (by name, type, etc.), and Thumbnail size.

Hint: Map a Material

Many materials include textures. However, if the texture has a very specific line or repeat pattern, you might need to change its Mapping as it is projected onto a surface, as shown in Figure 10–22.

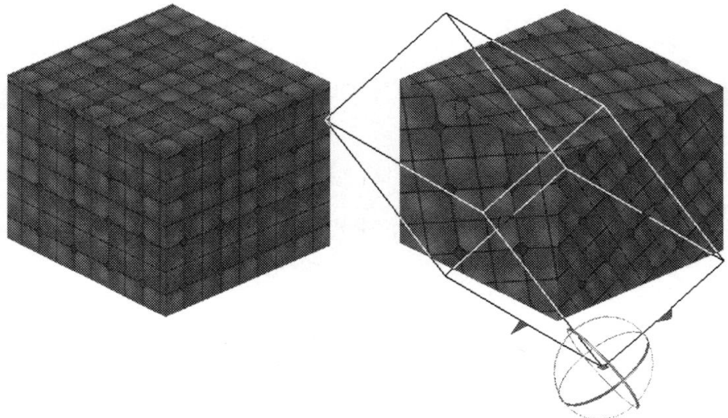

Figure 10–22

In the *Visualize* tab>Materials panel, select the mapping method that you want to use: **Planar**, **Box**, **Cylindrical**, or **Spherical**, as shown in Figure 10–23. Select the faces or objects, press <Enter>, and use grips to adjust the mapping as required. You can switch between the **Move** and **Rotate** modes.

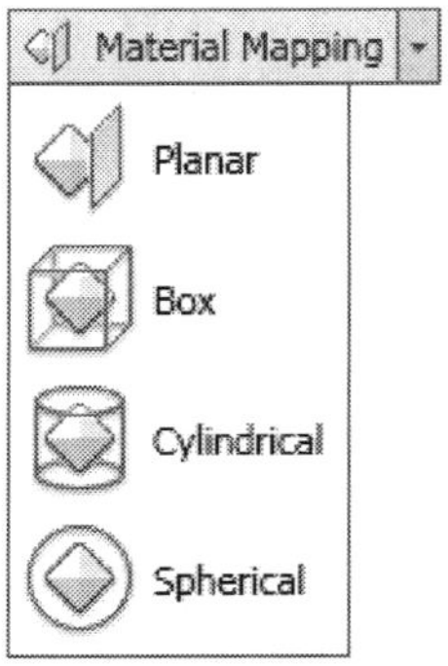

Figure 10–23

Attaching Materials by Layer

In complex models with many types of materials (such as architectural designs), attaching a material to each object would take too long. If you use a layering scheme when creating the objects, you can associate materials with each layer using the Material Attachment Options dialog box, as shown in Figure 10–24.

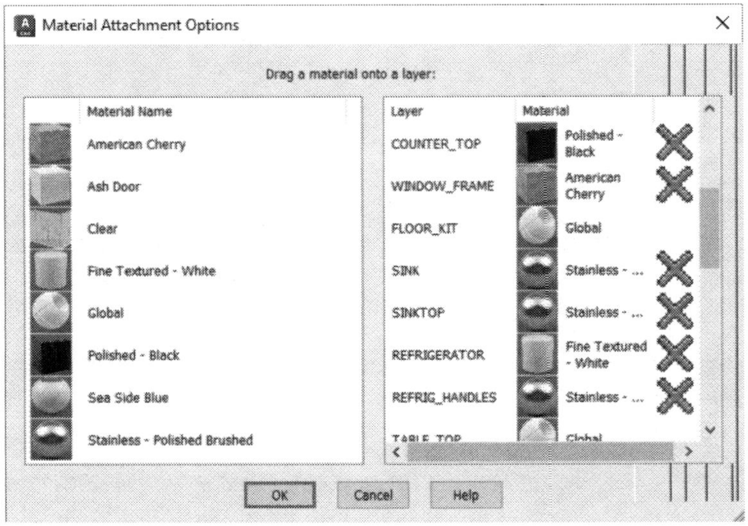

Figure 10–24

- The materials that you want to use must be loaded into the drawing before the **Attach By Layer** command is launched.

How To: Attach Materials by Layer

1. In the *Visualize* tab>expanded Materials panel, click (Attach By Layer).
2. In the Material Attachment Options dialog box, select a material in the left pane and drag-and-drop it onto a layer name in the right pane.
3. Continue attaching materials to layers as required.
4. Click **OK** to end the command.

- Materials attached to individual objects override materials attached by layer. You can change the assigned material to **ByLayer** in Properties.

Material Editor

The Material Editor enables you to modify the properties of materials. You can change the material's name, type, pattern, reflectivity, transparency, lighting, color, etc., as shown in Figure 10–25. The options vary depending on the type of material selected.

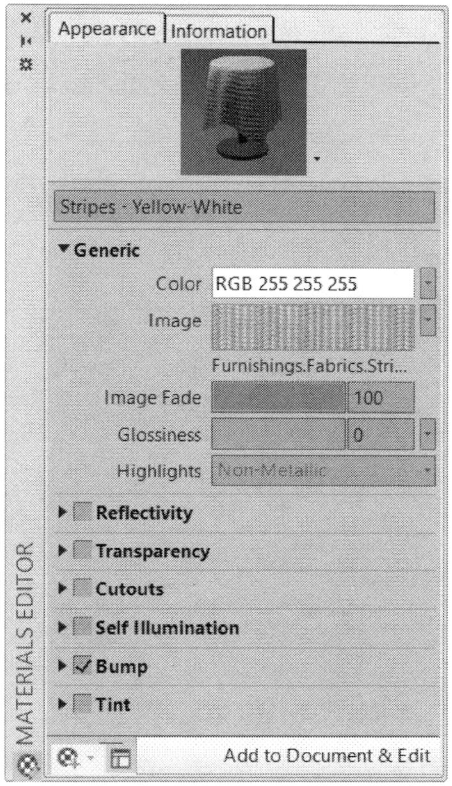

Figure 10–25

- You can open the Material Editor by right-clicking on a material in the *Document Materials* area and selecting **Edit**.

  You can also click (Material Editor) in the *View* tab>Palettes panel, or in the *Visualize* tab>Materials panel. You can also open the Material Editor for a particular material by hovering over that material swatch in the *Document Materials* area and clicking (Edit).

- The Material Editor enables you to modify existing materials or to duplicate the current material to create a custom copy.

Preview/Render Quality

A preview of the material displays at the top of the Material Editor. You can change how the material displays by selecting an option in the **Scene** category in the drop-down list next to the preview in the Material Editor palette, as shown in Figure 10–26. You can control the rendering quality by selecting **Quick**, **Draft**, and **Production** in the **Render Settings** category. You can also set various **Environments** in this list.

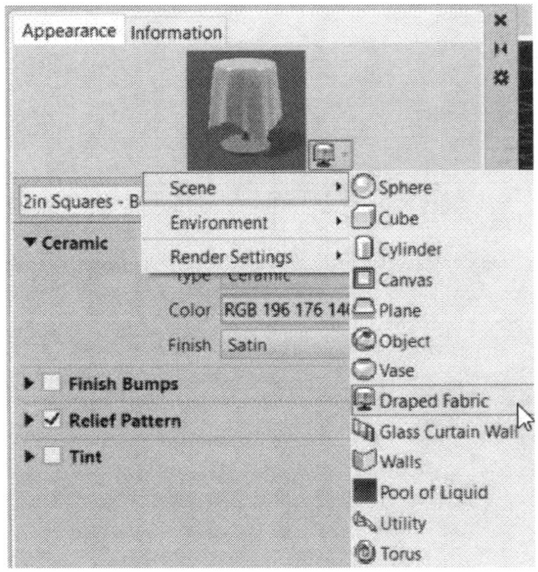

Figure 10–26

Material Type

You can create a new material type from the  (Create Material) drop-down list at the bottom left of the Material Editor palette, as shown in Figure 10–27. You can duplicate the existing material, select from a list of types, or create a generic material.

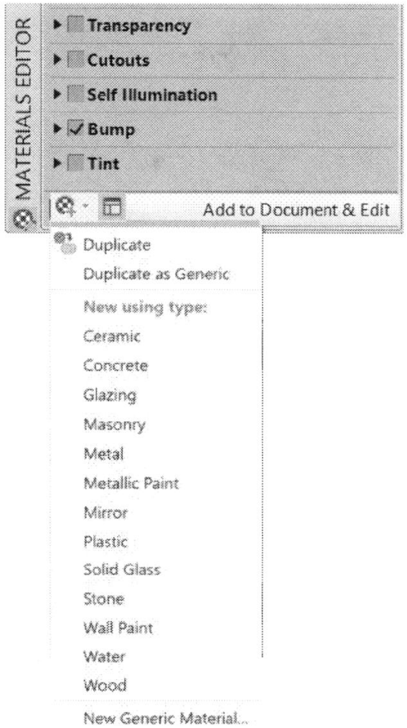

Figure 10–27

Properties

The Material Editor is divided into areas, each of which controls properties related to the type of material being modified or created. The *Type* area lists the type name and enables you to set its properties. The other areas control the *Reflectivity*, *Transparency*, *Cutouts*, *Self Illumination*, *Bump*, and *Tint* settings.

For the Generic Type, the settings are as follows:

Generic	Controls the color, image, glossiness and highlights of the material.
Reflectivity	Controls the amount of light reflected from the material directly at the camera or at an angle to the camera.
Transparency	Controls the amount of transparency, translucency, and refraction of the material. Also controls whether an image or texture are used with the transparency.
Cutouts	Uses an image or texture to make a material partially transparent. For example, this could be used to created lace or etched glass.

Self Illumination	Controls the color, brightness, and temperature of the light being transmitted through a transparent material.
Bump	Uses an image of the material or a texture to create a bump pattern and controls the relative height of the pattern.
Tint	Controls the hue and saturation value of the assigned color when mixed with white.

Texture Editor

The Texture Editor enables you to modify the appearance of the texture displayed on a material. Select a texture option in the second drop-down list in the Material Editor palette>*Generic* area, to open the Texture Editor. A preview of the texture and its properties display. The properties vary depending on the type of texture selected. For example, the Tiles texture and its properties are shown in Figure 10–28.

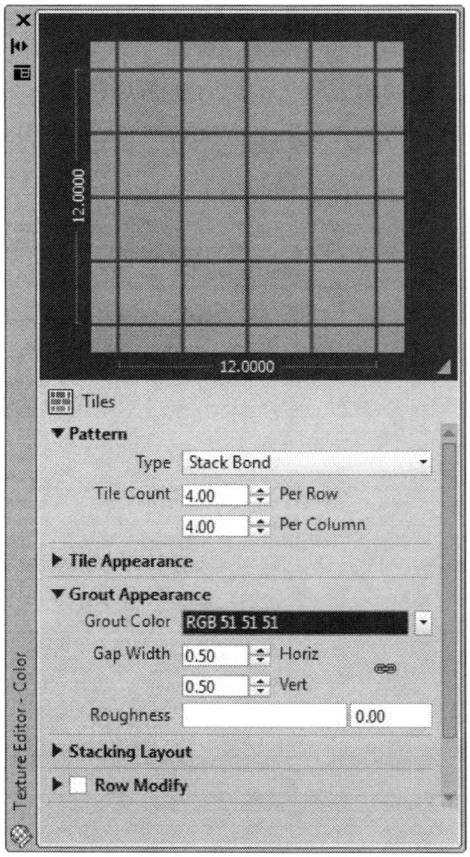

Figure 10–28

- You can control the texture's color, pattern, size, repeat, etc.

Practice 10b Working with Materials

Practice Objective

- Apply materials by layer and to objects faces to complete a realistic display.

In this practice, you will apply materials by layer and to objects faces to complete a realistic display, such as that shown in Figure 10–29. The exact selection of materials is up to you.

Figure 10–29

Task 1 - Add materials to objects and layers.

1. Open **Kitchen-3DMaterials.dwg**.
2. Switch to the **Dining Area** view.
3. In the *Visualize* tab>Materials panel, click (Materials Browser).

4. In the Materials Browser, in the *Libraries* area, expand the Autodesk Library, expand the **Flooring** category, and select the **Wood** subcategory to display the list of its materials, as shown in Figure 10–30.

5. Hover the cursor over **American Cherry**, then click (Add material to document). This adds the material to the *Document Materials* area, as shown in Figure 10–30.

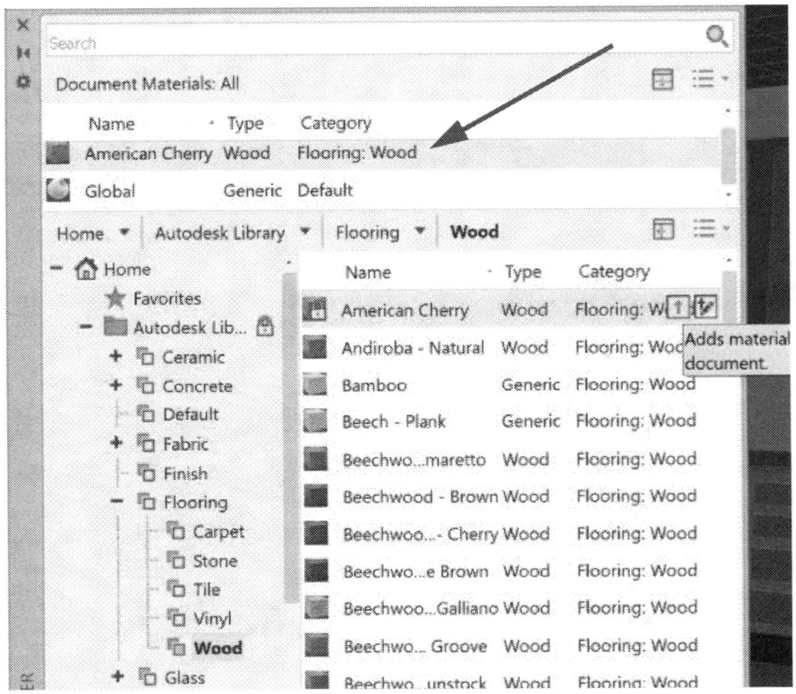

Figure 10–30

6. Add some ceramic, metal, plastic, fabric, and wood materials that will be used in the Kitchen and Dining Room.

7. Drag-and-drop some of the materials from the *Document Materials* area onto objects in the Kitchen and Dining Room views.

8. In the *Visualize* tab>expanded Materials panel, click (Attach By Layer).

If the material you want to use is not listed, close the Material Attachment Options dialog box, load the material, and open the dialog box to display the material.

9. In the Material Attachment Options dialog box, attach materials to the layers. For example, you can apply a wood material to the layer **CABINET**, a plastic material to the layer **REFRIGERATOR**, and a metal material to the layer **REFRIG_HANDLES**, as shown in Figure 10–31. Click **OK** to apply the changes to the drawing.

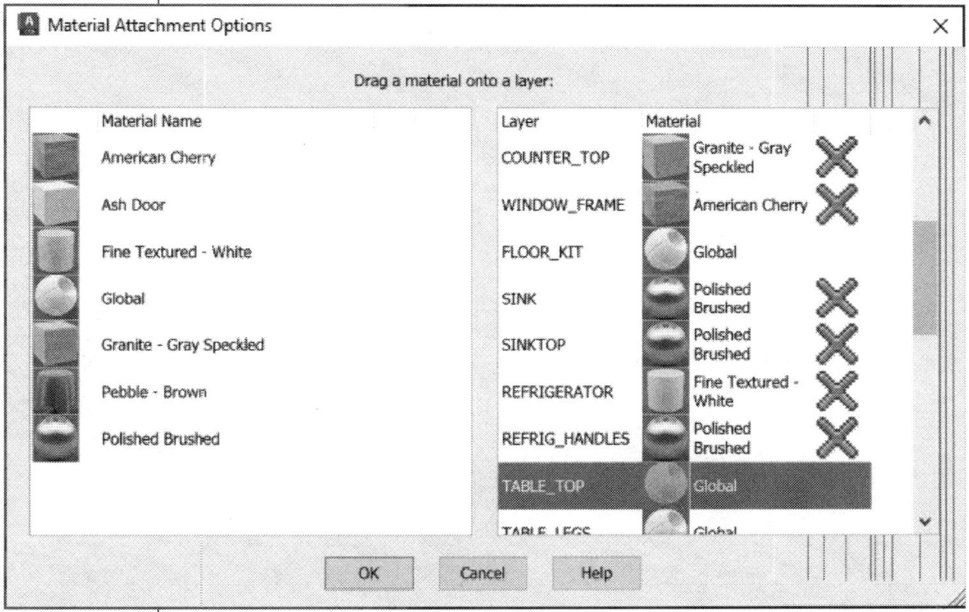

Figure 10–31

10. Save the drawing.

Task 2 - Modify materials and textures.

1. In the Materials Browser, in the Autodesk Library>Ceramic> Tile category, hover over **2in Squares - Beige** and click  (Add material to document).

2. In the *Document Materials* area, right-click on the **2in Squares - Beige** material and select **Edit**.

3. In the Materials Editor, expand the  (Create Material) drop-down list and select **Duplicate**.

4. Set the *Name* to **Backsplash**, as shown in Figure 10–32.
5. Set the *Type* to **Porcelain**, as shown in Figure 10–32.
6. Expand the Color drop-down list and select **Speckle**, as shown in Figure 10–32.
7. In the Texture Editor, expand the Color 1 drop-down list and select **Edit Color**. In the Select Color dialog box, switch to the *Index Color* tab and select the blue color (*Index color* **5**). Click **OK**.
8. Similarly set the *Color 2* to cyan color (*Index color* **4**).
9. Set the *Size* to **15**.
10. Close the Texture Editor. The new materials displays (as shown in Figure 10–32) in the Materials Editor.

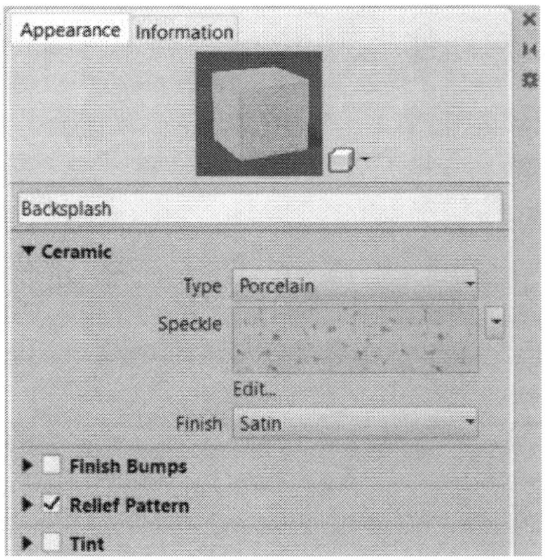

Figure 10–32

11. Close the Materials Editor.
12. Switch to **Kitchen** view.

13. Drag-and-drop the material **Backsplash** onto the backsplash area, as shown in Figure 10–33.

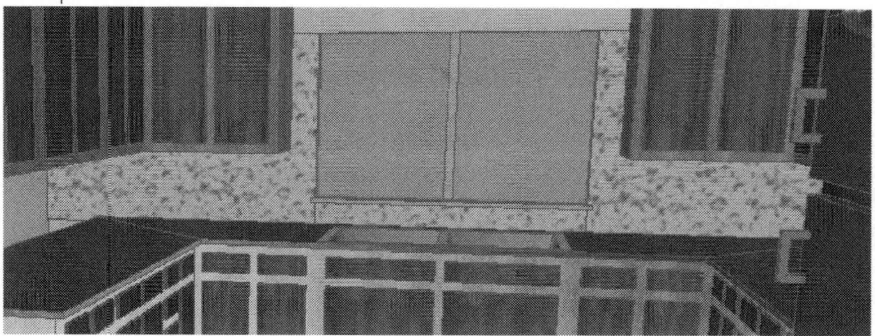

Figure 10–33

Task 3 - Create a library.

1. In the Materials Browser, expand (Libraries) and select **Create New Library**.
2. In the Create Library dialog box, navigate to your practice files folder and save the new library as **Dining Area**. The Dining Area library displays in the Materials Browser.
3. Expand (Libraries) and select **Create Category**. Name it **Flooring**.
4. Create categories for **Furniture** and **Walls** as well.
5. Drag-and-drop the materials that you applied to the floor to the Flooring category.
6. Drag-and-drop the appropriate materials to the other categories.
7. Save and close the drawing.

10.3 Specifying Light Sources

When you create realistic views, such as the example shown in Figure 10–34, the light sources and the shadows they cast are a major component of the display.

*The **Realistic** visual style automatically displays any materials and textures that are associated with objects in the viewport. However, the lights and shadows are toggled off to save regeneration time as you create and modify objects.*

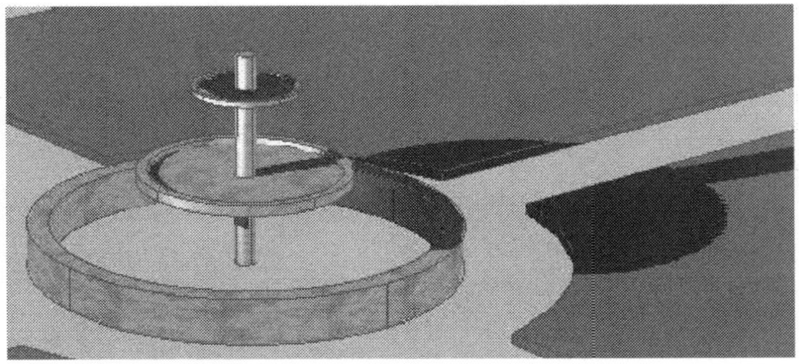

Figure 10–34

The AutoCAD software includes several sources of light to help you visualize your drawing:

- **Default Lighting:** Shines on all faces of the model as you move around the drawing.
- **Sunlight:** Defined by the location of the project and time of day.
- **User-defined lights:** Include **Distance**, **Point**, **Spotlights**, and **Weblight**, which can be added directly to the drawing.

Default Lighting

Default lighting illuminates a model without any specific focus. It is frequently used for mechanical drawings that do not need to display cast shadows.

- The default lighting source should be toggled off to display the sun or user-defined lights. Toggle off the default lighting by clicking  (Default Lighting) in the *Visualize* tab> expanded Lights panel.
- The first time you toggle the Sun or a user light, an alert box opens. Select **Always perform my current choice** and select **Turn off the default lighting (recommended)**.

Sunlight

One of the easiest lights to work with is the sun. All you need to do is toggle it on. Once it is on, you can set its location, date, and time. This is most effective if you also have shadows toggled on, as shown in Figure 10–35 for two different times of day.

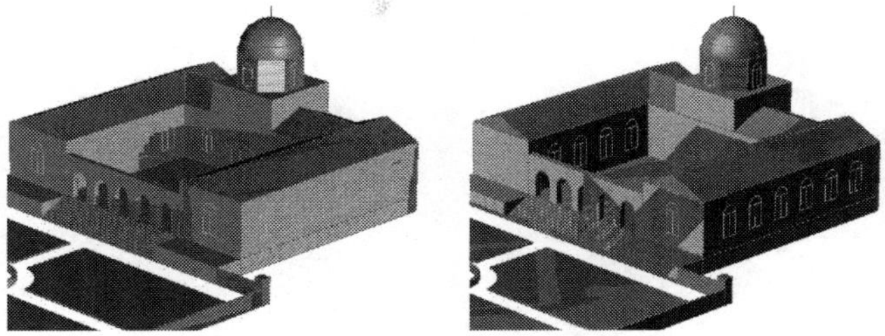

Figure 10–35

- In the *Visualize* tab>Lights panel and Sun & Location panel (shown in Figure 10–36), you can toggle on shadows, toggle on the sun, and set the location, date, and time.

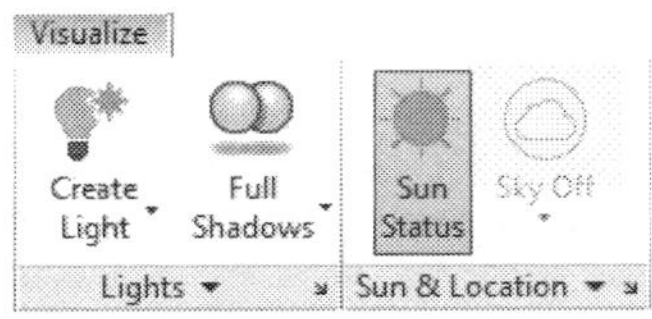

Figure 10–36

- The Sun Properties palette specifies the intensity and color of the sun, and its location, date, and time, as shown in Figure 10–37. You can open the palette by clicking [icon] in the Sun & Location panel.

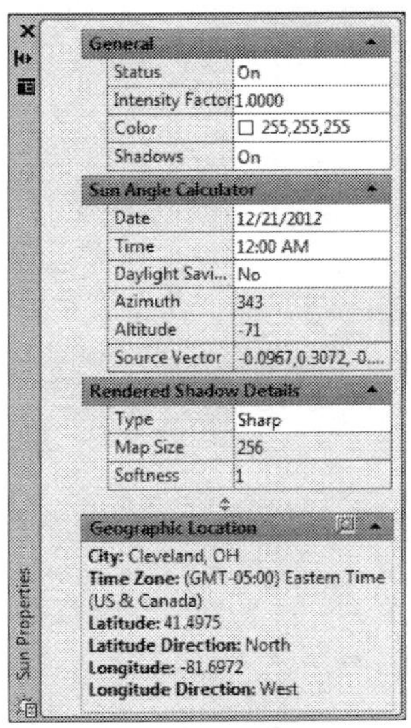

Figure 10–37

How To: Set the Geographic Location

1. In the *Visualize* tab>expanded Sun & Location panel, expand (Set Location) and click (From Map).
   - **From Map:** Specifies a location from a map or latitude and longitude location. When you click (From Map), the Online Map Data warning box opens as shown in Figure 10–38. To use Online Map Data, you must sign into your Autodesk account. Click **Yes** if you want to access the maps using your account. Click **No** if you do not have access to the internet and want to enter the latitude and longitude values manually.

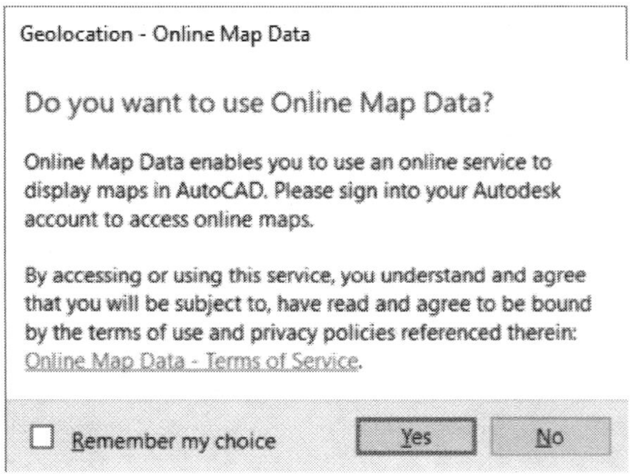

Figure 10–38

2. After you log in to Autodesk account or click **No** to use the non-internet option, the Geographic Location dialog box opens.
   - If using Online Map Data, use the mouse to zoom in on the required city on the map.

- Enter the location in the **Address** box which displays a list of locations. Hover your cursor on each location which pinpoints the location on the map and select **Drop Marker Here**. The required values of latitude and longitude are automatically displayed in the dialog box, as shown in Figure 10–39.
- You can also right-click in the Geographic Location dialog box and select **Drop Marker Here**.
- Click (Locate me) to enable the software to automatically zoom in on where your computer is located to make dropping the pin easier.

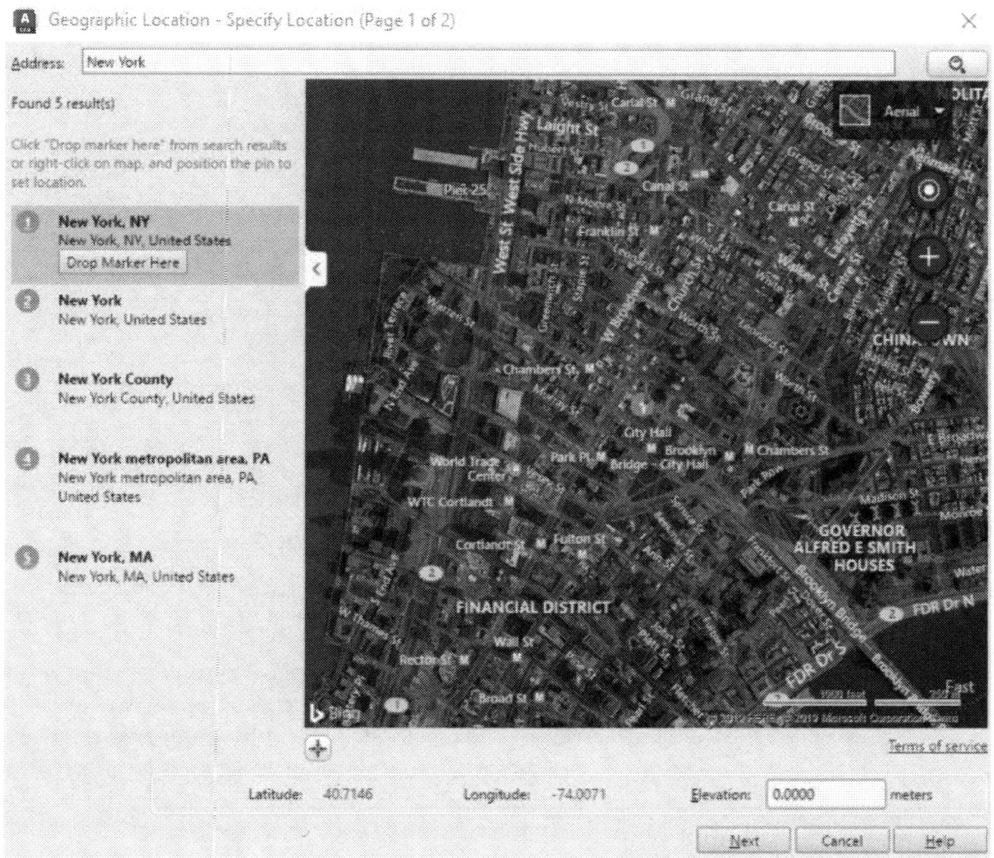

Figure 10–39

3. Click **Next**. In the Geographic Location - Set Coordinate System (Page 2 of 2) dialog box, in the *GIS Coordinate System* area, select the required coordinate system, as shown in Figure 10–40. For *Time Zone*, expand the drop-down list and select the required time zone. For *Drawing Unit*, expand the drop-down list and select the required units.

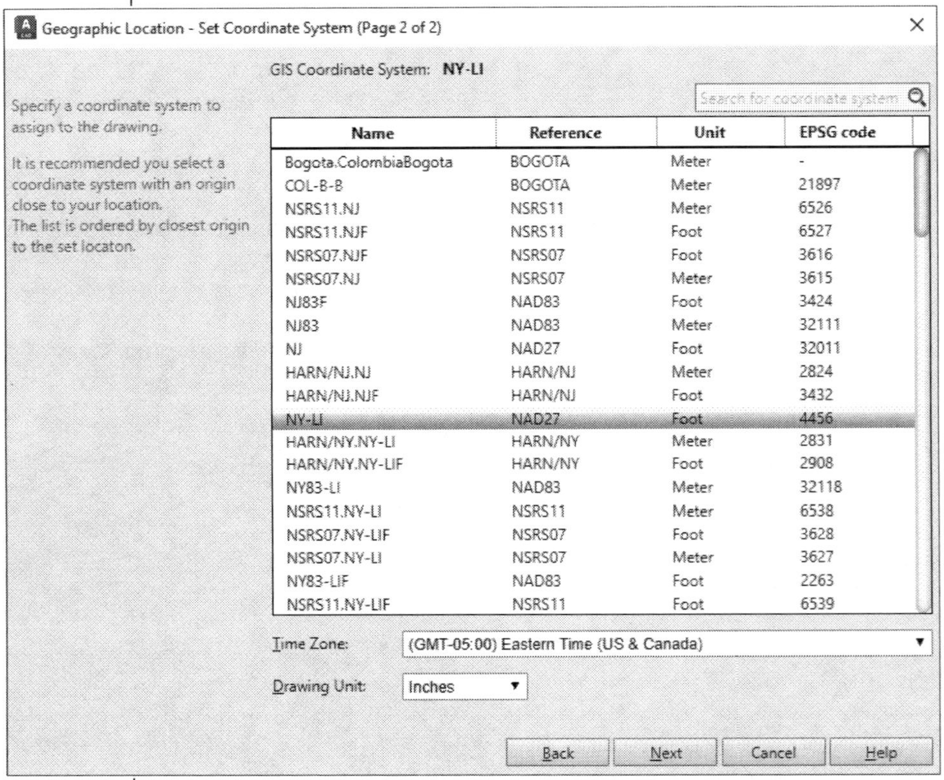

Figure 10–40

4. Click **Next**. In the drawing, select the location at which you want to place the Geographic Location.
5. Select a direction for North by entering an angle, selecting a point relative to the geographic location, or picking two points in the drawing. An icon is added to the drawing indicating the position of the Geographic Location.

- If a map is added to a drawing using Online Map Data, it is embedded in the drawing and can be used if you are not connected to your AutoCAD account or the internet.

- If a map is embedded in the drawing, you can use grips to move, resize and rotate its boundary. The *Map Image* contextual tab displays when the map image is selected. It enables you to adjust the contract, fading, and brightness of the image. If the image boundary is changed and you are logged into AutoCAD account, the map information automatically updates.
- When a drawing containing a map image is opened, the image does not update automatically. You need to use **Reload Image** or change the image boundaries to update the map image information.
- When using Online Map Data, an aerial map displays in the drawing. When you zoom in the image displays more clearly.
- You can also select the *Visualize* tab>Sun & Location panel, expand (Set Location) and click (From File) to import a .KML or .KMZ (zipped) file. These files are used by Google Earth and other 3D geospacial tools and include the latitude, longitude, and altitude of a location.
- If a Geographic Location already exists in the drawing, you can edit the current location, define a new location, or remove the location.

Geolocation Contextual Tab

The *Geolocation* contextual tab (shown in Figure 10–41) enables you to modify an existing geographic location.

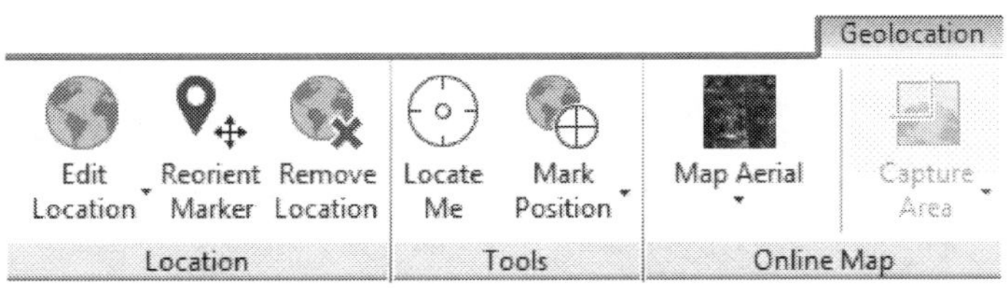

Figure 10–41

Location Panel

The Location panel enables you to edit, reorient, and remove the current geographic location, as shown in Figure 10–42.

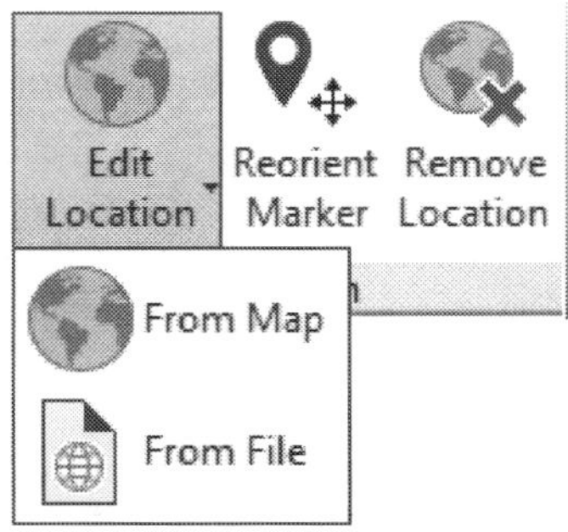

Figure 10–42

Tools Panel

The Tools panel enables you to mark a position using latitude and longitude, your current location, or a selected point, as shown in Figure 10–43. You can also use **Locate Me** to add a location marker at your current location.

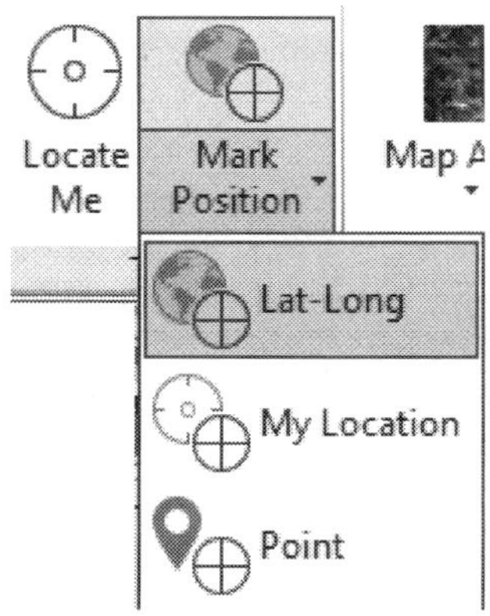

Figure 10–43

Online Map Panel

The Online Map panel enables you to control how the map displays and to capture an area or viewport for plotting, as shown in Figure 10–44.

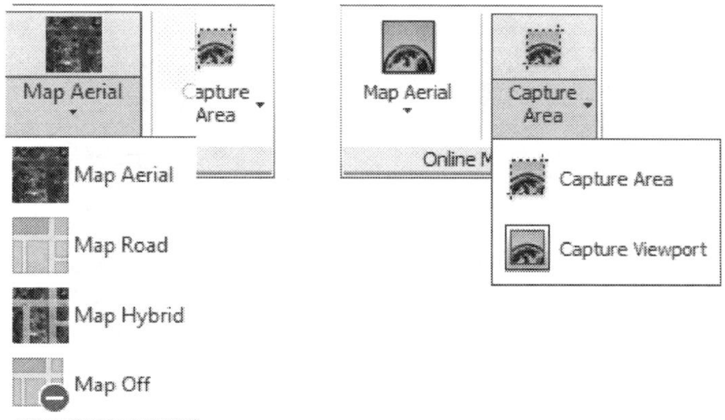

Figure 10–44

User-Defined Lights

Draw some 3D objects (such as boxes or cylinders) that can act as a stage or a frame to help you with positioning, or attach lights to objects that are already in your drawing.

User-defined lights can create more realistic views in a drawing. For example, you can place a **Point** light in a lamp to act as a light bulb or a **Spot** light to highlight materials and add shadows, as shown in Figure 10–45.

Figure 10–45

*As you place lights, you are prompted to set their options, such as their **Name**, **Intensity**, and **Color**. Setting these options is easier to modify using Properties after you have placed the light.*

Point Lights

A point light is like a light bulb. It radiates in all directions from the source and fades in intensity further from source, as shown in Figure 10–46. This fading is the rate of attenuation. Point lights are used for general lighting effects, such as light from a lamp.

Figure 10–46

How To: Place a Point Light

1. In the *Visualize* tab>Lights panel>Create Light flyout, click  (Point Light).
2. Specify the location of the light.
3. Select one of the options to modify as required or exit the command

Hint: Generic Lights and Photometric Lights

The AutoCAD software has two methods of controlling light intensity: *photometric* and *generic*. These can be set in the Units dialog box (usually in a template file) or in the *Visualize* tab>expanded Lights panel>Lighting Units flyout, as shown in Figure 10–47.

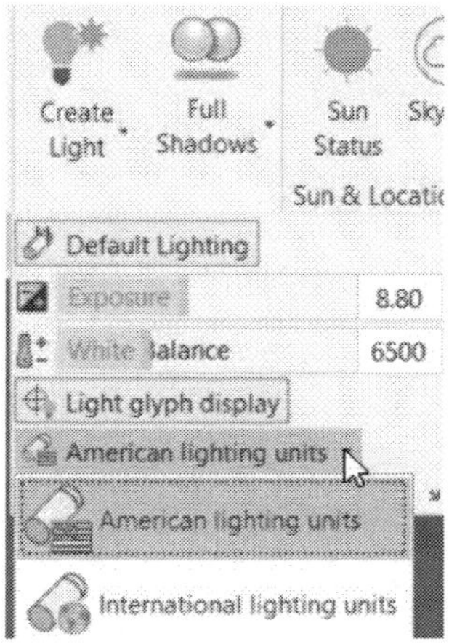

Figure 10–47

The **International** (lux) and **American** (foot candles) options enable photometric lighting.

- Additional photometric lights that have a precise intensity, color, and falloff rate are included in the Photometric Lights tool palettes, as shown in Figure 10–48.

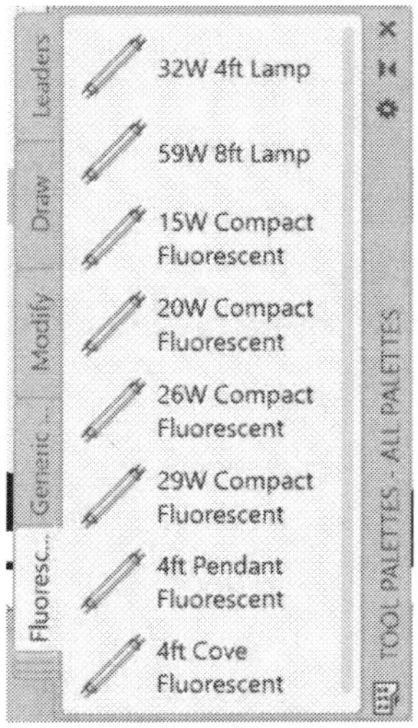

Figure 10–48

Spot Lights

A spot light is similar to a spot light used in the theater where you can focus a cone of light on a specific part. It focuses a cone of light on a specified part of the drawing. You can set the hot spot (the brightest point of light) and the falloff (the angle filled by the cone), as shown in Figure 10–49.

*Sometimes, spot lights do not display with the expected power. Change the Intensity Factor in the light's Properties to **1000**.*

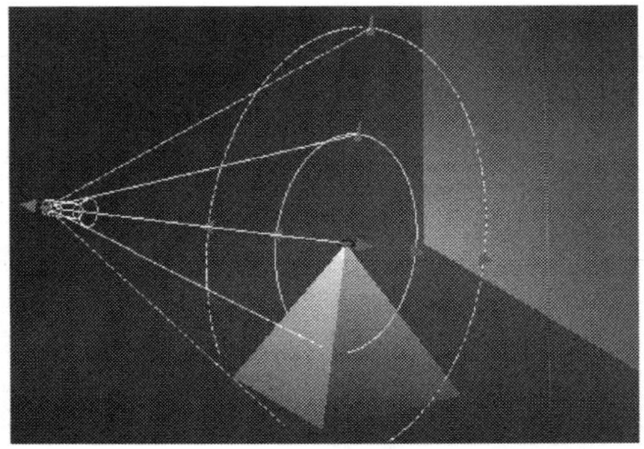

Figure 10–49

How To: Place a Spot Light

1. In the *Visualize* tab>Lights panel>Create Light flyout, click  (Spot Light).
2. Specify the source location of the light.
3. Specify the target location of the light.
4. Select one of the options to modify as required or exit the command.

Distant Lights

A distant light is similar to the light of the sun. The rays shine parallel in one direction and fall with the same brightness on all surfaces.

- Distant lights are only available when the *Lighting Units* in the drawing are set to **Generic**.

How To: Place a Distant Light

1. In the *Visualize* tab>Lights panel>Create Light flyout, click  (Distant Light).
2. Specify the light direction from point.
3. Specify the light direction to point.

4. Select one of the options to change as required or exit the command.

An additional distance light is available in the Generic Lights tool palette.

Hint: Weblight

(Weblight) can be found in the *Visualize* tab>Lights panel> Create Light flyout. Weblights are 3D representations of real-world light intensity distributions from a single light source. Their distribution is defined in a photometric data file in IES format.

Weblights display similar to Point Lights in Model Space and Viewports, as they are approximated as such here. The actual web distribution is only used in rendered images.

Modifying Lights

When you select the light name in the Lights in Model palette, it is selected in the drawing. When you double-click on the light name, it is selected and the Properties palette opens.

When you are ready to modify lights, you can select point and spot lights directly in the drawing or open the Lights in Model list, by clicking in the *Visualize* tab>Lights panel, to display a complete list of lights, as shown in Figure 10–50.

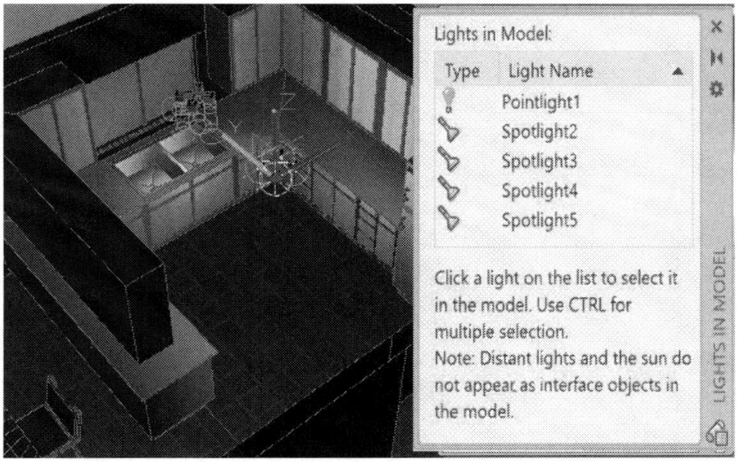

Figure 10–50

- All light options can be modified through Properties.
- To toggle individual lights off, select them and change their On/Off Status in Properties.

- You can change the *Exposure* and *White* Balance dynamically with slider bars in the expanded Lights panel, as shown in Figure 10–51.

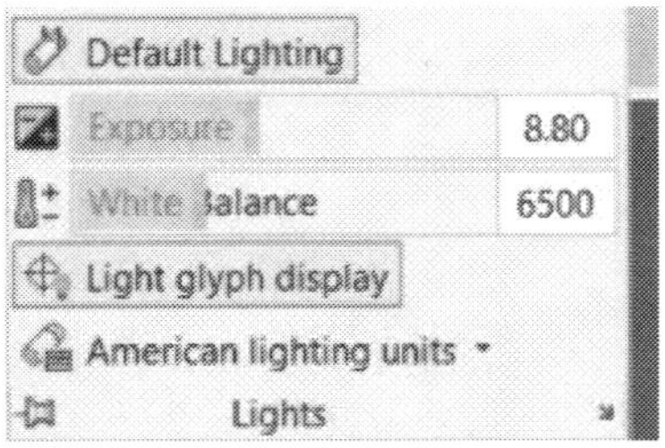

Figure 10–51

- Spot lights, point lights, and photometric webs display glyphs, as shown in Figure 10–52, which show you the locations of the lights and enable you to modify their locations and directions with grips. You can toggle them off and on using (Light glyph display) in the expanded Lights panel.

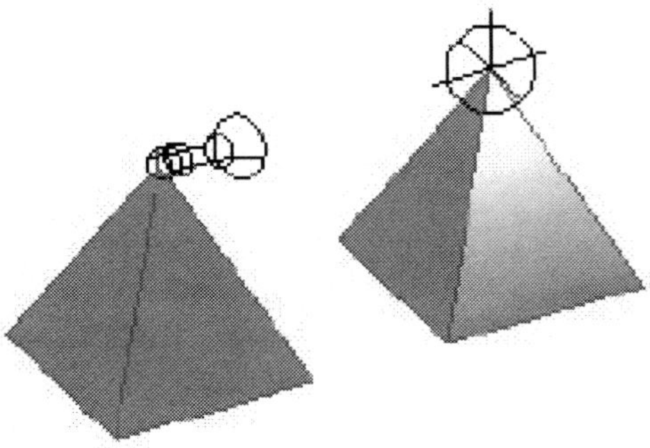

Figure 10–52

Practice 10c Creating a Sun Study

Practice Objective

- Create a sun study of a conceptual skyline to see how the shadows change over time.

In this practice, you will create a Sun Study of a conceptual skyline and see how the shadows change over time, as shown in Figure 10–53.

Figure 10–53

1. Open **Skyline-Sun.dwg**.
2. In the *Visualize* tab>Sun & Location panel, click (Sun Status). If the alert box displays, select **Turn off the default lighting (recommended)**.
3. In the Lighting - Sunlight and Exposure dialog box, click **Keep exposure settings**.
4. In the *Visualize* tab>Lights panel, expand (No Shadows) flyout and click (Ground Shadows).
5. In the expanded Sun & Location panel, expand (Set Location) and click (From Map).

6. If the Geolocation - Online Map Data dialog box opens, click Yes.

7. In the Geographic Location dialog box, in the *Address* bar, enter **New York** and press <Enter>. In the results area, hover your cursor over **New York, NY**, United States. Note that it should be close to City Hall in the map. Select **Drop Marker Here**, as shown in Figure 10–54 (the approximate values of *Latitude* and *Longitude* should be around **40 and** -**74**). Click **Next**.

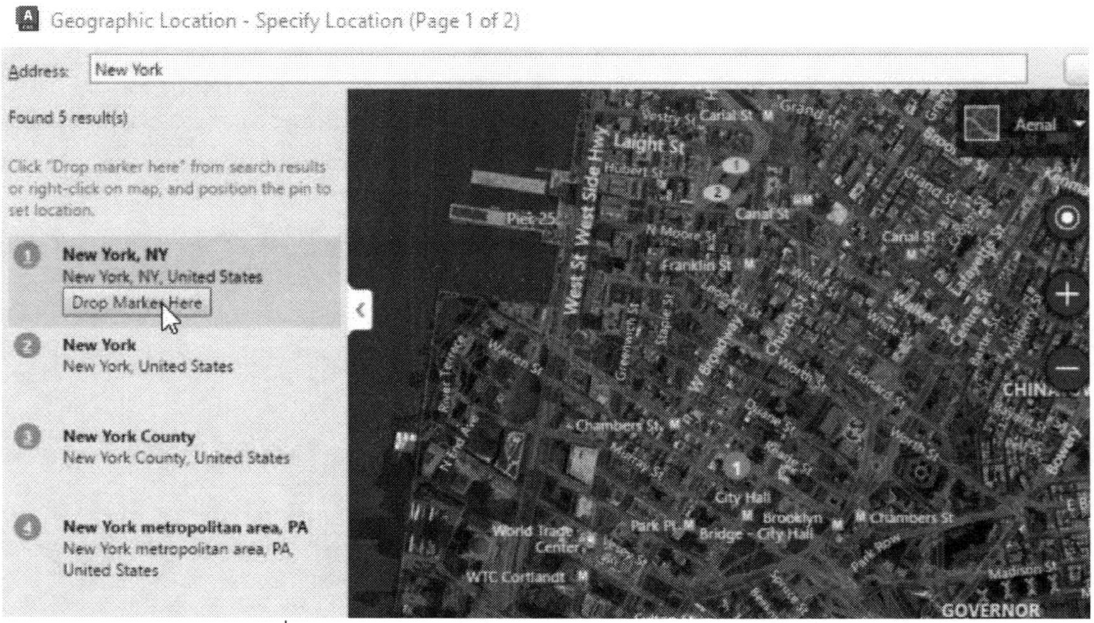

Figure 10–54

8. On Page 2 of 2, do the following:

   - Select the **NY83-LIF** for the GIS Coordinate System name.
   - For *Time Zone*, expand the drop-down list and select **(GMT-05:00) Eastern Time (US & Canada)**, if required.
   - For *Drawing Unit*, expand the drop-down list and select **Feet**.
   - In the Geographic Location - Unit Mismatch dialog box, click **Reset the units of the map to match the units of the drawing**.
   - Click **Next**.

9. In the drawing area, click a point near the UCS Icon to set the location.

10. Click a point vertically upwards to locate the North position. The Geographic Location displays in the drawing.

11. Select the *Visualize* tab. In the expanded Sun & Location panel, set the *Date* to today's date.

12. In the Sun & Location panel, move the *Time* slider bar and note how the light and shadows change over time, as shown in Figure 10–55.

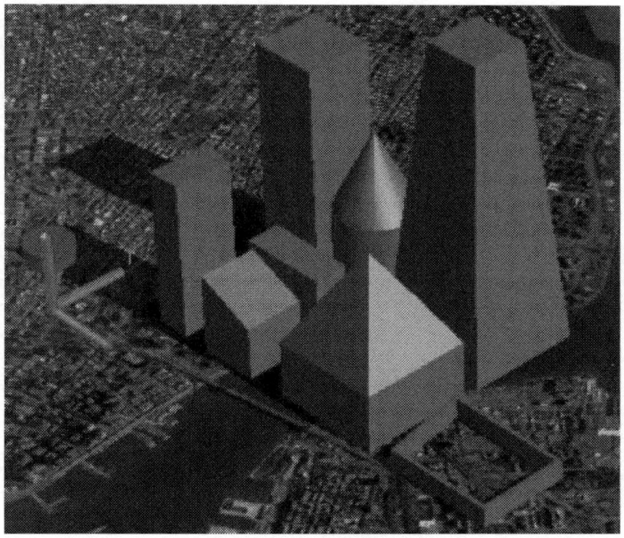

Figure 10–55

13. In the Lights panel, click (Full Shadows). Move the *Time* slider bar and note how the shadows impact the various buildings as the day progresses.

14. If time permits, try other dates, locations, and times.

15. Save and close the drawing.

Practice 10d Placing Lights in a Model

Practice Objective

- Place a point light, spot lights, and a photometric light in a model.

In this practice, you will place a point light and spot lights in a model. You will also add a Photometric Light from the tool palettes. The final view with lights is shown in Figure 10–56.

The backgrounds of the figures have been modified for printing clarity.

Figure 10–56

1. Open **Display.dwg**. This is a simple model with objects of different materials.
2. In the *Visualize* tab>Lights panel, expand **Create Light** flyout and click  (Point Light) and click near the center of the globe lamp on the display case to add a light. Press <Enter>. The room becomes washed out.

You might need to hover the cursor over the area in which the light-box is located to display its outline.

3. Toggle on the layer **Light-Box** and zoom out slightly. You should see the outline of a solid box. It has a glass material applied to it so that you can see the objects inside it.
4. Select the **Endpoint** osnap, and toggle on **Objects Snaps** and **3D Objects Snaps**.

5. In the *Visualize* tab>Lights panel, click (Spot Light). Click to the endpoint of a corner of the light box and drag to point to objects on the table (top point of the cone object) and press <Enter>. Similarly, add three more spotlights along the other corners of the light box, as shown in Figure 10–57.

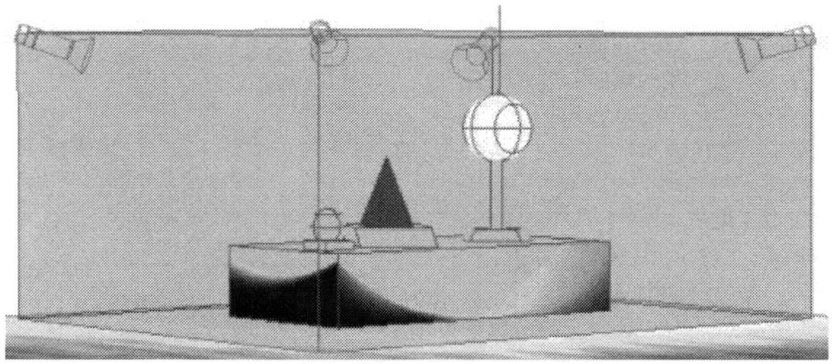

Figure 10–57

6. In the *Visualize* tab>Lights panel, click to open the Lights in Model palette. It displays four spot lights and one point light, as shown in Figure 10–58.

The numbering on the lights might be different in your drawing.

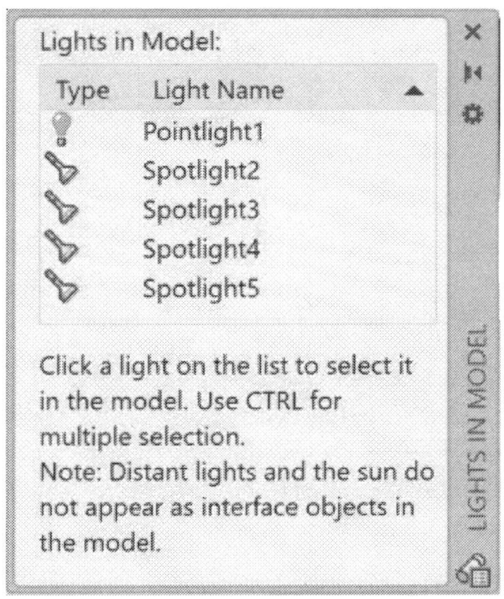

Figure 10–58

7. In the Lights in Model palette, select and right-click on **Pointlight1** and select **Delete Light**.

8. In the Lights in Model palette, select the four spot lights (use <Ctrl>). Right-click and select **Properties**. In the *Photometric properties* area, set the *Lamp Intensity* to **500,000 Cd**. Press <Esc> to clear the selection.

9. Open the Tool Palettes. Select the *Fluorescent* tab.

*To get the midpoint of the box, use the **Center of face** 3D object snap. Press <Ctrl> + the right mouse button to open the list of object snap overrides. You might also need to rotate the model and toggle off the ceiling layer.*

10. Add a **4 ft Pendant Fluorescent** light to the top middle of the light box, as shown in Figure 10–59:
    - Select the **Center of face** 3D object snap.
    - Orbit the model such that you are looking from the top.
    - Toggle off the layer **Ceiling**.
    - Place the **4 ft Pendant Fluorescent** light at the center of the top face.

Figure 10–59

11. In the *Visualize* tab>expanded Lights panel, toggle off  (Light glyph display) to hide the light objects.

12. In the *Home* tab>View panel, select the **Camera 1** view.

13. Toggle off the layer **Light-Box**.

14. Save the drawing.

10.4 Rendering Concepts

While you can display important 3D information using visual styles, materials, lights, and shadows, you sometimes need to create a more refined view to present to clients. You can do this by creating a rendered image, as shown in Figure 10–60. Creating rendered images takes time and skill, but you can do a few things to quickly obtain a rendering.

- Rendering tools are located in the 3D Modeling workspace in the *Visualize* tab>Render panel.

Figure 10–60

When selecting a render preset, hover the cursor over the preset to see the time required to render the view and how many rendering levels are applied, as shown in Figure 10–61.

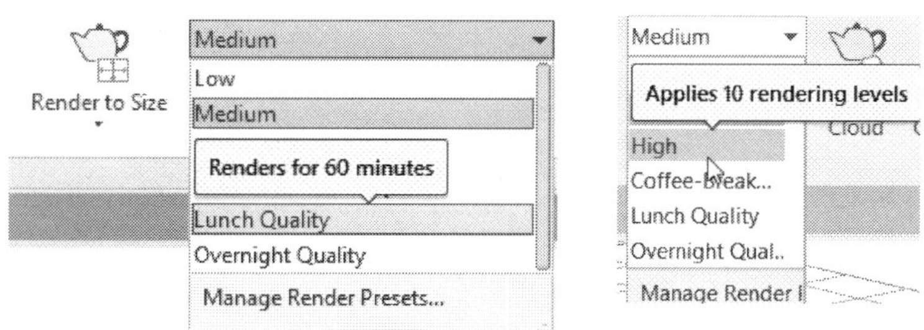

Figure 10–61

How To: Render a View

1. Set up the view with lights, materials, and shadows.
2. In the Render Presets Control, select an option as shown in Figure 10–62.

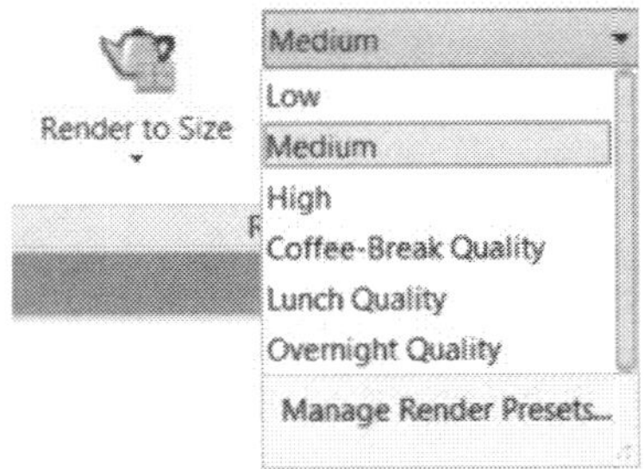

Figure 10–62

3. Start the **Render** command. The entire scene is rendered based on the Render Presets. By default, the Render dialog box opens displaying the results.

    - In the *Visualize* tab>Render panel, expand **Render in** and select **Region** (as shown in Figure 10–63) to only render a selected area in the drawing window. Click (Render to Size) and two points to create a window around the portion that you want to render. Use this when you are testing materials and lights. Type **Regen** or select a named or preset view to return to the drawing window.
    - In the *Visualize* tab>Render panel, select **Window**, and then click (Render to Size). The Render window opens, which enables you to preview, print, and save renderings.

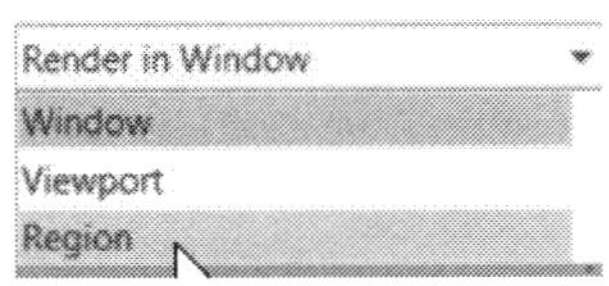

Figure 10–63

- Expand (Render to Size) to select the render output size and quality, as shown in Figure 10–64.

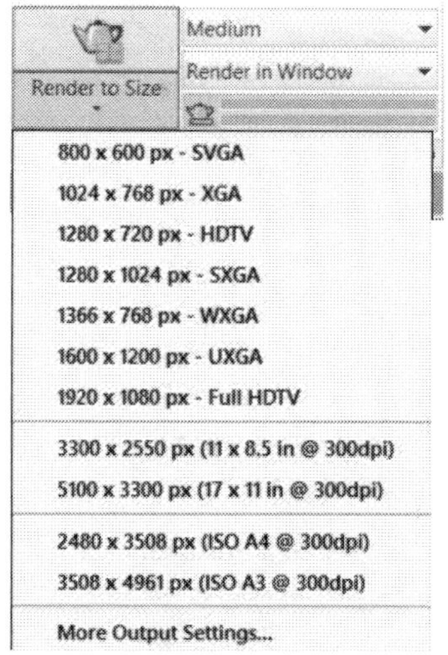

Figure 10–64

4. Click (Render to Size) to open the Render Window and start the rendering process.

How To: Save a Rendering to a File

*You can also right-click on an output file in the Render dialog box and select **Save**.*

1. In the *Visualize* tab>Render panel, click (Render to Size) to open the Render window. Alternatively, in the *Visualize* tab>expanded Render panel, click (Render Window).
2. In the Render window, click (Save).
3. In the Render Output File dialog box, assign a name, location, and file format. File formats include BMP, TGA, TIF, JPEG, and PNG. Click **Save**.

4. In the Image Options dialog box, select the *Color* quality and click **OK**. For example, the dialog box for a PNG image is shown in Figure 10–65.

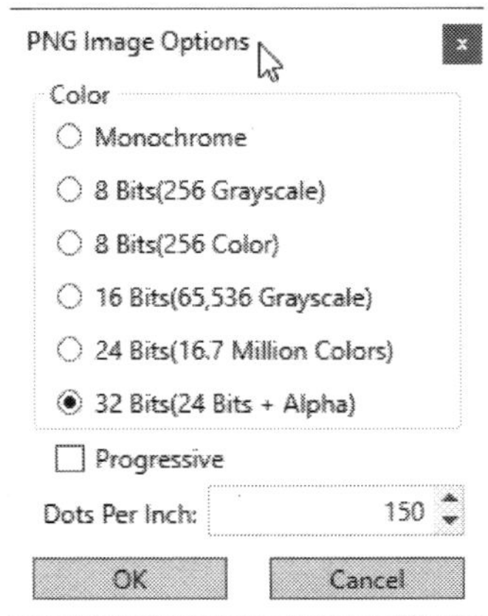

Figure 10–65

Adjusting the Exposure

Click (Render Environment and Exposure) in the *Visualize* tab>expanded Render panel to modify the brightness and contrast of the active view. You can also change the *White Balance* and background options, as shown in Figure 10–66. The active view displays the changes.

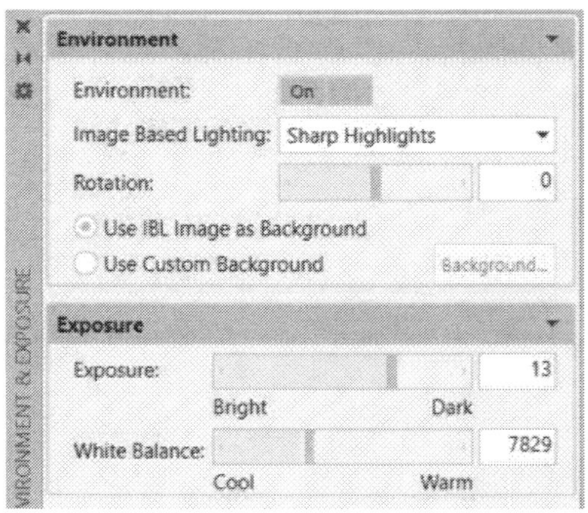

Figure 10–66

Render Presets Manager

Presets can be added or modified using (Render Presets Manager) in the *View* tab>Palettes panel. The Render Presets Manager palette enables you to set options, such as *Render Size*, *Render Duration*, and *Render Accuracy*, as shown in Figure 10–67. If you are going to render a view many times using similar settings, you can create a new Render Preset.

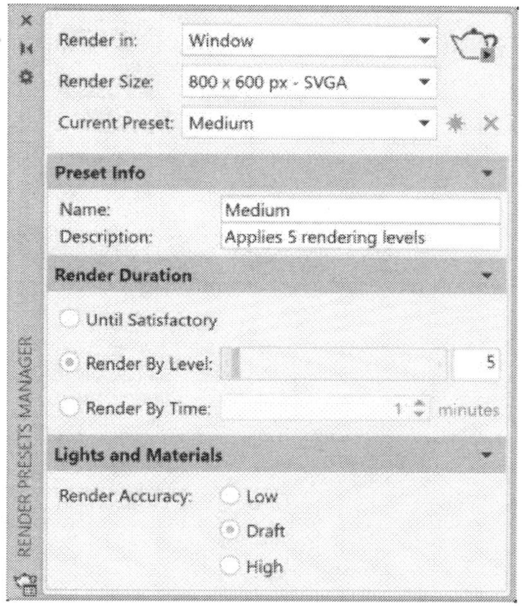

Figure 10–67

How To: Create Render Presets

1. In the *Visualize* tab>Render panel, click (Render Presets Manager).
2. In the Render Presets Manager palette, select an existing preset that is similar to the one you want to create and click (Create Copy).

3. Modify the settings as required, as shown in Figure 10–68.

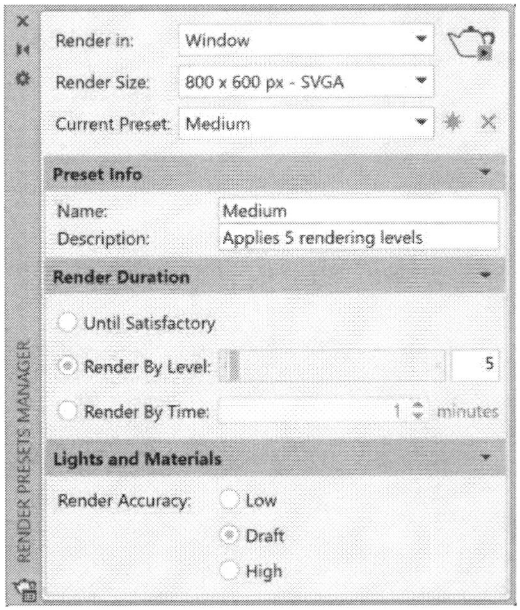

Figure 10–68

4. Close the Render Presets Manager. In the Render Presets Control, set the new preset to be active before rendering.

Practice 10e

Rendering Concepts

Practice Objective

- Render a view using the Draft preset and then render a region of a view using a higher preset.

In this practice, you will render a view using the **Low** preset and then render a region of a view using a higher preset, such as the one shown in Figure 10–69. If time permits, you can render a region using a higher setting.

Figure 10–69

1. Open **Condo-With-Skylight.dwg**.
2. In the *Home* tab>View panel, switch to the **Render View_330pm** view.
3. In the *Visualize* tab>expanded Render panel, click  (Render Environment and Exposure).
4. In the Render Environment & Exposure palette, set the following:
    - *Environment*: **On**
    - *Image Based Lighting*: **Sharp Highlights**
    - *Exposure*: **13**
    - *White Balance*: **7829** (Cool)

- Leave all other defaults, as shown in Figure 10–70.

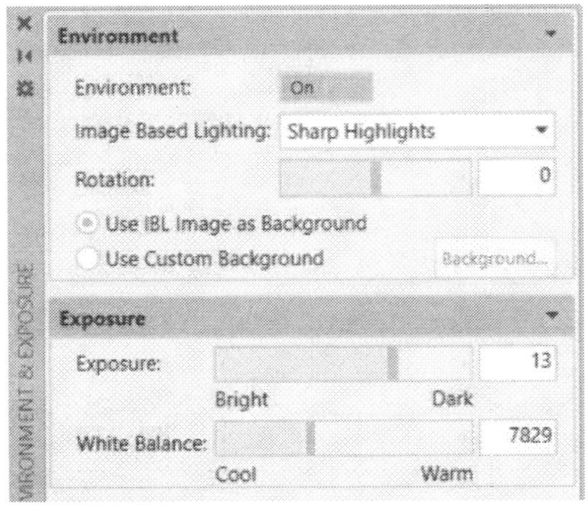

Figure 10–70

5. Close the Render Environment & Exposure palette.
6. In the *Visualize* tab>Render panel, do the following:
   - Set the *Render Preset* to **Low**.
   - Expand (Render to Size) and verify that **800 x 600 px - SVGA** is selected.
   - Click (Render to Size).

You might be required to install the image library.

7. The Render dialog box opens and the view is rendered quickly, but not very effectively, as shown in Figure 10–71.

Figure 10–71

*If **640 x 480 px** is not available, select **More Output Settings** and enter **640** and **480** as Width and Height and click **Render to Size**.*

You might be required to install the image library.

8. Change the *Render Preset* to **High**.

9. Expand (Render to Size) and select **640 x 480 px**.

10. In the *Visualize* tab>Render panel, click (Render to Size). The Render dialog box opens and the view is rendered. The process is slower, but the materials, lights, and shadows are much more realistic, as shown in Figure 10–72.

Figure 10–72

11. Save and close the drawing.

Chapter Review Questions

1. Which of the following is a preset visual style?
    a. Random
    b. Mesh
    c. Solid
    d. Sketchy
2. A point light is used for general lighting effects and a spot light is used to focus a cone of light on a specific part of a drawing.
    a. True
    b. False
3. How do you create a custom Material Library?
    a. In the *Insert* tab>Import panel, click **Import** and select the library.
    b. In the Application Menu, expand New and select **Library**.
    c. In the *Visualize* tab>Materials panel, click **Create New Library**.
    d. In the Materials Browser, expand  (Libraries) and select **Create New Library**.
4. Which visual style uses the **gooch** face style?
    a. **Realistic**
    b. **Conceptual**
    c. **Hidden**
    d. **Wireframe**
5. Which of the following **Render in** option enables you to render a selected area in the drawing window?
    a. **Viewport**
    b. **Window**
    c. **Region**
    d. **Rectangle**

6. How do you estimate the amount of time a view will need to render, or the number of rendering levels that will be applied?
    a. There is no way to estimate this.
    b. In the Render window, right-click and select **Render Time**.
    c. In the *Visualize* tab>expanded Render panel, click **Render Environment and Exposure**.
    d. When selecting a render preset, hover the cursor over the preset.
7. Where can you specify the intensity and color of the sun?
    a. Use the Tool Palettes>Sun & Location group.
    b. Use the Sun Properties palette.
    c. Use the tools in the *View* tab>Visual Styles panel.
    d. Use the tools in the expanded Sun & Location panel.

Command Summary

All ribbon names reference the 3D Modeling workspace.

Button	Command	Location
	Adjust Exposure	• **Ribbon:** *Visualize* tab>expanded Render panel
	Advanced Render Settings	• **Ribbon:** *Visualize* tab>Render panel settings arrow or *View* tab>Palettes panel
	Attach By Layer	• **Ribbon:** *Visualize* tab>expanded Materials panel
	Default Lighting	• **Ribbon:** *Visualize* tab>expanded Lights panel
	Distant Light	• **Ribbon:** *Visualize* tab>Lights panel> Create Light flyout
	Environment	• **Ribbon:** *Visualize* tab>expanded Render panel
	Full Shadows	• **Ribbon:** *Visualize* tab>Lights panel>No Shadows flyout
	Ground Shadows	• **Ribbon:** *Visualize* tab>Lights panel>No Shadows flyout
	Light Glyph Display	• **Ribbon:** *Visualize* tab>expanded Lights panel
	Material Editor	• **Ribbon:** *Visualize* tab>Materials panel settings arrow or *View* tab>Palettes panel
	Materials / Textures Off	• **Ribbon:** *Visualize* tab>Materials panel
	Materials / Textures On	• **Ribbon:** *Visualize* tab>Materials panel
	Materials Browser	• **Ribbon:** *Visualize* tab>Materials panel or *View* tab>Palettes panel
	Materials On/ Textures Off	• **Ribbon:** *Visualize* tab>Materials panel
	No Shadows	• **Ribbon:** *Visualize* tab>Lights panel
	Point Light	• **Ribbon:** *Visualize* tab>Lights panel> Create Light flyout
	Remove Materials	• **Ribbon:** *Visualize* tab>expanded Materials panel
	Render Environment and Exposure	• **Ribbon:** *Visualize* tab>Render panel • **Command Prompt:** renderexposure
	Render to Size	• **Ribbon:** *Visualize* tab>Render panel • **Command Prompt:** render

	Render Window	• **Ribbon:** *Visualize* tab>expanded Render panel • **Command Prompt:** renderwindow
	Save Render	• **Window:** Render
	Set Location	• **Ribbon:** *Visualize* tab>Sun & Location panel
	Spot Light	• **Ribbon:** *Visualize* tab>Lights panel> Create Light flyout
	Sun Status	• **Ribbon:** *Visualize* tab>Sun & Location panel
	Visual Style Manager	• **Ribbon:** *View* tab>Visual Styles panel bar settings arrow or *View* tab> Palettes panel
	Weblight	• **Ribbon:** *Visualize* tab>Lights panel> Create Light flyout

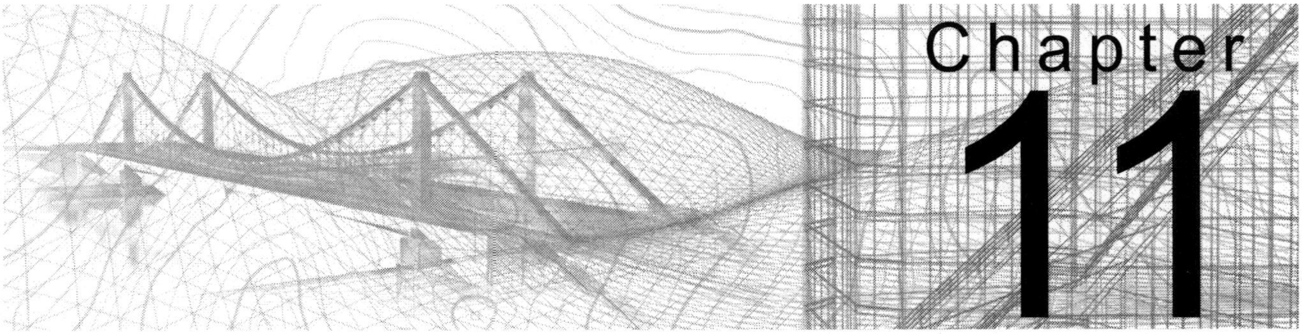

Working Drawings from 3D Models

In this chapter, you learn how to create multiple 3D viewports, create 2D views from 3D solids using Solid View, Solid Drawing, and Solid Profile. You also create technical drawings using Flatshot, import 3D models of various file formats, and create Automatic Model Documentation Views.

Learning Objectives in This Chapter

- Create multiple 3D viewports in a layout to help visualize the 3D model from different angles.
- Create hidden line views or a wireframe model of 3D objects.
- Create a flattened view of the solids in a specified view as they are projected onto the XY plane using the Flatshot command.
- Import different types of 3D models directly into the Model Space.
- Automatically generate intelligent documents based on 3D models created in the AutoCAD® or Autodesk® Inventor® software.
- Set up a drawing for printing in 3D.

11.1 Creating Multiple Viewports

The Viewports dialog box is a powerful tool that creates multiple tiled viewports, which help you to visualize your 3D model from different angles as you work in the **Model** tab or to set up multiple viewports in a **Layout** tab, as shown in Figure 11–1.

The viewports display the 3D model, not the 2D versions of the top, front, and side.

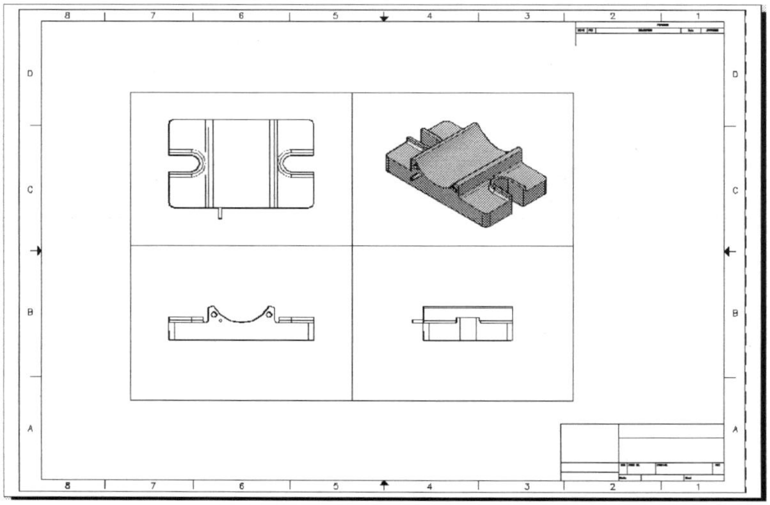

Figure 11–1

The **Rectangular**, **Polygonal**, and **From Object** commands for creating viewports each create a single viewport. The use of the **Viewports** command enables the creation of multiple viewports, each of specific views, all in a single command.

- (Viewports, New Viewports) opens the Viewports dialog box in the *New Viewports* tab. When a *Layout* tab is active, it can be found in the *Layout* tab>Layout Viewports panel.
- Visual styles only display in the drawing window. If you want the viewports to plot using a specific method, select and right-click on the viewport border, expand **Shade plot** and select the required method as shown in Figure 11–2.

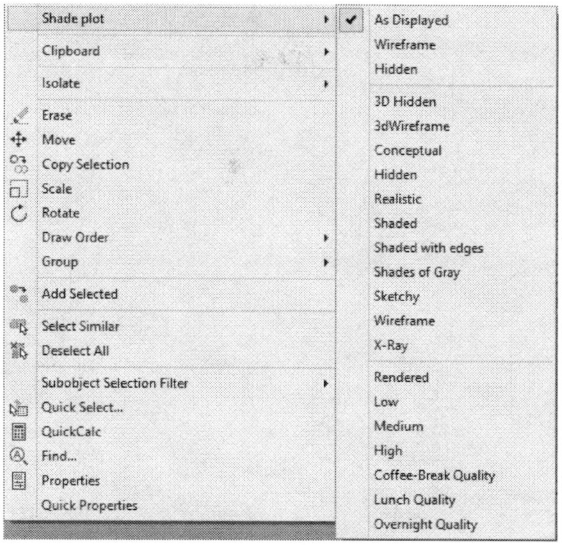

Figure 11–2

How To: Create Multiple 3D Viewports

1. Make a layout tab active.
2. In the *Layout* tab>Layout Viewports panel, click (Viewports, New Viewports). The Viewports dialog box should open to the *New Viewports* tab.
3. Change the *Setup* to **3D** and select the number of viewports you want to create.
4. Select each viewport preview and set *Change view to* and *Visual Style* as required, as shown in Figure 11–3.

If you want to have a border between each viewport on a layout, type a value in the Viewport Spacing.

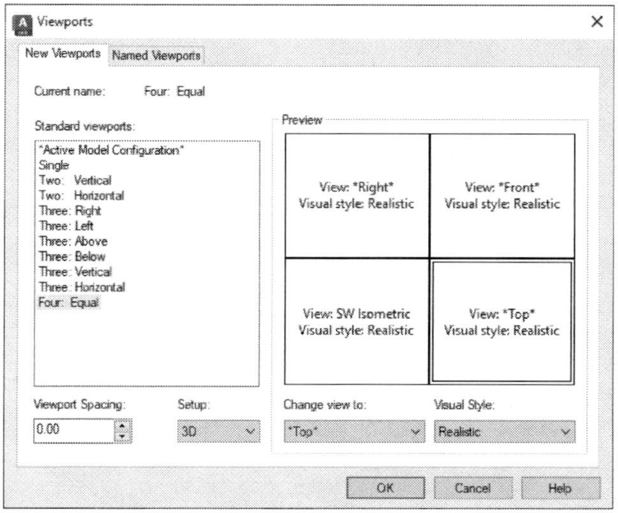

Figure 11–3

5. Click **OK**.
6. In the Paper Space layout, you are prompted for two points to define the extents of all of the viewports.
7. In the layout, use the scale (arrow) grip to scale each viewport as required, as shown in Figure 11–4.

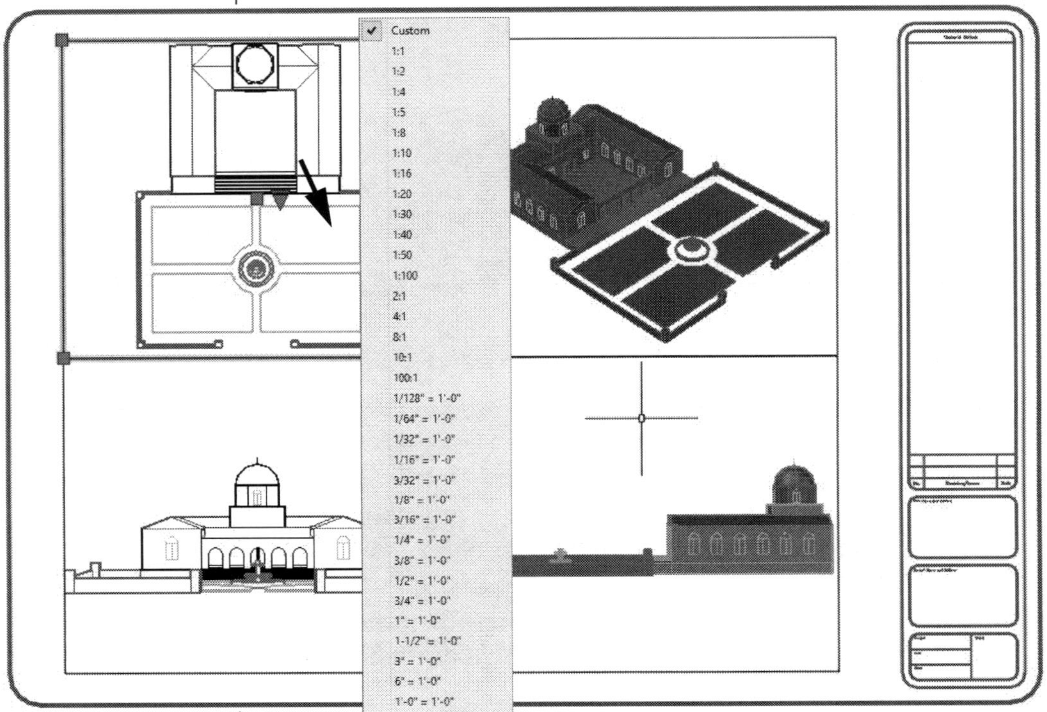

Figure 11–4

Practice 11a

Creating Multiple Viewports

Practice Objective

- Layout several views of a 3D model using the **Viewports** command.

In this practice, you will lay out several views of an architectural model for plotting, as shown in Figure 11–5.

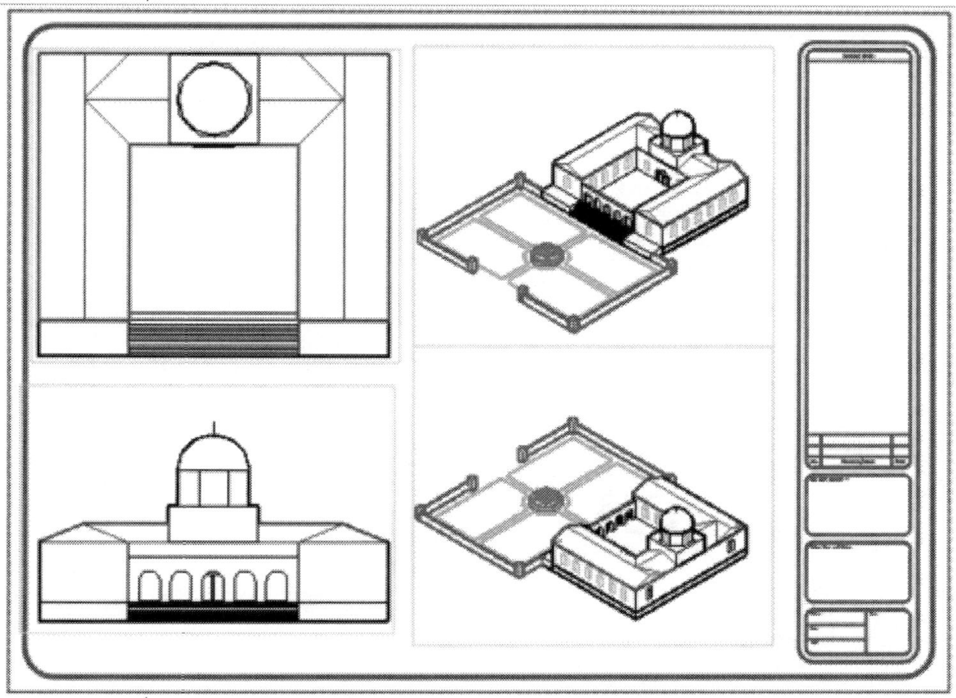

Figure 11–5

1. Open **Museum-Views.dwg**.
2. Switch to the **Layout1** layout tab.
3. In the *Layout* tab>Layout Viewports panel, click (Viewports, New Viewports).

4. In the Viewports dialog box, *New Viewports* tab, select **3D** in the *Setup* drop-down list. In the *Standard viewports* area, select **Four: Equal**, as shown in Figure 11–6.

5. In the *Preview* area, to set the viewports, click on the viewport to be changed and select the required view in the *Change view to* drop-down list. Set the two viewports on the left to be **Top** and **Front** views and set the two viewports on the right to be two different **Isometric** views, as shown in Figure 11–6.

6. Set all of them to use the **Hidden** visual style, as shown in Figure 11–6. Click **OK**.

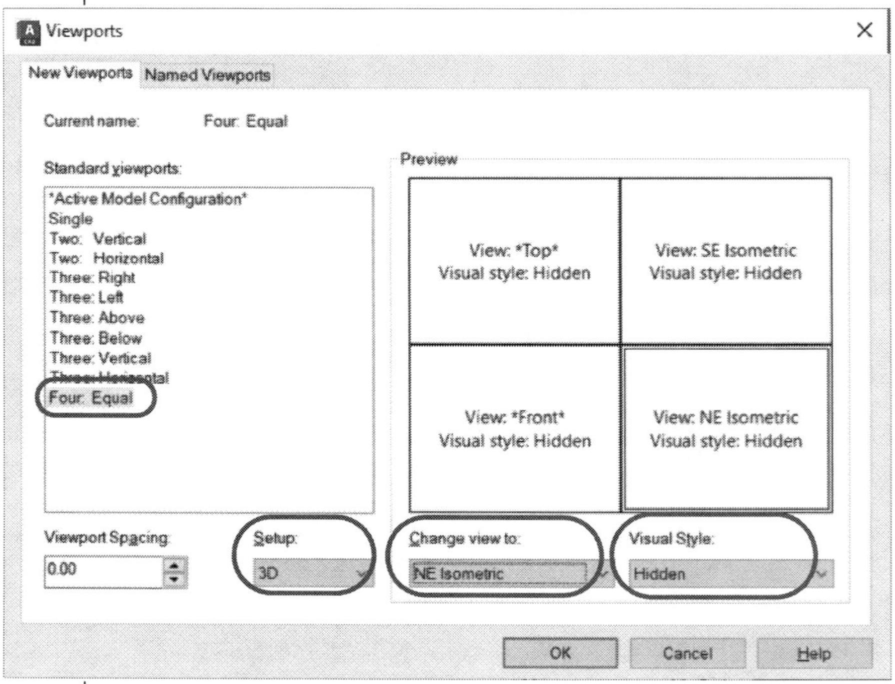

Figure 11–6

7. In the layout, select two opposite corners in the open area of the titleblock in which to place the four viewports, so that it fills up most of the sheet.

8. Make the top left viewport active by double-clicking inside it.

9. In the Layer Properties Manager, use **VP Freeze** to freeze the layers **Fountain**, **Garden Wall**, and **Lawns** for the viewport, as shown in Figure 11–7. Note that, in the viewport, the portions drawn on these layers are not displayed any longer.

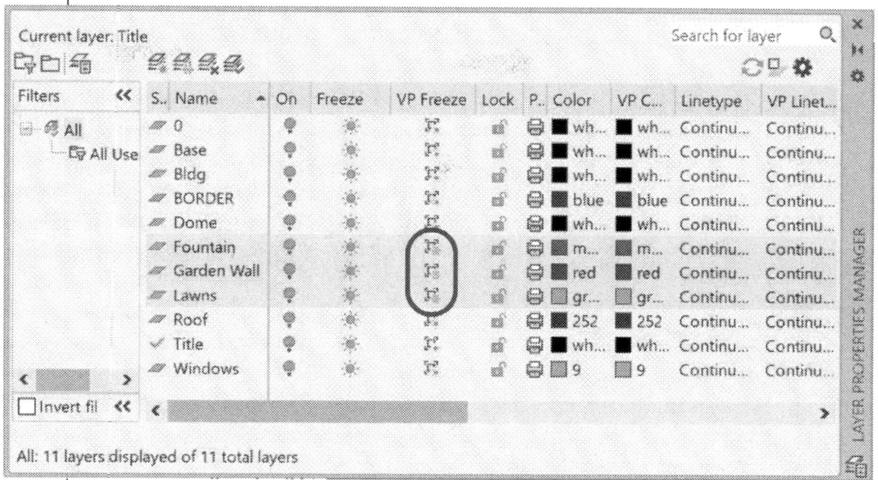

Figure 11–7

10. Make the **Front** viewport active and freeze (use **VP Freeze)** the same layers in that viewport.

11. Double-click on any part of the layout sheet to return to Paper space. Select the **Top** view to display its grips.

12. Set the scale of the **Top** view to **1/8"=1'-0"** using the triangular grip. Using the middle square grip, move the viewport down such that all the visible portion fits in the viewport area of the sheet. Then use the corner grips to make the viewport border small to fit around the displayed objects, as shown in Figure 11–8.

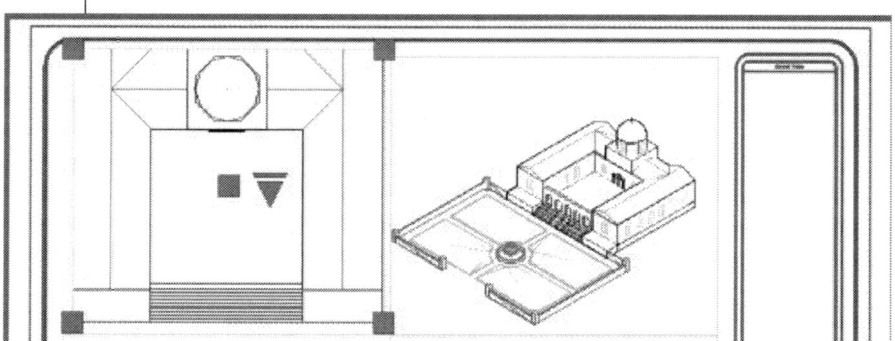

Figure 11–8

13. Do the same to the **Front** view. Then adjust the viewport locations as required to fit everything on the page.

14. Preview the plot to display the results.

15. Save and close the drawing.

11.2 2D Views from 3D Solids

A 3D solid model offers many advantages over 2D drawings, such as a better understanding of the model you are creating, the ability to apply properties to that model, and the ability to manufacture directly from the model. However, it is important to be able to create 2D views from the model as shown in Figure 11–9, without having to redraw the objects.

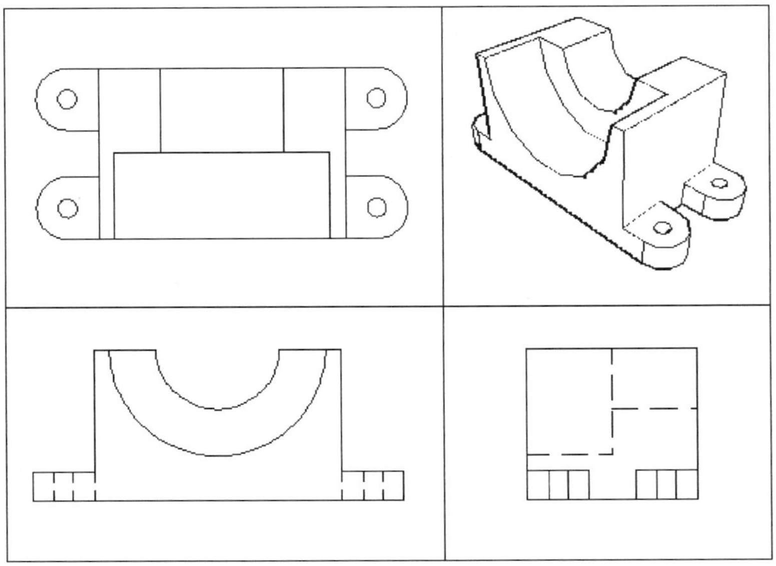

Figure 11–9

Three commands, found in the *Home* tab>expanded Modeling panel, can help you create the 2D views, as follows:

	**Solid View:** Creates orthographic and auxiliary views in a layout from the 3D solid model.
	**Solid Drawing:** Creates hidden line views and sections from the views. Only works in viewports that have been created by Solid View. Together, they enable you to quickly dimension the drawing in the standard 2D orthographic views of **Front**, **Left**, **Right**, **Top**, and **Auxiliary**.
	**Solid Profile:** Creates 2D drawings and 3D wireframes of solids in any floating viewports, regardless of how the viewports were created.

Creating Hidden Line Views

*An **Auxiliary** view is based on an angled surface on the solid.*

*The section hatching is not displayed until you use **Solid Drawing** on the viewport.*

Creating hidden line views of 3D objects on a layout is a two-step process. First, you use **Solid View** to set up orthographic, auxiliary, or section floating viewports, as shown in Figure 11–10. Then, you use **Solid Drawing** to create 2D objects of those views.

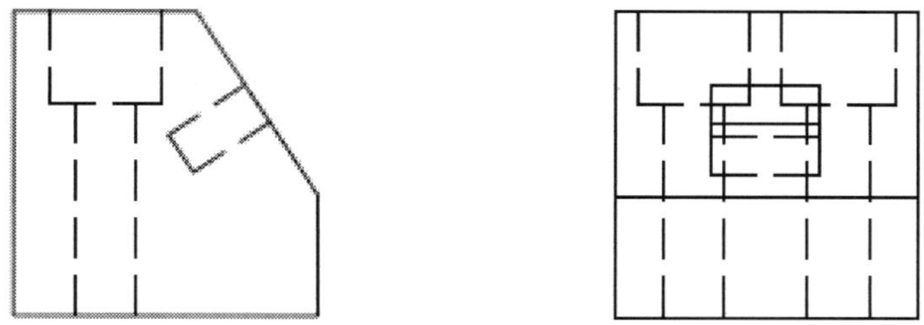

Orthographic Views

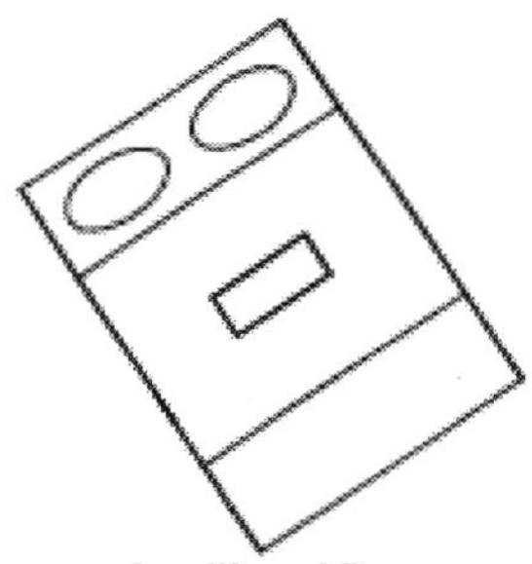

Auxiliary View

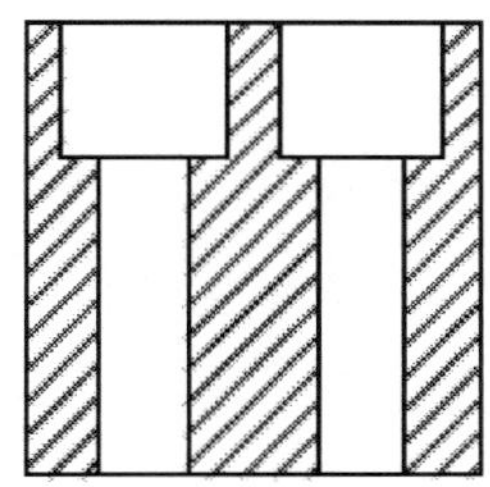

Section View

Figure 11–10

How To: Set Up Solid Viewports

1. Switch to a layout.
2. In the *Home* tab>expanded Modeling panel, click (Solid View).
3. For the first viewport on a sheet, select **UCS** and the type of UCS (**World**, **Current**, or **Named**) from which you want to take the view.
4. Enter the view scale.
5. Specify a view center (location of the viewport). You can select this several times until the object is at the correct point in the drawing window and then press <Enter>.
6. Specify the first and opposite corners of the viewport.
7. Enter a view name for the viewport and press <Enter>.
8. To create additional views, select **Ortho**.
9. Specify the side of the viewport you want to project.
10. Specify the view center and press <Enter>.

11. Select two points to define the boundaries of the viewport, as shown in Figure 11–11.

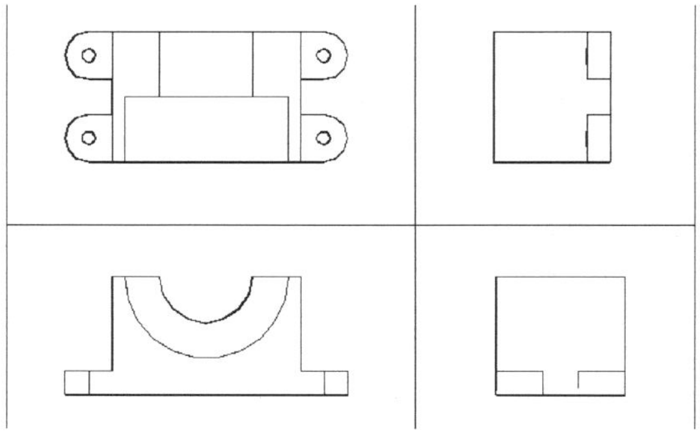

Figure 11–11

12. Continue to select other **Ortho**, **Auxiliary**, or **Section** views.
13. Press <Enter> to end the command.

- Once the viewport has been created with **Solid View**, you can stretch or clip it to change its shape.

How To: Set Up the Solid Drawing

1. In the *Home* tab>expanded Modeling panel, click (Solid Drawing).
2. Select the viewports to draw.
3. The command draws the 2D shapes on the 3D solids. It automatically freezes the layer that contains the 2D shapes in all of the other viewports. If you thaw the layers in all of the viewports or return to the **Model** tab, the 2D shapes display as shown in Figure 11–12.

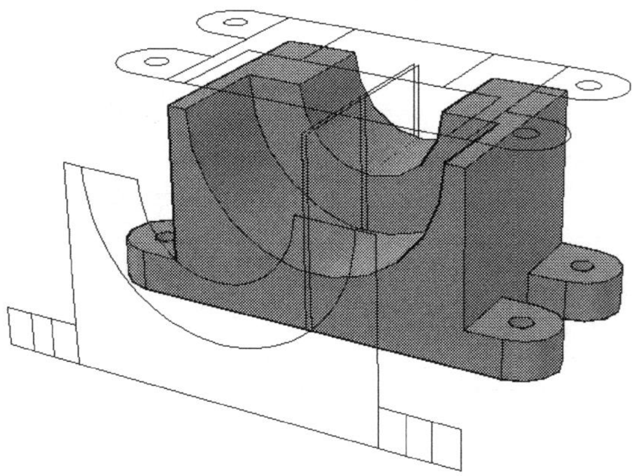

Figure 11–12

- **Solid Drawing** does not delete existing solids.

Hint: Layers in Solid View

Solid View creates a viewport and several layers. The viewport is placed on the **Vports** layer, which is created if required.

Each viewport is given a name. This name is used to create four layers per viewport: <name>-DIM (dimensions), <name>-HAT (hatching), <name>-HID (hidden lines), and <name>-VIS (visible lines).

- Do not put anything else on these layers (except for the layer **Dimensions**), because **Solid Drawing** automatically deletes and updates the information stored on them.
- Change the linetype for the -HID layers so that they display with hidden lines, as shown in Figure 11–13.

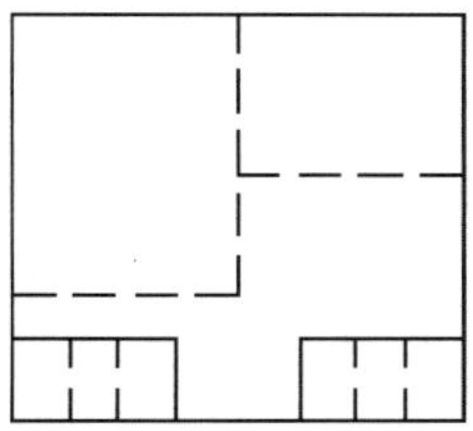

Figure 11–13

- You can change the color of any of the layers as required.
- Hatching created in sectional views uses the current values set in the **Hatch** command. Double-click on the hatching to modify it once it is in the drawing.

Creating Profiles from Solids

Tangential edges are not true edges. They are lines that are drawn where the slope of the edge changes (e.g., in a fillet, where the arc meets the flat edge). You can select whether or not to include those lines in the profile.

Another way of creating hidden line views is to create profiles with the **Solid Profile** command. This creates a similar result to using **Solid View** and **Solid Drawing**. **Solid Profile** is most often used to create a wireframe model from a solid, as shown in Figure 11–14.

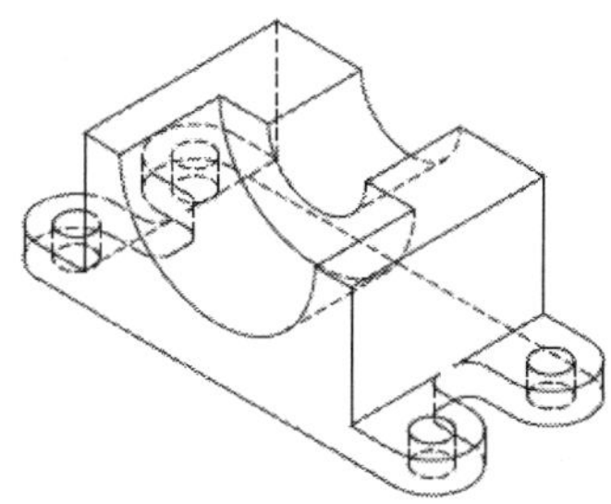

Figure 11–14

How To: Set Up a Profile View

1. In a layout, create a viewport and arrange the model as you want it to display.
2. In the *Home* tab>expanded Modeling panel, click  (Solid Profile) and select the objects in the viewport that you want to copy to a profile.
3. If you want to display hidden profile lines on a separate layer, enter **Yes** at the prompt.
4. If you want to project profile lines onto a plane, enter **Yes** at the prompt.
5. If you want to delete the tangential edges, enter **Yes** at the prompt.

- **Solid Profile** does not create viewports. Instead, it creates anonymous blocks of the profile and hidden lines. The blocks are created on top of the original model and can be moved as required, as shown in Figure 11–15.

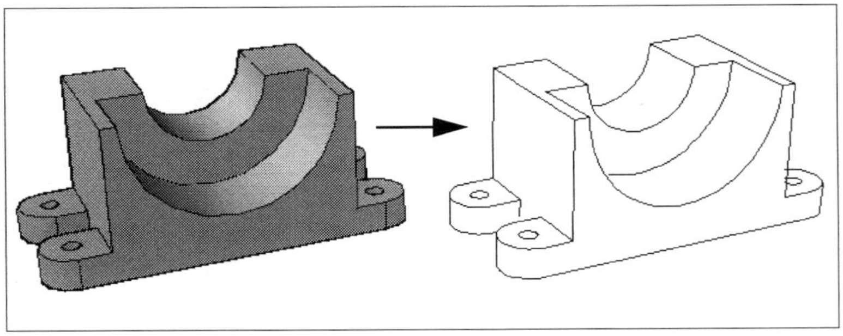

Figure 11–15

- If you display hidden lines on a separate layer, the layer is called **PH-<handle>** and all other lines display on the layer **PV-<handle>**. The **<handle>** is a number supplied by the AutoCAD® software.

- If you project profile lines onto a plane, a 2D shape is created, as with **Solid Drawing**. If you do not project the profile lines onto a plane, **Solid Profile** creates a portion of the wireframe model from the solid. In either case, **Solid Profile** does not delete the solid.

Practice 11b 2D Views from 3D Solids

Practice Objectives

- Create 2D views of a solid model using the **Solid View** and **Solid Drawing** commands.
- Create a profile from a solid model using the **Solid Profile** command.

In this practice, you will use **Solid View** and **Solid Drawing** to create 2D views of a solid model in Paper Space, as shown in Figure 11–16. You will also use **Solid Profile** to create a profile from the solid model.

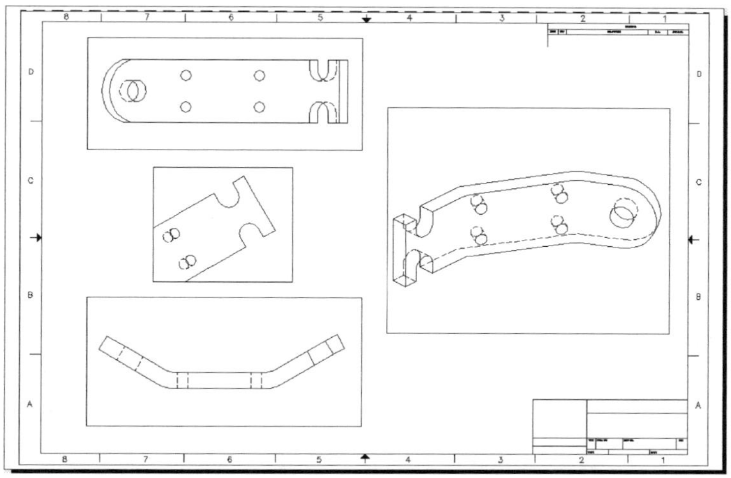

Figure 11–16

Task 1 - Create a viewport from the UCS.

1. Open **Constr.dwg**.
2. Set the Visual Style to **2D Wireframe** and switch to the **Layout1** layout tab.
3. In the *Home* tab>expanded Modeling panel, click (Solid View).

The 2D drawings are actually created on top of the model. The viewports control which layers display.

You can keep clicking to reposition the model.

   - For *option*, select **Ucs** and then select **Current** to create a view based on the current Ucs. Press <Enter> to accept a *View scale* of **1.0000**.
   - For the *view center*, select a point towards the lower left corner of the layout. If the object is not at the required location (as shown in Figure 11–16), click again to reset the location. When satisfied with the location, press <Enter>.

- Select two diagonally opposite corner points for the viewport such that the entire object is inside the viewport.
- Name the viewport **Front**.

4. Stay in the command and for *option*, select **Auxiliary**, as shown in Figure 11–17.

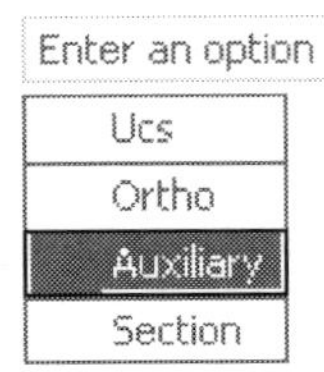

Figure 11–17

- For the first and second points on the inclined plane, use the **Nearest** object snap to select two points along the same surface on the slanted portion of the right side of the object, as shown in Figure 11–18.
- Select a point above the part as the side from which to view.
- Select a point above the first viewport as the location of the view center and press <Enter>. Note that the complete object is displayed. Some portion might overlap the Front viewport and some portion might also be outside the sheet.
- Select two diagonally opposite corners around the right side of the part to create a viewport for only the selected portion, as shown in Figure 11–18.
- Name the viewport **Aux**.

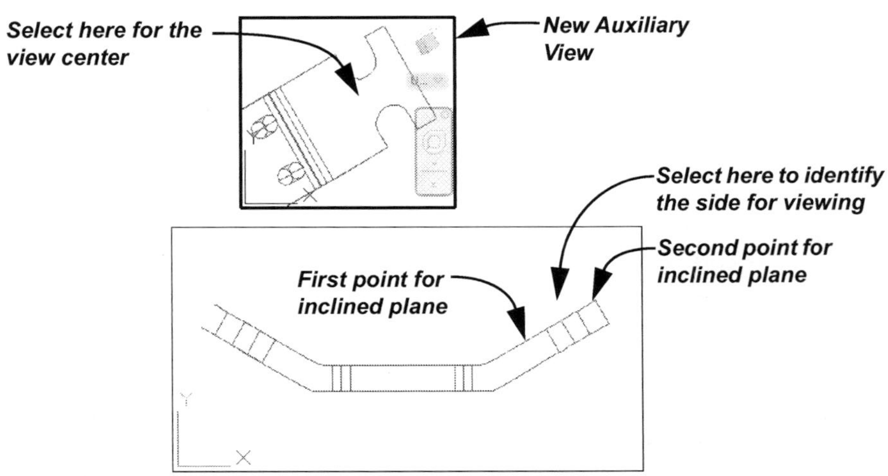

Figure 11–18

5. Stay in the **Solid View** command and select **Ortho**.
   - Specify the top of the Front viewport as the side of the viewport to project.
   - For the view center, select a point above the Aux view that was created in Step 4 (as shown in Figure 11–16) and press <Enter>.
   - Select the two diagonally opposite corner points for the viewport such that the entire object is enclosed within it.
   - Name the viewport **Top** and press <Enter>.
   - Press <Enter> to complete the command.

Task 2 - Create 2D objects of each view.

1. In the *Home* tab>expanded Modeling panel, click  (Solid Drawing).
2. Select the three viewports and press <Enter> to end the command. Note that all the three views display as profiles without the original 3D objects.

Task 3 - Create profiles from solids.

1. Set the layer **VPORTS** to be current.
2. In the *Layout* tab>Layout Viewports pane, click

    (Viewports, Rectangular) and select two points along the right side of the other three viewports. This creates a single new viewport.
3. Double-click inside the new viewport to make it active.
4. Use **Orbit** to display the model in the new viewport so that it is similar to that shown in Figure 11–19.

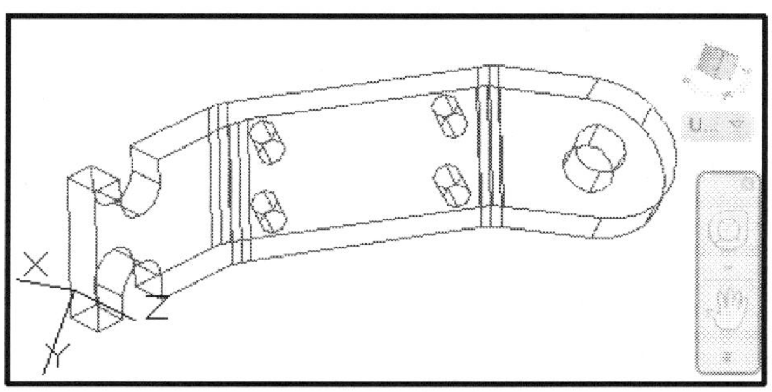

Figure 11–19

Note the newly created profile view in Model Space.

5. With the new viewport still active, in the *Home* tab>expanded Modeling panel, click  (Solid Profile). At the *Select objects:* prompt, select the 3D part in the viewport. Accept the defaults for all of the remaining prompts.
6. In Layer Properties Manager, for the layer **Part**, select **VP Freeze** to freeze the layer in the new viewport. The new profile displays in the viewport without the original 3D object.
7. Save and close the drawing.

11.3 Creating Technical Drawings with Flatshot

Flatshot creates a flattened view of all of the solids in a specified view as they are projected onto the XY plane. Simplifying a drawing is very useful when creating technical illustrations, such as part diagrams or assembly instructions. The new 2D objects are placed in a block and inserted into the drawing. You can then view the block in the top view to correctly display its representation, as shown on the right in Figure 11–20.

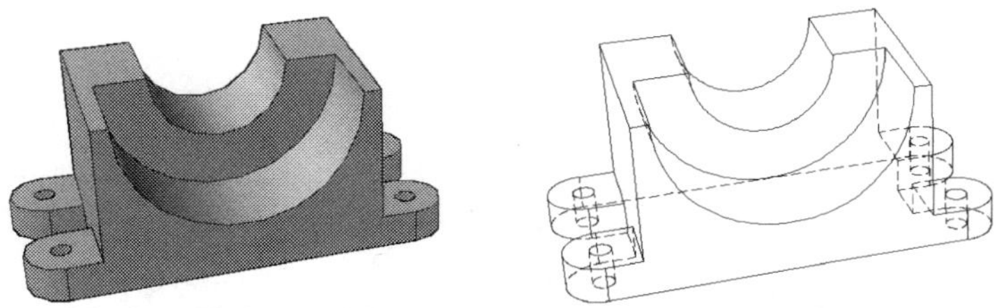

3D view of the model ***Top view of flatshot***

Figure 11–20

- **Flatshot** selects all of the solids or surfaces in a view. Therefore, you should toggle off or freeze any layers of objects that you do not want to select.

- When first inserted, the new block that is created by **Flatshot** does not look correct. This is because the block is actually flat against the XY plane, but is being viewed in the current 3D view. Switch to the **Top** view and the block displays correctly.

- **Flatshot** is not designed to replace the **Solid Profile** command, which creates a profile view of an object in Paper Space.

- You must be in a **Parallel** view with the UCS set to **World** for this command to work correctly.

How To: Create a Flatshot

1. Freeze the layers of the objects that you do not want to select.
2. Set the view and verify that the UCS is set to **World**.
3. In the *Home* tab>expanded Section panel, click  (Flatshot).

4. In the Flatshot dialog box, specify whether you are creating a new block, replacing an existing block, or exporting the block to a file, as shown in Figure 11–21.

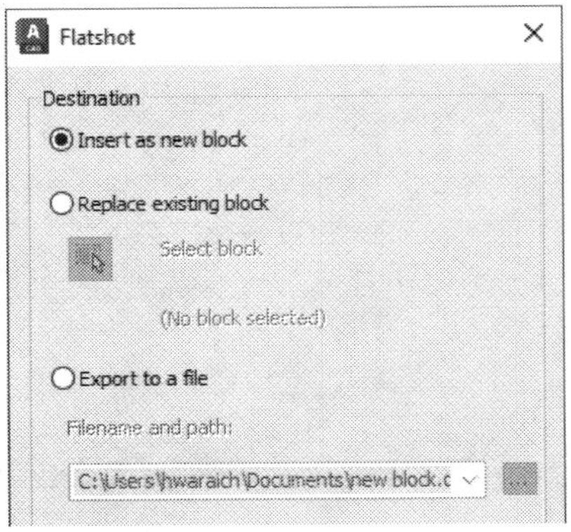

Figure 11–21

5. Specify the color and linetype of the foreground objects, as shown in Figure 11–22.

Figure 11–22

6. If you want to display hidden lines, select **Show** in the *Obscured Lines* area, as shown in Figure 11–23. Also, specify the color and linetype for the obscured objects.

Figure 11–23

7. Specify whether you want to **Include tangential edges**, as shown in Figure 11–24.

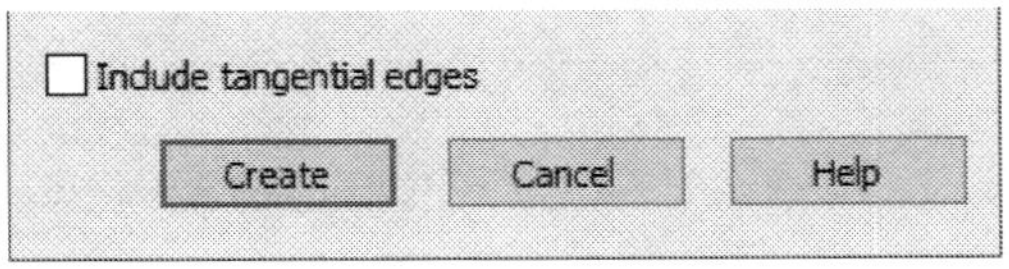

Figure 11–24

8. Click **Create**.

9. Specify an insertion point, X- and Y-scale, and rotation angle.
10. The view does not look correct in the view from which you created the flatshot. Switch to the **Top** view to display the flatshot accurately.

- If you have updated the model, you can replace the existing block with the updated block rather than creating a new one.

- You can save the block as a drawing file. Select **Export to a file** and specify the name and location of the file.

- Section objects do not impact blocks created using **Flatshot**.

- You can make changes to the objects created by **Flatshot** using **Block Editor** (**bedit**) or **Edit Block in Place** (**refedit**). You can also explode the block. To rename the block, click (Save Block As) in the *Block Editor* contextual tab> expanded Open/Save panel.

Practice 11c Creating Technical Drawings with Flatshot

Practice Objective

- Create flatshots of two different angles of a 3D model using the **Flatshot** command.

In this practice, you will create two different flatshots of a house and place them beside the house, as shown in Figure 11–25.

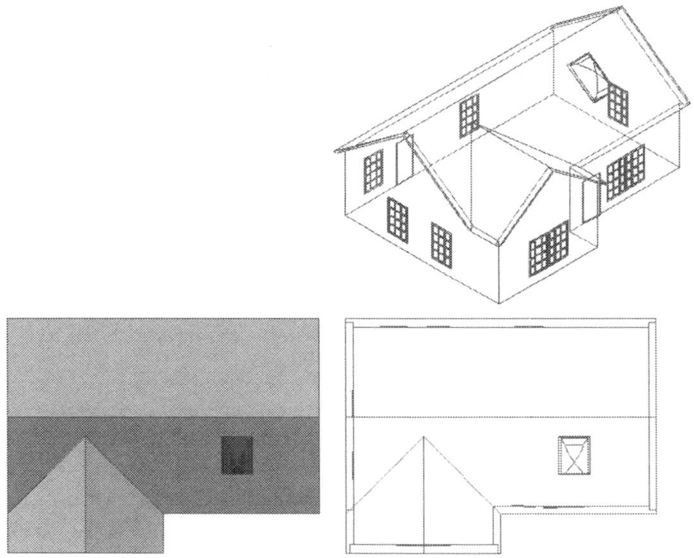

Figure 11–25

1. Open **Workshop.dwg**.
2. In the *Home* tab>View panel, expand the **3D Navigation** drop-down list, and switch to the **Top** view.
3. Make the layer **Window** current, if required . In the *Home* tab>expanded Section panel, click (Flatshot).
4. In the Flatshot dialog box, accept the defaults and click **Create**.

You might need to zoom out to see the flatshot model with the cursor.

5. Place the flatshot to the right side of the house and accept the default scale and rotation values.
6. Change to the **SW Isometric** view and click (Flatshot).

*If **Hidden2** is not in the list, click **Other** from the list and then use the **Load** option to load the linetype, making it available in the list.*

7. In the Flatshot dialog box, in the *Foreground lines* area, set the *Color* to **Blue**.
8. In the *Obscured lines* area, set the *Linetype* to **Hidden2**. Click **Create**.
9. Place the flatshot above and near the previous flatshot. Accept the default scale and rotation values.
10. Switch to the **Top** view. Both flatshot views should display.
11. Save and close the drawing.

Practice 11d Mechanical Project - Saddle

Practice Objective

- Layout a 3D solid model for plotting by creating hidden line views and a realistic view.

In this project, you will lay out a 3D solid model for plotting, create hidden line views, and specify a viewport displaying a realistic visual style, as shown in Figure 11–26.

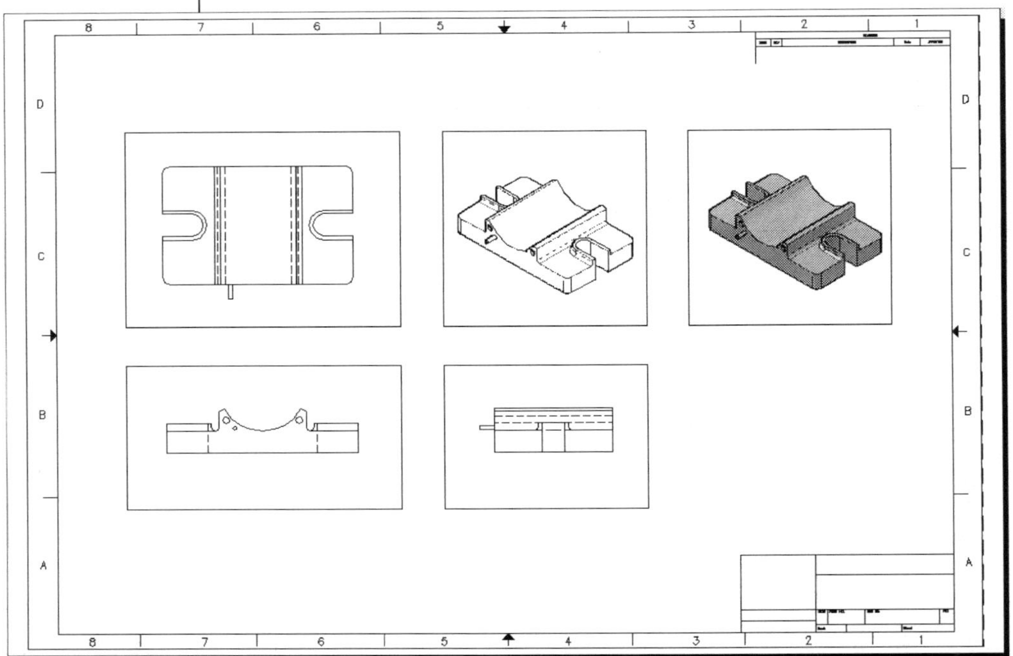

Figure 11–26

1. Open **Saddle.dwg**.
2. Switch to **Layout1**.
3. Use (Solid View), (Solid Drawing), and (Solid Profile) to display the views of the drawing at a *scale* of **1:1**.
4. Add another viewport and set it to display the drawing in an isometric or other 3D view. Set the *Visual Style* to **Realistic**.
5. Save and close the drawing.

11.4 3D Model Import

In addition to creating 3D models in Model Space, the AutoCAD software can import a large number of types of 3D models. You can directly import the following types of files: Autodesk® Inventor®, CATIA, NX, Parasolid, Pro/ENGINEER, Rhino, SolidWorks, IGES, and STEP, as shown in Figure 11–27. Once imported, you can freely modify the data using standard editing tools found in the AutoCAD software.

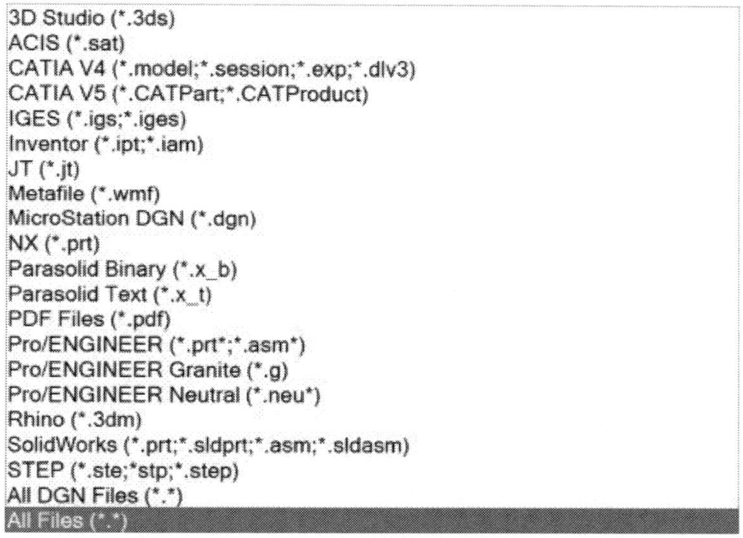

Figure 11–27

- To import a file, click (Import) in the *Insert* tab>Import panel, to open the Import File dialog box. In the *Files of type* drop-down list, select the required file format to import.
- After the import operation completes in the background, a bubble notification displays with a link to the file to be imported.
- The enhanced **Import** command supports surfaces, solids, 2D, and 3D wire geometry from these available file formats.
- The data being imported is translated to native geometry in the AutoCAD software, and inserted into the drawing as blocks.
- Any original parts or assemblies in the original file are maintained and replicated as nested blocks.

11.5 Automatic Model Documentation

You can automatically generate intelligent documents based on models created in the AutoCAD software, Autodesk® Inventor® software, or imported 3D models, as shown in Figure 11–28. Instead of manually adding individual viewports on layout tabs for each view to document 3D models, some other tools are used to perform similar tasks automatically.

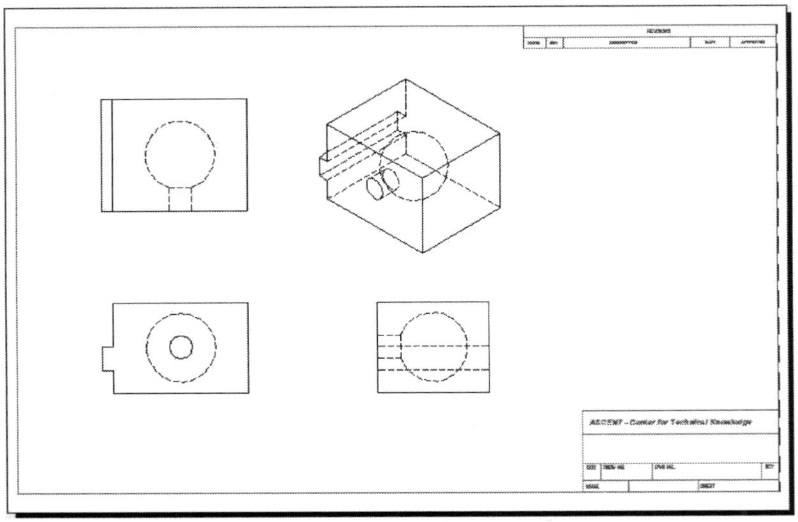

Figure 11–28

- Just like viewports, if the model updates the views are updated automatically.
- The tools for automatic model documentation are located in the *Layout* tab on the ribbon, as shown in Figure 11–29.

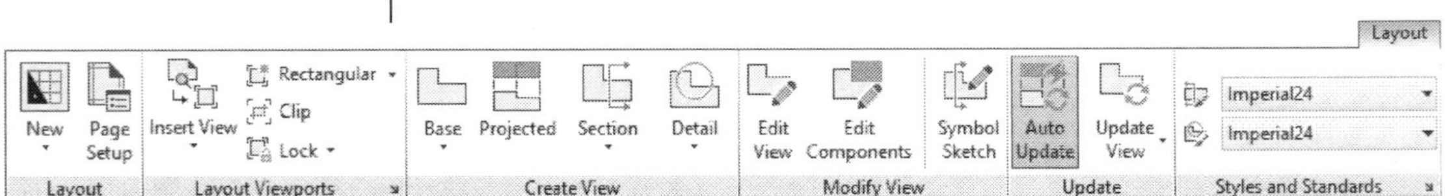

Figure 11–29

Hint: Interface Settings

If all the panels in the *Layout* tab are not available, then you are required to manually load the **MODELDOC** group for user interface settings. Use **CUILOAD** command which opens the Load/Unload Customizations dialog box. In the dialog box, click **Browse** to open the Select Customizations dialog box. Select **ModelDoc.cuix** file and click **Open**. The filename and its location path is listed in the File Name box. Click **Load** and note that **MODELDOC** is listed in the *Loaded Customization Groups* area as shown in Figure 11–30. Click **Close**.

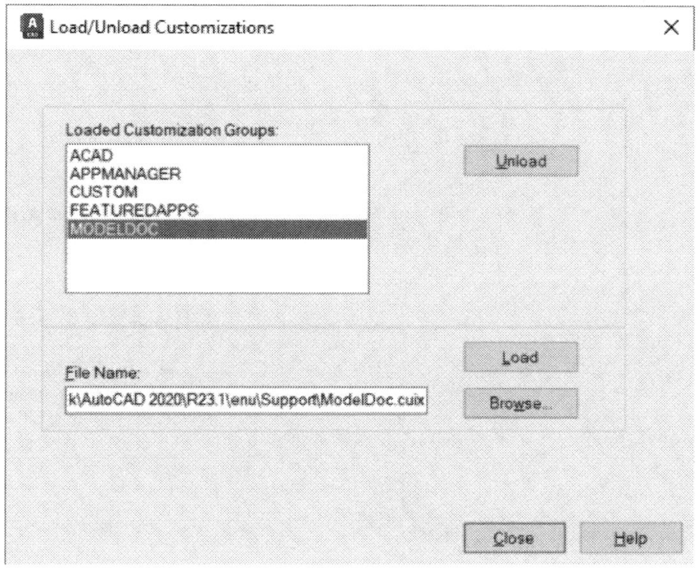

Figure 11–30

For Windows 10, the cuix files are located in:
C:\Users\<username>\AppData\Roaming\Autodesk\AutoCAD <version>\<release>\<language>\Support

Adding Base Views

The first view must always be a Base view, as shown in Figure 11–31. After that, additional views can be added or modified as required.

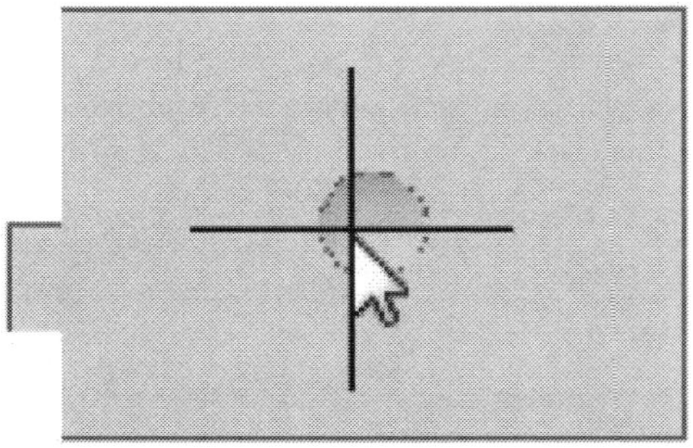

Figure 11–31

- You can place a Base view of an existing 3D model created in or imported into Model Space. If there is no 3D model in Model Space, you are prompted to select an external 3D model that was created in the Autodesk Inventor software.

How To: Add a Base View

1. Have a 3D model created and ready in Model Space or a ready to use Model file that was created in the Autodesk Inventor software.
2. Switch to a Layout tab in Paper Space.
3. In the *Layout* tab>Create View panel, click (Base View from Model Space) or (Base View from Inventor).
   - If you click Base View from Model Space and there is no 3D model in Model Space, the Select File dialog box opens.
   - If you click Base View from Inventor, you are required to select and open a model that was created in the Autodesk Inventor software.
4. In the *Drawing View Creation* tab shown in Figure 11–32, make any **Orientation** or **Appearance** modifications.

Figure 11–32

- If you are using a model that was created in the Autodesk Inventor software, it also includes a Representation panel.

5. A scaled preview of the model is attached to the cursor, as shown in Figure 11–33. Select a location in Paper Space to place the Base view.

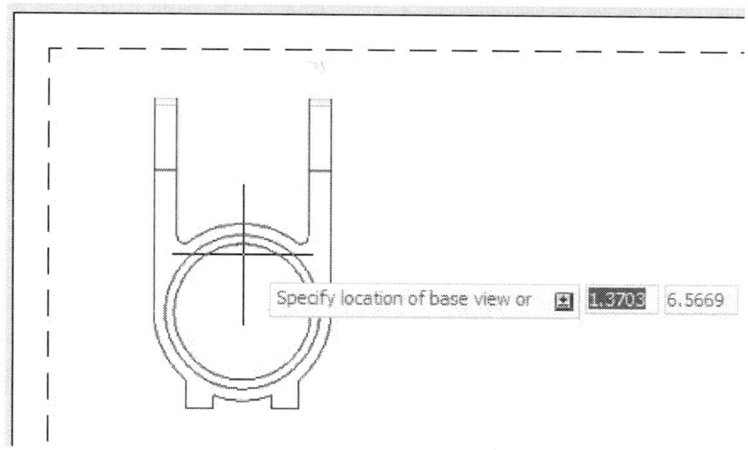

Figure 11–33

6. Press <Enter> to complete the command and continue or in the *Drawing View Creation* tab>Create panel, click (OK).

Options for Placing a Base View

Before you place the base view, you can select some options and settings from the *Drawing View Creation* contextual tab, Command Line, or Dynamic Inputs.

- **Orientation:** Sets the base view orientation to **Top**, **Bottom**, **Left**, **Right**, **Front**, **Back**, or one of four Isometric views. The preview changes accordingly, as shown in Figure 11–34.

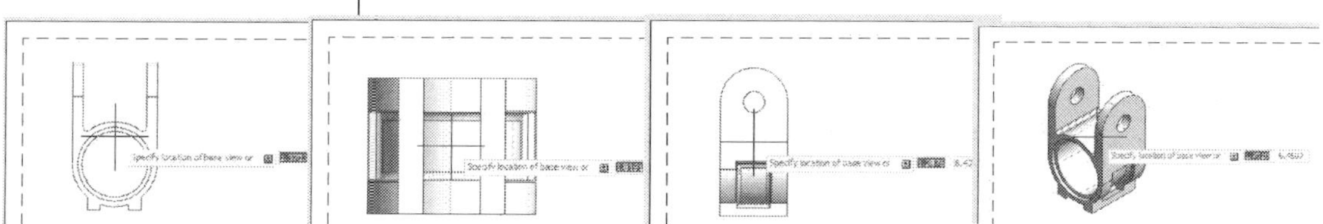

Figure 11–34

- **Type:** (At Command Prompt only.) Controls whether to place the base view only, or to be able to place and create projected views immediately after placing the base view.
- **Select:** (At Command Prompt only.) It can be used with **Base View From Model Space** command only. Enables you to specify which 3D objects are to be represented in the base view.
- Other settings include **Scale**, **View Style**, and **Object Visibility**.
- After you have placed the Base view, you can still move it using grips or the **Move** command in the Modify panel before ending the command.

Adding Projected Views

A Projected view is a view created by projecting from a base view in one of eight possible directions: four orthographic and four isometric, as shown in Figure 11–35.

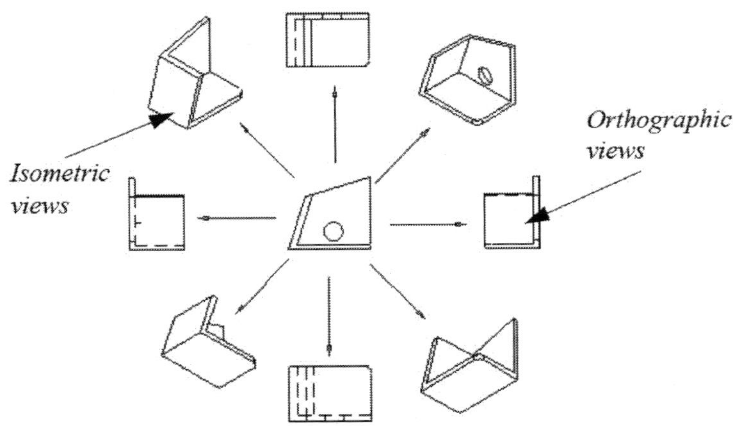

Figure 11–35

- The orthographic views are the top, bottom, and side views. These views align with the base view and are dependent on that view.
- The isometric views are the diagonal views. These views are not dependent on the location of the base view.
- Projected views are drawn using the base view's projection angle (first angle or third angle).

There are two ways to place a Projected view: continue and automatically place it after placing a Base view, or place it at a later time using the **Project View** command.

How To: Add Projected Views

1. Have an existing base view in Paper Space.
2. In the *Layout* tab>Create View panel, click (Projected View).
3. Select a parent view from which to project.
4. Drag the cursor to the required location around the parent view. When the preview displays as required, click in the location, as shown in Figure 11–36.

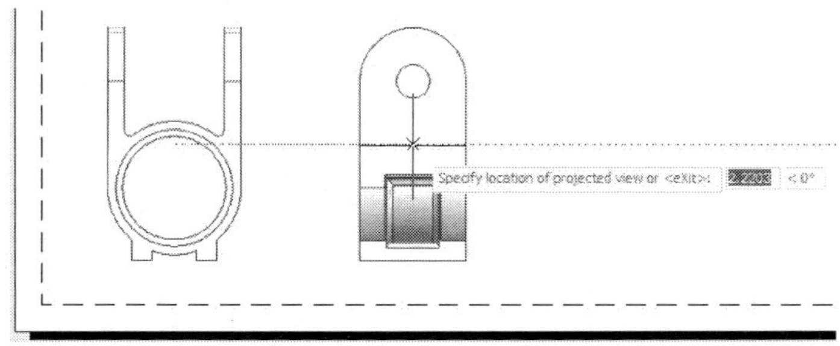

Figure 11–36

5. Continue to place additional projected views as required. Press <Enter> when done. You can always add more later.
6. Press <Enter> to complete the command.

- When the command is complete, the views take their final form based on their appearance settings, as shown in Figure 11–37.

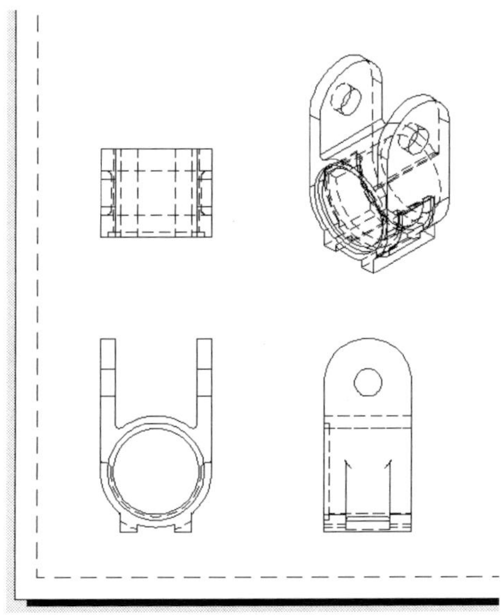

Figure 11–37

- During the creation of projected views, a parent/child relationship is formed between the selected view and the projected views.
- When placing a base view, if its *Type* is set to **Base and Projected**, you can immediately place projected views after the base view is placed.
- Each view created is a new drawing view object and includes a non-printing boundary similar to a viewport. Their properties can be modified in the Properties palette, as shown in Figure 11–38.

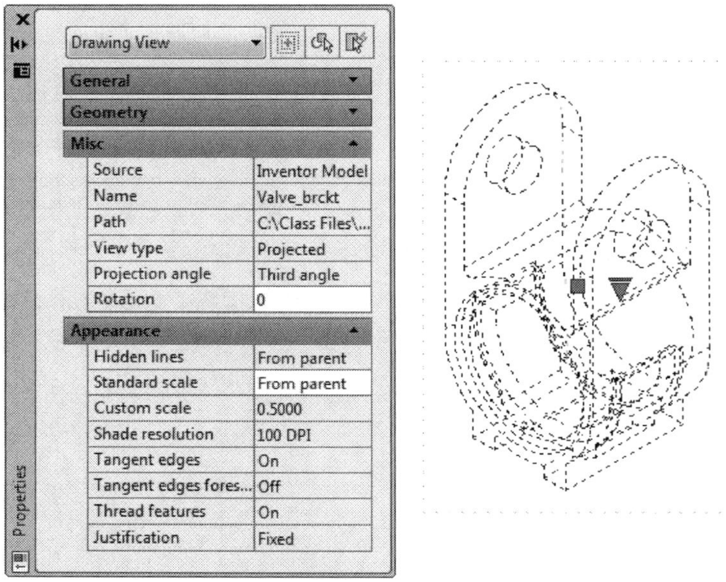

Figure 11–38

- When a drawing contains drawing views,  (Drawing Views) displays in the Status Bar on the bottom right, as shown in Figure 11–39.

Figure 11–39

Editing Drawing Views

There are several ways to edit drawing views. Selecting a view, displays a square grip, an arrow drop-down list grip at its center, and the *Drawing View* contextual tab. The square grip enables you to move the view. The arrow drop-down list grip enables you to change its scale, as shown in Figure 11–40. The *Drawing View* contextual tab gives access to creating a Projected, Section, or Detail view based on it, editing and updating it.

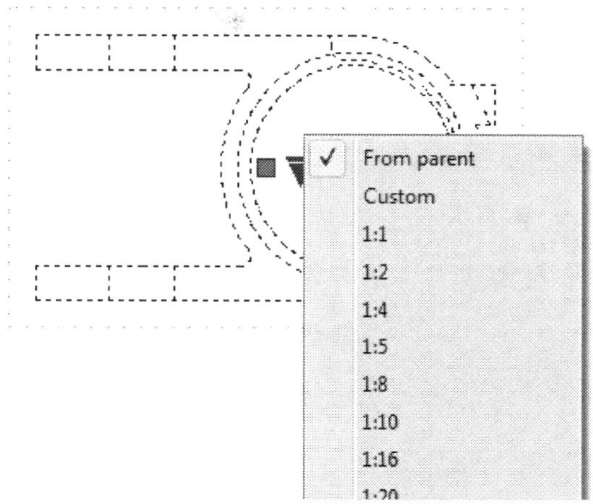

Figure 11–40

In the *Layout* tab>Modify View panel, click (Edit View) and select a view to edit or double-click on the Drawing view that you want to edit. Both methods display the *Drawing View Editor* contextual tab, as shown in Figure 11–41.

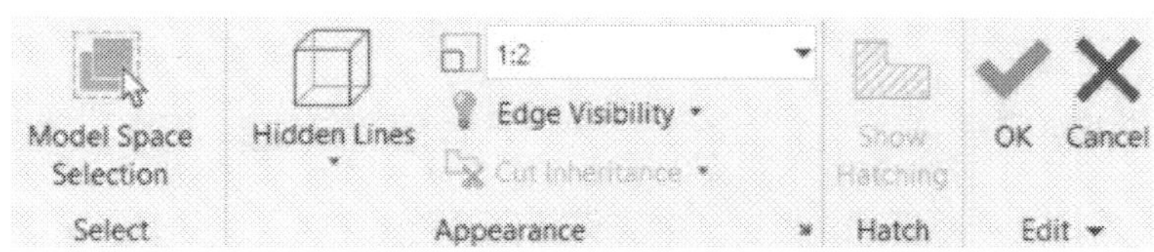

Figure 11–41

- When you edit a parent view, the changes are applied to the parent and all of its child views.
- When making multiple changes in a single view, to ease up system performance, toggle on (Defer Updates) in the *Drawing View Editor* contextual tab>expanded Edit panel. When you are done, they all propagate down to the rest of the views.

- When the source 3D model is modified, a bubble notification displays. Click the link in the bubble to update the views, or click (Update View) or (Update all Views) in the *Layout* tab>Update panel, to update a view or all views.

Practice 11e Creating Automatic Model Documentation

Practice Objectives

- Import a 3D model in STEP file format and create its 2D model views.
- Import a 3D model from the Autodesk Inventor software, and create and edit its 2D model views.

In this practice, you will import a 3D model in STEP file format and create automatic 2D model views of the imported STEP model, as shown in Figure 11–42. You will also import a model that was created in the Autodesk Inventor software, create 2D model views, and edit the drawing views as shown in Figure 11–42.

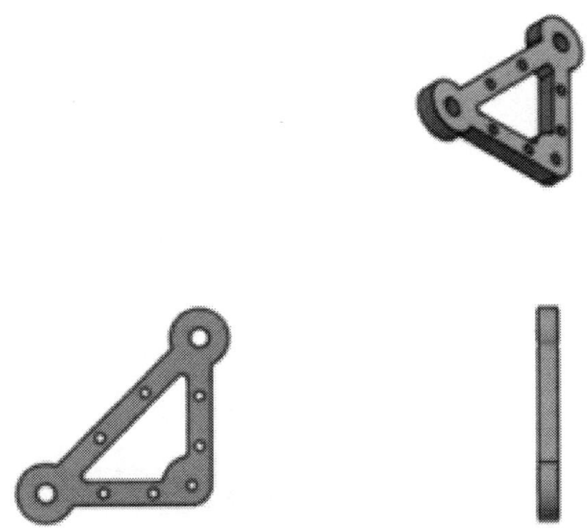

Figure 11–42

Task 1 - Import STEP File.

1. Open **Mechanical-3D.dwg**.
2. In the *Insert* tab>Import panel, click  (Import).
3. In the Import File dialog box, navigate to the practice files folder.

4. Expand the Files of type drop-down list and note the available types. Select the **STEP** file format.

5. Select **Mounting-Bracket.stp** and click **Open**.

6. In the Import- Processing Background Job alert box that opens, click **Close**.

7. An Import Job Complete icon and an *Import File processing complete* bubble display in the Status Bar. Click the link in the bubble.

8. The mounting bracket displays in the drawing window, as shown in Figure 11–43. Zoom extents to display the entire model as required.

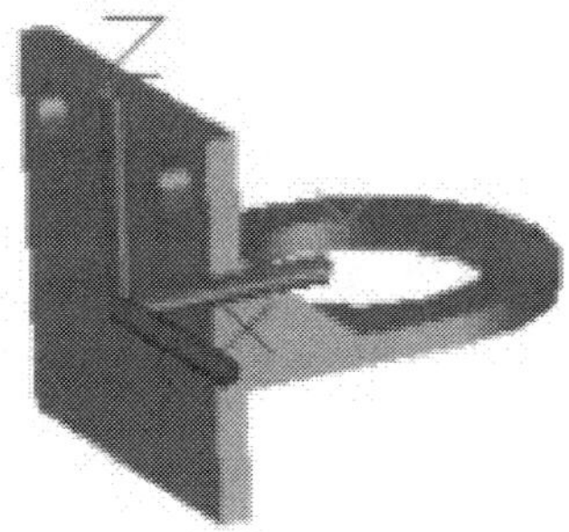

Figure 11–43

9. Orbit around to view the model from various sides.

10. Save the file.

Task 2 - Create a Base View and Projected Views.

1. Switch to the **B-Sized** layout tab and delete the existing viewport.

2. In the *Layout* tab>Create View panel, expand  (Base) and click  (From Model Space).

3. The Front view of the mounting bracket is attached to the cursor. Move the cursor near the bottom left corner of the drawing and click to place the view, as shown in Figure 11–44.

The Front orientation becomes the Base view.

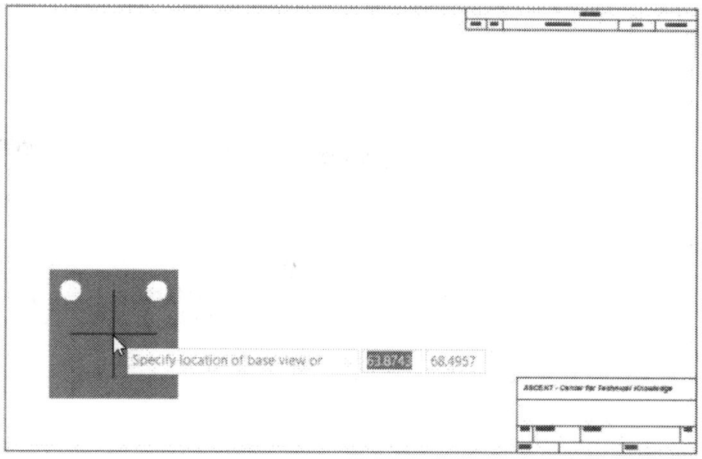

Figure 11–44

4. Press <Enter>. Move the cursor to the right and click, as shown in Figure 11–45. This automatically creates one of the side projected views.

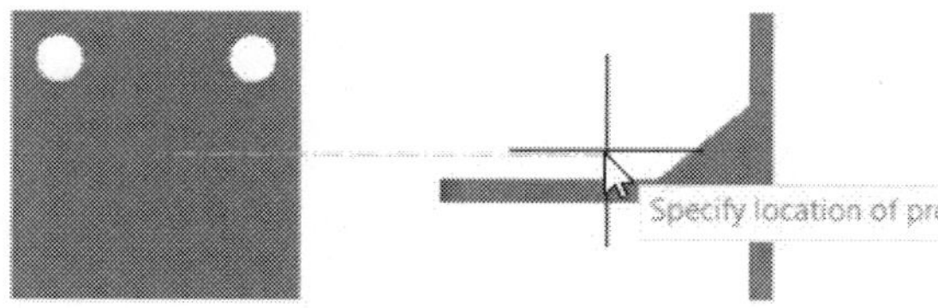

Figure 11–45

5. Move the cursor and add one top view and one isometric view, as shown in Figure 11–46.

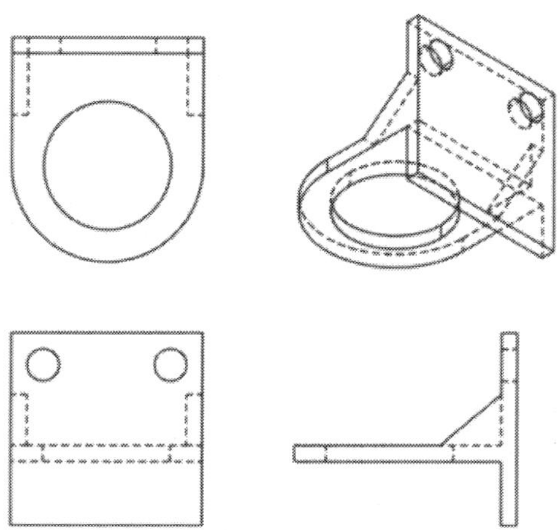

Figure 11–46

6. Press <Enter> to end the command.
7. Save and close the file.

Task 3 - Create drawing views from file created in the Autodesk Inventor software.

1. Open **Inventor-3D.dwg**.
2. Switch to the **B-Sized** layout tab and delete any existing viewports.
3. In the *Layout* tab>Create View panel, expand (Base) and click (From Model Space).
4. The Select File dialog box opens because this drawing does not contain a 3D model in Model Space. Select **P5-12-Plate-Web.ipt** from your Practice Files folder and click **Open**.
5. In the *Drawing View Creation* contextual tab>Orientation panel, select **Back**. In the Appearance panel, set (Scale) to **1:2**.
6. In the drawing window, right-click and select **Type** and then select **Base only** (or type the options at the Command Prompt).
7. Select a location near the bottom left corner of the drawing to place the base view, as shown in Figure 11–47, and press <Enter>. You are not given the option to continue to add projected views because you selected **Base only** as the *Type*.

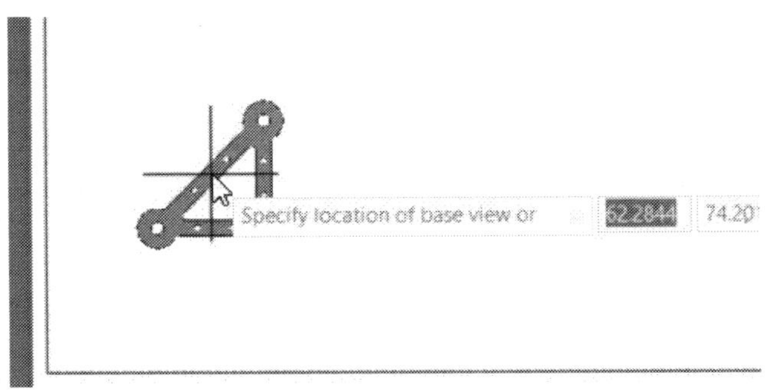

Figure 11–47

8. In the *Layout* tab>Create View panel, click (Projected).

9. At the *Select parent view:* prompt, select the base view that you just added and place two projected views, one to the right side, and the other up and to the right for an isometric view, as shown in Figure 11–48. Press <Enter>.

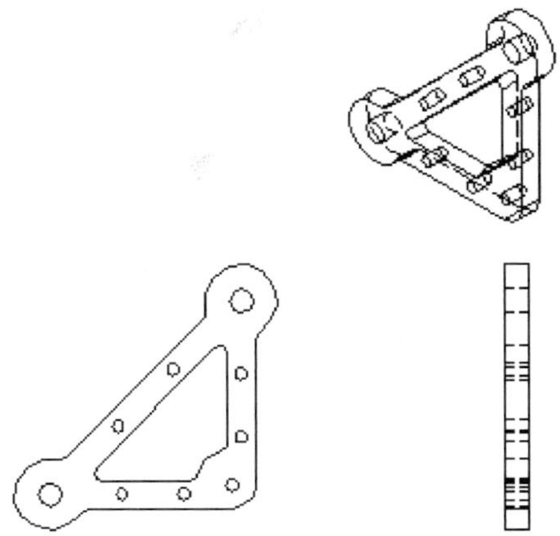

Figure 11–48

10. In the *Layout* tab>Modify View panel, click (Edit View).
11. At the *Select view:* prompt, select the base view.
12. In the *Drawing View Editor* contextual tab>Appearance panel, expand (View Style) and click (Shaded with visible lines).
13. Press <Enter> to exit the **Edit View** command. The final views are shown in Figure 11–49.

*Because you changed the parent view, the two child views follow the parent and, all three views automatically update to **Shaded**, as shown in Figure 11–49.*

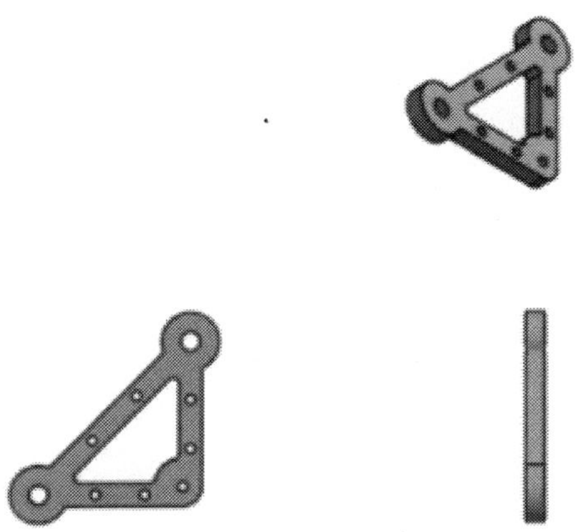

Figure 11–49

14. Save and close the file.

11.6 3D Printing

3D printers are used to print 3D models. Whether you want to print a scaled model of your design or a part of an actual product, you can now do it directly from the AutoCAD software. There are multiple ways to send 3D solid objects and watertight meshes to 3D printers.

3D Print Service

When sending your model to a 3D Print Service, the model is saved as a binary STL file. The file is then sent to a 3D printing service provider. They print the model and send it to the address you indicate during the ordering process.

How To: Send a 3D Model to Print

1. In the Application Menu>expand **Publish** and click  (Send to 3D Print Service).
2. In the 3D Printing - Prepare Model for Printing dialog box, click **Continue**.
3. In the drawing, select the 3D part(s) you want to print and press <Enter>.
4. In the 3D Print Options dialog box, set the Output dimensions, as shown in Figure 11–50. Click **OK**.
    - Click  (Select objects) to reselect or add more objects.
    - Click  (Quick select) to select all object types with the properties you define as the filter.

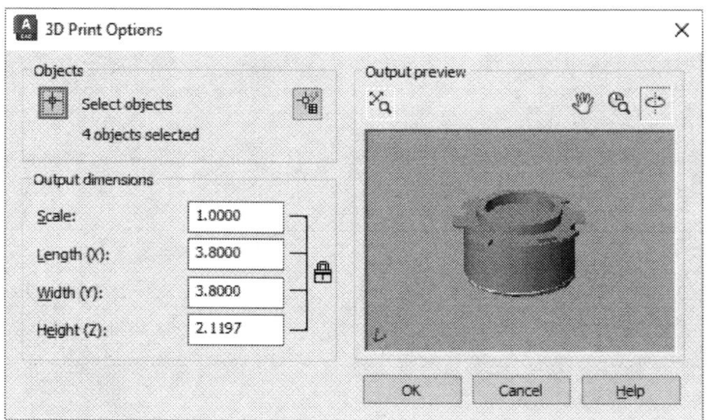

Figure 11–50

5. Save the drawing as an STL file.
6. You can send the file for 3D printing service provider.

Practice 11f

Send a 3D Model to Print

Practice Objective

- Create an STL file to send a 3D model to print.

In this practice, you will import a 3D model in STEP file format and create automatic 2D model views of the imported STEP model. You will then import a model that was created in the Autodesk Inventor software, create 2D model views, and edit the drawing views, as shown in Figure 11–51.

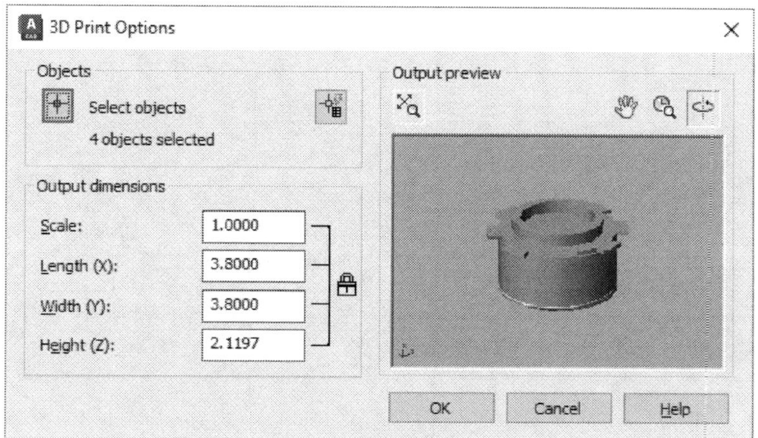

Figure 11–51

Task 1 - Create an STP file.

1. Open **Print-3D.dwg**.
2. In the Application Menu, expand **Publish**, click (Send to 3D Print Service).
3. In the 3D Printing - Prepare Model for Printing dialog box, click **Continue**.
4. In the drawing, select all the parts and press <Enter>.

5. In the 3D Print Options dialog box, in the *Output dimensions* area, verify that *Scale* is set as **1**, as shown in Figure 11–52. Click **OK**.

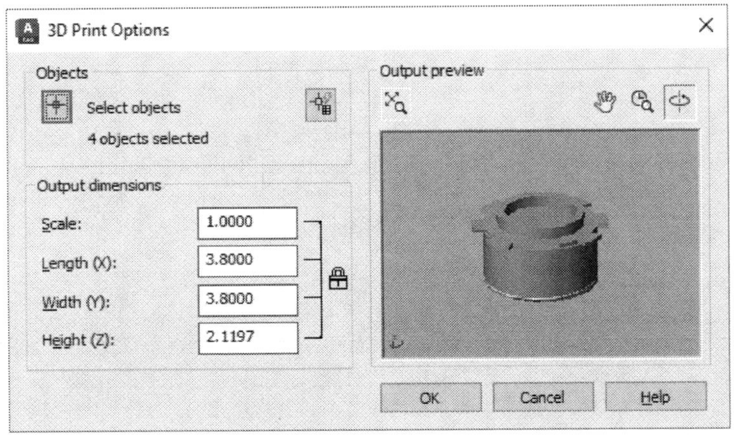

Figure 11–52

6. In the Create STL file dialog box, browse to your practice files folder. Set the *File name* to **Assembly** and click **Save**.

7. You can send the file for 3D printing service provider.

Chapter Review Questions

1. What is the maximum number of viewports that you can create at one time using the Viewports dialog box?
   a. One
   b. Two
   c. Four
   d. Unlimited
2. What does the **Solid Drawing** command do?
   a. Creates hidden line views and deletes existing solids.
   b. Creates a viewport containing an orthographic or auxiliary view of a 3D solid model.
   c. Creates 2D drawings and 3D wireframes of solids in a floating viewport.
   d. Creates hidden line views and sections in viewports that are created using **Solid View**.
3. When using **Flatshot**, which option do you set if you want to display hidden lines?
   a. Linetype
   b. In the *Obscured Lines* area, select **Show**
   c. Include tangential edges
   d. Color
4. **Solid Profile** creates a viewport containing an anonymous block of the profile and hidden lines.
   a. True
   b. False
5. The **Flatshot** command selects all solids and surfaces in a view.
   a. True
   b. False

6. Which of the following methods do you use to create a 2D hidden line view from a 3D Solid?
    a. In Paper Space, run **Solid Drawing** and then **Solid View**.
    b. In Model Space, run **Solid View** and then **Solid Drawing**.
    c. In Model Space, run **Solid Drawing** and then **Solid View**.
    d. In Paper Space, run **Solid View** and then **Solid Drawing**.
7. What type of file do you send to a 3D print service provider?
    a. .DWG
    b. .DWT
    c. .STL
    d. .3dP

Command Summary

All ribbon names reference the 3D Modeling workspace.

Button	Command	Location
	**Base View From File**	• **Ribbon:** *Layout* tab>Create View panel>Base drop-down list
	**Base View From Model Space**	• **Ribbon:** *Layout* tab>Create View panel>Base drop-down list
	**Edit View**	• **Ribbon:** *Layout* tab>Modify View panel
	**Flatshot**	• **Ribbon:** *Home* tab>expanded Section panel
	**Import**	• **Ribbon:** *Insert* tab>Import panel
	**New Viewports**	• **Ribbon:** *Layout* tab>Layout Viewports panel
	**Projected View**	• **Ribbon:** *Layout* tab>Create View panel
	**Send to 3D Print Service**	• **Application Menu**>Publish • **Command Prompt:** 3DPrintService
	**Solid Drawing**	• **Ribbon:** *Home* tab>expanded Modeling panel
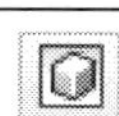	**Solid Profile**	• **Ribbon:** *Home* tab>expanded Modeling panel
	**Solid View**	• **Ribbon:** *Home* tab>expanded Modeling panel

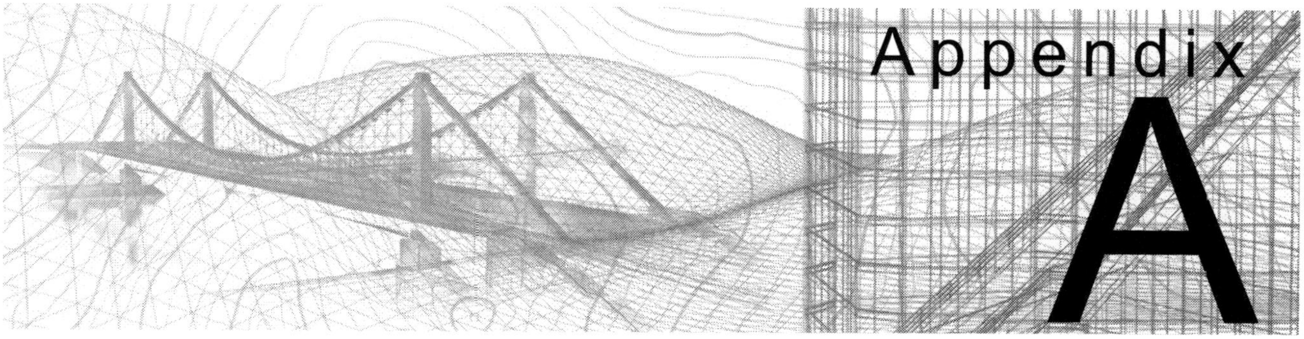

Appendix A

Skills Assessment

The following assessment has been provided to test your skills and understanding of the topics covered in this learning guide. Select the best answer for each question.

1. Which tools change the view of a model so that it displays a hidden line, wireframe, or realistic look?
   a. Render
   b. Shademode
   c. Visual Styles
   d. Named Views
2. Which of the following objects is considered a solid primitive? (Select all that apply.)
   a. Extrusion
   b. Wedge
   c. Revolve
   d. Cylinder
3. You can modify solid objects that have been subtracted from other solid objects.
   a. True
   b. False

4. Which command creates a single solid object from a 2D element and then either creates a void in it or adds a shape to it, maintaining it as a single solid?
   a. **Extrude**
   b. **PressPull**
   c. **Subtract**
   d. **Convert to Solid**

5. Which two object types must be in a drawing before you can create a sweep?
   a. A region and a line
   b. A solid and a surface
   c. A 2D object and a 3D object
   d. A path and a profile

6. How do you select a face on a solid?
   a. Hold <Ctrl> as you select the face.
   b. Use the **Face selection** option.
   c. Draw a window around the face.
   d. Edit the Solid History.

7. What **Smoothness Level** obtains the most rounded edges in a mesh model?
   a. 0
   b. 2
   c. 4
   d. 6

8. Which command hollows out a solid?
   a. **Separate**
   b. **Shell**
   c. **Imprint**
   d. **Clean**

9. What object must be in a drawing before you can view a Live Section?
   a. A camera
   b. A section plane
   c. A cutting plane
   d. A section visual style
10. How do you apply existing materials to the objects in a drawing?
   a. Drag-and-drop materials from the Materials Browser.
   b. Select **Load...** in the Materials Browser.
   c. Drag-and-drop the material from DesignCenter.
   d. Start the **Load Materials** command.
11. How can you adjust the location of the sun in your model? (Select all that apply.)
   a. Change the geographic location.
   b. Move the sun light glyph.
   c. Adjust the time of day in the ribbon.
   d. Adjust the date in the ribbon.
12. Which of the following commands can you use to create different 2D views from a 3D model in a layout? (Select all that apply.)
   a. **Solid View**
   b. **Solid Profile**
   c. **Solid Drawing**
   d. **Solid Layout**
13. Which UCS command option changes the drawing plane from a UCS (user coordinate system) to the default coordinate system (UCS home position)?
   a. **Origin**
   b. **World**
   c. **View**
   d. **Icon**

14. When you run the **Interference Checking** command, it always results in one or more new solids that indicate interference.

    a. True

    b. False

15. What is the the first view from which you can generate additional views of a 3D model in a layout?

    a. Projected view

    b. Initial view

    c. Base view

    d. Profile view

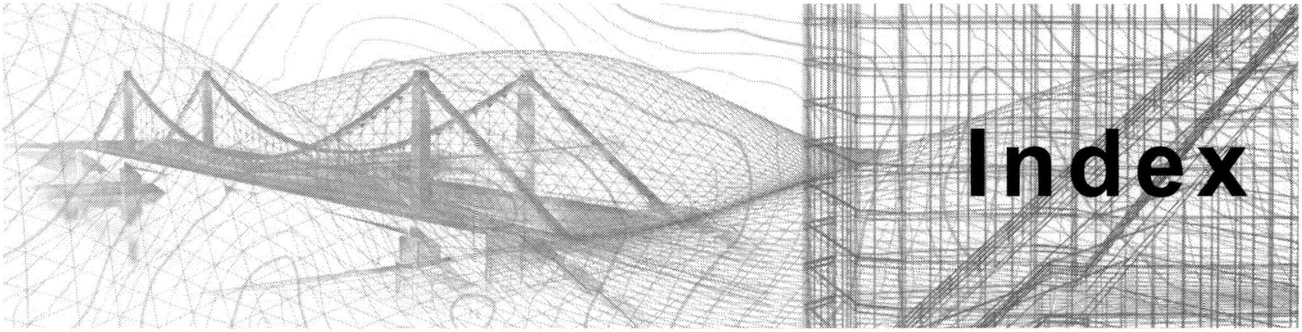

Index

G

H

I

L

M

N

O

P

R

S

Made in the USA
Monee, IL
13 September 2026

62976614R00240